The St. Louis Cardinals
in the 1940s

ALSO BY MEL R. FREESE
AND FROM McFARLAND

Magic Numbers: Baseball's Best Single-Season Hitters,
Decade-by-Decade (1998)

Charmed Circle: Twenty-Game–Winning Pitchers
in Baseball's 20th Century (1997)

The St. Louis Cardinals in the 1940s

MEL R. FREESE

McFarland & Company, Inc., Publishers
Jefferson, North Carolina, and London

LIBRARY OF CONGRESS CATALOGUING-IN-PUBLICATION DATA

Freese, Mel R., 1933–
    The St. Louis Cardinals in the 1940s / Mel R. Freese.
       p.   cm.
    Includes bibliographical references and index.

    ISBN 978-0-7864-2644-7
    (softcover : 50# alkaline paper) ∞

    1. St. Louis Cardinals (Baseball team)—History. I. Title.
GV875.S3F747   2007
796.357'640977866—dc22   2006035086

British Library cataloguing data are available

Cover photograph: Enos Slaughter of the St. Louis Cardinals,
World Series game October 15, 1946 at St. Louis; Umpire is Al
Barlick *(AP Photo)*

Manufactured in the United States of America

*McFarland & Company, Inc., Publishers
  Box 611, Jefferson, North Carolina 28640
   www.mcfarlandpub.com*

This book is dedicated to the memory of
Bob Broeg, a true friend,
fellow SABRite, Hall of Fame journalist,
and the greatest and most knowledgeable
Cardinals fan of all time. I owe many thanks to Bob
for his past assistance and encouragement
in my writing of Cardinals baseball books.

Acknowledgments

I would like to thank Steve Geitschier, archivist at the *St. Louis Sporting News* for all his support during my research in writing this book. His help and comments have been invaluable. I would also like to thank my fellow members of the Bob Broeg SABR chapter in St. Louis for their comments when I reviewed the book with them.

Thanks to all the authors who wrote the books from which I drew material and references. They helped make this book possible.

In numerous conversations I gleaned many interesting facts, stories and insights into this great period of the St. Louis Cardinals. Bob Broeg had the greatest knowledge of anyone regarding the Cardinals and he guided and assisted me in telling of many of these tales. His help was greatly appreciated and he will be truly missed not only as a SABRite, but as a great personal friend.

Last, but not least, a million thanks to my wife, Martha, who patiently waited while I researched and wrote the book. It was finished while we were packing to move out of state. Her patience and assistance helped me through this trying period.

Contents

Preface

A dynasty can apply to a kingdom, a country, a business or as in sports to a specific team. This book provides a close look at the great St. Louis Cardinals clubs of the 1940s—clubs that enjoyed a level of success some, including the author, have characterized as dynastic. The reader can decide if this team truly deserves the honor of that title.

During the decade of the 1940s the Cardinals had the best record in baseball, averaging 96 victories per season. That total would have won the pennant 22 times over the first 49 years of the twentieth century. They won four pennants, three World Series titles, finished second five times and third once. The other great franchise of the time was of course the Yankees, who won five series, finished third place four times and fourth once.

When reviewing the team's seasons and the events that happened it was quite conceivable that with a few breaks they could have won three or four more pennants. The reader may draw his or her own conclusions, but as the years unfold and the events show themselves many will concur with the conclusions.

While this book is about the St. Louis Cardinals in the 1940s, other events are also explored. Of course the biggest was World War II and the impact it had on baseball and the lives of the players. This subject will be covered on a number of occasions as will those players classified as 4F and what their role should have been.

The subject of the Pacific Coast League wanting major league status or at least several major league franchises is a theme that runs throughout this book. The reader will find the position of the PCL as well as organized baseball's viewpoint, and how it was handled.

There is also an in-depth look at the death of Commissioner Kenesaw Mountain Landis and his impact on the game. We will look at what baseball was like when he was commissioner, and what followed after his death. In the final analysis, what was his legacy for the game?

Discussion will also revolve around the reserve clause and how the owners and players viewed it in the 1940s, as well as the establishment of a minimum salary and the beginnings of baseball's pension plan. This era also covered the first attempt of the twentieth century at a player's union, how it was handled, and the players' reactions.

This was the decade that saw baseball integrated, and how the Negro ball player was received by fans, players and teammates. As our story ends some conclusions were drawn as to what the future held for the Negro in baseball. Everyone knows what happened, but looking at it as if it were still 1949 might lead to some different conclusions.

We will also look at the first attempt at a strike by some ballplayers, how it was handled and the effect it had on the game at the time. This was also the era when a number of players jumped to the Mexican League. We will look at how this impacted the game. We'll see how the amnesty issue was addressed when they wanted to return, along with how the other players reacted.

This book was not only a great research project but a labor of love.

ONE

1940

Beginning of the Forgotten Dynasty

Many writers, pundits, baseball observers and fans thought that the best team did not represent the National League in the 1939 World Series. The consensus was the St. Louis Cardinals were the best club. The team led the league in batting average (.294), runs (778), hits (1601), doubles (332), triples (62), RBIs (732) and slugging percentage (.432). In addition they had the second best ERA (only Cincinnati's was lower, bulwarked by the work of Bucky Walters and Paul Derringer). The Cardinals staff was deeper in strength and ability.[1]

A slow start and then a bump in mid-season prevented them from taking the title. From August 1 through September 28 (when they were officially eliminated), St. Louis was 43–17 versus Cincinnati's 36–25. They had reduced the lead from 12 games to 2½ when they met the Reds for a four game set. Cincinnati won the first game 3–0, not scoring after the third inning. The Cardinals' Morton Cooper and Bill McGee shut them out in a double-header the next day, giving the team 24 consecutive scoreless innings.

In game four Cincinnati led 4–3 in the bottom of the seventh when Joe Medwick hit a double, but was out trying for a triple. Two singles and an infield hit followed, but no runs were scored in the inning. Faulty base running cost the team a big inning and possible victory. They had one more chance when rookie Johnny Hopp (just up from the minors) hit a pinch-hit double for pitcher Curt Davis, but was picked off at second on a missed bunt attempt. The Cardinals stranded 11 runners and thus ended their chances. Three games were left, but their season was basically ended.

High hopes ran for 1940 as they had strong hitting throughout the lineup. Johnny Mize led the league in batting (.349), home runs (28) and slugging percentage (.626). Enos Slaughter batted .320 in his second season and led the league with 52 doubles. Medwick hit .332 with 117 RBIs (second in the league) and his 48 doubles also took second place. Terry Moore, besides his great defensive play, batted .295 with 17 home runs.

Stu Martin played second and batted .268 with 80 RBIs, while Jimmy Brown split time between short and second playing 147 games, hitting .298 and scoring 88 runs. Don Gutteridge played third base and batted .269. The catching duties were handled by Mickey Owen, who played stellar defense while batting .259. Don Padgett was a fill-in catcher and first baseman, batting .399 in 233 at-bats.

The pitching staff had six pitchers with 10 or more victories, led by Davis with 22. Bob Bowman and Lon Warneke each won 13, while Cooper and McGee each grabbed a dozen wins. Bob Weiland rounded out the sextet with 10 victories. Thus the staff had quality and depth.

The Yankees steamrolled the Reds in four games, but during the season failed to draw 1,000,000 people because of their fourth straight runaway title. General Manager Ed Barrow refused to play night games, even though it would have helped home and road attendance.

Walters won the National League MVP with Mize second. In the American League Joe DiMaggio won, despite missing 32 games. In just 120 games DiMaggio batted .381, scored 108 runs, had 126 RBIs, 32 doubles, 6 triples and 30 home runs. His statistics plus defense and team leadership qualified him for the MVP award.

When we address salaries in these chapters the reader should multiply the number by approximately 20 to get a relationship to current dollars. Cincinnati had a payroll of $169,000 and expected it to rise substantially for 1940, as many players had excellent seasons.

Brooklyn's general manager, Larry McPhail, proposed a playoff system for all 16 teams that would run concurrently with the World Series. The concept was the second place teams in each league would play each other, the third place teams the same and on down through the eighth place clubs. The victories (including the World Series) would be totaled and the league with the most wins would receive a silver trophy.[2]

It was pretty obvious to even a novice that this plan would not fly. Not much interest could be generated watching the eighth place Philadelphia Phillies (45–106) play the last place St. Louis Browns (42–112). The idea died almost as quickly as it was born.

Cardinals owner Sam Breadon proposed that baseball be played on a six day week. Each Sunday would have a doubleheader and then single games on Tuesday through Saturday. Monday would be an off day and this would allow the players to spend time with their families when in their home towns.

This idea had a lot of merit and was adopted and used during the 1940s and 1950s on a fairly consistent basis.

Breadon said that no player was worth $200,000. That was the market value placed on Medwick by opposing teams who were interested in acquiring the slugging outfielder. The value would consist of cash and players to be traded for Medwick. Since Medwick was one of the main cogs of the team, especially in the power department, Breadon (as much as he liked money) wasn't ready to part with Medwick.

Manager Ray Blades thought if the team had one shortcoming it was in the lack of complete games by the pitching staff. The team had only 45, the fewest in the league. The club had 32 saves in a day when saves were not a common occurrence. The starting pitcher was expected to go nine innings on most occasions. The New York Giants were the only other club with as many as 20 saves. The other six clubs had between nine and 15. This tells the reader how pitching staffs were handled during this era.

Blades pointed out the team used 364 pitchers in 155 games (over two per game). He would be shocked by today's standards. In their 45 complete games the team was 44–1 and when using two pitchers they were 26–20. If three or more pitchers were used the team was 23–40 and therein lies the key reason they didn't overtake Cincinnati. It was Blades' aim to get more complete games and two pitcher games out of his staff in 1940.

The Giants, Brooklyn Dodgers and Chicago Cubs all had their respective eyes on Medwick. Each wanted to see him in their lineup, as they believed he could either help deliver a pennant or move the team up in the standings. Breadon held firm that Medwick was not for sale or trade.

Blades said with a few changes the team could win the pennant next season. There was already a strong contender in place and it just needed a little fine tuning. He planned to let Brown, Gutteridge, Martin and rookie Joe Orengo vie for the infield positions. A dark horse was third baseman Robert Schmidt, who led the Northern League with a .441 average and had been promoted to Columbus, an AA farm team.

There were also several impressive pitching prospects to add to an already excellent pitching staff. The three most promising pitchers were Murray Dickson (22–15), Harry Brecheen (18–7) and Ernie White (15–7). Two other pitchers, Ken Raffensberger and Elwin "Preacher" Roe, would also be in the potential mix.

Commissioner Kenesaw M. Landis assailed the chain store or chain gang farm system, as he visualized it. He opposed interlocking farm systems and working agreements. He was against further expansion of the farm system. Cardinals general manager Branch Rickey, who founded the farm system, assailed Landis, saying "a ban on working agreements would lead to only 15 minor leagues from the current 41–43."[3]

Rickey had developed the farm system in the early 1920s because the

Cardinals didn't have the financial wherewithal to compete with the large teams, i.e. New York and Chicago. It had been a savior to many teams, especially St. Louis. From 1926 through 1939 the club won five pennants, three World Championships and finished second four times. Without the farm system that would not have been possible. Each league would have been dominated by the big and powerfully rich clubs.

Rickey told Landis his ideas would stymie minor league growth, lead to stagnation and eventual club dissolution and league closings. Rickey opposed Landis' "share the wealth" concept which he was trying to get the American League to force onto the New York Yankees. This would also impact the St. Louis Cardinals, who had 26 farm teams.

At the other end of the spectrum was a team like the St. Louis Browns, who had never won a pennant and spent most of the century in the lower realms of the second division. 1939 was another good example as the club finished 42–112, a season in which they gave up almost seven runs per game.

The Cardinals' rookie pitcher Bob Bowman (pitched in 48 games in 1939) stated it sure beat working in a coal mine. That was what Bowman did before he turned to pitching. He learned his pitching while working in the coal mines and played for one of the coal mine teams. Since coal miners as a lot were a rowdy, tough and ready bunch, he once had to have a police escort off the field after his team had defeated an opposing club. He said he would keep his pit job until he was certain that he would have a successful career.

Rickey was rapidly nearing his goal of making the Cardinals farm system self sufficient for the Cardinals and their affiliates. His goal was that the team would be 100 percent "our boys" or as close as possible. He realized there were times when you might have a player that was not a home grown product (what a change from today's game). Opportunities presented themselves and you couldn't pass up a bargain or good opportunity.

The Cardinals had just five players that were not from their farm system. They were Davis, Warneke, Weiland, Clyde Shoun (who led the league in saves with nine and appearances with 53) and veteran infielder Lyn Lary. Each was a pick-up in a trade and all but Lary had paid fine dividends to the club.

Many fine new players moved up to the major club each season while others were sent to affiliates for further seasoning. Rickey's goal was to have at least eight new youngsters every year and move out non-developed players and older veterans. In this manner the team always had a youthful bent to it, was hungry and aggressive. If you developed your players properly then you were always bringing in new good talent. Rickey's philosophy had been to trade a player not when he was going downhill, but when he still had value. In that manner you could receive a good price and either good prospects or a capable veteran in his place.[4]

Another potential pitcher for 1940 was Max Lanier, a late season call-up that appeared in seven games, posting a 2–1 mark with a 2.37 ERA. This was exactly the type of player to which Rickey referred. Lanier said he had taken up golf and it had helped him as a pitcher. It took his mind off his worries, made him more relaxed and as a result more efficient on the pitching mound.

Landis was back into the act again and laid down laws for farms, working agreements and the players. In the process the Detroit Tigers lost 91 players and had to pay an additional 15. This loss was estimated at $500,000. The Cardinals, Yankees and other clubs were worried that this could spread and wondered how it would affect them. They banded together to see what action could be taken in defense of their properties.[5]

Medwick made $18,000 in 1938 and wanted reinstated to his 1937 salary of $20,000. The reader should bear in mind this was long before (some 35 years) the end of the reserve clause and long term contracts virtually did not exist. Medwick had been reduced at the end of 1938 because he slumped from 1937, his MVP season.

Medwick had his greatest season in 1937 and led in virtually every category. He led in at-bats (633), runs (111), hits (237), doubles (56), home runs (31), average (.374), slugging percentage (.641), and total bases (406). He also had 10 triples. In 1938 Medwick batted .322, scored 100 runs, led with 47 doubles, had 6 triples, 21 home runs, led with 122 RBIs and had a .536 slugging percentage. Admittedly not as good as 1937, but still a fine season. Imagine a player putting up numbers like that today and then being given a 10 percent pay cut? Ludicrous!

Mize earned $13,000 in 1938 and after his standout 1939 season wanted a raise to $17,500. Others, including Slaughter and Moore, who had good seasons, also were expecting raises. Breadon and Rickey were trying to keep the lid on. They already saw that Cincinnati had to give about $50,000 more this season. That was almost a 30 percent increase.

Rickey continued arguing with Landis over his policies and handling of the minor league teams and the affiliates. Rickey said the farm system was the lifeblood of a major league team and without it, they would flounder and so would the minor league teams and leagues. Landis' revolutionary plan would have created a clearing house for players (a precursor to free agency). This meant teams like the Cardinals and Yankees couldn't dominate. What has to be remembered is that these clubs spent millions of dollars (over many seasons) in building these teams and farm systems. It would have been a virtual crime to have wrecked that system which made the game thrive.

Many officials of lower leagues stated that they could not survive without financial support from the major league teams. They told Landis that they could not work or operate without some type of working agreement with a major league ball club. The survival of the minors was tied to the success of the major league teams. Finally, minor league teams won concessions from Landis on player movement. This seemed to temporarily settle the tempest in a teapot situation.[6]

In the National League the St. Louis Cardinals and the Brooklyn Dodgers had led the opposition against Landis with the result that the specialization plan was tabled for the present. During the winter meetings several key decisions were made. The sacrifice fly was abolished and the farm system draft problem was worked out to everyone's satisfaction. For now the minor league system remained intact.

The St. Louis Browns were trying to pressure the Cardinals to play more night games. The Browns owned Sportsman Park, but the Cardinals paid rent. The Browns wanted to increase the night games to 14, but it would have cost $140,000 for more lighting and the Cardinals would have had to share the cost. Currently St. Louis plays seven night games a year, which can be worth 100,000 to 200,000 fans with a pennant contending team. The Cardinals finally acquiesced and told the Browns they could be ready by May 15 to play the additional games.

The Rowland rating system predicted that the order of finish in the National League would be Chicago, St. Louis, Cincinnati and Pittsburgh, in that order. This was a surprise as most writers had picked either St. Louis or Cincinnati to win it all. Some had even picked Brooklyn, which finished third in 1939.

All major league teams with the exception of the St. Louis Browns (who trained in Texas) took spring training in either California or Florida.

With high pennant hopes and based on their 1939 performance the Cardinals' payroll increased by 15 percent, about half of Cincinnati's. Medwick was unhappy, as his pay offer was the same as 1939 ($18,000). He said he would be a holdout as he wanted $20,000. Medwick wanted to play for the Cardinals, but wanted fair treatment. The fans would have hated to see Medwick traded, as he had been extremely popular as well as a highly oiled cog in the Cardinals' machinery since 1933.

Breadon's final offer was $18,000 and an impasse was reached. Lynn King (defensive replacement for Medwick) was released. This move strengthened Medwick's position. He always resented being taken out for a defensive move and now saw this as a tribute to his defensive skills. Therefore, Medwick believed this gave greater support to his case and he should be paid $20,000.

As Blades looked at spring training and his roster he saw little competition in the outfield. It was set with Medwick in left, Moore in center and Slaughter holding down right field. The problem was the infield and Blades was leaning towards putting Brown at second and having open competition for third base and shortstop.

Blades listed as the key goals for the Cardinals to win the pennant:

1. A bolstered infield, improved both defensively and offensively
2. Added pitching strength, expected to come from young rookie pitchers
3. More reserve punch in the outfield.

Blades believed if these objectives were achieved then the Cardinals would win the National League pennant. One of the key people considered was Hopp, who was also a fine defensive first baseman.

The infield mix consisted of a combination of veterans and rookies. The veterans were Martin and Gutteridge, while the rookies were Marty Marion, Eddie Lake, Joe Orengo, Robert Repass and Joe Sturdy. Marion was the best defensive short stop, but the question was could he hit major league pitching. With the other power in the lineup, Marion batting .250 would be acceptable, when you considered his defensive skills.

Orengo spent some time with the team in 1939, but was sent back to the minors to work on his swing. Instead of a smooth level swing that would generate line drives, as he was not a power hitter, Orengo had an uppercut swing which led to pop fly and easy outfield fly balls. If he could overcome this problem, Orengo could be a valuable asset to the team.

Among the young pitchers Blades was looking closely at Francis "Red" Barrett, Brecheen, Dickson, White, Roe and Lanier. The latter was given the best chance to make the major club, especially based on his late 1939 performance.

At this juncture the Cardinals looked like the pick of the league, but they needed a solid double play combination. In 1939 they used Brown at short and Martin at second, but those were not their best positions. Brown was an excellent third baseman or second baseman. He should have been at one of the two places. This was why it was so critical that Marion be able to hit major league pitching at an acceptable pace. Probably the best would have been Marion at short and Brown at second and then let the rest battle for third base.

One has to wonder which were the real Cardinals? Were they the April to July team of 1939 which went 45–42? Or were the real Cardinals the August–September club that was 47–19 and the best team in baseball? The pace they set in those two months generated 110 victories for a full season. This tied the record of the 1927 New York Yankees (considered by many the greatest ball club of all time).

The catching looked to be in the hands of Mickey Owen (a good defensive player, but only a .250 hitter) or Don Padgett, he with a blistering bat, but weak with the glove. The Cardinals had experimented with him as a catcher to get his bat in the lineup. He was an outfielder by trade, but couldn't break into the Cardinals' lineup.

The Cardinals dropped seven in a row during spring training, using reserves as Medwick was now officially a holdout. Moore had a kink in a muscle in his left shoulder and Slaughter a sore toe. Thus the entire starting outfield wasn't playing. Those seven losses included two to the Cincinnati Reds. Thus far the hitting had been slow to come around and the vaunted pitching staff had been hit hard. Blades considered playing Hopp in left field if Medwick was still a holdout come opening day.

Meanwhile the Cincinnati team had its own problems with two key players on the injured list. Vince DiMaggio and Lombardi were out for several days. Ironically, DiMaggio would be traded to Pittsburgh early in the season.

As spring training was drawing to a close, Blades began making some critical decisions. He would play Brown at third and Marion at short, but still needed a second baseman. He wanted to keep Gutteridge and Martin as reserves. Lake needed more experience, so Orengo was probably the best of the lot, but didn't compare to Cincinnati's Lonnie Frey.

The outfield was in good condition with Hopp, Pepper Martin and newcomer Morris "Red" Jones. Blades still needed one of the young pitchers (Dickson, White, Brecheen or Lanier) to step up and be able to take the ball every fifth day. The favorite still seemed to be Lanier, but no decision was made at this point.

Medwick grudgingly accepted $18,000. He felt it was better that than quit baseball. Any other job he would have made $15,000–$16,000 less for 12 months and this was pay for six months. Breadon believed a firm stand on holdouts, not only with Medwick, but all players, would help in future years. The players would know that once Breadon made a final offer, that was it. Take it or sit out.

The team's attitude and spirit were much better with Medwick back and ready to play. Players usually sympathize with each other, but Medwick had been his own worst enemy and received small consolation from his teammates. He took a West Coast trip with Dodgers manager Leo Durocher and then told him that Breadon either had to trade him or lose $200,000 (the value placed on Medwick).

Medwick underestimated Breadon's grit and determination, as he neither traded Medwick nor paid him $20,000. Then when Medwick visited before signing he left the box during a Cardinals–Dodgers game and visited Durocher for 30 minutes (they had been teammates in the 1930s, including the 1934 World Series champions).[7]

A fan finally convinced Medwick to return. He said the only person he was hurting in the long run was Joe Medwick. The players were glad to have Joe back as he was a great hitter and player. They realized without him in the lineup their chances of going all the way were greatly diminished.

Mize and Brown were both out with knee injuries and it looked like they would miss opening day. Hopp could play first base, but was no Johnny Mize at the plate. Hopp was a speedy line drive type hitter. Third base was an even bigger problem. The choice was Gutteridge or Martin; the former played there most of 1939. Orengo could also start at third.

John Carmichael (a Chicago expert) picked Cincinnati, St. Louis, New York and Brooklyn, in that order. In the American League he picked New York, Boston, Detroit and Cleveland. He liked the Cardinals and they had loads of power, but the infield was unsettled and there were some question marks regarding the pitching staff, thus he picked them second. Should either of the latter two have become rapidly settled then St. Louis was the favorite.

The Cincinnati catchers declared that Walters was better than in 1939 (remember he won 27) and Derringer was just as good (he had 25 victories). They would also get more help from other members of the staff this season. Help was seen in the form of Joe Beggs, Elmer Riddle, Whitey Moore and Junior Thompson. The latter two had a combined 26–17 mark in 1939. There was also the possibility that Johnny (double no-hit) Vander Meer could come back strong. If this developed Cincinnati might be untouchable. Walters declared he was aiming for 30 wins.

Just as in politics and many other areas there were numerous polls or groups that made projections. The latest group probably had the most credibility, since it was the baseball scribes. Two hundred and sixty-six writers picked a St. Louis–New York World Series. They last met in 1928. In the National League the group picked St. Louis, Cincinnati, Brooklyn and Pittsburgh. Their American League choices were New York, Boston, Cleveland and last year's winner, Detroit, to finish fourth.

The season didn't begin well for the Redbirds. Blades was not happy with the team in the early going. Medwick was out with an ailing back. Mize was overweight with leg and shoulder problems and Brown was playing with a gimpy knee. To further complicate the situation the Cardinals had a lot of idleness due to several rainouts. These coupled with a slow start meant the team didn't get its first victory until April 23.

Martin was playing second base, but feeling the pain of twinges from his appendectomy. Meanwhile it seemed Mike McCormick (Frank's younger brother) had nailed down the left field job that eight men held for Cincinnati in 1939. After the first week St. Louis was just 1–4, while Cincinnati was 3–0 and Pittsburgh and Brooklyn each 2–0.

Brooklyn headed east and won eight straight with seven complete games. Their powerful extra-base hitting and stellar defense paved the way to victory. The Reds allowed fewer runs than last season, just over two per game. Beggs showed class in relief roles. After two weeks Brooklyn was 8–0, Cincinnati 5–2 and St. Louis struggling at 4–6.

The fans were becoming disenchanted with Blades' style of managing and booing at the continuous pitching changes. The Cardinals had used 41 pitchers in the first 14 games. Remember Brooklyn had seven complete games in their first eight starts. Davis had no complete games in his first four starts and Warneke just one in the same number of games. It wasn't until May 14 that the Cardinals got their first complete game and it was by McGee.

Meanwhile Medwick, while hitting a ton, was feuding with his teammates, especially Moore. Medwick, Mize, Slaughter, Martin and Padgett all hit well over .300, although the latter left a lot to be desired defensively. There was a bad omen as the team lost its first series to Brooklyn. If they were going to be serious contenders they had to beat Cincinnati and Brooklyn in head to head competition.

In the early going only reliever Jack Russell (age 34) and 24-year-old Lanier had winning records. Each were 1–0. The next best was Shoun at 2–2.

In contrast we look at Cincinnati and their strategy was to let the opponents beat themselves. They used tight pitching and defense to lead the way. In their first 12 games the team had eight errorless games. They gave the opponent very little in opportunities. Their enemies had to make their own breaks. They had also shown daring on the base paths, stealing and taking the extra base.

Walters was 3–0 with three complete games, Derringer was 2–1 with three complete games and Thompson was 2–1 with two complete games. Brooklyn was setting the pace with an 11–1 mark, while Cincinnati was close behind at 10–3. The Cardinals were last at 5–10. These were the standings on the morning of May 9.

It looked like the ship had been righted and was ready to sail when they drubbed Brooklyn 18–2. Then they lost three straight to Cincinnati. The Reds were ahead of their 1939 pace (10–9) with the best record in baseball at 15–4, while Brooklyn was hot on their heels at 14–5. St. Louis had climbed out of the cellar, but were only 8–13.

When you analyze the team, the hitting can't be faulted. Seven men— Owen, Martin, Medwick, Slaughter, Marion (a real surprise at .347), Padgett and Mize—were all at or over .300. Certainly Medwick, Slaughter and Mize would finish over .300, and maybe even Padgett. The key question was how close the others could stay to that mark. In 1939 the team had a .294 league leading average and also led in runs scored.

Injuries had hurt. When Moore was not in center field the team had a problem. While Hopp covered ground, he didn't have the throwing arm or the finesse of Moore. But then who did? The big downfall had been the pitching, as only two pitchers were at or above .500. McGee was 2–1 and Shoun at 2–2. It was a cold day when Shoun didn't warm up or get in a game as the fireman. He was on pace to set the major league mark for game appearances. He had been in 16 of the first 27 games. Last season Shoun pitched in 53 games and was 3–1 with a league high nine saves.

The Cardinals went through a six game losing streak, three to Cincinnati, two to the lowly Phillies and one to Brooklyn. The slump was finally stopped by a five home run game. The team made only seven hits, but all were for extra bases as they defeated the Dodgers. Moore and Mize each hit two home runs and Orengo one. Orengo added a double and Mize a triple. Orengo hit home runs in consecutive winning games.

Brown was out of the lineup again. This time he had a broken nose and though it had healed, Brown had great difficulty in breathing. Last season Brown missed only eight games, playing in 147. He was on pace to play in far less this year, as he had been saddled with numerous injuries. Orengo and Martin performed good fill-in roles.

Brooklyn's pitching was strong at the start, but had started to decline as did their fortunes. The club had mustered just two complete games in 14 starts after the impressive seven complete games in eight starts. At the same time their hitters took this time to take a fiesta. Thus Brooklyn was hit with a double whammy.

Meanwhile Cincinnati continued on its breakneck pace. The Reds had been errorless in 14 of their first 25 games. Manager Bill McKechnie was not worried about the three man rotation as the reserves had held up well. Walters, Derringer and Thompson were the main cogs at present. These three were 14–4 in 20 starts. Overall the Reds were a major league best at 18–6–1 in their first 25 games.

Meanwhile St. Louis had no pitcher over .500. Shoun and McGee were 2–2 while White and Lanier were 1–1. The Cardinals' hitting continued to be strong led by Medwick at .353, Slaughter at .333 and Mize at .323 with 12 home runs. Padgett, Owen, Orengo and Martin all were still over .300. On the morning of May 23 Cincinnati was 18–7, Brooklyn not far behind (after their terrible slump) at 15–8 and St. Louis was a pitiful 10–17.

Landis had been made commissioner in 1920 following the infamous Black Sox scandal and had ruled baseball with an iron hand. While some owners resented his methods, most agreed that his actions had been instrumental in saving the game and returning it to favor and an honorable position among the public. Landis continued to stress the need for vigilance against gambling in the game. When a person looks forward some 50 or 60 years it can be understood why Pete Rose was barred from the game. The roots of gambling run deep in the game of baseball.

The hopes of the Cincinnati Reds and Brooklyn Dodgers continued to soar. The Reds were climbing as Derringer was showing his form of 1939, while Johnny Rizzo, acquired in a trade from Pittsburgh, had taken over left field from McCormick, who was relegated to the bench. A hot start by Rizzo landed him the job.

Walters seemed headed for his 30 victories as he was 7–0 with seven complete games. Meanwhile, the Dodgers were making their move on the arms of veterans or second line pitchers. Sixteen year veteran Freddy Fitzsimmons was 3–0 as a spot starter, while Newell Kimball, Vito Tamulis and Tot Pressnell were combined for a 5–1 mark in relief. Johnny Hudson had been doing a good job filling in for the injured Peewee Reese. The starters recently had their problems, but the team was 18–8 overall.

The Cardinals had a southpaw at Houston in the Texas League that was being called the next Carl Hubbell or Bill Hallahan. His name was Howard Pollett (nicknamed Howie) and he was 19 years old with a 10–0 mark. He might soon be seen in a Cardinals uniform. If not this season certainly in 1941.

A can't miss tag had been put on him, although sometimes that can be a curse instead of a blessing.

By the end of May Cincinnati was 20–8 followed hotly by Brooklyn at 22–9. If Philadelphia weren't in the league St. Louis would be last with their 11–20 record. Breadon continues to support Blades, saying, "It was not his fault. Injuries, pitching failures have caused the slow start by St. Louis." Breadon tells fans, "While we are disappointed we are sticking with Blades." How often have we heard the front office give vocal support to a manager only to see him dismissed shortly thereafter? It was often the death knell.[8]

Breadon continued to deny that Medwick would be traded. We might trade somebody, he said, but at this point we don't know who or what for and to what team. Medwick, after a hot start, had really cooled down. As of June 2 he had gone 15 consecutive at-bats without a hit. This was certainly not the only reason the Cardinals were 14–22 versus a 23–13 mark in 1939, but it was a major contributing factor.

Pitching and defense continued to pace the Cincinnati ball club. Although they had a decent hitting attack (third in the league in scoring) it was the former that kept the club atop the standings. Beggs and Moore had been the keys to the Reds' relief corps. Walters continued to roll with a 9–0 mark and a sparkling 1.83 ERA. Meanwhile Whitt Wyatt and Van Lingle Mungo had arm trouble and this decimated the Dodgers' starting corps. Mungo would be limited to seven games for the season. Reese continued on the injured list, but the Dodgers' team spirit and drive remained at a high pitch.

At the end of the first week of June Cincinnati was 26–11 followed closely by Brooklyn at 24–11. St. Louis was a dismal 14–25. Only McGee (4–3) and Lanier (3–1) owned winning records. Three days (June 7) after saying he supported Blades, Breadon replaced him with Billy Southworth. Breadon had become disenchanted with Blades. Southworth had taken over the 1929 Cardinals from McKechnie after he lost the 1928 World Series in four straight to the New York Yankees. Sure hope it doesn't happen to Tony La Russa for 2006.

Mike Gonzales became interim manager until Southworth could join the team and was 1–5 during his short tour of duty. Veteran outfielder Estel Crabtree replaced Southworth as manager of the Rochester Red Wings. He would also serve time as an outfielder. Rickey had known nothing of this; in fact he had stated that no changes were in the near future. This showed another widening of the breach between Breadon and himself. The chasm would eventually reach the point where it could not be repaired.[9]

A failure by Cincinnati groundskeepers to take down protective shields on lights deprived center fielder Harry Craft of a game winning home run. The game would have ended 3–2 in the bottom of the ninth. Instead Brooklyn won the game 4–3 in the 11th and handed Walters his first defeat of the season. Next day Cincinnati got revenge, defeating Brooklyn 23–2. Brooklyn reliever Carl Doyle showed he was no major league pitcher, allowing 14 runs, 16 hits and 4 hit batters in 4 innings. Fitzsimmons allowed five runs in the first innings and took the loss. Doyle appeared in only three games for Brooklyn and finished with a 20.5 ERA. Somehow the Cardinals acquired him in a trade. Why has never really been determined. During his tenure with St. Louis he appeared in 21 games, five as a starter and was 3–3 with a 5.89 ERA until a broken wrist sidelined him for the balance of the season. This would be his last season in the majors.

Orengo, Medwick, Mize and Owen were all still over .300 while Russell (2–1) and McGee (4–3) were the only pitchers over .500. As the middle of June approached Brooklyn had taken over first place by percentage points with a 29–13 mark, while Cincinnati was 31–14. New York at 26–15 and Chicago 26–22 rounded out the first division. St. Louis came in at a dismal 15–30, waiting hopefully for Southworth and any magic that he could work.

Over in the American League the attention was momentarily taken from the pennant race and focused on the fireworks between Cleveland manager Oscar Vitt and his ballplayers. They were staging a protest, almost a strike. This was something unheard of in 1940. We have to wait over 30 plus years before players rise up in protest and strike. The players signed a petition asking for the ouster of Vitt, who was a hard nosed manager. Club president Alva Barrett held a meeting with the players and a truce was called and the affidavit was withdrawn. For now there was a tenuous truce. However, fireworks would re-erupt at a later date.[10]

Meanwhile back in the National League St. Louis was having fireworks of their own. They had traded the ever popular hard hitting Medwick and last season's 22 game winner Davis to the Brooklyn Dodgers for $125,000 cash and a few ham sandwiches (as one writer put it). The Cardinals received Ernie Koy (a good defensive outfielder, hitting .229), while Medwick was at .304. Koy would play left field and turn in an acceptable performance, but lacked Medwick's potent bat. Medwick because of his petulance had fallen out of favor with Breadon.

Other players received in the trade were pitcher Sam Nahem, who remained at Louisville, and Bert Hass, a bright future prospect that would stay with Montreal. These were Brooklyn farm teams, but the players would report to the Cardinals in 1941. They also picked up the aforementioned Doyle. Medwick's hitting had declined after a hot start. He was also in the fans' doghouse as they didn't think he showed the necessary drive and team spirit. Many thought he had lost a step in the outfield and on that basis and as had been Cardinals practice (trade a player while he still had some value) the deal was made. Also there had been the salary dispute that still rankled Breadon and Rickey.

Larry McPhail had offered $200,000 cash for Medwick in 1939. When the team jumped in as a contender this was when McPhail thought it was time to make the move for Medwick. He reasoned if the team could acquire the hard hitting Medwick, who had a career average of .336 and had 100 plus RBIs every season except his rookie year (he had 93 in 1933), it would solidify the club and give Brooklyn a great shot at the pennant. Many had been tried in left field, but with little success.

At the end of the third week of June Cincinnati regained the lead with a 36–17 mark followed by Brooklyn at 32–16 and surprising New York was now 31–17. The Cardinals had won their first five games under Southworth and were now at 20–30. The club still had four hitters at .310 or better, but no pitcher was over .500. The best marks were McGee (4–4), Russell (2–2), and Shoun (3–3). Southworth knew if the team was to make a move the pitching had to find its 1939 form. Thus far that had been lacking.

As the end of June approached it found Cincinnati still in a team hitting slump, but their Sunday play and winning double-headers kept the team moving ahead. They were 14–2 on Sundays. In two days the club had gone from first to third in losing three straight to the lowly Philadelphia Phillies and the hot surging New York Giants. This represented their longest losing streak of the season. Then the Reds took three in a row from the Giants at the Polo Grounds and climbed back into first place.

Cincinnati's two Sunday defeats were in split double-headers. The club had won the other seven double-headers it played. The balance of the week the team was 24–18, thus their Sunday play and success in double-headers had kept them in first place.

In Brooklyn an altercation in an elevator between pitcher Bowman of the Cardinals and Medwick supposedly led to an instant in the game that day. Medwick was beaned by a pitch from Bowman. Bowman said it was unintentional, but the Dodgers believed it was deliberate based on what happened at the hotel earlier in the day. Medwick would recover and have several more fine seasons, but would never again be the hard hitting aggressive player of the 1930s. Many observers believe the beaning made him a little leery at the plate. Age is sometimes cited as the factor for his decline, but that was hard to accept as Medwick was just 28 (the prime years of a player are supposed to be 28–32). Owen was ejected from the game for punching Durocher following the beaning of Medwick.

The Dodgers had further troubles when hot-tempered pitcher Luke Hamlin, in a temper tantrum, went home after blowing two leads. He wasn't the loser in one game as the Dodgers lost it in extra innings. Dodgers management told him to stay home until he changed his attitude and got his temper under control. Otherwise the team didn't want him back. He later apologized and returned to the club.

As June ended it found Cincinnati having pitching problems as Walters, who started the season 9–0, was now 9–4. It couldn't be expected that he would continue undefeated with an ERA well below two runs per game. There was disappointment that he hadn't won a game in three weeks. Cincinnati was back on top at 38–20, Brooklyn at 34–19 and New York remained in the chase at 33–21. St. Louis was 22–32 (they were 7–2 under Southworth).

St. Louis hosted its first All Star Game and three players from the two St. Louis teams were chosen—Mize and Moore from the Cardinals and George McQuinn from the Browns. Cincinnati placed four on the All Star squad and Brooklyn six, including Medwick. The players, coaches and managers selected the team. They could not vote for members of their own clubs. The voting would be returned to the fans after this season. The National League posted the first shutout in All Star Game history, winning 4–0.

After the All Star Game the Cardinals were hopeful they could make their big push. Brown was now back in the lineup after a long illness. Brown was not only a steady defender and an excellent hitter, but also an aggressive hard nosed infielder, cut in the mold of Terry Moore. He gave no quarter and asked none. The pitching staff looked ready to take charge with McGee, Shoun, Cooper, Bowman and Warneke to lead the way. Mize led the majors with 20 home runs to pace the hitting attack. It would not be an easy task as the club was 15 games out of first place and still under .500.

St. Louis first represented the city in the old American Association in the 1880s as the St. Louis Browns. They won four consecutive championships from 1885–1888. In 1892 they joined the National League and became the St. Louis Cardinals, except for one season in 1900 when they were known as the St. Louis Perfectos (the reason is one of those mysteries that remains unsolved).

At the second milestone in the pennant race (July 14th) Cincinnati continued setting the pace at 41–22, Brooklyn was 39–21 and New York was still playing over .600 ball at 36–22. St. Louis was still well below .500 at 25–34. The team was 10–4 under Southworth.

For the first 70 games of the season Cincinnati pitching held opponents to a composite .229 average with less than one hit per inning. Walters had allowed 107 hits in 146 innings, Derringer 136 in 150 innings, Thompson 94 in 126 innings and Jim Turner 81 in 86 innings. The big four had been key reasons Cincinnati was in first place. They also had an excellent defense, making the fewest errors in the league and allowing the least unearned runs. The team's batting improved and now all the pieces seemed to fit together.

The Giants started a slide as fans hopes began to rise but then fall as the team began to falter. The big letdown was their pitching staff as none of their key five starters would have a winning record. Hal Schumacher would be tops at 13–13; Harry Gumbert finished at 12–14; Carl Hubbell, hoping for a comeback and 15–18 victories turned in a 11–12 mark; Cliff Melton, starting and relieving, would finish at 11–12; and Bill Lohroman would only be able to crank out a 10–15 mark. All the starters would be used in relief, most only three to five games, except Melton who would make 16 relief appearances to compliment his 21 starts. From a high point of 36–22, New York finished the season at 72–80 and in sixth place. They were just 36–58 the remainder of the season.

As mid–July approached Cincinnati held a one-half game edge on Brooklyn, 48–23 to 47–23. New York was at 42–29 (having lost seven of their previous 13). The Cardinals had slipped to 13 under .500 at 27–40. Some wondered if the magic of Southworth had worn off or disappeared as the Cardinals lost five of seven and now were just 12–11 under his reign.

Thus far Lanier had been the biggest pitching disappointment. He was expected to win 15–18 games and was struggling to stay at .500. Pittsburgh swept the Cardinals in four games at St. Louis and jumped into the first division, pushing St. Louis further behind. Cincinnati at this point was ahead of their 1939 pace. The club was 20–4 in double-headers (winning eight and splitting four). The Reds were 17–3 on Sundays and 33–21 the balance of the week. It should be noted the latter was a .636 winning pace. They were .630 in their 1939 pennant winning season.

Southworth was running the team on his own as he had a straight contract with no ten day release clause, which traditionally had been the manner in which contracts were written. This gave him the flexibility to play his own game, make his own moves, and maneuver in the manner he wanted. He decided Padgett was not a catcher and played him in the outfield, hoping he would regain his hitting form of 1939 (remember he hit .399 in 233 at-bats).

Southworth was also considering moving Mize to the outfield as he was a poor defensive first baseman, as he moved very slowly and poorly on ground balls. The question was then how would he fare in the outfield? Would fly balls go for singles, and the latter for doubles and triples with Mize in left or right? Also if his goal was to have an all left hand batting outfield against right hand pitchers this meant benching the best defensive center fielder in baseball. Rickey didn't like the idea, and neither did many fans.

Southworth, after further careful study, decided to leave Mize at first and use Hopp on occasion as a late inning defensive replacement. He had to have Mize's big bat in the lineup. On the good news side was Slaughter's emergence from a long slump that saw his average drop from the .350s to the .260s.

Rickey didn't like some of the moves or decisions that Southworth made, but had little control over the situation. He particularly didn't like the idea of Mize moving to the outfield and Moore on the bench. There Southworth did acquiesce. Southworth conferred almost daily with Breadon but not Rickey (and this is another sore point for him). Marion and Orengo had been making a good double play combination.

The pitching was still spotty although McGee picked up his seventh win (high on the team). Shoun (4–4) and Russell (3–3) were the only other pitchers at .500. With almost half the season gone it didn't look bright and rosy for the Redbirds.

As the middle of July passed Cincinnati opened a small lead on the Dodgers. They were three games up with their 51–24 mark compared to Brooklyn's 48–27. New York was still third at 42–32. Their real slide hadn't begun, as the club was 9–10 for the last 19 games. St. Louis, on the strength of a 5–1 week, moved to within nine games under .500 at 32–41, with Southworth now at 17–12, but they were now 18 games out of first place.

The Reds' 55 victories in their first 80 games was the best record in the National League since 1919. Their double-header win over New York was their ninth of the season. Meanwhile, on a long road trip, Brooklyn lost six games by one run which led to just an 11–9 record; hard to keep pace with Cincinnati at that rate. Medwick was booed lustily when he came to St. Louis and he responded with a home run into the left field bleachers. Although he was not hitting his usual high average, Medwick was hitting for power and driving in runs. The pitching of the Dodgers during their slump held up, but the hitting let them down.

The Cardinals continued their drive toward .500 and respectability with a 9–3 stretch. Mize hit his major league leading 25th home run and could hit 45 or more. Slaughter continued his resurgence at the plate as in one game he hit two home runs and added a single. Martin, Owen and Orengo were all over .300. Mize was just under .300, but his power more than made up for the difference.

Pitching was driving the top two contenders with Walters at 12–4, Derringer 12–7 and Thompson 10–6. Brooklyn had Fitzsimmons at 8–1 and Tamulis (relieving and starting) at 6–1. With one week left in July Cincinnati was 55–25, Brooklyn now five games behind despite a very fine record (51–31) and New York was beginning its slide at 44–36. St. Louis was now 37–43, just six games under .500 and 22–14 since Southworth took over the helm of the team.

The injury jinx hit Cincinnati as Lombardi sprained an ankle and Thompson was hurt and missed a few games. Despite this they won six games over four days against Brooklyn and New York. In an effort to strengthen their team the Dodgers called up Pete Reiser and got pitcher Les Grissom from the New York Yankees to bolster a slumping team. Reiser had been a Cardinals farm hand, but in 1937 Landis declared him a free agent because the Cardinals had violated signing regulations. Grissom fashioned only a 2–5 record with Brooklyn, but Reiser would prove to be a real star, beginning in 1941.

St. Louis continued its drive toward the .500 mark with a 5–2 week and was hopeful for the return of Moore to the lineup. It certainly was a different outfield with Moore in center field. Martin and Orengo were the only St. Louis batters over .300, but Mize was at .296 besides leading the majors in home runs. Slaughter had raised his average to a respectable .283, but he wouldn't be satisfied until he scaled the .300 mark.

Brooklyn's pitching had been led by the ageless Fitzsimmons (he was actually 38). In his 16th season he had a 202–139 career mark. He was considered a fizzle when he first came to the majors. As July closed Brooklyn, with a very excellent 54–34 record, had now fallen eight games behind the red hot Cincinnati team that was 62–26 and continued on a pace to win 110 games. New York was 48–36, as they would only be 24–44 the balance of the season. St. Louis was just four games under .500 at 41–45.

Since Southworth took over the team they had been 32–18, a .640 pace, making the team 47–48 and only one-half game out of fourth place. It had been a long, hard struggle, digging out of the deep hole the club was in after the first seven weeks. Meanwhile Cincinnati had run into problems of their own as Lombardi was still out and with Thompson missing some starts this had thrown their pitching staff into turmoil. Moore pitched two good games, but lost them both. The Reds dropped eight of 12 games and lost their first double-header of the season.

In a tragic note, reserve catcher Willard Hershberger committed suicide by slitting his throat. He thought he was letting the team down and couldn't take the pressure. His father had committed suicide and Hershberger used to say he would too. The Reds vowed to give his widowed mother a full share of whatever postseason earnings the team had.[11]

The job of catching full time fell to Hershberger when Lombardi was injured and he couldn't handle the pressure. He didn't believe he was doing a good job, when in fact, the team and management were pleased with his performance. He was batting .309 with 26 RBIs in just 123 at-bats. The latter was a pace that would produce 125–130 RBIs in a season. The pitching staff was very satisfied with the way he called the game.

In the last words he spoke to a teammate he told Derringer at the hotel, "I'll be out soon and get four for four today." McKechnie had told his players they had a mentally sick man and must not play jokes on him as he couldn't handle it. They needed to do everything to encourage and praise him and make him as upbeat as possible. Hershberger knew Lombardi was ready to resume catcher the day he destroyed himself. It was a real shock to the team as Hershberger had no financial worries, but did have this mental problem. The entire team was shaken by the tragedy and resolved to win the pennant.

Koy (previously labeled a good fielder but not a hitter) had responded with the bat very well, hitting .294, Moore was at .284 and Slaughter at .281. Thus the outfield was starting to be productive again. In fact all three finished over the .300 mark. St. Louis had seen some improvement in pitching as McGee was 10–6, Warneke 8–7, Shoun 7–5 and Bowman at 4–3.

Fitzsimmons at 10–1 had the best winning percentage in the league and teammate Tamulis was second at 8–1. Ironically, the latter did not win another game the rest of the season. Cincinnati was paced by Walters at 15–6, although hopes for a 30 win season had faded. Derringer was also 15–6, thus both seem certain to repeat as 20 game winners. Jim Turner has turned in a sparkling

10–3 mark up to this point. Cincinnati's slump may have cost them the chance at 110 wins, but they still had a very fine 63–33 mark, six games ahead of Brooklyn at 58–40 (which had slipped below .600) and New York at 51–41.

The Dodgers' Wyatt was at 12–9 and led the league in strikeouts and shutouts (5). At the start of the season he had knee trouble and it was questionable how much value he would be. In 1939 he was limited to 14 starts, but was 8–3 with a 2.31 ERA. Therefore the Dodgers were counting on Wyatt for possibly a 20 win season. Medwick returned to the lineup, but his punch was missing. Reese continued to shine at short stop when he was able to play.

Breadon realized that the chances of St. Louis over taking Cincinnati were rather slim but saw a bright ray of hope for 1941. The young pitching talent in the Cardinals farm system beamed bright for the future. Pollet was 18–4 and Krist, after arm trouble in the spring of 1939, fashioned a 17–8 record. Then there was Brecheen, Dickson, White and Munger to consider for the future.

It looked like history was repeating itself for Cincinnati. In 1939 they had a big slump in August and the month started off the same way this season. They lost two double-headers in early August and through the 11th the team was just 5–7. Meanwhile St. Louis was riding the hot bats of Martin (.340), Mize (.318 and 81 RBIs), Koy (.313), Orengo (.309), Hopp (.297), Moore (.283), Marion (.281) and Slaughter, who had slipped back to .279. Martin, while hot now, would end the season at only .238, which killed any future chances for a full time position.

The Cardinals' pitching showed McGee (11–6), Warneke (9–7) and Shoun (7–7). Other leading pitchers in the league were Walters at 15–7, Derringer at 16–8 and Fitzsimmons at 11–2. As mid–August approached Cincinnati's lead had shrunk to 4½ games as the Dodgers were at 62–42, while Cincinnati had slipped to 66–37. It was not so much that Brooklyn got extremely hot, but Cincinnati slumped. New York was now 55–49 and St. Louis went into a tailspin of their own and dropped below .500 at 49–52.

From the American League there was a good news–bad news situation. First the good news. Cleveland catcher Rollie Hemsley set a major league mark for catchers, handling 450 chances without a miscue. His string was broken on July 18, 1940. Hemsley once had a severe drinking problem, but quit and his career blossomed. The sour note side involved the young slugging outfielder of Boston, Ted Williams. He demanded to be traded. He said he was unhappy and felt unappreciated in Boston and wanted to go to New York or Detroit. Naturally both teams would like to have had him, temper tantrums included. He didn't like the city, fans and hated all sportswriters, especially those in Boston. These situations occurred repeatedly throughout his career, as Williams developed a love-hate relationship with Boston.

Reese broke a bone in his heel and was lost for the season. The Dodgers, since their last trip west, were only 14–14. The only thing that kept them from falling completely out of the race was that Cincinnati during this time lost 12 of their first 20 games in August, including two double-headers in eight days to St. Louis. They lost the double-headers on August 11 and August 18. A bad break cost them the first double-header loss. On Saturday, August 17, Frey and Bill Werber hit solo home runs and Lombardi and Ival Goodman hit doubles for a 3–0 first inning lead. Then the heavens opened and it rained continuously until the game was called.

Cooper had been the pitcher in that game. In game one the next day Cooper again started and this time held Cincinnati to one run in nine innings and won the game. What a difference from pitchers today. Can anyone imagine a pitcher starting one day, pitching one inning and the game was rained out, so he starts the next day? Today his next start would be after four days' rest.

Starting August 18, Cincinnati played the next 21 games at home where they were 39–14 versus 29–27 on the road. Brooklyn was just the reverse. They were 36–17 on the road, but only 29–28 at home. However, the Reds needed their hitting and pitching to return. Walters had lost five of six, Turner three of four, Thompson was kayoed in his last two starts, but someone else took the loss. Cincinnati stood at 69–41, Brooklyn just four back at 65–45, New York at 56–51 while St. Louis had moved back to .500, 54–54.

The Cardinals' hitters continued to hit with the best in the league and with a resurgence of their pitching they had moved into the first division. Under Southworth the team was 39–24. Warneke was 10–7 while McGee was 11–7. Fitzsimmons was the top percentage pitcher in the league at 12–2, while Walters and Derringer had each won 16 games in their quest for another 20 win season.

The Cardinals, with a seven game winning season, moved to a season high seven games over .500 and were .662 under Southworth. The flag, however, seemed out of reach, although second place could be a possibility. On June 14 when Southworth took over, Cincinnati was 32–15, Brooklyn 31–13 and St. Louis 15–30. Since that time St. Louis was 46–24, while Cincinnati was 42–28 and Brooklyn two games under .500 at 36–38. This gave St. Louis its best record in the National League since June 14. Unfortunately the first two months of the season also counted.

Roy Stockton of the *St. Louis Post Dispatch* said at some point St. Louis would put the same team on the field and keep it all season. Orengo had played second, short and third, as had Brown, and Martin had played second and third. Only Marion had played just shortstop. The same steady infield would go a long way for making a solid, consistent, winning team. Warneke won his eighth in a row for his 13th of the season (at one point he was 5–7). Padgett was doing a lot of the catching because of his potential bat (although hitting only in the .240s). Owen relieved in late innings for defensive purposes.

At this point the Dodgers' main concern was to hold onto second place, as they looked over their shoulders and saw the onrushing Cardinals. Brooklyn's chances of catching Cincinnati seemed to have dimmed considerably. Reiser was hitting close to .300 besides playing a superb outfield. He also filled in a few games at shortstop and third base. The Cardinals had six players over .300 with Slaughter at .287 and Marion a surprising .281. By the end of August Cincinnati had a seven and one-half game bulge on Brooklyn. The Reds were 75–44 while Brooklyn was 67–51 and St. Louis trailed the Dodgers by five games with a 61–55 mark.

The major leagues were given the first pitch of draft eligible age under military regulations. Uncle Sam said all single players of good physical and mental health would be classified 1-A. Married players or those single players with dependents would initially have a 3-A classification. Of course, this changed as wartime emergency conditions changed. There would be a lottery system and every eligible male in the country would have a number assigned and then a random drawing would determine the order in which they were taken. A low draft number didn't mean you went first; it's the order in which it is taken. For example, you could have had number 50, but it might be drawn on the 2500th pick while another person could have number 2000 but it might be chosen on the 75th pick. It came down to the luck of the draw. If we got into a full scale war there was certain to be more refinement to the draft system.[12]

Even though Cincinnati played only .500 ball in August and left the door open, no one entered. Cincinnati was on the hot seat, but they lacked the killer instinct. They bore down hard in must-win tilts, and then let up in easier games. A good example was on August 28 when they wanted a victory at muddy Crosley Field and beat Brooklyn 9–2 as Derringer broke a five game losing streak. The next day they left five men who had doubled stranded and lost 6–2. They lacked the same sense of intensity. The killer instinct wasn't there.

Lombardi was back on the injured list when hit by a Bill Lee (Chicago) pitch on the little finger of his left hand. Forty year old Jimmy Wilson took over catching duties and handled the job admirably. In Brooklyn Reiser was the man of the hour, as he hit close to .300 and fielded brilliantly. Next season he would probably play left or right field (he would actually become the center fielder). They beat the Giants three in a row at home. Each team always wanted to finish ahead of the other. Both being in New York City made for a natural rivalry. They needed this sweep as it followed a 3–7 road trip to St. Louis, Chicago and Cincinnati (where they were 2–2).

Meanwhile McGee picked up his 14th victory and fourth shutout, but the Cardinals express was slowed by rain in Pittsburgh. They lost one game and tied the other (which since it would have no meaning in the final standings was not played). The chances of first or second, especially the former, were pretty slim. Still it would be a good season if they finished third when we consider where the team started and was after almost two months of the season.

The Cardinals also considered bringing up Pollet, who was 19–6. Mize was the August player of the month as he now had 38 home runs. For the month Mize batted .315, hit seven doubles, seven home runs and had 23 RBIs. He played through several injuries and was considered a good team man. Seven of the Cardinals regulars were at or above .285, with four over .300.

McGee and Warneke were both 13–8, as the former's eight game winning streak was just broken. Shoun was 10–8 and Cooper, after a slow start, was at 9–9. Other top pitchers in the league were: Fitzsimmons (13–2 and the top winning percentage), Truett "Rip" Sewell of Pittsburgh at 12–3, Walters at 18–9, Derringer at 17–12, Turner at 10–6 and Chicago's Claude Passeau, en route to a 20 win season, was 17–11. As they entered September it now just seemed a matter of time before Cincinnati took it all. With their 80–46 mark they had an eight game bulge on Brooklyn at 72–54. St. Louis was 64–58.

In the American League mutiny was taking place, as trouble once again brewed in the Indians' tepee. The alleged rebels took over again and the Indians dropped six in a row. It was simple: they hated Vitt. Some of the players present (most notably Hal Trosky and Johnny Allen) made a strong denial of any rebellion or mutiny. Bob Feller, Jeff Heath and Ben Chapman had no knowledge of the meeting.

In any event, the net result was a half hearted run for the pennant and they lost to Detroit by one game, as the Tigers' Floyd Giebel outdueled Feller on the final day of the season. Giebel played in the majors only from 1939–41 and had a career mark of 3–1, while Feller won 266 games and probably lost 100 more victories because of his four years in military service during World War II. As has often been said, baseball was a game of strange oddities and events that take place.[13]

The Dodgers seemed to have second fairly well clinched, but first place was out of sight. Their hope now was for Medwick to hit .300 or better and for Dixie Walker win the batting title. The former would happen, but not the latter, although Walker would win a title a few years hence. Fitzsimmons finished with a brilliant season, appearing in 20 games, starting 18, completing 11 and having a 16–2 record and 2.82 ERA. His winning percentage of .889 was the best in the majors. Reiser, with his hustle, dash and verve, became the spark plug of the team and next year would be its star.

On September 8 Mize hit three home runs in a game for the fourth time in his career, making him the first player to turn the trick more than three times. Even great sluggers such as Babe Ruth, Lou Gehrig, Hank Greenberg or Jimmie Foxx had not accomplished this feat. These three home runs gave him 41 for the season, the most by a National Leaguer since Hack Wilson's

56 in 1930. Mize would hit only two more home runs the rest of the season, but still led the majors with 43.[14]

The Cardinals were in danger of losing third place as they dropped three of four games to Pittsburgh. The Redbirds called up several players (including Krist; Walker Cooper, younger brother of Mort; and Frank "Creepy" Crespi). All three of these players would figure prominently in the Cardinals' pennant titles of 1942–44.

Cincinnati continued to show their grit, true colors and determination. Against both the Chicago Cubs and the Pittsburgh Pirates they overcame leads to win games. Wilson continued to do a fine job behind home plate, replacing the injured Lombardi. With just over three weeks to play the standings were Cincinnati (84–47), Brooklyn (79–55), Pittsburgh (67–61) and St. Louis (66–62).

Just when the Reds thought they had their slugging catcher back full time, Lombardi suffered another injury. He hurt his ankle going after a foul ball in a game against Brooklyn. These series of injuries would limit him to three at-bats in the World Series, as the catching duties fell on the broad shoulders of 40 year old Wilson.

On September 15 Cincinnati defeated Brooklyn 13–2, and then after a game that ended in a 1–1 tie called because of darkness after 11 innings on the 16th, they won 4–3 in 10 innings the next day. They hadn't clinched, but were close. Walters got number 20, while Derringer notched his 19th victory. After a bad August, Cincinnati rebounded to win 20 of the first 24 in September and put the pennant out of reach. It was just a matter of time before they officially clinched the title.

Slaughter was still at .285, but a late season surge would put him over .300 at .306. He finished with 25 doubles, 13 triples and 17 home runs. The disappointing statistic was his doubles. The total was less than half his league leading 52 in 1939. St. Louis ended the season with five regulars at .300 or better and a fifth (reserve Pepper Martin) hit .316. Mize plus the entire Cardinals outfield all were over .300. Orengo was close at .297. Martin, after strong hitting, fell to .238. Koy was a pleasant surprise, batting .310 and driving in 53 runs in 348 at-bats, a pace of about 90 RBIs a season.

On the pitching side the complete games under Southworth improved from 45 to 71. His hook wasn't as quick as Blades.' He let his starters in longer and let them learn to work their way out of trouble. This paid big dividends over the next five seasons. McGee and Warneke were each 16–10, but the former had only 11 complete games in 31 starts while the latter had 17 in the same number of starts.

Shoun appeared in 54 games, starting 19 and completing 13 and finishing at 13–11, while Cooper was in 38 games, 29 as a starter, of which he completed 16, and was 11–12. He deserved a better fate, at least 15 victories. Lanier, used mostly in relief, was 9–6 with a fine 3.34 ERA.

Mize led the league with 43 home runs, 137 RBIs and a .636 slugging percentage. Moore was voted the most popular Cardinals player. The Cardinals won 19 of their last 26 games to finish seven and one-half games in front of Pittsburgh. The final Cardinals mark was 84–69, with Southworth coming in at 69–39, tied for the best in the National League after June 14th.

Walters led the league again in victories with a 22–10 mark. He also had the most complete games at 29 and an ERA of 2.48. Derringer was 20–12 with 26 complete games and a 3.05 ERA. Thompson came on with his best mark at 16–9, 3.32 ERA, and Turner at 14–7 with a 2.89 ERA. A couple of other pitchers deserve honorable mention. Passeau, pitching for 75–79 Chicago, finished at 20–13, while Sewell had the second best winning percentage with a 16–5 mark for Pittsburgh. Without Sewell Pittsburgh was 60–71. The Reds won the pennant on tight pitching and defense. They held their opponents to a .240 batting average and set a major league record for fewest errors in a season.

They had 77 errorless games and made only 117 errors all season. The previous major league record was 124 errors in 155 games by the Philadelphia Athletics in 1932. The National League record had been established by the Chicago Cubs in 1938 with 135 errors in 154 games. The Reds allowed only 492 runs (450 earned) and held opponents to three runs or less in 90 games. That was how they won the pennant.

The final standings showed Cincinnati at 100–53, Brooklyn at 88–65 and St. Louis at 84–69. From June 14 on St. Louis was 69–39 as was Cincinnati, while Brooklyn was just 58–52. A better start and St. Louis might have gone to the World Series instead of Cincinnati. At the end if St. Louis wasn't the better team, at least it was just as good. It was the second straight season it could have been St. Louis in the World Series.

Frank McCormick was voted MVP, giving Cincinnati this honor three years in a row. Mize was second for the second consecutive season. McCormick batted .309, had 109 RBIs and provided team leadership to the Reds.

The World Series would feature Cincinnati's pitching and tight defense versus Detroit's power. The latter could throw two good pitchers against Cincinnati. They had Bobo Newsom, 21–5, winning percentage .808, 2.63 ERA, and Schoolboy Rowe, 16–3, .842 winning percentage, 3.46 ERA. These two had the number one and two best winning percentages. However, after their combined 37–8 mark, the rest of the staff was just 53–56.

Detroit outscored Cincinnati by 181 runs and had a .286 batting mark to the Reds' .266. Detroit hit 134 home runs to Cincinnati's 89. McCormick led Cincinnati with 19 while Greenberg hit 41 and Rudy York 33 for the Tigers. However, games were won on the field, not on paper.

When the series was over Cincinnati prevailed, four games to three. Walters and Derringer each won two games and it turned out to be a low scoring affair. Cincinnati scored just 22 runs to Detroit's 28. Cincinnati's

ERA was 3.69, while Detroit was at an even 3.00. Detroit won by scores of 7–2 (game one), 7–4 (game three) and 8–0 (game five). In the other four games Detroit scored just six runs, while Cincinnati scored 16.

The future for 1941 looked bright for the Cardinals. If they could overcome these horrible starts and play the full season the way they did in August and September in 1939 or from June 14, 1940, forward, there was no reason they couldn't win it all. There was a wealth of young talent in the Cardinals organization, especially in the pitching area and come 1941 we would see some of this. So until next season, enjoy the winter and we will see you in spring training.

TWO

1941

Almost Number One

The Cardinals' cage was loaded and gilded for the next season. Their Columbus farm team had two full stocks of infielders. Rickey said in the past few years they had taken some misfits into spring training and started slowly and that hurt their chances for the pennant. By the time the team was in place the hole was too deep to crawl out of. In both 1939 and 1940 the Cardinals had the best record in baseball in August and September; unfortunately they didn't play that well in April through July. Southworth said things would be different this coming season.

The Cardinals would bring several new pitchers to spring training and they got long looks. Among them were Murray Dickson, Harry "The Cat" Brecheen and Ernie White. Each had standout seasons this past year. It was also expected that Walker Cooper, brother of Morton Cooper, would be the regular catcher.

Cincinnati had a fine team and demonstrated it in the World Series as they came from behind three times to defeat Detroit four games to three. Paul Derringer and Bucky Walters each won two games.

In the minor league draft the Cardinals felt an ill wind as they lost four players out of their organization. Fortunately with a network of 26 teams and an abundance of talent they could better stand the loss than other clubs, but it still hurt, as they could be losing another Joe Medwick or Johnny Mize.

For the season the Cardinals' attendance was 330,000 and it should be remembered the country still hadn't recovered from the Depression as the unemployment rate was over 10 percent. Imagine if we faced such a situation today. There would be virtual panic in the streets. The Cardinals played seven night games and drew 81,000 for an average of 13,000, while their day games drew an average of 3,500. It must be remembered that they had only around 55 playing dates due to the large number of double-headers played (one every Sunday). Taking that into consideration the day rate was around 4,500. More night games could put the team over the 500,000 mark, especially if they got off to a good start and were contending for the pennant all year.

The future looked bright for both St. Louis teams as they placed three players on the all rookie team. Joe Orengo split his time at shortstop, second base and third base for the Cardinals and batted .287. Meanwhile, the St. Louis Browns' center fielder, Walt Judnich (who batted .303, 24 home runs and 89 RBIs), and catcher Bob Swift (hit .244 in 139 games) were on the all rookie team. Based on these and other talents it looked like the 1941 campaign boded well for both St. Louis teams.

Cardinals owner Sam Breadon had to make some tough decisions and one was giving 36 year old Pepper Martin his unconditional release. Martin was a star of the 1930s team and had a spectacular 1931 World Series. Breadon hated to see Martin leave, but said the game belongs to the young and that time waits for no one. Breadon admired Martin's dash, verve and gas house style of play. The team was high on Harry Walker as his replacement.

Thousands of players, both major and minor leaguers, signed up for the draft if and when the United States went to war. They were all ready to fight for their country. A patriotic fervor ran strong among the athletes. For now there would be no abandonment of baseball considered unless war broke out. In World War I baseball went on, albeit on a shortened season.[1]

There was a debate over whether ballplayers should serve. Some said the game was essential to the welfare and morale of the country and servicemen. Others believed there should be no favor granted to athletes. However, their career is different than others. As they approach 30, their income begins to decline and is almost gone by 35, as most players are either out of the game or close to retirement by this time. It made for an interesting hot stove topic over the winter months.[2]

Owners were considering raising team limits from 25 to 28 players. This was because of a potential loss of players to the draft. The military granted no exceptions to single ballplayers. Married ballplayers might be treated differently, depending upon the needs and demands of the armed forces.

In the American League rumors persisted that Ted Williams would be traded to the Chicago White Sox for pitcher Johnny Rigney and outfielder Taffy Wright. Both Williams and Rigney were alike, as each had great talent, but difficult temperaments and could be hard to handle. Each was considered a maverick in his own right.

The Cardinals planned to bring pitchers Sam Nahem (acquired in the Medwick trade) and Howard Krist to spring training. Nahem had 10 complete games in 15 starts and a microscopic 1.63 ERA. After a sore arm in 1939 everyone thought Krist was through, but he was doctored back into shape and was 22–9, with 18 complete games and a 1.71 ERA for Houston this past season. He would be 25 in February.

The Cardinals again were looking at their infield and wanted to get a set lineup from opening day and not be shifting players from one position to another. This had been a problem in the past two years. They believed they had an ace in the deck in Steve Mesner, as in six seasons in the minors he batted between .320 and .336. The only rap was that he lacked power.

Jimmy Brown seemed set at second base, although he had gone to spring training every season without a regular job and had to fight for his position, but was always in the lineup on opening day. The others in the mix for shortstop and third base were Marty Marion, Stu Martin, Eddie Lake, Frank Crespi, Don Gutteridge and Orengo. Marion was the regular shortstop and was the best defensively while hitting a surprising .278 this past year. Martin saw duty at third base and short, while Gutteridge was a reserve infielder. It looked like an interesting spring in the battle for infield positions.[3]

Few leading players were included in the early draft numbers. Most stars subject to initial call were married or had dependents. There was much uncertainty as the order in which numbers were called was not an absolute criteria. Other factors such as district, quotas and number of volunteers all came into play. Terry Moore's draft number was 713, but was number 3108 called, while Orengo had draft number 2822 and was number 2035 drawn. The system at that time took players based on number draw and not their draft number. The draft number was for the purpose of assigning everyone a number and then drawing to determine the sequence in which they would be taken. A somewhat cumbersome method.[4]

Frank McCormick of Cincinnati won the MVP, becoming the third Cincinnati player in three years to win the coveted award. Mize was second again. Bucky Walters was the winner in 1939 and Ernie Lombardi copped the prize in 1938.

There had been a proposal to move Al Lang Field to a new location in St. Petersburg. The citizens of St. Petersburg balked and both the New York Yankees and the St. Louis Cardinals lent their support. Both teams had been going there for years and didn't want to move to a new park. As it turned out, all parties were satisfied.

Based on 1941 Orengo might have wanted to play all games at night. He batted .287 for the season, but hit .452 at night, going 14 for 31. He had told Rickey that he was an outfielder and Rickey asked if Orengo had ever played shortstop. Orengo said, "No, I don't like it." Rickey then said to Orengo, "That's fine. You are our shortstop. Go get a uniform."

There was a built in safeguard against conscription for the minor leagues. Each team was permitted to replace any draftee with any available player. The majors' policy was to smile and take it when it came to the draft. Commissioner Kenesaw M. Landis steered the game away from asking favors.

National League president Ford Frick said they were ready to do their bit for the country and New York Yankees president Ed Barrow said the American League would make whatever sacrifices were needed.[5]

Breadon and Ricky were both silent on trades. It is not that they were avoiding trades, they just weren't looking for anything in particular at that time. They both said they would listen to anything from any team if they thought their club could be improved. From the Medwick trade the Cardinals received Ernie Koy, who hit .310 in 93 games. They also got Bert Haas, who was expected to be a bright star in the future. Certainly let us not forget the $140,000 cash the team received. That certainly helped fill the coffers.

The New York Giants wanted Don Padgett, even though he slumped from .399 in 1939 to .242 in 1940. They believed with regular outfield duty his hitting would return. In 1937 he was a regular outfielder for St. Louis and batted .314 with 10 home runs and 74 RBIs in 123 games. The next season Slaughter became the right fielder and Padgett was used as a fourth outfielder, reserve first baseman, part-time catcher and pinch hitter. While his average slipped to .271, he did have 65 RBIs in 388 at-bats.

Brown was in St. Louis to undergo surgery on his nose. It was broken on April 25 in Pittsburgh by a bad hop ground ball. It didn't heal properly and then he broke it again later in the season and had difficulty breathing. The hope was that the operation would correct his problem, help his breathing and make him available for everyday duty.

Another player wanted by several teams was catcher Mickey Owen. He was a great handler of pitchers and a fine defensive catcher. He also batted .284 in 117 games this past season. Somewhere along the line Owen displeased his bosses and now was potential trade bait, especially with young Cooper coming to the majors. The Dodgers, Giants and Cubs all had an interest in Owen. Bill McGee was also in the trade news, as the Giants coveted him. This was what happened when you had not only a team loaded with talent, but a farm system that kept turning them out like popcorn.

Orengo was traded to the Giants for cash and two players to be named in the spring. He would play third base for New York. Orengo had been in the Cardinals system since 1934 and finally made it as a reserve in 1940 and finished the season as the regular third baseman. It was management's feeling there was enough other infield talent available to let Orengo go to another team.

St. Louis was interested in power hitting catcher Harry Danning of the Giants. Danning was not only a fine hitter, but also an excellent receiver. However the Cardinals would had to have given up too much talent to acquire him. The Giants wanted a pitcher and outfielder, either McGee or Cooper. Pitching held the balance of power in the league and Breadon and Rickey both knew the Cardinals were in the driver's seat when it came to that category. They could have traded Owen and a pitcher for Danning and still had enough pitching strength to make a run for the pennant.

There were 4,520 players in 43 leagues in the minors. This represented an increase of 183 players over 1940, as the minors continued to grow and expand.[6]

The current thinking was that the Dodgers would try to trade for Owen at the winter meetings. They had already added pitcher Kirby Highbe, who won 14 games and had 20 complete games for last place Philadelphia (50–103). The trade to acquire Owen would involve three teams. Owen would go to the Dodgers, who would send pitchers Luke Hamlin and Tot Pressnell to the Cardinals and the Redbirds would ship Orengo to the Giants and get Danning from them. However, the Orengo trade was made before this came about.

Breadon said it was hard to get money on a big cash deal. The team had to operate on 330,000 attendance this past season and with the large farm system they supported, the Cardinals needed all the cash they could get. He finally sold Owen to the Dodgers for $65,000, Martin to Pittsburgh for $25,000 and pitcher Bob Bowman to the Giants for $25,000. These types of deals netted St. Louis $160,000. The Cards had acquired Pressnell from the Dodgers, but then sold him to Chicago for cash. More money for the coffers.

Bowman was 13–5 for St. Louis in 1939 and only 7–5 this past year. Part of his decline was due to a side injury. Unfortunately for the Giants neither he nor Orengo provided dividends in 1941. Bowman was 6–7 with a 5.74 ERA and Orengo hit .214 in 252 at-bats as a reserve infielder.

Landis made a plea to uphold the integrity of the game and morale of the nation in the wake of war. He said the major and minor leagues should not be in a dispute with each other. The two organizations must work together for the benefit of everyone.[7]

Landis' contract was extended through 1946, ending speculation he would retire or be replaced. Frick's contract as National League president was extended for four years. Another decision made at the winter meetings was that night games would be limited to seven per city. This didn't apply to Chicago since they had no lights.

In the American League Joe DiMaggio won another batting title, while Hank Greenberg led in home runs, doubles, RBIs (150) and total bases and Williams was the leader in runs scored. In general hitting was down in both leagues.

Cincinnati set a new major league fielding record in 1940 with a .981 average. They had the leader at first (McCormick), second (Lonnie Frey), third (Bill Werber), catching (Lombardi) and center field (Harry Craft). The latter set a new record at .997 with just one error in 109 games. The Reds set a new record for fewest errors in a season with 117.

In the pitching department Walters led in victories (22), complete games (29) and ERA (2.42). Chicago's Claude Passeau was runner up in ERA, as he posted a 20–13 record for a sub .500 team. Freddy Fitzsimmons set a new winning percentage mark at .889 on his 16–2 record.

The Cardinals had a good season, not only on the field, but financially as well. Aided by the cash from trades they were able to pay a dividend of $7.00 per share and this cost about $70,000. There was 18 percent of the stock outstanding, with Breadon owning the balance.

Rickey and Southworth believed the Cardinals had a strong team and they were favored by many observers to win the National League pennant. Rickey believed Mesner and Crespi a better combination for third and second base than the traded Martin and Orengo. Cooper was considered a strong catcher, as well as an excellent hitter. All he needed was a little seasoning and development which he would get with the parent team.

The Cardinals boasted a strong pitching staff and an excellent outfield, which had Moore in center and Enos Slaughter in right field. Left field was open and Koy would be challenged by Harry Walker and Johnny Hopp for the job. First base was in the capable hands of Mize. He was the leading slugger in the league for the third consecutive season. He led with 43 home runs, 137 RBIs, 368 total bases and a .636 slugging percentage.

Southworth planned to bring 20 young pitchers to camp. They were Nahem (8–6, 1.63 ERA); Ernie White (13–4, 2.25 ERA); Krist (22–9, 1.17 ERA); Max Surkont (19–5, 2.50 ERA); Newt Kimball 7–8, 2.61 ERA); Newak (12–7, 2.27 ERA); Brecheen (18–9, 2.75 ERA); Pintar (11–9, 2.77 ERA); Fred Gornicki (19–10, 3.21 ERA); Dickson (17–8, 3.33 ERA), Herschel Lyons (1–12, 3.38 ERA); Cy Vandenberg (6–8, 4.79 ERA); Johnny Grodzicki (8–3, 3.79 ERA); Ira Hutchinson (1–7, 4.28 ERA); and Elwin "Preacher" Roe (3–8, 3.94 ERA). He would also have veterans Lon Warneke, Cooper, McGee and Clyde Shoun.

Krist was the cream of the crop. He was one of the pitchers most likely to earn a spot on the team. Krist had arm trouble for two years, but was now fully recovered. Other strong candidates were Nahem, White, Dickson and Brecheen.

Mize planned on being in camp early, probably when the pitchers and catchers arrived. Since he had a tendency to put on weight, especially around the middle, he wanted to get in some extra training and exercise. His goal was to lose 12–15 pounds. His batting goal was to better his 43 home runs of last season. Some thought that he was a strong candidate to challenge the Babe's mark of 60 home runs some day.

The Detroit Tigers just found out that Greenberg had a low number and expected to be called up in May or June 1941. Some felt he might just volunteer and due to his situation the ban on trades for pennant winning teams (Detroit and Cincinnati) would be lifted for his club, should he go into military service. Both leagues had ruled that pennant winners couldn't make trades to strengthen their teams. It was sort of a parity concept. Since losing Greenberg changed that scenario and was a real blow to Detroit's chance to repeat, the ban would be lifted.[8]

Another situation developing in the American League involved DiMaggio and his pay. Despite hitting .352 he was offered the same pay as the prior year ($32,500). Other players took pay cuts. The reasons cited were his average dipped 29 points; however, he drove in seven more runs and hit one more home run. Imagine this happening to a player today.

Rickey gave Gutteridge his outright release. He would later become a member of the 1944 pennant winning St. Louis Browns and be their regular second baseman. He was the eighth member of the 1940 team to be traded, sold or released. This was in keeping with Rickey's philosophy of turnover and bringing in new and young blood.

Rickey also had at spring training a new pitching machine that could throw pitches at various speeds. It gave the hitters more of a feel of a regular ball game and get them better prepared for the season. It could also fire the ball at a given spot. It really gave the player game like conditions.[9]

Many major leaguers had low draft numbers and several could have been gone by next summer. Bob Feller had a high number, but was more than willing to go and do his duty. Morris Arnovich, who played with Cincinnati in 1940, and pitcher Sid Hudson of the Washington Senators could have missed the season due to their draft numbers.

It was in the Cards this season to improve and go all the way if the recruits lent the hand that they seemed capable of doing. Mesner seemed to be the solution to the third base problem. If he didn't pan out they could always fall back on reliable Brown, who seemingly went to spring training every year without a job and finished starting someplace. Other strong candidates to improve the team were Crespi, Walker Cooper, Walker, White, Krist, Dickson and Lake.

Rickey had always believed in no less than eight and maybe as many as 12 new players each year to keep the team young, active and hungry. With their vast farm system and wealth of talent the Cardinals had been able to do this. Many clubs didn't have this luxury. If he didn't get a regular job, Lake would probably remain as a reserve.[10]

The Cardinals had 12 Sunday double-headers this season with seven night games. The park was vacant most Mondays, as that was a day off. The only exception would be if there were rainouts and it became necessary to use Monday to play a make up game. Traditionally the club had scheduled double-headers to cover a postponed game. It is interesting to see how their strategy turned out that season.

Pete Reiser was tabbed as the next Dodgers superstar. The 22 year old Reiser batted .293 in 58 games for Brooklyn in 1940. He could bat or throw with either hand, although he was now primarily a left hand hitter and right hand thrower. He was originally in the Cardinals chain, but this was one that got away from Rickey. He was lost when Landis freed several players. He was born in St. Louis and signed in 1937 and Landis ruled in 1938 the signing was illegal and St. Louis lost Reiser. Rickey was still grumbling over this one.[11]

Mize got $17,500 for the season, making him the highest paid Cardinal. The team would have a low payroll since most new players would not average much over $3,500 per year. This was another thing that bringing in young players did. It kept the payroll low and as long as the talent was there it didn't hurt the team. The only negative could be that of breaking up the potential of the previous team. Today we call it chemistry. In those days it was clubhouse atmosphere.

Southworth saw the Reds as strong contenders again, especially with a pitching staff that was headed by Walters and Derringer and had a rejuvenated Johnny Vander Meer. Other teams battling for first division could be Brooklyn, Chicago and Pittsburgh. Southworth believed St. Louis could take it all if the young pitching developed the way he thought it would.

The Cardinals become upset with Landis' ruling. He was constantly ruling against St. Louis and the Yankees because of their large farm systems, which he called chain store or chain gang operations. Thirteen players under the Redbird roster came under fire. Landis ruled all players purchased after August 15 and before the draft deadline were being covered up by the parent team only to be able to send them back to the minors when necessary.[12]

His ruling provided for a sheriff's sale on these players. Waivers had to be sought before the players could be sent to the minors. Rickey was extremely upset. The players had passed the waiver gauntlet by April 3. This meant that a player went at draft price of the league to which he was being sent. This would be a penalty to a major league club.

We were talking about W. Cooper, Walker, Lyons, Grodzicki, Pintar, Surkont, outfielder Garden Gillenwater, and Gornicki. Some still stayed, but those not could be claimed by a lower major league team at a low price. This would not only have been a loss of talent, but the compensation would be far less than their value.

Breadon said it was unfair simply because a team spent money and time in efficient development of players in a farm system, only to lose them at the whim of Commissioner Landis. Simply because the Cardinals had a large chain should not have been reason to penalize the team. All clubs had players under this new rule, but the Cardinals had the most and would be hit the hardest.

There was much debate and heated discussion over this subject. Injuries could penalize a team and then they would have already lost a valuable player because of this ruling, when he could have replaced the injured man. It would help some teams and hurt others. To make matters even worse, Landis wanted to make it retroactive. We all know the government couldn't pass retroactive laws, known as ex post facto. How could Landis do this? Of course he had been the czar of baseball since 1921. While he had done a lot of good, he had also ruled with an iron fist.

The National League wanted a change in the draft ruling from the government as all clubs were opposed to the way it was written. They didn't object to the draft for the military, just the manner in which it was handled. The league would also present a plan for playing army teams and send it to the War Department. The object was to entertain troops and show their patriotic spirit.

The team looked great to Breadon, Rickey and Southworth and they entered the season with high hopes. They expected Mesner to start at third and to use Hopp as a combination outfielder-first baseman. He would play some outfield, relive the regulars when they were injured or needed rest, back up Mize and pinch-hit.

Arnovich said he was rejected by the army after he tried to enlist. A report had been circulated that he had asked for deferment. Some teammates and fans were upset by this story until it was set straight. Arnovich had false teeth and the army at that time wouldn't take men with false teeth. Arnovich was embarrassed to admit he had false teeth.

Veteran catcher Gus Mancuso was to be the key man on the Cardinals "Kiddie Corps." He would help tutor Cooper behind the plate as well as work with the young pitchers. His influence would go a long way to keeping the young pitching staff relaxed, calm and steady.

Southworth saw Mesner at third base, Marion at short and Brown at second. He believed one of his starters would come from the group of 15 young pitchers still with the club. At least four rookies had to make the pitching staff and be successful for the Cardinals to succeed. Mancuso said he believed Cooper should be a 20 game winner.

His job was to work with Mort Cooper and help him over the hump. In the past when Cooper was in trouble, Owen would signal for his curve which from Cooper was nothing more than a wrinkle. The batters then would tee off on Cooper. Mancuso went with the fastball, which was Cooper's meat and potatoes. Lanier was also in the running for a starting pitching slot.

Breadon rated the outfield as the best ever, although that was hard to say when they had Medwick in left and now had Koy. While Koy was a good defensive player and hit .310 last season, he was no Medwick and certainly didn't have his power. Still with Moore in center and Slaughter in right there was a pretty solid combination. Should Koy falter, there was Walker or Hopp ready to step in and fill the job.

Landis, under great pressure, finally relented and revoked his order requiring waivers for draft eligible players sent back to the minors. He did believe that warning legislation should be passed to stop this abuse and evil, as he saw it. The draft we are talking about was not the military, but drafting of players from minor league clubs or those involved in trades that become eligible to be drafted by other teams.[13]

Meanwhile in the American League another time bomb had been defused, at least temporarily. Williams hopefully penned finis to his feud with reporters. He dropped in on correspondents and wiped the slates clean. However, throughout his career, he would be in constant turmoil with the press, especially in Boston. Theirs would be a love-hate relationship.

Grodzicki pushed ahead of other hurlers. The 24 year old Polish boy was from a Pennsylvania coal camp. It was a Cinderella story. During the early part of the season with Rochester in 1940 he had influenza and was now on the comeback trail. In his first nine innings he allowed no runs and two hits. Dizzy Dean and Schoolboy Rowe inspired him to be a pitcher. He had no experience as a pitcher prior to winning a scholarship to Ray Doan's school in 1936.

Uncle Sam told Washington's Buddy Lewis to get ready to report for his physical. He could be the first call up in the majors.

Neither the National nor the American League wanted to give the minor leagues a voice in selecting a replacement for Landis when his contract expired on January 12, 1946. That would make 25 years that he had been the commissioner. In fact, he was the first and had been the only one in the job. Many thought times had changed in the past 25 years and that a Landis type was not now needed.

As the start of the season neared, Southworth was not happy with Mesner. He was considering Brown at third base and Crespi at second. After the team was just 4–8 in spring training, Southworth was taking a harder look at Mesner. He carried 188 pounds and didn't seem to have the bounce in his step to get to grounders on a timely basis. Also he totally lacked power. He batted .336 last season with zero home runs.

The Cardinals were pioneering again in farm system methods. They had developed a training program from officials for their own clubs in a business college of the game. There were courses in publicity, sales promotion, administration and advertising. Leave it to Breadon and Rickey to come up with new systems and new ways to make money. They might not always have loved each other, but they had been a successful duo for almost 25 years.

Southworth made his final decision. Naturally, Mize at first, but Crespi would be at second, Marion at short and Brown at third with Cooper behind the plate. The outfield would be Moore, Slaughter and Hopp. Koy would get only 40 at-bats with St. Louis and be dispatched to Cincinnati.

Rickey stated this would be the best Cardinals outfield in their history. Even better than the 1926 of Chick Hafey, Taylor Douthit and Billy Southworth. While the outfield would be good it wouldn't approach the one the team utilized in 1942. That would have Moore, Slaughter and a youngster named Stan Musial.

Grodzicki had been highly impressive in spring training. The Cardinals were high on him even though he had just a 3–3 record last year. Southworth said he had all the tools to be a winning big league pitcher. His career almost ended last year at Rochester because of influenza and pneumonia. He spent the winter in the Panama Canal Zone and the warm weather cured him. He was now touted as a number one prospect. He could fade by Memorial Day, but for now he was the second coming of Bob Feller, Pete Alexander and Christy Mathewson.

In other spring news the Cardinals sent Haas back to Montreal. It was beginning to look like Mesner would be the third baseman with Lake and Crespi as reserves. Walker seemed to have nailed down the left field job. Warneke announced his goal was 20 wins.

Everyone was touting the Cardinals as the team to beat in the National League. However, after they lost eight of their first 12 spring games, Southworth tore his infield apart and put Crespi at second baseman and Brown at third. He said Brown had slowed a step and couldn't turn the double play the way Crespi could. Mesner was out at third as he had no power. Although he hit .336 in the Pacific Coast League, he had no home runs.

Rickey said, "We will start and finish with this squad, unless of course something unforeseen develops." The Cardinals had a history of creating unforeseen situations either by choice or invitation. The team would stand pat with their present talent. The young pitching had looked very good, so now the key question was, who would be kept and who would get sent back? Koy had now moved into the spotlight to challenge Walker for the left field job.

The experts picked Cincinnati to win a third straight flag with Brooklyn second, and St. Louis third followed by Pittsburgh and Chicago. Cincinnati got the nod because of their strong pitching, led by Bucky Walters and Paul Derringer. This duo had won 94 games the past two seasons, 49 by Walters and 45 by Derringer. Shades of the Dean brothers.

The United States was likely to keep the draft from making heavy inroads into the majors. Current restrictions were only one man per club could be drafted in any one season. This deferment until fall was among many proposals. President Roosevelt knew the value of sports and wanted to keep the game intact.[14]

The Cardinals opened the season in fine fashion on the road by winning three straight at Cincinnati. Cooper and Warneke got two of the victories. Then the club came home and dropped two straight to Chicago with both McGee and Shoun getting hit hard. Crespi had impressed with his hustle, spirit, fielding and hitting in the first week of the season. Koy started off fine, hitting two home runs, and then fizzled. Walker replaced Koy in left field and was installed in the lead off position.

The Cardinals made some adjustments on their roster by sending pitcher Herschel Lyons and Vanderberg to Rochester. Lyons pitched in one game and would never return to the majors. They also sent Roe to Columbus as Southworth was pruning his staff in preparation for the pennant drive.

Cooper's second victory of the season on April 27 put St. Louis in first place. Lanier also gained his second victory, his first as a starter, joining

Cooper and Warneke with two victories each. Nahem beat Pittsburgh as a starter and Hutchinson had sparkled in relief in helping Warneke obtain win number two.

As April drew to a close the Cardinals had four batters at .350 or above, paced by Slaughter's .382. Moore, Crespi and Cooper were the other three hitters in this rare atmosphere. It was shaping up like a real dogfight as Brooklyn had started strong at 11–4, St. Louis was 8–3 and New York close behind at 8–4. It looked like it would prove to be an interesting summer.

After sending several pitchers to the minors, Southworth had decided to reduce the rest of his staff through a process of attrition and personal elimination. He had several good young pitchers and couldn't decide which ones to keep and who to send back to the minors. He hit upon a simple idea. He would let them pitch themselves either into a major league job or back to one of the Cardinals' minor league affiliates.

However, his program backfired on him, although it was with good news. None of the pitchers were eliminating themselves. Nahem had defeated the Pirates on three hits and Krist followed suit with the same. Instead of finding pitchers to option out he was finding starters. He next started Gornicki who shut out Philadelphia. White was his next project and he defeated Boston 5–1. Now he had more starters than he needed. It was a nice dilemma to have.

However the problem was he couldn't start seven pitchers during the season. None of them would get sufficient work. By May 6 the team had run up a 10 game winning streak, including 12 straight on the road. During that 10 game streak, seven different pitchers had started. Only Cooper and Lanier made two starts. Hutchinson was also doing a good job in relief.

The success was not limited to the pitching staff, as the Cardinals had five batters over .300, with Brown the latest addition at .303. Crespi was a key player at second and he and Marion formed a terrific double play combination. Mancuso had been the catcher during the 10 game streak, since Cooper was still learning his trade. He would eventually be the starting catcher. By the middle of May the Cardinals were 15–3 with Brooklyn at 15–6. It looked like a two team fight.

The sportswriters were calling the Cardinals the best young team in baseball. The club had pitching, hitting, speed and defense. Some didn't believe this highly talented team had reached its potential. The only question was would these young daredevils be able to stand up under the pressure of a pennant drive. Southworth said yes as he had a nice blend of veterans on the team. There was Slaughter, Moore, Mancuso, Mize, Morton Cooper and Warneke. All had been through pennant fights before.

The Cardinals' young pitching staff of Nahem, Gornicki, Grodzicki, Krist and White were 8–2, with the two defeats suffered by Grodzicki and White. Grodzicki said he was playing baseball only because of a scholarship awarded him by *The Sporting News* through the Ray Doan school of baseball.

Dizzy Dean and Schoolboy Rowe were at that school and they inspired him to become a pitcher.

Cardinal scout Joe Mathes signed him and sent him to New Iberia in the Evangline League in the spring of 1936. In 1937 he won 18 games for Houston, but got the nickname "Right handed Bill Hallahan" because he walked 174 men. He slipped to 8–7 the next season and then was sick in 1939–40 and was starting all over. The Cardinals viewed him as one of the bright pitching prospects of the future.

All good things must end and so did the Cardinals' 10 game winning streak. It happened with a loud bang as they dropped three straight. Nahem, with relief help from Hutchinson, defeated Pittsburgh to stop the losing streak. The Cardinals were leading the league in hitting and defense and had turned 29 double plays. Crespi made his first error on May 7, while Slaughter looked like a strong challenger for the batting title. Brooklyn jumped back in front with a 20–6 mark, while St. Louis was 17–6. Both teams were on a pace to win over 100 games.

In an effort to strengthen the team and also bring the squad within the player limit they made several moves. They traded McGee (16 game winner in 1940, but 0–1 with a 5.14 ERA in four games this year) to New York for veteran pitcher Harry Gumbert, cash and Paul Dean. The latter was then optioned to Sacramento. The Cardinals then sold Koy to Cincinnati for an undisclosed amount of cash. It was considered significant since Cincinnati forced the trade. Koy would not be missed as Hopp had performed well in the outfield and could also play first base.

Koy had figured to be a part-timer at best and the team already had six outfielders. For that reason the Cardinals also sent Walker to Columbus. At one time it looked like he would be the regular left fielder, but the team believed he needed one more season in the minors. There he got a chance to play every day. They expected him back to stay by next year.

The regular outfield now consisted of Hopp, Moore and Slaughter with Crabtree, Padgett and Triplett as reserves. McGee left the team with mixed emotions, as both Breadon and Rickey liked him. He always seemed on the verge of being a 20 game winner, but never quite made it. Last season was his best. He had been with the Cardinals on and off since 1935.

Rickey thought Dean could make a comeback. He was only 27 and theoretically could have eight to 10 more years of pitching left, if he could overcome his shoulder and arm problems. Rickey believed sending him to Pepper Martin could help. He was always a pal of the Dean brothers and whenever they got into trouble, Martin was the first to their rescue.

Gumbert paid big dividends by shutting out Boston 7–0 in his first start. The Cardinals continued a combination of hitting and pitching that put them in first place. They had five .300 plus hitters with Cooper at 5–1, Warneke 4–0, Nahem 3–0 and Grodzicki and Lanier at 2–1 each. The Cardinals regained first place with a 20–8 mark, while Brooklyn was close behind at 22–9. Cincinnati, last year's pennant winner, was in sixth place at 12–16. Hard to figure with that pitching staff headed by Walters and Derringer.

The Cardinals and Dodgers were the class of the league and already eight games ahead of Cincinnati (winners in 1939–40). The situation was probably best expressed by a minor league player and former national table tennis champion, Bud Blattner, who would become a fair infielder and a great play-by-play broadcaster. He said, surviving his last years in the minors at Sacramento under Martin as an unorthodox manager, "If you had taken an All-Star team of our top farm clubs, I honestly think we could have finished third in the National League to St. Louis and Brooklyn."[15]

Not only was there a clash on the field between St. Louis and Brooklyn there was also a difference in the way the two teams approached baseball and the building of a ball club. Brooklyn's philosophy was to buy the players they needed. A look at their lineup quickly shows that. Dolph Camilli, Billy Herman, Dixie Walker, Cookie Lavagetto, Mickey Owen and Medwick in their starting lineup all came to the team via trade or sale.

This doesn't include Pete Reiser, who was a Cardinals farm hand, but never played for the big club. Their two pitching aces, Whit Wyatt and Kirby Higbe, were not home grown products. Curt Davis, Luke Hamlin, Freddy Fitzsimmons and Hugh Casey were all products of other teams. Although Casey pitched practically his entire career with Brooklyn, he started in the Cincinnati organization. Brooklyn believed it could buy or trade for a pennant.

The Cardinals' philosophy was to develop their own players and then sell the excess. Since 1940 they had received $368,500 for players sold. This did not count the players they received in talent. Admittedly the Cardinals gave up more in talent than they got, but with the wealth of young talent in their farm system, they believed it would serve them well. This strategy worked fine as long as they had an extensive farm system that produced good young talent.

The Cardinals had been successful with such a system, as indicated by their record, since 1926. It would continue to serve them well for the 1940s. However, when television began forcing the closing of minor league markets and farm systems shrank in size, the Cardinals would suffer during the 1950s. However, for now the Redbirds flew high with their vaunted and valued farm system.

The team was strong with pitching and carried 11 pitchers. It was the first time the team had carried more than nine, said Rickey, but they had such a rich staff it was difficult to decide who to send down. Currently the team was carrying only six bench players. As the season progressed Southworth believed he would need at least one more bat on the bench.

Rickey, Breadon and Southworth all believed it was pennant time for St.

Louis. This was especially true after they won six in a row from Brooklyn and Pittsburgh. They had now defeated Pittsburgh eight of eight this season. The Cardinals had their second major injury (the second of many for the season) when Crespi fractured the third finger on his right hand trying to make a double play.

Brown took over at second and Mesner played third in the interim. Just a week before the Cardinals lost catcher Cooper with a fractured bone in his shoulder and a dislocated collarbone in a collision. In time these became telling injuries and would come back to haunt the team. Southworth finally decided to trim his pitching staff and in a surprise move Gornicki was optioned to Rochester and Grodzicki to Columbus. They were sent out so they could get more work, by pitching every fourth or fifth day. The team decided to keep White. Many fans thought that White should have been sent out and one of the other two retained.

Southworth kept White because Lanier was the only other left hander on the staff. The fans didn't think that was a good enough reason. Brooklyn was loaded with heavy hitting left hand batters; Camilli, Reiser and Dixie Walker were three of the four top hitters on the team.

The New York Giants were hesitant to make any more trades with St. Louis as the last few had not fared so well for them. McGee, Bowman and Orengo had all fallen below expectations, while Gumbert had gotten off to a good start for St. Louis. Rickey and Breadon had always been known as good horse traders and rarely came out on the losing end.

The Cardinals march toward the pennant continued, fueled by a fine pitching staff that was a mixture of veterans and young arms. It was a much improved staff over 1940. The team had also developed some excellent hitters with seven hitters at .290 or greater, led by Mize at .353 and Slaughter at .352. The catching and handling of the pitchers was much improved over 1940. For these reasons St. Louis was starting to put some daylight between themselves and Brooklyn. They were 27–9, three and one-half games ahead of Brooklyn (23–12).

The Dodgers continued to stick to their spend and build policy while the Cardinals continued their farm system program. Both teams were playing extremely well and despite an 11 game winning streak the Cardinals couldn't open any daylight with Brooklyn. During that 11 game streak they came back several times from deficits of two and four runs to win games. They took two from Brooklyn, four from Pittsburgh, three from Chicago and two from Cincinnati for the streak. On Memorial Day 25,632 saw the Cardinals win a double-header from Cincinnati. They were far ahead of last season's attendance.

More injuries continued to plague the team and one had to wonder how long they could continue at their present pace without some tell tale effects. Mize was out with injuries and his big bat would be missed in the lineup.

Hopp had moved to first base and did a good job fielding and hitting. While Hopp was a better fielder, faster and hit .300, he lacked the long ball power of Mize.

The team did get some good news when Crespi returned to the lineup. Neither Mesner nor Lake hit very well in his absence. With Cooper out Mancuso had been an outstanding one man catching department. While Padgett spelled him occasionally behind the plate, that was not his forte. He, Triplett and Crabtree alternated in the outfield when Hopp was at first base. Cooper was the leader on the staff at 6–1 and Gumbert was 3–0 since joining the team.

On June 7 the Cardinals wore protective helmets for the first time. Since the severe beaning of Medwick last year, several teams had taken to using batting helmets. However, at this time it was not a common practice and many batters considered them a hindrance and nuisance. On that day the Cardinals banged out 19 hits in annihilating New York 11–2. White, in relief of Nahem, pitched eight innings of four hit relief ball to gain his second victory.

The team continued to play great baseball, despite the numerous injuries. Mize now had a broken bone in his finger and would miss several games. With Hopp at first, Padgett and Triplett platooned in left field. However, neither was the equal of Hopp as an outfielder. The team still had seven players at .293 or better while the pitching continued to sparkle. Warneke was now 7–1, Cooper 6–3 (losing his last two decisions) while Krist and Nahem were 4–0. Despite all these heroics Brooklyn still trailed by just one game.

There was an axiom in baseball which said a team was no stronger than its reserves. Sort of akin to the old bromide that a chain was only as strong as its weakest link. The Cardinals had an excellent outfield, first base and catching reserves, but were weak on the infield. As long as Brown, Marion and Crespi could play, the team was fine. If one went down there were problems, as both Mesner and Lake had not done the job.

Brown broke his hand sliding into third base in completing a triple. This would necessitate some lineup changes. They alternated Lake and Mesner at third, but neither hit very much. Mesner was hitting .145 and Lake .105. They even tried Crabtree at third for one game, and while he was a good hitter, Crabtree was no third baseman. The team could only hope for a speedy recovery from Brown. Half of the infield was now in sick bay, although Hopp did a fine job filling in for Mize.

The Cardinals led the league in hitting at .288 and in defense at .978. They, Cincinnati and Brooklyn were virtually tied for team ERA honors. This had enabled the team to build a two and one-half game bulge on Brooklyn, but not for long since the Dodgers were a hot ball club.

On June 13, 15,700 saw Lanier best Wyatt 1–0. In a double-header with Brooklyn on June 15, 34,543 showed up and saw Warneke lose the opener 8–1. However, the crowd went home happy as White won the nightcap 5–3.

Brooklyn was a hot team until a lefty pitched. The fans were now beginning to see Southworth's strategy in keeping White.

The Cardinals received a double blow as they dropped three of four to New York, wiping out their first place edge. Southworth said that was an obstacle they could overcome. The second one did not look as easy. Cooper, who was fast becoming the best pitcher on the team, was in jeopardy of being lost for the season. He had calcified cartilage growth on his right elbow and was operated on on June 23. Cooper was off to a great start and then slumped, but much of that was blamed on his elbow problem.

He would be out at least six weeks, but could be out for the season. Most pitchers after having this type of operation were out at least one year and sometimes longer. There was more danger of re-injuring the arm and possibly doing permanent damage by pitching too soon. Most did not expect Cooper back until next season. He was 7–3, with a chance for 20 victories.

Cooper didn't have his customary zip in his last several starts and that was when it was noticed that something was seriously wrong with him. Both Coopers were now on the disabled list. The Cardinals, rather than call up one of their pitchers from the minors because of their longstanding policy of not interfering with teams in the pennant race, purchased Bill Crouch (2–3) from Philadelphia. Crouch was a right hander with a 6–3 career record who had pitched mostly in relief.

White, who had been given little regard by the experts in spring training, won the only game from New York when he pitched his second consecutive two hit shut out. That gave him 26 consecutive scoreless innings. He had eight against New York in relief, then nine against Brooklyn and now nine more against New York.

With Cooper out, the big four starting rotation would be Warneke, Gumbert, Lanier and White. If one of them faltered then someone else would be given a chance. The team got some good news in that Mize was back in the lineup; however, although hitting for average he was not delivering the long ball.

Brown was expected to be out for two more weeks. Mesner had moved into third, because Lake didn't hit. However, Mesner's average wasn't much higher. While neither performed very well for St. Louis, both would play for several years in the majors. Mesner became Cincinnati's third baseman from 1943–45, averaging around .255. Lake played in the majors until 1950, with 1945–47 his best seasons when he played shortstop for the Red Sox and Detroit and drew over 100 walks each season. Although he didn't hit for the Cardinals he did show the ability to coax a walk. He had 76 official plate appearances for the season and would also draw 22 walks.

At this point in time the Cardinals had not renewed Rickey's five year $50,000 per season contract. Normally it was renewed one year in advance. Breadon said this didn't mean he wasn't going to be back. Breadon didn't think it was such a good idea at this time to tie up such a contract with the outlook of the nation the way it was. At Rickey's age it was hard to understand what impact the draft or possible war could have on him.

Perhaps Breadon now thought he could run the team without Rickey. One must remember the farm system was basically Rickey's idea and that was what had made the Cardinals so successful for the past two decades. It was the reason they were in first place. Despite all their injuries the team clung to a one-half game lead over Brooklyn heading into the final week of June.[16]

The Cardinals had just completed a 10–6 homestand, not bad when you consider all their problems and injuries. They would be on the road until July 22. That would be a very telling trip for the team. However, they started the trip without one of their key reserves as Padgett was left behind with a very severe case of tonsillitis. The Cardinals' reserves and regulars continued their hitting onslaught while White picked up some of the pitching slack left by Cooper's absence. At the July 4 mark both St. Louis and Brooklyn were 47–23.

The Cardinals hit a slump and lost five in a row, as their bats developed holes in them. St. Louis fans took it calmly. They were confident the team would bounce back and the hitters would start batting like they had for the first half of the season. The pitching, however, continued to hold up. On July 11 Pittsburgh defeated St. Louis for their first victory over them this year.

The five losses in a row were three in Chicago and two in Cincinnati. Lanier lost the first game 2–1 on two unearned runs. Then they dropped a double-header 6–5 and 5–2. Lake's error (subbing for Brown) gave Chicago the victory in game one. Padgett (giving Mancuso a rest in game two) made a key error in that defeat. In Cincinnati Nahem lost 2–1 on two unearned runs and then Elmer Riddle defeated them 3–0.

The Cardinals' usual stellar defense led to four of the five defeats. Two of the games were lost when substitutes (Lake and Padgett) made key errors. A few key hits would have won four of the games despite the fielding problems. Those five defeats enabled Brooklyn to open a three game lead on St. Louis.

Brown and Cooper were both due back soon. The losing streak was broken on July 12, the day Brown returned. On the next day the Cardinals took a double-header from Philadelphia, the very day Walker Cooper returned. Warneke was now a 10 game winner and had a chance for 20 wins. Lanier, White and Gumbert each had won six. It was especially gratifying in White's case, as he was in the bullpen for much of the first six weeks. At this juncture Mize had an excellent chance to lead the league in batting. He was at .348.

Despite their recent recovery Brooklyn had a three and one-half game lead on St. Louis. They were 54–26 while St. Louis was 51–30. Both teams could win over 100 games. It had happened only twice this century. In 1909 the Chicago Cubs won 104 while Pittsburgh won 110. In 1915 the Boston Red Sox won 101 and Detroit won 100.

The Cardinals finished their road trip at 9–9 after dropping six of the first seven. They won two games in Brooklyn and took a double-header from Boston on July 20. In game one at Brooklyn, St. Louis won 7–4 before 32,265. Warneke, in relief of Lanier, won in 12 innings. He pitched from the eighth through the 12th innings. White took the second game of the double-header 6–1 and was now 7–3.

Warneke then won his 12th game in relief at Boston. However, there was more bad news for St. Louis as Moore pulled a shoulder muscle in a 10–6 loss to Boston on July 19. This was the seventh major injury this year for the team, with Mize being out twice. Southworth just shook his head wondering what else could happen with two and one-half months left to go.

However, thanks to their recent surge, a renewal of the hitting, continued fine pitching and the two victories at Brooklyn, St. Louis was right back on the heels of the Dodgers. Brooklyn was 57–30 and St. Louis was 56–31. New York continued in third at 44–37, but would soon collapse. Cincinnati, after its terrible start, was now 46–39. They had been playing well in excess of .600 ball since the first month. Unfortunately for them so were St. Louis and Brooklyn, plus these two teams had a hot start.

White had become the fair haired boy on the Cardinals' pitching staff and a new hero to St. Louis fans. He won four games in five days. Shades of Dizzy. He won three games in three days against New York. This stretch put the Cardinals back in first place. It all started on July 22 when he pitched 5⅔ innings against New York and won.

Then the next day he pitched a hitless 12th and the Cardinals won in the last of the inning 5–4. On July 24 he relieved in the 10th inning and fanned Gabby Hartnett and Johnny Rucker, leaving Dick Bartell stranded at third. The Cardinals then scored the winning run in the bottom of the 10th on a hit by Brown for a 3–2 victory.

White rested on the 25th as Jim Tobin and Boston shut out St. Louis 8–0 before the largest crowd (22,933) of the year. The next day he defeated Boston 9–2 in a complete game. Early in the season many criticized Southworth for sending Gornicki and Grodzicki to the minors and keeping White. Now he was their hero with an 11–3 record and a good chance for 20 victories.

On July 27 the Cardinals got embroiled in a slugfest and lost 12–10 as Warneke was hit hard. However they won the second game behind their good luck charm Krist, who was now 8–0. In his first four seasons in the majors he posted a 37–9 record, used mostly in relief, although making an occasional start.

The pitchers were receiving much of the glory and deservedly so, but there were other important contributors on the team. The stellar defensive play of Crespi (who led second basemen with 94 double plays) and Brown at third had been critical. The hitting of Hopp, Mize, Moore, Slaughter and Cooper had been a big factor in the team's success. Cooper was hit hard in the first game of the July 29 double-header, but he showed no ill effects of the operation. As the month drew to a close St. Louis (61–33) enjoyed a two game edge on Brooklyn (59–35). Pittsburgh and Cincinnati were now tied for third, as New York had slipped to fifth.

The team, although winning, had not been getting many complete games over the past three weeks. Early season sensations like Nahem and Gumbert had faded. Recently Warneke, Lanier and Shoun were not finishing what they started. Shoun was a double duty pitcher in 1940, appearing in a league high 54 games, completing 13 of 19 starts as he finished 13–11. He was a major disappointment this year. He ended at 3–5 with a 5.66 ERA, appearing in 26 games and failing to complete any of his six starts.

Finally in an August 3 double-header against Philadelphia with Cooper leading the way the Cardinals got a complete game win 6–1. Cooper was back after just six weeks to the amazement of everyone. This seemed to wake up Warneke who also pitched a complete game 6–1 victory and was now 13–5.

The next day Krist also pitched a complete game, albeit not very pretty as he went 9–0 in an 11–7 victory over Philadelphia. Warneke had been throwing the home run ball and weakening in the late innings, but not in the double-header. The Cardinals had power, skill afield and were running fools. With Cooper back and showing no ill effects of his operation, the pitching looked great. Slaughter led the team with 12 home runs, which was sort of a strange position for him. Mize had 10, which put him in unfamiliar territory at this stage of the season. He was hitting .323, but not getting the long ball. Some think his reduction of power was brought on by the various injuries he had had this season.

The Cardinals' attendance was now at 408,793 and Breadon was smiling brightly. Maybe he would now renew Rickey's contract with the Redbirds drawing so well and being in first place. Whatever the differences were between the two it was hoped they could be worked out. St. Louis would have hated to lose Rickey and see him work his magic for someone else.

Cooper had now won four in a row, three straight since returning from his operation. He followed up his victory at Philadelphia with a 3–2 win over Cincinnati on August 7 and then three days later beat Pittsburgh 4–2. Cooper was now 10–3, and although his chance for 20 was gone because of the six weeks he lost, a good season was still in the offing.

Another pitcher who was headed for a great season and possibly 20 wins was White. He had now won eight in a row after defeating Chicago 4–2 on August 4 and then stopping Pittsburgh 3–2 on August 10. He was now 14–3 for the season. Cooper, White and Warneke gave the Cardinals an unmatched big three in the league. The Dodgers had Wyatt and Higbe, but didn't have a third starter to compare to the Redbirds.

Just when it looked like all the dark clouds were gone, disaster struck again. The team had both Coopers back, Brown and Crespi were playing, Mize and Moore were in the lineup. Then the worse possible thing happened. Slaughter, who was leading the team in most offensive categories, broke his collarbone. It was feared he could be lost for the season. The team had good outfield reserves, but none of his caliber.

Slaughter and Moore both were going after a long hard hit drive and the latter made a great catch, but as he did they collided and Slaughter broke his collarbone. This was a severe blow. He was hitting .312 with 13 home runs and 74 RBIs. He was on a pace to hit 20 home runs and drive in 120. Not only were his offense and defense missed, but also his all out hustle and hard play. He could have played for the Gas House Gang. He was cut from that mold.

In an effort to strengthen the infield reserves the Cardinals send Mesner to Rochester and called up veteran Floyd "Pep" Young. He was a former Pirate, having played for them from 1933 to 1940. Cincinnati had him at the start of this season and now he was in the Cardinals chain. Unfortunately he did not help the situation, batting just twice as a pinch hitter and going hitless.

As mid–August approached St. Louis and Brooklyn were in a virtual dead heat for first place. Not only had St. Louis being drawing great, but so had Brooklyn, who led the league in attendance. Brooklyn would probably draw 1,200,000 or double most teams in the majors.

Hopp was a real Gas Houser. He could have played for the original Gas House Gang, as he was another of the current players who were cut from that mold. He did belly flop slides, had skill, courage and a fine batting eye. The phrase Gas House implied courage, fight, speed and hell bent action. It was no misnomer. They came to play and so did Hopp. He was one of Rickey's boys.

Rickey broke his own rule when he called pitching ace Howard Pollet up from Houston, even though they were in a pennant race. However, their situations were different. They had a 24 game lead. Pollet was 20–3 with 1.09 ERA and five shutouts. Rickey realized he could still incur the wrath of the fans as Houston would then play for the Dixie World Series, which pitted the winner of the Texas League (Houston) against the winner of the Southern Association.

White's eight game winning streak was ended by Pittsburgh 3–2. Cooper gained his 11th victory the next day, but Warneke lost the second game. The schedule favored the Cardinals the rest of the way as starting with a Labor Day double-header on September 1 with Pittsburgh all their games were at home except for one trip to Pittsburgh and two to Chicago.

It would be a race to the wire and the Dodgers may have had the edge. They would play Boston (seventh place) and Philadelphia (last and eventual losers of 111 games) during the last two series of the season while the Cardinals played Pittsburgh and Chicago, decidedly tougher opponents. Also the Cardinals were without the services of their star right fielder, Slaughter. The team was braced for an all out drive to the wire.

The team continued its lusty hitting as Hopp, Mize, Slaughter, Brown and Moore were all at .310 or greater. White was a 14 game winner, Warneke had 13 and Cooper 11 to pace the mound staff. With six weeks to play White and Warneke both had a chance for 20 victories. Brooklyn held a one game edge on St. Louis.

As if things weren't bad enough Moore was beaned in Boston, just ten days after Slaughter was injured. He was hit by a pitch from Art Johnson. He missed the Philadelphia and Brooklyn trip. It was thought he might be able to return in another week, but that was up to the doctors. Hopp was then hurt in Philadelphia sliding into second base when Bobby Bragan stepped on his hand. It was badly cut, bruised and lacerated, but he got back into the game during the Brooklyn series.

The team was now down to three outfielders until Hopp could return. A reserve outfield of Crabtree, Triplett and Padgett was fine, maybe even excellent. But it was not a good starting outfield, especially for a team competing for a pennant. Crabtree was hitting .462 when Slaughter went down. That was based on 29 for 62, much of that as a pinch hitter and spot starter.

Southworth, who was 48 and hadn't played since 1935 when managing the Class B Asheville team, took batting practice in case the team needed him. This was the type of spirit that was in Southworth and the Cardinals that carried them all season through so much adversity. If playing on sheer intestinal fortitude or just plain guts could win the pennant, then the Redbirds were home free.

Pollet won his first start on August 20, the day Moore got hurt, 3–2 over Boston in the second game of the double-header. White had won his 15th in the first game. On August 24 he got win number 16 over Brooklyn in the first game of a double-header, but Pollet lost 3–2 in the nightcap. When Warneke defeated Philadelphia on August 22 it was his first victory since July 20. An entire month without winning one game.

The Cardinals still had Mize, Hopp, Slaughter, Moore and Brown over the .300 mark. On the mound White was inching closer to 20 wins as he was now 16–4, Warneke 14–7 and Cooper at 11–4. Lanier, who had been counted on for at least 15 victories, and Gumbert were both 7–6. Marion was the only regular who had not been injured and had played every game. After Moore's beaning all the Cardinals players began wearing their batting helmets.

On August 30 Warneke no-hit Cincinnati 2–0 for his 15th victory. It was the first Cardinals no-hitter since Paul Dean in 1934. Pollet had been brilliant in his first four starts and was 3–1 and easily could have been 4–0. The team won seven in a row and were back in first place, despite Slaughter and Moore not being in the lineup.

The Cardinals played Pittsburgh in a double-header before 34,812, the largest crowd in two years. White, improving his chances for 20 victories, won the first game 5–3 and Pollet was the winner in game two, 6–2. Moore, suffering from headaches and a punctured ear drum from being beaned, hoped to be back by mid–September. Slaughter was hoping for the same date of return.

Breadon, Rickey and Southworth hoped they could return and be ready for the stretch drive. The Cardinals outfield situation was a major problem with the two of them injured. The only reliable outfielder was Hopp. Triplett could hit, but was only a fair outfielder. Neither Padgett nor Crabtree would win accolades as fielders and both had stopped hitting. Crabtree finished the season at .341 (57 for 167), but batted just .267 when called on for regular duty. That hurt.

The Cardinals had a one-half game edge on Brooklyn with 25 to play. Most of Brooklyn's remaining games were against the weaker teams. They also had the two leading winners in the league in Wyatt and Higbe, each with 18 wins at this time.

The team was hoping that the return of Slaughter and Moore could propel them to the pennant. The team had fought so hard against so much adversity that to fall by the wayside now would be a terrible loss. At home they were 42–18, whereas on the road they were 41–29. Their road record had not been very good since the early going. They started 14–3 on the road, but were just 27–26 since that time. Fortunately 17 of their last 24 games were at home.

The Cardinals had the jitters on September fourth and lost a double-header to the Cubs. Their usual fine defense made seven errors in the two games, five in game two. They were also tight at the plate, being shut out twice in three games including the home opener against Cincinnati on September 6. They were shut out by Johnny Vander Meer of the Reds on two hits as he fanned 14. Claude Passeau of the Cubs also shut them out. After splitting a double-header with Cincinnati on September 7 the team had fallen three games off the pace.

The pressure was on the young players, especially with all the injuries, and it was starting to show. The showdown series with Brooklyn was September 11 through 13. It had a World Series atmosphere due to the many requests from out-of-town scribes. Extra press seats were provided in the grandstand.

The three game set drew 69,774 and the fans got their money's worth. The games were filled with great pitching and thrills. The fans got everything they wanted except three Cardinals victories, which would have put them back in first place. Brooklyn took the series two games to one and now the fans were all but conceding the pennant.

In game one White was the heartbreaking loser in 11 innings 6–4. He should have won the game in regulation play 4–1, but three unearned runs kept Brooklyn in the game. Pollet won the next day 4–3 despite errors. The final game was a great pitching duel between Wyatt and Cooper. Cooper pitched no-hit ball for 7⅓ innings then Walker got a double and Herman after two swing strikes doubled for the only run of the game and a 1–0 Dodgers win.

The Cardinals got a bad break in the fifth when Crespi doubled and Marion grounded to Reese, who threw to third to get Crespi, who was going to slide. The ball hit him in the head and knocked him out and rolled toward the St. Louis dugout. Had he not been knocked unconscious the Cardinals would have scored and had Marion at second with no outs. Wyatt then fanned Mancuso and Cooper and got Brown on a ground out.

Southworth, not one to grouse or complain, saw where the team could have just as easily won all three games. It also would have been a different series had Slaughter and Moore been available. Just when everyone was writing the Cardinals off they came storming back once more. They took a double-header from the Giants as Warneke got number 17 in a 1–0 victory over Carl Hubbell.

Moore played in the first game against New York, but was hitless, although playing a flawless center field. Slaughter pinch-hit against Brooklyn and New York. Crabtree was hitting just .233 for the past 15 games. What a difference that had made. White lost his last three decisions while Cooper was the loser in four of six. Their defeats were not a matter of poor pitching, but a lack of hitting.

Even though Moore returned to the lineup he wasn't the same hitter. The effects of the beaning clearly showed in his hitting. It would be next season before he returned to normal. Meanwhile Mize was injured again, the third time this year. He was hurt on September 19 when he stretched out too far to tag first after fielding a grounder. He injured his shoulder and when he was able to return to the lineup he couldn't muster his power swing.

The courageous Cardinals fought to the bitter end. Just when it looked like it was all over they came roaring back one more time. The Cardinals took a double-header over the Cubs and Southworth was rewarded with a new contract for 1942 for the great season he had put together. Breadon said regardless of what happened Southworth and the Cardinals had done a superb job.

It looked like it was all over on September 20 when Chicago scored six in the ninth to defeat St. Louis 7–3. Brooklyn took two from the futile Philadelphia team and everyone was counting the Cardinals out and the Dodgers in. Once more they bounced back and took a double-header from Chicago the next day while Philadelphia defeated Brooklyn. They were just one game out.

Finally the Dodgers nailed down the pennant with a 100–54 record. The Cardinals finished at 97–56, with one game not played, a truly gallant effort against almost unbelievable odds. Time and time again during the season the team kept fighting back against all kinds of adversity. They truly earned their spurs, this young fighting reincarnation of the Gas House Gang.

In late September the Cardinals called up a young outfielder from Rochester. His name was Stanley Frank Musial. In 1940 he was a 19 year old pitcher and center fielder for the Daytona Beach Class C team. In August of that year he injured his shoulder making a diving catch. Everyone thought his career was over.

However, he could hit so he was assigned to Springfield in the Western Association, where he hit .379 in the Class C league. He then went to Rochester (AAA) and batted .326. Rickey called him up and except for a year in the navy he would remain for 22 years. He was six for his first 10 and 12 for his first 22.

In a double-header against Chicago Musial doubled and singled twice in the first game. In the ninth inning, while the Cubs' first baseman argued over a close play, Musial raced home from second with the winning run. In the second game he had two more hits and made two diving catches. This prompted Chicago manager and former Cardinals catcher Jimmy Wilson to comment, "Nobody, but nobody, can be that good." But as many found out, he was for 22 years.[17]

Musial batted .426 for the remainder of the season and many said if he had been brought up one or two weeks sooner St. Louis would have won the pennant, despite all the adversity. He would have played in the Brooklyn games, a team whose pitching he would terrorize down through the years. In fact it was in Brooklyn where his famous nickname, "The Man," was born when fans started yelling, "Oh, no! Here comes that man again."[18]

In summing up the Cardinals' season no one needed to hang their head in shame. A team picked for third came within an eyelash of winning it all. Only the injuries stopped them. This in no way was meant to demean the Dodgers, who had a great team and also put up a magnificent spirited fight. However, they did not have the injuries that St. Louis sustained. In fact five of the Dodgers were ex–Cardinals. They were Medwick, Owen, Davis, Reiser and manager Leo Durocher.

Injuries are part of the game and all teams experience them, but when they become excessive it is almost impossible to overcome them. The only serious injury the Dodgers sustained was to veteran pitcher Freddy Fitzsimmons who had elbow problems and appeared in only 13 games. At age 39 he didn't figure to appear in much more than 20 games, thus he made two-thirds of what the Dodgers counted him for. From 1935 to 1940 Fitzsimmons had appeared in from 17 to 28 games. He had not been in over 30 since 1934 when he appeared in 38 games.

Meanwhile the Cardinals had their regular lineup together for just 23 games. Only Marion escaped the injury jinx. The Cardinals had 12 major injuries. Minor or routine injuries were not considered. Mize was out three times, Brown was out twice, while Hopp, Mancuso and Crespi each had a period that they could not play. Then there was Slaughter's broken collarbone which rendered him virtually useless for the last seven weeks and Moore's beaning which left him at less than full strength for the last six weeks of the season.

The Coopers were both out for extended stays. Pitcher Mort missed six weeks when his elbow was operated on and brother Walker, counted on to be the number one catcher, appeared in only 63 games as a catcher. The Dodgers' Owen was in 128. The Dodgers averaged 140 games per regular while the Cardinals averaged 124.

The team had just three short periods where the entire team played together: from May 4 to May 18 for 12 games, for seven games from July 27 to August 3, and four games from August 6 to August 10.

The Cardinals would gain their revenge in 1942 in another hotly contested race with the Dodgers, but this time the victory would be theirs. Brooklyn would win 104 games, but St. Louis would set its team record at 106. They took 43 of the last 51 games to win and come from as far behind as 10½ games in mid–August. They then completed the season by defeating the Yankees four games to one in the World Series after New York had taken the opener.

This would be Rickey's last season with the Cardinals and while there were some within the organization that were glad to see him go, in time his loss would be greatly felt. Breadon would sell the club in 1947 and while new owners Bob Hannegan and Fred Saigh wanted to build pennant winners, they didn't have a genius like Rickey at the helm guiding the ship.

Rickey would take his genius to Brooklyn and after the 1942 season, Brooklyn would flounder for a couple of years, but by 1946 they were back on track and starting in 1947 they would win six pennants in 10 years. Unfortunately they won only one World Series, losing to the Yankees each time. One can only think those pennants, or at least several of them, could have belonged to St. Louis had Rickey remained and worked his magic there as he had for 20 years.

One final observation about the 1941 Cardinals and that was their fighting spirit. This was the period when the "Cardinals type" was used generally by baseball men to describe any young, eager, fast athlete who played hungrily and a bit recklessly.

THREE

1942

The Cardinals' Victory Garden

A decision was made that would likely keep the draft from making heavy inroads into major league baseball. The decision was that no more than one man would be taken from each team and the deferment was until fall 1941. However, the picture would change should the United States become actively involved in the war. President Roosevelt knew the value of the sport to the American public.[1]

Headlines in various papers read, "It's in the Cards to win in 1942." The team was destined to be an even stronger club as they would have Stan Musial for a full season and the pitching was going to be even better than in 1941. Various National League teams said St. Louis should have been in the World Series, as they were the better of the two teams. This was the same story as in 1939. It seems like St. Louis had taken the role of a bridesmaid, but never a bride. All forecasts were that would change in 1942.

The Cardinals planned to bring up some of the best young talent in the minors. The pitchers that they would take to spring training were Murray Dickson, Fred Gornicki, Johnny Grodzicki, Harry "The Cat" Brecheen, Max Surkont, and Freddy Martin (teammate of Howard Pollet at Houston). There was also talk that Mize would be traded, despite being very valuable and the most potent hitter in the league. Mize was extremely popular with the St. Louis fans. His weakness was his fielding, as Mize covered very little ground. The Cardinals planned to bring Johnny Hopp and Ray Sanders (both first basemen) to spring training. It looked like a message was being sent.

The Brooklyn Dodgers, the reigning champs, took great resentment at the statements that the best team was not in the World Series. They said they had won the pennant and the right to be there. Regarding that comment and that the Cardinals were shoo-ins for 1942, the Dodgers' attitude was just wait and see until all the games have been played.

Bob Feller told the Cleveland Indians that he was close to being drafted, but would not ask for a deferment. This was much to the chagrin of Cleveland, which lost the pennant by one game in 1940. In 1941, they slumped to 75–79, but Feller was 25–13. Feller felt that it was his duty to serve his country if it needed him.

Rumors continued to circulate that Branch Rickey (often at odds with Cardinals owner Sam Breadon, who liked the limelight and resented all the accolades that went to Rickey) would leave the Cardinals and move to the St. Louis Browns and do for them what he did for the Cardinals. The program was that he would run the club with President Donald Barnes and Bill DeWitt would be farm director. It would then be Rickey's responsibility to build a farm system like he did with the Cardinals.[2]

Over in the American League the Detroit Tigers lost pitcher Fred Hutchinson to the Navy for four years. Hutchinson was to be inducted in the Army on November third so he enlisted in the Navy for four years. Detroit had planned on his being an important part of their 1942 pitching staff. On the positive side the return of Hank Greenberg from his one year tour of duty was expected to help the Tigers' offense.

Another reason most scribes and observers picked St. Louis for 1942 was the young arms that would be added to an already outstanding pitching staff. They would have Pollet for a full season. He came up in September and was 5–2 with a 1.93 ERA. At Houston he had set a new ERA mark in 1941 at 1.16, while teammate Martin set a new record by winning his first 13 starts.

Some of the public raised concern over some of the Cardinals working at the small arms plant on Goodfellow Avenue in the off-season. The plant employed Walker and Morton Cooper, Enos Slaughter, Terry Moore and Ernie White. Opponents argued that at least Slaughter and Morton Cooper made enough money in the off-season that they didn't have to work at the small arms plant and take jobs from more needy people.[3]

Many people were still unemployed or making a very low wage and could use one of those good paying jobs at a defense plant, was the argument. Those who supported the players said they had to eat in the six month off-season, so they had the same right to the jobs as anyone else. Also it was a patriotic duty, doing defense work. Still others claimed that some made enough playing ball to carry them through the entire year. The issue never became a serious one and soon was forgotten as we entered the war.[4]

Southworth planned to bring to spring training 11 pitchers that were 175–99 in the minors in 1941, all at Class A or above. In 1941 there was quite a howl of disapproval from fans when Grodzicki and Gornicki were sent back to the minors and White was kept. However, when White turned in a 17–7, 2.40 ERA season all that was forgotten, as he was one of the mainstays of the staff and became a St. Louis hero.

The records of the six key pitchers Southworth planned to bring were: Dickson (21–11), Grodzicki (19–5), Brecheen (16–6), George "Red" Munger (17–16), Gornicki (13–9) and Surkont (10–6).

Rumors of a Mize trade continued to circulate, especially when it was known that two good fielding first basemen (Hopp and Sanders) were going to be at spring training. While they both lacked the power of Mize they were solid line drive hitters with speed and the ability to hit .300 or better. Mize's home run total dropped from 43 in 1940 to 16 in 1941 and he played in 29 fewer games, which did have some impact on his total, but didn't tell the full story. Mize batted .317 with 100 RBIs. His would be a hard bat to replace in the lineup.

Trade rumors weren't the only ones circulating about the Cardinals. It continued to be said that Rickey would leave the Cardinals and join the Browns. Rickey would bring money and talent to the team. His current contract with the Cardinals ran through 1942, but had not been extended. In the past Rickey had always received a new five year contract the season before the old one was to expire. It didn't happen this past year.[5]

Breadon hadn't done it because he thought he could run the club and the farm system and also receive all the glory. Breadon commented, "I haven't been in baseball for 25 years without learning a few things. Certainly I have learned a few things." Breadon was no longer actively engaged in any other activity or enterprise and therefore said he could devote his full time to operating the Cardinals.

All National League teams were extremely jealous of Cardinals pitching and wanted to bid on some of the pitchers. They were willing to negotiate a trade or purchase a pitcher outright. All the clubs were well aware of the Cardinals' policy of selling excess talent since they had the largest farm system in the league. It was more than double the size of any other club.

The Brooklyn Dodgers were interested in one of the five left handers on the Cardinals and were quickly told that neither Pollet nor White were available. The team might possibly consider Lanier, Shoun or Brecheen, the Dodgers were advised. However, at this time they were told no trade was possible until the Cardinals saw what the draft brought. Lanier pitched in tough luck last season and was slowed down by several injuries. Being a heavy set fellow Lanier was prone to bruise or injure easily.

The entire picture on the draft would change with the Japanese bombing of Pearl Harbor. Martin had already been drafted on November fourth. Babe Young of the Giants was told to be ready to go to the Army and Greenberg was headed back after the bombing of Pearl Harbor. He would eventually spend four and one-half years in the service, which kept him from achieving some very high levels in home runs, RBIs and other categories. Still in just 9½ seasons he hit 331 home runs, scored 1051 runs, had 1276 RBIs and a career average of .312. Twice he hit 50 or more home runs (once 58). He is also tied for number one in RBIs per game at .92.[6]

Organized baseball was ready to spark war morale similar to the action that was taken in World War I (1917–18). One of the first things they wanted to do was limit the number of night games, as this would help the blackout situation. The St. Louis Browns had been fighting for 14 night games for the season, but that was now futile with the war effort being put forward. Breadon had initially fought against night baseball expansion, stating that if it was expanded to 14 games per team it would eventually kill night baseball.[7]

Rumors had persisted that Barnes wanted to move the St. Louis Browns to Los Angeles. They would have played at Wrigley Field in Los Angeles, but that field was owned by the Chicago Cubs. With the war now on that move was tabled for the duration.

The situation now was that more players were headed for military service and the ruling of one player per team became passé. Cecil Travis and Sid Hudson of the Washington Senators were both reclassified as 1-A. Grodzicki would follow Martin into the service. These men would be just the first few of hundreds of major leaguers and thousands of minor leaguers that would eventually serve their country.

The Cardinals finally turned loose one of their pitching prospects when they sold Gornicki to Pittsburgh for cash and outfielder-third baseman Deb Garms and catcher Ray Mueller. The latter two were immediately assigned to Sacramento of the Pacific Coast League. Mueller would later become a Cincinnati Reds player and set a major league record for consecutive games caught. Garms had won a disputed batting title in 1940 with a .355 mark, but had only 358 at-bats. He did however play in 103 games to make the qualifier of appearing in at least 100 games.

The Giants said if Young went into the Army they wanted either Mize or Hopp from the Cardinals. The Cardinals acquiesced and traded Mize to the Giants for $60,000 cash, pitcher Hank Lohrman, catcher Ken O'Dea and first baseman Johnnie McCarthy (who was sent to Columbus to replace Sanders). The trade surprised Breadon, as Rickey made it after Breadon had left the meeting in Chicago.

Rickey had been working on a deal with the Dodgers to get first baseman Dolph Camilli and catcher Herman Franks, but it fell through. Mize, once considered a good team man, irked Southworth during the last weeks of the season when he had an arm injury, didn't dress and sit on the bench, but instead put on street clothes and sat in the grandstand or press box. This also irked and irritated many of his teammates.

Mize also didn't go on one road trip and all this did was add more fuel to an already building fire. Southworth said he could have used him as a pinch hitter or even as a late inning replacement. Mize, even in his best days, never covered much ground at first base. Many players felt, despite all the injuries and mishaps the team had, they still could have won had Mize played through some of his injuries and been available for pinch-hitting duty. It would have taken only a few more wins to take it all. Mize would prove to be a good fit for the Polo Grounds and the short right field line.[8]

The Cardinals unloaded another old face when they sold Don Padgett to the Dodgers for $25,000. He thought it was utopia, as he envisioned he would now get a chance to play as a regular. Once a player had been a regular and then became a back up he yearned for the chance to be in the starting line again on a daily basis. Before Padgett could play a game for the Dodgers he was called into military service.

The major leagues did everything they could to carry on as if operating in normal times. They provided a lot of equipment to the services for use by the military teams. They were certainly not the only operation that supported and gave help to the military. The tobacco companies provided free cigarettes to the military for the duration of the war.

Billy Southworth was named manager of the year for 1941, even though his team finished second. The award was based on the job he did with the cloud and the adversity they overcame and just missed winning it all by a hair. Had they not suffered the injuries and mishaps, they would have taken it all.

More players from the majors and minors entered the service as the list continued to grow. One of the biggest losses occurred to the Cleveland Indians when their ace right hander, Bob Feller, the best pitcher in baseball, volunteered for the Navy. His draft number wasn't up, but Feller strongly believed it was his duty and obligation to serve. He would later win eight battle stars, as he saw considerable combat, although he also played service ball.

Breadon had double objectives for 1942. He wanted to help maintain the security of the United States and be sure that they were protected from tyranny the country was facing. On another level he wanted to win the pennant and World Series, which he felt they should have had in 1939 and 1941—at least the pennant.[9]

As spring training approached the Cardinals were pinning their pitching hopes on Cooper (13–9), White, (17–7), Warneke (17–9), Harry Gumbert (11–5), Lanier (10–8) (who pitched in a lot of tough luck), and Howard Krist (10–0). The veteran players viewed 1942 as the "V" season as the youngsters got the draft call or enlisted. A hot race was predicted between St. Louis and Brooklyn just as it was in 1941.

Ted Williams was changed to a 3A classification from 1A. He had a 3A as he was his mother's sole support, but was reclassified to 1A. This was a major blow to the Boston Red Sox.

President Roosevelt told Baseball Commissioner Kenesaw Landis to "stay in there and pitch." The president said "it was best for the country to keep baseball going." He gave it a "green light" and sent a letter to organized baseball expressing strong sentiment for the game as a morale builder for both the military and the general public. It was to become known as the "green light" letter. It gave the true feeling that 5,000 or 6,000 baseball players were a recreational and morale boost for 20,000,000 people. This comment rallied the support of the entire country. It was a rally around the flag situation and worked like a charm.[10]

The shaky structure of the minor leagues was such (with so many young players) that the game was saved by night baseball. The National League decided to set aside the seven game limit and push for a 14 game night schedule. National League president Ford Frick hinted that the American League might sanction unlimited night baseball. This would mean two games a week in two team cities, except Chicago, as the Cubs were not equipped to play night baseball. In New York it would mean sometimes as many as four night games a week when the Yankees were in town as there were two National League teams in the city.

At first it was thought some teams might play less than 14 games, while others played more. This could have led to some very disturbing and conflicting situations, especially in terms of scheduling and transportation, which was to become very difficult to secure, as the military had all the preference. Breadon believed that the 14 game schedule would be established as the war's time limit. The Cubs had planned on installing lights and playing night baseball, but those plans were thwarted by the war. Materials and men needed to do the job would not be available. Breadon also thought that he should keep on searching for talent, as the war wouldn't last forever.

Sanders was tagged a natural. He had speed, was a good defensive player and a solid line drive hitter with some power. Sanders had played in only four regulation games before age 20. Then he turned to organized baseball and became a professional. He then spent four years in the Cardinals chain and now at the age of 25 was ready to make his bow in the major leagues. Sanders' story was that of a player baseball discovered and not vice versa.

Army and Naval officers joined the president in their support of baseball. They believed it was a great morale booster and it would have a detrimental effect on the troops if the game were curtailed. For years the military had service teams and they went a long way in building esprit de corps in the service. Now in time of war it became extremely important the game continue, as most servicemen were great baseball fans.[11]

Rickey said he didn't see anything hidden in the Mize deal, but if it turned out Mize was damaged goods then he would be willing to nullify the deal. However, he didn't expect the Giants to do that as there were a lot of good years left in Mize, which history was later to bear out.

The Cardinals didn't have any crack holdouts, so the club was ready for spring training. The highest paid players, in order, were Warneke, Moore, Slaughter and Jimmy Brown. Musial was expected to crowd into the outfield picture. It was assumed the starting outfield, going left to right, would be Musial, Moore and Slaughter. There were other candidates fighting for outfield positions on the team, even if as reserves. They were Erv Dusak, Estel Crabtree, Coaker Triplett, Harry Walker and Hopp. The latter could also do duty as a first baseman, which gave him a leg up on his competition. Southworth said there was no way to keep the fine hitting, fielding, running and throwing of Musial on the bench. He was a prophet of the first degree.

Southworth said Sanders would be his first baseman and if he faltered, then Hopp would take over. The real chore that faced Southworth was the selection of his pitching staff, as he had to whittle the fine corps down to a group of nine or 10 men. The decision would have been even tougher if Martin and Grodzicki were still there, but both were in the service.

The team overall looked even stronger than in 1941. The club had Musial from the start of the season and he always played right field, but could handle left and if Moore needed a rest could fill in at center field. The infield reserves were a large improvement over Steve Mesner and Eddie Lake. Buddy Blattner was able to play all three infield positions. The team also had Crespi, who could play second or short, and Brown was adept at all three infield positions. He would divide his time at all three, getting 606 at-bats for the season, the most in the league. George "Whitey" Kurowski would eventually establish himself as a power hitting third baseman and until his arm injury shortened his career provided the right hand punch to go with the Cardinals' strong left hand hitting lineup.

The first casualty of the war as far as organized baseball was concerned occurred in the United States. It was a non-combat related fatality. Lt. Gordon E. Houston of McCloud Field near Tacoma, Washington, was killed in a single seater plane while on a routine training flight mission. Before the war would end there would be many more fatalities, several in combat.[12]

President Roosevelt had recently instructed General Lewis B. Hershey, head of the Selective Service Board, to reclassify Williams to 3A. Williams had not asked for the deferment, but the appeals board at Minneapolis did it on its own volition. All five members of the draft board had voted 1A, but the appeals board overruled the decision. The 3A classification was because Williams was the sole support for his mother. While the Boston Red Sox were pleased Williams hoped that the fans understood he had not asked for this and was not trying to shirk his responsibility. The Williams case would test fans' sportsmanship. Ted said he had "nothing to be ashamed of" and could keep his chin and head up proudly. Williams would eventually serve and distinguish himself as a combat pilot.[13]

As spring training advanced Southworth restated his analysis of the team. He called it stronger than in 1941 as they had a better outfield with Musial,

Moore and Slaughter. The infield of Brown, Crespi and Marion outranked what the club had the prior season and now they had Kurowski and Blattner as reserves. Walker Cooper would be solid as the everyday catcher and Sanders would play first. If he faltered Hopp was right behind him. Both were speedy, fine defensive players that were also line drive hitters. Musial was called the second edition of Paul Warner of the Pittsburgh Pirates.

Southworth's toughest job was in cutting pitchers. He had so many dazzling arms it was a difficult decision to make as to who was to be kept and who to send down. With Medwick and Mize gone the Cardinals' hitters were labeled "banjo hitters." Southworth said maybe so, but they had great speed and would always score from second on a single. The team would go from first to third on a single and stretch hits into doubles and triples. This was to be the forte and attack of the St. Louis Cardinals as the National League and later the New York Yankees discovered.

In spring training Southworth and his team were red faced because of their poor hitting. Someone remarked, "You may be able to score from first on a double or go from first to third on a single, but you first have to get on base." In one stretch the team scored just four runs in 36 innings. However, the pitching remained airtight. The club just needed someone to hit a few over the fence and Southworth told the scribes and anyone else interested that it would all come together. The team would be fine.

Southworth was placing all his chips on his remarkable pitching staff. Brecheen had been trying to make the team for three seasons, but had two disadvantages. Many thought his size, 5' 10" and 160 pounds, worked against him and that he couldn't win consistently against major league hitters. The other problem Brecheen faced was the Cardinals already had three left hand pitchers with Lanier, White and Pollet, all proven winners.

In the first 19 spring training games the Cardinals' pitchers allowed just 52 runs, the best in the major leagues Southworth told whoever would listen. However, the hitting remained below par. Someone remarked you can't pitch shutouts every day. The pitching alignment looked like Cooper, Warneke, Gumbert, Krist, White, Lanier and Pollet. That left three spots open. Southworth had to choose between Dickson, Brecheen, Surkont, Munger, Lohrman, Shoun and Hutchinson. Cooper said, "I'll win 20 games this season or throw my glove away."

Musial started off hot in the spring and then cooled off causing alarm among the manager and coaches. The question now became was he just a flash in the pan that happened last September or was he just having a slump, like many hitters do. Southworth said he would be patient with his young phenom, as he still remembered his dazzling September.

Some good news did come out of spring training as the Cardinals defeated the Yankees six games to three in spring play. Was this a forerunner of October? This gave the St. Petersburg title to St. Louis, marking the first time in 17 years that New York had not won the championship. The last time the Yankees lost the St. Pete crown was in 1926 to the Boston Braves, who finished seventh in the National League. That season the Cardinals won their first 20th century pennant and defeated the Yankees four games to three in one of the all time classic World Series. Was this an omen of things to come?[14]

As observers looked at the Dodgers team they seemed stronger than in 1941. The only question was their veteran pitching staff, which loomed as a potential problem. Southworth continued to contend that St. Louis was the team to beat. Many observers agreed with Southworth as they analyzed the Cardinals team. There was a fighting spirit on the club that was reminiscent of the Gas House Gang. Remember, Moore was a member of the 1935–36 Gas House Gang, before it was completely broken up. Walker promised that he would beat out Musial for the left field position. While he would be a good contributor to the club, that would not and did not happen.

As the season drew near Southworth made some final critical decisions. He would open with Marion at short and Crespi at second (same combination as in 1941). Brown would have the third base assignment (also his 1941 role). Ever since spring 1937 Brown had gone to spring training as sort of an odd man out, looking for a job. This had been true regardless of his previous year's performance, but he always came away with a starting position. This spring proved no different. Southworth solved his pitching dilemma by sending Hutchinson, Surkont, Munger and Al Jurisch to the minors for further seasoning. Musial was being called the next Medwick or Chick Hafey or compared to some other great hitters. However, the fact that he had not hit well in the spring also raised the question was he just a morning glory that bloomed and quickly faded? Time would tell.

President Roosevelt told the nation, "Let's go America. Let's play ball."[15] He had decided it would be best for America to keep the game going. More than 95 percent of the servicemen said, "Keep them playing. Let's not take away all our fun." The military and the civilians alike said, "The United States needs baseball. It is an American institution. Let's not let these tyrannical societies destroy what we have built. During World War I more than half of the ballplayers entered service before the war ended." Today the minor league chains can keep the majors going with a continuous flow of talent. The game was in a stronger position due to the farm system than 25 years ago.

Most baseball scribes picked the Cardinals and Yankees to meet in the fall classic. If this came true it would be the third time they played. Each had won one previously. The Cardinals triumphed in 1926 and the Yankees returned the favor in 1928. However, veteran sportswriter Tom Meany (who predicted the Yankees-Dodgers Series in 1941 with the Red Sox and Cardinals second) had the same prediction for 1941. History would show who was correct.

The St. Louis fans had been hyped up for months about all the pennant talk and the constant barrage of writing that spoke so eloquently of the Cardinals. Pennant fever had been building almost since the World Series ended. It cooled a little when the Cardinals had a slump in the spring, but it was reignited during the Cardinal-Brown spring series. The Cardinals showed the dash and flavor that characterized their 1941 play. Musial hit in the series as he did in September and Sanders won the first base job. This meant Hopp and Walker went to the bench, although both would see a lot of action before the battle was won.

The Cardinals opened the season by taking two of three from Chicago at home, but then quickly reversed themselves by losing two of three at Pittsburgh. Except for one game, which was an 11–6 rout of the Cubs, the Cardinals still were not hitting like everyone thought them capable. The pitching, which everyone conceded was their strong suit, was very good, but you still had to score runs to win. There was a casualty among the pitchers, as Pollet had a sore arm and didn't look like the September pitcher everyone had seen. Also many were saying Hopp should be at first in place of Sanders.

The Dodgers were playing excellent ball even with Camilli and Peewee Reese out with injuries. The Dodgers headed west for their first foray with an 11–3 mark. The Cardinals dropped three one run games in a week and Pittsburgh's Ken Heintzelman shut out the team for a second time. This was pointing out the futility of the team against left hand pitching. Remember the core of the club was left handed—Musial, Slaughter, Hopp, Walker and Sanders. Southworth sat out Musial against a Chicago left hander and in one of the games against Heintzelman. His concern was twofold. He didn't want to destroy Musial's confidence against left hand pitchers and also could he really hit left hand pitching? Southworth was handling Musial delicately at this juncture in his career.

April ended with the standings showing Brooklyn first with their 11–3 record, followed by Pittsburgh at 7–5 and Chicago and New York tied at 7–6. The highly praised and talented St. Louis Cardinals were limping along at 5–6. The pitching from Cooper, Warneke, Gumbert, Lanier, White and Johnny Beazley had been excellent. The hitting was spotty with only Sanders, Slaughter, Moore and Brown contributing. However, there was a dearth of home runs.

The number from organized baseball in the military continued to grow, but they said don't stop the game. This would be a recurring theme for the next three and one-half years. The Army and Navy all said keep the game going. To the servicemen, the only item that rated higher than baseball was their letters from home. "Don't let us down. We want baseball," they said.[16]

It was beginning to look like that left hand pitching would keep the Cardinals from winning the pennant. Teams were now altering their rotations to save left handers for the Cardinals, as at this juncture they had no power right hand bat, like Medwick. Many observers now believed the Cardinals would also regret the Mize deal. He was a power hitter and although left handed, he could hit any type of pitching. Mize finished the season with 26 home runs, a .305 average and a league high 110 RBIs. It looked like the Cardinals had made a big mistake in trading Mize and relying on two speedy, fancy fielding men to alternate at first base. Both were also left hand hitters. The final analysis at this point was the Cardinals had great pitching, but couldn't hit. This was Cincinnati's fate in 1941.

The early going was rough for St. Louis and a lot of scorn and criticism was directed at Southworth. They said he kept some of the wrong pitchers, that he should have kept so and so here and sent so and so back. Sanders might hit some, but not like Mize and although a good fielder, he had a weak throwing arm. Warneke couldn't finish what he started and if he couldn't complete games now, what would happen when July and August arrived? Cooper was just so-so at this point and many were saying when they operated on his arm they took his fastball. Musial was hitting just .275 with only three RBIs in the first 13 games. These were the comments being made and the pennant fever had dwindled to a small flame.

Southworth was not one to panic and knew that fans were fickle. He said a few victories, a few base hits and all that would change. The question was when would it happen? Pretty soon, most were saying, or Brooklyn would be so far ahead it would be too late. Was this the shades of another 1940, was the question now being asked.

The St. Louis pitching staff said that Moore was the best friend a pitcher ever had. He saved many a game for a pitcher and some of the catches he made belonged in the Hall of Fame. Moore had received a serious beaning in 1941, but had now recovered and was at this juncture enjoying one of the finest seasons of his career. Moore was considered the finest center fielder in the National League, if not in the majors. His career average was .284 and while he couldn't hit with Joe DiMaggio, he would never have to take a back seat to him in the outfield. Moore finished only grade school and got a job to support his mother. He was the youngest of six boys and never thought about playing baseball until he was 16 years old. Moore began his ball playing as a pitcher, but hurt his arm and had to move to the outfield. He started playing in the Industrial League with the Bemis Bag Company, where he had a job as a flunkey, as Moore told it. Then a scout signed him with the Cardinals and he was now in his eighth major league campaign. What a heartwarming story.[17]

The Cardinals were relying on their pitching to keep them afloat. They had the best pitching record in the majors, allowing the fewest runs per game at 3.3. However, their hitting still hadn't caught up to the pitching and as a result the club was just 12–12. Brooklyn was number two in pitching in the league at 3.8 runs per game. Their Larry French had just been the man of the hour. In his 14th season he defeated Pollet 3–1 in 11 innings at Flatbush, allowing just four singles. That put Brooklyn atop the standings at 17–7, with St. Louis tied with Cincinnati five games out. Sandwiched in between were Pittsburgh at 16–11 and Boston at 13–12. All the fans kept saying if only the hitting would come alive, with our pitching no one could beat us. They were getting impatient.

At this time St. Louis didn't look like pennant winners when Johnny Vander Meer beat them 5–2, to make the sixth left hander to defeat them this season. Southworth's favored team seemed to be going nowhere. The Cardinals' hitting frustrations continued as in a Sunday doubleheader they were shut out. In game one Cooper pitched magnificently, but lost to Cincinnati's Ray Starr, 1–0. In the nightcap Bucky Walters took Beazley's measure 3–0. The only game the Cardinals won in the four game set was game one behind Warneke, 5–2. The team allowed only 10 runs in four games, but lost three as they scored just seven runs. No matter how great you pitch, you still have to score runs, was what everyone was saying. The Cardinals optioned Dusak to Rochester and sold Shoun to Cincinnati and Lohrman was sent back to the Giants.

Cooper (.324), Musial (starting to hit, but only nine RBIs .317), Brown (.317), Sanders (.310) and Slaughter at .303: You would think with five .300 hitters the team would have a better record. They had scored 89 runs in 21 games, but Brooklyn in their first 22 scored 122. Therein lay the difference. The Cardinals were leading the league in doubles and triples, but sixth in home runs and only sixth in runs scored. With their pitching superiority they should have been in first place. Medwick (.296), Pete Reiser (.304) and Dixie Walker (Harry's older brother) at .340 paced the Dodgers' attack.

After the first 31 games (one-fifth of the season) the Cardinals were a hard team to figure. They had allowed the fewest runs, but were last in double plays, last in fielding and third in team batting, but only fifth in runs scored. They led in doubles and triples but trailed Boston, Brooklyn, New York, Philadelphia and Cincinnati in home runs. With their great speed and daring on the base paths they were only fourth in stolen bases. Southworth said his was not a team to steal bases, but take the extra base. This was his philosophy. On another team the Cardinals would have had several of the league's leading base stealers. Crespi was still not hitting and Marion was only at .150. Southworth was thinking of benching Crespi, putting Brown at second and Kurowski at third. He still believed that once the lineup was set and jelled the team would start winning consistently. The fans were wondering. As the third week of May ended the standings showed Brooklyn in a potential runaway at 24–8. Then came Boston (17–15), Pittsburgh (15–14) and St. Louis (16–15), seven and one-half games out with only one-fifth of the season played. At this pace it looked like a long season for St. Louis, picked by many as the best team in the league.

Williams and the Navy finally saw eye to eye. He was listed as 1A, but it could be two or three months before his call up. More devastating news to St. Louis as Slaughter was reclassified from 3A (because he was married) to 1A. He took his physical and was told he would be given a reporting date later. His loss would be a devastating blow to the St. Louis attack. He was a career .300 hitter, bettering the mark the last four seasons after his rookie .276 season in 1938. When the season started Slaughter was in the deferred class, but because of his separation from his wife he was now reclassified as 1A.

It finally looked like the team was ready to make its move when it went on a five game winning streak. They won three in New York, Cooper blanked Brooklyn in the only game played there and the Cardinals won the first game of a homestand against Cincinnati on Musial's three home run. The next day the club dropped a double-header to the Reds by scores of 3–2 and 2–0. In game one they made five hits and in game two Vander Meer held them to three hits, making the ninth loss to left hand pitching. Southworth was riled at the play and attitude of one player and fined him, but would not tell the press his name. His only response was, "I'm through killing players with kindness."

The Cardinals' injury problems in May rekindled the bitter memories of 1941. White won a game, but was still nursing a sore arm. Musial injured his leg sliding in a game in Chicago on May 21 and had to be carried off the field. Crespi wasn't hitting, thus Brown was shifted to second and Kurowski installed at third. This move would eventually pay big dividends, not only in 1942 but through 1947 as he became the team's main right hand power hitter. That was until his bad right arm prematurely ended his career. Sanders was replaced at first with Hopp, hoping his Gas House spirit would rekindle the ball club.

At this juncture Brooklyn led the league with a 27–11 mark with Boston second at 22–17, and the Cards third with 20–17 followed by Cincinnati at 18–19. It had been musical chairs for the first six weeks in the first division. With the exception of Brooklyn the following teams had been in and out of the first division: St. Louis, Boston, Cincinnati, Pittsburgh, Chicago and New York. Only poor Philadelphia didn't qualify, as they would finish the season at 42–109. Slaughter was at .321, Cooper at .319 and O'Dea as a reserve at .300. Musial had moved to .292 with Moore, Brown and Sanders all in the 280s or 290s. The hitting was starting to show some life, but pitching still carried the club.

O'Dea was back with the Cardinals, as he had started in their system. He was more than just a back up catcher, almost a co-catcher with Cooper. His experience would help develop Cooper into one of the premier catchers in the league. While O'Dea was not a power hitter, his hits were often timely. He was also a master at handling pitchers and an all around asset to the team.

It looked like the team was making its move as Pollet won two straight strong starts, shutting out the Cubs and defeating New York 4–1. The club now seemed to have second place in their firm grasp and looked like the team predicted to win it all. Cooper won the second game of a double-header 2–0 over the Giants for his sixth victory. The Cardinals' pitching was great and would have to remain that way if the Cardinals were to win it all. The Dodgers had Whit Wyatt, Kirby Higbe, Larry French and Curt Davis setting a bristling pace. Wyatt and Higbe weren't pitching as frequently as in 1941, but were getting more help from other staff members. French was used in relief and as a starter and would respond with a 15–4 season, with three of the losses coming at the hands of St. Louis.

Despite their brisk play and being in second at 29–20, the club still trailed the Dodgers by seven games. The Dodgers were setting a fast pace a la 1941 at 37–14 and were on a course to win 111–112 games. Cincinnati (28–24) and New York (26–26) rounded out the first division. The Dodgers' edge seemed to lie in their veterans' expertise. They had Medwick, Mickey Owen, Billy Herman, Walker, French, Higbe, Wyatt, and Johnny Allen. Cooler heads were paying big dividends. The Dodgers would prove a tough team to catch, as Medwick, Walker, Reiser and Owen were all over .300 with Walker the lowest at .311.

Slaughter was at .309 and Cooper at .300 as was Musial, however with only 15 RBIs. He would get 57 RBIs in the next 102 games. Had he started that well Musial would have racked up 85–90 RBIs for the season. The Dodgers were paced on the pitching mound by French (4–0), Kimball and Webber (2–0), Davis (7–1), Ed Head (5–1), Wyatt (4–1), Higbe (4–4), Casey (3–3) and Allen (3–4). Casey wouldn't lose a game the rest of the season, winning three more, but appearing in 50 games and leading the league with 13 saves. That was a high total for an era when pitchers were expected to go nine innings. Allen would be 7–2 for the rest of the season. Meanwhile St. Louis' mainstays were Cooper (6–3), Beazley (5–3), Lanier and Pollet (3–2), White (3–3) and Gumbert (2–3).

In early to mid–June from one Sunday through the next the Cardinals could only play three games. First hitting had slowed down the team, now it was rain. The team won all three games with Cooper getting credit for two of the victories. Financially these were a devastating loss to Breadon and the team. Three postponed Dodgers games cost about $65,000 of which $40,000 would have been the Cardinals' share. They would be rescheduled as part of a double-header on July 18 with a regular double-header on July 19. This would help recoup some of the loss. The team also lost a double-header in Philadelphia because of rain.

More problems surfaced for the team, but they were off the field this time. They had been criticized for sending Crabtree to Rochester and losing a valuable pinch hitter. He had originally been sent to Rochester on May 25 to serve as manager and play the outfield. However, his health problems wouldn't permit him to perform double duty, therefore they recalled him to be used as a pinch hitter. Catcher Ray Hayworth replaced him. They also sent Blattner to Rochester. This didn't end the Crabtree saga. It was just beginning.

A snag developed when they tried to recall Crabtree. He had been optioned out twice 12 years earlier and when the Cards sent him out on May 25 that was the third time (the limit a player could be optioned). That meant he either had to remain with Rochester through the draft period or become a free agent. The key question became, who overlooked the fact he had been optioned twice twelve years earlier? To complicate the problem Crabtree was upset with the story that he was sent to Rochester to manage, but couldn't play as a regular because he wasn't in condition to do so. Crabtree contended that his condition was no different than in 1941.[18]

The plot thickened as Crabtree earned twice Hayworth's salary and it could be better earned by having him as a pinch hitter and reserve outfielder in St. Louis (a role he performed admirably in 1941, batting .341). This led to a deeper problem—the feud between Breadon and Rickey. It had been brewing since 1940 when Breadon replaced Blades as manager with Southworth without discussing it with Rickey. The loss of Rickey would prove to be devastating, as he was a genius and the mastermind of the farm system. He would eventually do for the Dodgers what he did for St. Louis and many of the pennants Brooklyn won between 1947 and 1956 could have belonged to St. Louis if personalities and egos hadn't gotten in the way.[19]

Meanwhile, on the field, around the latter part of June, Brooklyn continued their blistering pace with a 38–16 mark while St. Louis was 32–20. Cincinnati (29–27) and New York (30–29) continued to hang on to their first division spots.

A game between the Cleveland Indians and thirteen soldiers and ten sailors was scheduled for July 7 in Cleveland. All 25 players were former major leaguers, including Feller, who would pitch against his former teammates. The game was a sell out and all proceeds went to the Army and Navy Relief Fund.

As a five game series began in Flatbush the Cardinals had a seven game winning streak and Medwick was riding a 25 game hitting streak. The first game started with a bang or perhaps one should say a brawl. Medwick was on first and Lanier made a wild pitch, but Cooper recovered in time to throw out Medwick at second. Medwick came into Marion with spikes high and this precipitated a wild melee and brawl. To make matters worse the Cards lost four of five to Brooklyn and this further darkened their pennant chances. The only game won by St. Louis was Cooper's fifth shutout and ninth victory of the season, 11–0. St. Louis fans were rapidly losing the pennant fever. The team that was predicted to win it all was disappointing their loyal following.

At this point Cooper was 9–3 and could have been 11–1 as two of his losses were 1–0. If Cooper were to win 20 games he would be the first Cardinal since Davis copped 22 in 1939. Cooper might have made it last season, when he finished 13–9, but arm surgery kept him out of action for six weeks and then he was slow in rounding into form. Cooper was a throwback to Dizzy Dean. His attitude was, "Give me the ball, get me a run or two and I'll win the game." Also Cooper was willing to start today and relieve tomorrow, a la Dean. During the 1939–1941 season he appeared in 112 games, starting 80. Part of that may have been necessity with staff injuries, part the pitching philosophy of the time: use your starter to save a crucial game. However, part of it also was Cooper's willingness to do whatever the team needed to win. That was the old Gas House Gang spirit.

The batting race at this point was narrowed to Reiser at .338 and Medwick with .333. Medwick may have lost some of his power, as he would hit only four home runs for the season, but still drove in 96. He could still hit for a high average. Kurowski, given a chance to play as a regular, was hitting .318 and Slaughter was at .300. Musial had slipped below .300, but more disturbing was he had just 17 RBIs in the first 55 games. He would get 55 in the next 99 to finish at 72. Had Musial been this hot earlier, not only would he have finished with 85–90 RBIs, but the Cardinals might have won another five or six games. Remember they lost a lot of one run games early in the season.

The Dodgers continued to dominate the hitting in the league and had the best won-lost record. Claude Passeau of the Cubs was the league's top winner at 10–3, as he aimed for his second 20 win season. His first was in 1940. Warneke was at 5–2 and Beazley at 6–3 to help Cooper. The two left handers (Pollet and White) on whom the Cardinals depended had been little help due to sore arms. Pollet had been in just seven games and was 4–2, while White was only 2–2. As July approached it looked like Brooklyn (43–17) was ready to bury St. Louis (35–24) as they were seven and one-half games out of first. Cincinnati (33–26) and New York (32–31) completed the first division.

The Dodgers placed seven players on the all star squad, which was the most of any team in the National League. No team had ever had that many on an all star squad before. In fact the Dodgers probably could have placed even more. This would be the only time in Musial's career he would not be chosen for the all star game. He would eventually play in 24 all star games, as for several years there would be two games. The proceeds from this game, which totaled over $68,000, went to the Navy Relief Fund, another fine gesture on the part of major league baseball as it continued to try to do its part in helping during the national emergency.

At the All Star break the Dodgers were setting a remarkable pace at 48–18. They were still on pace to win 111–112 games. St. Louis had now fallen 9½ games out at 37–27 and most fans had conceded the race to the Dodgers. The euphoria that surrounded the team coming into the season had dissipated.

Cincinnati (38–32) and New York (34–33) clung precariously to their first division slots.

The Dodgers headed west for a big road trip, during which time they hoped to settle the race before they returned home. They would play 16 games of which five were double-headers. They played two double-headers in St. Louis and one each in Chicago, Cincinnati and Pittsburgh. They also had two night games in Cincinnati and Pittsburgh and two day games in Chicago. At this juncture in 1941 St. Louis and Brooklyn were each 48–24. It was a different story this season as St. Louis was 43–29 and eight and one-half games behind Brooklyn (52–21). When the Cardinals got too close for comfort the Dodgers put them in their place by winning four of five in Brooklyn.

St. Louis had to win at least three out of four games in the upcoming two double-headers. A split would just leave them where they were. Anything else would spell certain doom for the team. White and Pollet were far off the pace expected, as both were nursing sore arms. Beazley and Gumbert had helped by picking up some of the slack. At this point Beazley had been used mostly in relief with only one of his seven victories as a starter. He would now be in the daily starting rotation. Musial was hitting .330 and led the team in hitting, but the rest had fallen dramatically and the club was back to depending primarily on its pitching. Cooper had dropped to .283, Slaughter down to .274 and Moore to .265. Sanders and Hopp continued to alternate at first base as neither one could seem to hit consistently enough to claim the job full time. One day Sanders looked like a power hitter and the next day nothing. He lacked consistency.

Another reason the Dodgers were at the top was their pitching. They allowed just 3.2 runs per game, with only St. Louis better at 2.9. However, the hitting was the difference at this point. Medwick and Reiser were tied for the league lead at .342. Ray Starr of Cincinnati and Cooper were both 11–3. Starr would be just 4–10 the balance of the season, finishing at 15–13. Passeau was the league leader at 12–5 and Cliff Melton of the Giants was 10–5. No Dodger had 10 victories, but they had a wealth of pitchers with five or more.

As stated, the Dodgers were on a pace to win 111–112 games and even if they had played only .500 ball the rest of the way (which was highly unlikely) the team would still finish at 94–60, which based on the Cardinals' current pace would still have given the Dodgers the flag by one or two games. The team's pace slackened only slightly as they were 55–22 (110–44 pace), but they were now nine games in front of St. Louis. Entering the series the Dodgers figured if they could win three of four it would put them 11 games ahead and just about bury St. Louis. Even a split would serve them well as they would maintain their nine game advantage.

The American League All Stars played a team of military former major leaguers and defeated them 5–0. However, that was not the big story. The proceeds from this game and the All Star game netted $192,000 and all the money went to the Navy Relief Fund, another fine chartable showing by the major leagues.

Commissioner Landis gave Crabtree his free agency and he sat at home in Nelsonville, Ohio, neither accepting nor rejecting the Cardinals contract. Crabtree denied he had health problems. Southworth said he would "like him back" as he could use him as a pinch hitter and a sometime reserve outfielder. Southworth thought after relaying those comments to Crabtree he would resign his contract. However, he became adamant and wouldn't budge. Rickey had gone to see Crabtree personally, but failed to get his signature. Crabtree was not mad at the Cardinals, as he said "they always treated me fairly." He just wanted the story set straight for the Rochester fans.[20]

Meanwhile the wars on the baseball field continued. Brooklyn did well on their 21 game road trip except for dropping three of four in St. Louis, which allowed them to climb within six and one-half games of the Dodgers. However, the Dodgers now had most of the month of August in Brooklyn, except for a side trip to Boston, Philadelphia and New York. The Dodgers lost more than just three games in St. Louis. The team sustained serious injuries to Reiser when he cracked into the center field wall and would be out about 10 days with a concussion. This was to be the history of Reiser. A player that might have achieved the Hall of Fame but for countless injuries, many from running into concrete outfield walls. These were the days before padded walls. As a result his career was shortened and he never achieved his full potential. Another casualty was relief ace Casey, who would be out two weeks with a cracked little finger on his right hand suffered when hit by a line drive off the bat of Musial. Perhaps the Cardinals did more damage than just taking three of four from the Dodgers.

Breadon got the fans riled when he sold Warneke to the Cubs, from whom they had acquired him in the Dean trade. Cries of cheapskate, miser and penny pincher were heard. The fans felt what little chance they had left for the pennant were gone. The fans liked Warneke and with Pollet and White with sore arms they needed him. This was another example of selling a player when he still had some potential left. Breadon said this would allow Beazley to remain in the rotation on a full time basis, which it seemed he already was with the sore arm pitchers the team had.

Warneke had a 6–4 record when traded, certainly not a losing position or detriment to the team. Breadon said the veteran had lost something off his pitches and could no longer go the distance. The record showed he had made 12 starts and completed five. Maybe not in the class with Cooper, but certainly better than White, Pollet and Gumbert would achieve for the season. During his tenure Warneke was always a winning pitcher. His record for the five and one-half seasons was 83–51 (a pace that would make a team 96–58 for the season and win many a pennant). He was 18–11 in 1937, 13–8 in 1938, 13–7 in 1939, 16–10 in 1940 and 17–9 in 1941.

Rickey was in the east when the trade was made and his only comment was, "He was a fine man and a fine pitcher." It is interesting to note that during this time Pollet had been knocked out for the fourth straight game and still nursed a sore arm. For the season White, Pollet and Gumbert would finish at 23–15, completing 17 of 51 starts. Compare that to Warneke's record.[21]

The club could fall back on Krist, who was 10–0 in 1941, but they preferred him in a relief situation. At this point in his career Krist was 19–2 (9–2 for this season). His reaching the majors was delayed by illness, injury and a sore arm. Elbow surgery saved his career and he eventually made it to stay with St. Louis in 1941. While he could be a starter, his specialty was as a relief hurler. One of the victories over Brooklyn was achieved by White, a 7–4 win over French that saddled him with his first loss of the season after 10 straight victories. As July ended Brooklyn was 67–28, followed by St. Louis at 59–34 (seven games out) with Cincinnati (50–44) and New York (47–44) still staying in the first division.

The statistics show why the Dodgers were in first. Reiser was leading the league in batting at .350 and Medwick was third at .335. Sandwiched in between was Ernie Lombardi at .348. However, the Dodgers' pitching was the shining star, as all 11 pitchers were over .500. French (11–1) and Wyatt (12–5) paced the way. Higbe was 10–8, Davis 11–5 and Allen 10–5. The Cardinals had Kurowski at .325, Musial at .320 and Cooper at .308. Slaughter had come back to life and was up to .298. Cooper and Beazley led the mound corps at 12–4 and 11–4, respectively. Lanier, White and Pollet were all stuck at 4–4 each. Other big winners in the league were Passeau at 14–7, Walters 12–6 (he would be just 3–8 the rest of the season), Melton (11–7), Starr (13–7) and Rip Sewell (10–8).

Brooklyn seemed home free as 21 of their remaining 59 games were against seventh place Boston and eighth place Philadelphia, while the Cardinals had only 12 games left against those two clubs, but 24 against first division teams. The schedule, as almost everything else, seemed to favor the Dodgers. The Dodgers took two of three in Brooklyn and the Cardinals were now 2–7 against Brooklyn on their home field. If you can't beat the team you should then it is time to call the mortician. The Cards continue to be hurt by their one run game record, which was 12–22. After Brooklyn they split four games with the Giants at the Polo Grounds. Cooper got his 13th victory after arm, side and mental worries. He decided that he would wear number 14 when he next pitched, as he had never won over 13 in his career and being superstitious he would switch from his number 13 and try number 14. Lanier began showing new life and tacked on his seventh win.

The Cardinals were superior to the Dodgers in slugging, doubles, triples, batting average and even home runs, but they trailed in the all important RBIs. They got them on base, but the Dodgers brought more home. Therein lay the story. By the second week of August, St. Louis had fallen 10 games behind Brooklyn (74–30), while the Redbirds were 62–38. While they were playing at .600, Brooklyn was over .700 and on a pace to win 108 games. It looked like Katy bar the gate.

Crabtree told the Cardinals he would rejoin the team in Pittsburgh the next Friday and Southworth was pleased. The next day he sent a telegram to Breadon saying he changed his mind and couldn't play the rest of the season. Southworth was totally irritated with the entire situation. Crabtree had been optioned three times and he either stayed with Rochester or he was a free agent per Commissioner Landis. He had a serious kidney operation in 1940 and was concerned about his health, although publicly denying he had health problems. The Cardinals decided they were finished with Crabtree. Let him go his way.

Kurowski, who couldn't even doze on a Pullman, seemed to have found his berth at third base. An arm injury as a child (his right arm was shorter than his left arm) almost ended his career before it began. He had a serious injury, falling off a horse onto broken glass and it developed into osteomyelitis, leaving hideous scar and a shortened right arm.

Marion had been on a hitting tear, batting over .300 to raise his average to .291. He had been at .159 and as late as June was batting just .180. The Cardinals won three of four and so did Brooklyn. They couldn't seem to make up any ground. On June 24 they were nine games out of first and almost two months later they were eight games out. Someone commented they would never catch the Dodgers at that rate. At that pace they wouldn't catch them until November 1943.

Cooper got his 14th victory by wearing number 14. It was his plan to wear a progressive number each team he pitched. Beazley also picked up victory number 14, while Krist got his 10th against Cincinnati. The Cardinals, as August neared an end, had closed the gap to seven and one-half games. There was a large hill, if not a mountain, to climb. St. Louis had just 40 games to play and Brooklyn 41. Brooklyn was 79–34 while St. Louis was 72–42. New York had now taken over third (64–53), where they would finish and Cincinnati was fourth, their final resting place.

The Cardinals in mid–August, when still eight and one-half games out, came up with their victory song. It was a Spike Jones novelty number, *Pass the Biscuits, Mirandy*. Walker took a liking to the song and it soon became the Cardinals' victory chant. It was played and sung after each victory. A new Cardinals band had been formed to lead the parade down the stretch drive. Dr. Harrison J. Weaver (the trainer) played the mandolin while Musial played a slide whistle or kept time with coat-hanger drumsticks.[22]

Rickey said that "the game should go on at all levels, majors and minors." Executives at all levels agreed with him. Rickey said, "We should continue even if the talent pool became shallow and at a subordination of profits." If the call had come from any other executive than a salaried person it might have been received even more warmly. Some whose livelihoods depended on the game and were heavily invested had to consider the profit and loss statements. The chief fear of the independent minor league teams was, as always, lack of players, but even more so under the current conditions. They gave the same comment, however, that it was not time to worry about profits. It was time to re-organize loops in some way. The general consensus was to look for expansion after the war.[23]

Back in the baseball wars, the Cardinals smashed three jinxes on August 16, 17 and 18 as they won their first three decisions of the season over Vander Meer, Starr and Passeau. In game one they knocked out Vander Meer with a five run 5th. He had won three in a row including two shutouts against St. Louis as Beazley was the winner, 6–3. The next day, Starr, who also had two shutouts against the Cards, lost to Krist 5–2. On the 18th the Cardinals defeated Passeau (who had been 2–0 against them) 5–0 behind Lanier. It looked like the Cardinals express was coming down the track with a full head of steam and everyone was jumping on the band wagon, or should we say train.

During their eight game winning streak Hopp took over first base from Sanders and seemed to have found his batting eye. He played like an old Gas House Gang member. Another player that would have fit right in with the Gas House Gang, Slaughter had started hitting and was a long shot to take the batting title. The team was 6–1 in the week ending August 26 and was trying to hang on and catch the Dodgers.

On August 23 Cooper was 15–6 wearing number 14 (he should have had number 16) and lost in relief. He said after that he would change numbers each time he pitched based on which victory he was trying for. Also during that eight game winning streak Beazley picked up his 15th victory and Lanier got number 11. At one point the edge was whittled to six and one-half games. Brooklyn was 84–36 and St. Louis 78–43, with only 34 games left for the Dodgers and 33 for the Cardinals.

The race for the batting title was a heated one. Reiser, due to injuries, had fallen out of the race although remaining over .300. Lombardi now led with .325, followed closely by Medwick (.323) and Slaughter and Musial (both at .319). Slaughter also had 77 RBIs and Musial had 44. Slaughter would get 21 and Musial 28 in the final 33 games. Walker was .313, Cooper .302 and Marion and Moore both at .288. It all came down to the pitching. Brooklyn had French (12–1), Wyatt (14–4), Davis (13–5) and Higbe (11–9), while St. Louis had Cooper (15–7), Beazley (15–5), Lanier (11–6) and Krist (11–3). The Cardinals needed some help from Pollet, Gumbert and White.

The Dodgers, while starting to stumble, counted on two developments to help them. First, there was the acquisition of Bobo Newsom that would give them enough victories to put them over the top. He came from Washington where he was 11–17 with a 4.92 ERA. It was questionable with figures like that how much help he would be. The other consideration was that Reiser was not too seriously hurt and could play the balance of the season at the level he had been. They acquired Newsom on August 31, making him eligible for World Series play.

The Dodgers were just 3–5 in the last week of August and St. Louis fans said please put that obit about the Cardinals' flag chances on a lower rack. The team was 25–8 in August, marking the fourth straight season the team had a torrid August. This had been a trademark of Cardinals clubs, getting hot in August and September and coming from behind. Three weeks ago the death knell was being written about the Cardinals as they were eight and one-half games out of first. By the end of the month they had narrowed the gap to three and one-half games. To get to that point they beat the Dodgers three out of four, swept Philadelphia in three and won a double-header from Boston. Ironically the only game the Dodgers won was the finale, which if the Cards had won, would have cut the lead to just one and one-half games. Each game head to head was worth two in the standings. The Dodgers defeated Lanier, who had beaten them four times previously.

The odds were still against St. Louis as Brooklyn had seven games with the pitiful, woefully weak last place Philadelphia team. The club would score only 394 runs for the season (just over 2.5 per game—shades of the deadball era). Danny Litwhiler led the team with 56 RBIs. The team batting average was just .232. Pitcher Tom Hughes hurled 19 complete games in 31 starts, posted a fine 3.06 ERA, but was just 12–18. Once again a bad start looked like it would doom St. Louis. It happened in 1939 and again in 1940.

Kurowski, after a hot start, slumped, but now seemed on his way back. All members of the team were now contributing. After his 1A classification, Slaughter enlisted in the Army Air Force and would leave in January. Beazley wanted to be a boxer, but his mother kayoed the idea. He had never played sandlot ball until going into organized baseball at age 17. He had been in organized ball since 1937 and now at age 22 he was in the majors. His record in 1941 at New Orleans was 16–12 and his current record was 17–5, better than any of the four seasons he had in the minors.

Ray Blades, former Cardinals outfielder and manager, was his manager at New Orleans and was credited with making Beazley a better pitcher. His handling and tutelage of Johnny was what made him from a thrower into a pitcher. Johnny's idea had been to rare back and try to fog the ball by the batter. Blades showed him it was more than that and at the major league level you couldn't win consistently doing that. You had to have other things going for you. Blades taught Beazley how to pitch to spots, hitters' weaknesses and the like. He had started out in the Cincinnati system and was later transferred to the Cardinals. Beazley was just 13–23 with Cincinnati farm teams in 1937–38. He developed a sore arm in 1939 and in 1940 became a Cardinal and then came 1941 and his hook up with Blades and his development as a pitcher.

Heading into the last few weeks Lanier was 12–6, Krist was 11–3, Cooper 16–7 and the aforementioned Beazley 17–5. Brooklyn had Wyatt at 15–4, French at 13–3, Davis at 14–5 and Higbe at 12–9. Other big winners in the league included Passeau at 17–9, who would miss his 20 win season, going just 2–5 down the stretch. Vander Meer was 15–9 and would end at 18–12. Brooklyn still was atop the roost at 88–40 while St. Louis was 85–44, three and one-half games back. Brooklyn had 26 to play and St. Louis just 25.

Pennant fever was running high in the Mississippi River town (St. Louis), but time was running out on the home town favorites. The showdown with the Dodgers would be on September 11 and 12. They had to win both or it would be very difficult to catch the Dodgers. In the last ten days of the season Brooklyn played Philadelphia seven times, so a split was to their advantage, not St. Louis's. The Cardinals took a Labor Day double-header and reduced the lead to two and one-half games. St. Louis was 8–3 against Brooklyn at home, but only 2–7 on the road. Southworth had Cooper and Lanier ready to pitch the two games.

When told things didn't look good Southworth reminded sportswriters of teams that had come from behind in late August and early September to win the pennant. Southworth cited the 1930 Cardinals, the 1921 Giants, the 1934 Cardinals, the 1935 Cubs and the 1936 Giants all were seven and one-half to 10 games back and still won. On the homestand just completed the Cardinals were 19–3 and strangely Lanier lost two of the games and Cooper the other one. On the plus side, both Pollet and White showed some return to their 1941 form.

In the last 12 games the Dodgers had scored just 39 runs and were leaning heavily on their pitching staff. They hoped Newsom could help put them over the top. His final mark as a Dodger was 2–2, with a 3.38 ERA in eight games, five as a starter. Bobo said on the last day of road trip, "Get one run and old Bobo will do the rest." The Dodgers got two, but one would have been enough as he shut out Cincinnati on four hits, while fanning eight. A strange statistic was that neither Brooklyn nor their opponents hit a home run in those 12 games.

An interesting event happened at a game in the Polo Grounds where Walker hit two home runs (he had only six for the season, four here) and Arky Vaughn hit his first of the year. Normally you would figure Wyatt would win with that type of support, but he too gave up a home run. Unfortunately it was to Babe Young with the bases loaded and he took his fifth defeat instead of claiming his 16th victory.

As they approached the showdown Slaughter had taken over the batting lead at .324, Lombardi was .320 and Musial .314. Moore, Marion, Cooper and Walker were all between .282 and .312 for the Cardinals. The Dodgers' starters heading into the final two and one-half weeks were Wyatt (17–5), French (13–4), Davis (15–5) and Higbe (14–9). This quartet would be just

6–5 down the stretch. For St. Louis Cooper was 18–7, Beazley was 17–5, Lanier 12–7 and Krist 11–3. This quartet would be 11–2 in the final two and one-half weeks remaining. That would prove to be the difference.

As the teams neared the showdown series the standings showed Brooklyn still first at 93–43, while St. Louis was 91–46, two and one-half games out of first. The spirited Redbird dash had reminded fans of the 1930 and 1934 Cardinals ball clubs. On September 11 Cooper defeated Wyatt, 3–0 for his 20th win of the season and Cooper said, "I get to keep my baseball glove," recalling a comment he made in spring training about throwing his glove away if he didn't win 20 games this year. Lanier then took the Dodgers' measure 2–1. That gave Cooper and Lanier each five victories over Brooklyn. Cooper allowed just 10 runs in 53 innings against the Dodgers.

On September 13 St. Louis split a double-header with Philadelphia while the Dodgers dropped a pair to Cincinnati. This put St. Louis in first place for the first time that season. Breadon shouted, "We're in—we're home free." Whether they failed against the Yankees in the World Series or not didn't matter. This club had written another chapter in the thrilling history of the St. Louis Cardinals. They were 10 out on August 10 and now they were a game in front. This was reminiscent of 1930 and 1934. This team was a courageous, hustling team, fighting every day tooth and nail, refusing to be counted out. The Cardinals knocked the Dodgers out of first in 1930 with a three game sweep and they kept reeling and finished fourth. This season the worst they could do was second place.

Breadon called Southworth the best manager ever. He would be 272–143 for two and three-fourths seasons when this campaign ended. Southworth had said when Brooklyn was playing over .700 ball, "They haven't had their slump, we had ours. Never saw a team yet, no matter how good, didn't have a slump somewhere along the way." He went on to point out the fight wasn't over as Brooklyn still had seven games with Philadelphia. The Yankees said they wanted a subway series. That way travel problems could be avoided and besides they wanted to play Brooklyn again. However, the Yankees said they could beat anybody, so bring them on. They would eat those words.

However, the fight wasn't over. Brooklyn still had 12 games to play and St. Louis 11 and the Cardinals' lead was just one and one-half games. They were 96–47 and Brooklyn was 94–48.

During this stretch drive the Cardinals had made their own breaks. The gallant Cardinals arrived home to a huge, cheering, rabid crowd of fans that greeted them at Union Station. The team was 13–3 while gone. They had left St. Louis on September 3 three and one-half games out of first and returned home on September 21 with a two and one-half game lead. While they had pretty good pennant insurance, Southworth wasn't talking World Series yet.

On September 19 Breadon said they couldn't accept any more requests for World Series tickets as they were sold out. He added that he wished they had a larger park.

The Cardinals ended their road trip by splitting a double-header in Chicago to their largest crowd of the season. They swept Cincinnati in three games, split that Labor Day double-header with Pittsburgh, won the two crucial games in Brooklyn and won the only game played in New York. Philadelphia and Boston played St. Louis tough, but the Cardinals took three of four from Philadelphia and both from Boston. In one game in Philadelphia the Cardinals rallied for four runs in the ninth to win. They were being called the "come from behind kids," their new sobriquet. In the Chicago double-header the Cardinals scored only one run, but it was enough for Cooper's 21st victory and ninth shutout. In game two Passeau shut down the Cardinals 2–0, marking the first time they had been shut out since Starr did it on May 24.

Brooklyn fans couldn't understand what happened to their "beloved bums." Shivers, shakes and snarls hit Flatbush. The hitting slump, pitching lapse and Cards' surge was ending Brooklyn's pennant and World Series dream. From September 3 to September 22 Brooklyn was just 7–10, while St. Louis was 14–3. Most of the Dodgers' wins came against second division teams.

However, there still was a glimmer of hope as St. Louis held a two and one-half game lead with a 101–48 record, while Brooklyn was 98–50.

Kurowski was hailed as a miracle of modern medical science. Dr. Robert Hyland said by all rights Kurowski shouldn't be able to have hardly any strength in his right arm, let alone perform at the major league level. There were three inches of bone missing from his wrist to his forearm. Somehow the muscles grew in there and held the arm together. Kurowski would be a power hitting third baseman for the club through 1947, then the arm would give out and after that season he would not be able to perform adequately.[24]

With all the hoopla and enjoyment over the Cardinals' triumph the attention had not been focused on Rickey. Now it returned in the form of his being wooed by the Brooklyn Dodgers. Breadon had given permission for Rickey to leave and have discussions with the Dodgers. The key question was could Brooklyn afford Rickey? Breadon didn't mind losing Rickey as he wanted to run the whole show and receive the recognition. While he wouldn't be around in later years, the Cardinals would suffer because of the loss of Rickey and his genius. However, that was another story for later in the day.

The Cardinals finished the season two games in front of Brooklyn, winning their final five and ending at 106–48. They had to win all five because Brooklyn won its last six and ended at 104–50. The Dodgers' 104 victories and no pennant tied the 1909 Cubs, who also won 104 and lost 49 while finishing second to Pittsburgh, who was 110–42.

The Cardinals took the pennant with a 43–8 record down the stretch.

Brooklyn didn't necessarily fall apart, as they were 31–20, a pennant winning clip in many a season. The Cardinals led the league in team batting (.268), runs scored (755), doubles (282), triples (69), slugging percentage (.379), defense and the best ERA, 2.55. Cooper copped the MVP award with a 22–7, 1.77 ERA and 10 shutouts. Rookie Beazley was 21–6 with a 2.14 ERA.

Slaughter finished second in the batting with .318 and Musial (his first full season) was third at .315. Lombardi won the batting title at .330, but had only 309 at-bats. However, under the rules in existence then (a player had to appear in 100 games) he qualified, playing 103 games. Slaughter had 591 at-bats and led the league with 188 hits. He also scored 100 runs, had 17 triples 13 home runs and 98 RBIs. Lombardi had 102 hits, 11 home runs and 46 RBIs. Hitting throughout the league was off from prior seasons. Southworth later said he was wrong in not playing Musial early in the season against certain left hand pitchers. Musial proved he could hit them no matter what side they threw from.

This team was considered the finest in the Cardinals' history and a culmination of Rickey's prized and fabled farm system. They brought home the bacon in grand style. The greatest feature of this team was the assembling of one of the finest pitching staffs and greatest outfields ever on a ball diamond. It was no telling how far this team would have gone had World War II not intervened.

The next challenge for St. Louis was the famed New York Yankees, who said they could beat anybody. For eight innings in game one in St. Louis it looked that way as Red Ruffing held the St. Louis Swifties hitless for 7⅔ innings. Moore got the first hit in the eighth, but it meant nothing. In the ninth inning the Cardinals gave the Yankees a sample of what the National League had seen for 154 games and why St. Louis won 106. Down 7–0, they rallied for four runs before the Yankees could get the side retired.

It didn't look like anything would happen as Hopp flied out to open the inning. Sanders pinch-hit for Kurowski (who had fanned three times) and walked on four pitches. Marion tripled in the first run and O'Dea, pinch hitting for Lanier, singled home Marion. Brown singled and that kayoed Ruffing. In came Spud Chandler (16–5 on the season) and Moore greeted him with a single to score Crespi (running for O'Dea). Slaughter got an infield hit and Musial was up next. In a game in early September he had hit a grand slam home run in Pittsburgh. Could he do it again? This wasn't to be the time, although he hit the ball hard but right at Buddy Hassett for the final out.

This was all the spark and fire the Cardinals needed. In game two Beazley had a 3–0 lead, but weakened in the eighth and the Yankees scored three times (two on Charlie "King Kong" Keller's home run). It looked like the momentum had shifted. In the bottom of the eighth the first two men were easy outs and then, as would happen so often during the next ten years, Slaughter and Musial took charge. Slaughter doubled and Musial singled for what would prove to be the winning run, as Beazley held the Yankees in check in the ninth, but not without some great defensive help. Bill Dickey singled and Tuck Stainback ran for him and when Hassett singled Stainback headed for third, but Slaughter's great throw cut him down.

The Series now moved to New York and all the Yankees said, "It will never come back to St. Louis." And they were right. The Cardinals won game three, 2–0 behind the six hit pitching of sore armed White, who had been just 7–5 during the season, although a 2.53 ERA. White was aided by great catches from Moore, Slaughter and Musial. Game four proved to be a slugfest won by St. Louis, 9–6. The Cardinals scored six runs in the fourth on six hits as Musial got two. He started the rally with a single and ended with a run scoring double. Cooper couldn't stand the prosperity and was batted out on the box in the sixth inning. Lanier was the winner with a solid relief performance.

Now it was the Cardinals with three wins and the Yankees one and if they lost their prophesy would come true, the Series would not return to St. Louis. Ruffing (winner of game one) faced Beazley (winner of game two). Phil Rizzuto homered in the first and Slaughter tied it in the fourth. Red Rolfe, DiMaggio and Keller singled in the fourth to put the Yankees back in the lead, but in the sixth Moore and Slaughter singled and Cooper scored Moore with a sacrifice fly. It stayed tied 2–2 until the top of the ninth. Then with two out, Kurowski hit a two run homer that gave the Cardinals their 4–2 triumph and they became the first team to defeat New York in a World Series since they did it in 1926. No, there wouldn't be a return to St. Louis to play ball, only to a whooping, cheering, fanatic St. Louis crowd to welcome home the new world champions.

As said earlier it was sad that the war would break up this club. They would never be together as a group again. By the time the war ended in 1945, many would be gone or have lost their skills, but we are getting ahead of our story. It would have been interesting to see what this team could have accomplished. Then far greater and more important things were taking place and had to be addressed and that was fighting and winning World War II and destroying Germany and Japan's military forces.

It suffices to say that missing from the 1943 roster would be Moore, Slaughter, Beazley and Crespi. Others would join them as time progressed. We give a final salute to a great team and a great season.

FOUR

1943

Cards Run Away and Hide

Following their dynamic and overwhelming victory in the 1942 World Series, fans thronged to St. Louis' Union Station to greet the homecoming champions. Thousands packed the station to pay homage to the fabulous St. Louis Swifties. This was a thrilling climax to a great season. A team that was 10 games out in the second week of August not only won 43 of their final 51 games and achieved a team record 106 victories, they also defeated the mighty New York Yankees, who last lost in a World Series in 1926. The winner that time was also St. Louis.

Now with this euphoria behind them, the club had to turn to looking forward to 1943. The first casualty of the new season would happen months before the campaign began. Branch Rickey, the father of the farm system, left St. Louis and joined the Brooklyn Dodgers in a similar capacity. There was mixed emotion on his part as well as the fans of St. Louis about Rickey's departure.

Rickey was extremely reluctant to leave the city as he had many strong ties to the town. Rickey had been with the Cardinals for 24 years as president, general manager and field manager. He was the father of the farm system, which made the Cardinals into the premier team of the National League and one that had defeated the powerful New York Yankees in two of three World Series. Rickey was so popular there was a contingent that wanted him to run for governor or the U. S. Senate on the Republican ticket.[1]

This move and change had been forecast at least two years earlier (1940). Owner Sam Breadon now felt that he was fully capable of running both the team and the farm system. Some fans and pundits claimed that he was jealous of all the glory heaped on Rickey, but then the man deserved it for what he had achieved. In 17 seasons the Cardinals had won six pennants, four world titles and finished second four times. The fabled farm system had produced some of the greatest players of all time, many later to be enshrined in the Hall of Fame. A list of just a few will tell the story: Rogers Hornsby, Jim Bottomley, Jess "Pop" Haines, Dizzy Dean, Joe Medwick, Chick Hafey and Johnny Mize. Of course from the current team you would find Stan Musial and Enos Slaughter.

The key question now was could Breadon do with the farm system what Rickey accomplished? Rickey was a true genius, as history had shown. There was still a lot of talent left in the system and therefore Breadon could be safe for several years, producing championship teams or at least constantly remaining in the pennant race. The real test for Breadon was could he find the talent to continue the dominance in the National League that his team had enjoyed for almost two decades? As the situation was viewed people wondered whether Breadon had the moxie and skill of Rickey to continue the job and trend established. Time would answer that question.[2]

Pitcher Morton Cooper was the MVP of the league with a 22–7 won-lost mark, 1.77 ERA and a league high 10 shutouts. This was one of the finest seasons put together by a pitcher in many years.[3] Enos Slaughter was second in the voting as he batted .318 (second in the league), led with 188 hits and 13 triples and also amassed 98 RBIs (a high total for a light hitting season).[4]

On the financial side the World Series saved the Cardinals. The farm system lost $100,000 and Columbus was the only team to be in the black. It had been suggested the losses could have been as high as $150,000. It was expensive running a 26 team farm system. Breadon knew that he had to tighten up the system, as well as continue to produce star players and winning teams.

Breadon said there would be a general reorganization of the farm system, making it not only more competitive (it already the top system), but also more profitable. This would be by design if not brought on by World War II as players left for military service. The truth was that Rickey had not had his own way for some time. Breadon believed he had capable people on whom he could rely.

The key people were Bill Wallingham, his nephew; Joe Mathes, head scout; and Eddie Dyer, manager of Columbus. The Columbus team had given St. Louis manager Billy Southworth and 14 of their 1942 players. They were Terry Moore, Slaughter, and the Cooper brothers, Max Lanier, Ernie White, Ray Sanders, Harry Walker, Cooker Triplett and Murray Dickson. All of them had come direct from Columbus, while Musial, George "Whitey" Kurowksi, Frank Crespi and Emil Verban had all spent time at Columbus.

Several of the Cardinals went into defense plant work in the off-season and others donated blood. Hopp and White both were working at the small arms plant in St. Louis.

The Dodgers fans were saying of the Cardinals' Series victory, "See what we had to beat." Others were saying, "Maybe St. Louis has turned the Yankees around," meaning maybe they wouldn't be such a dominant, cocky force in the American League after the bashing handed them by St. Louis.[5] Meanwhile Durocher was in a precarious position, as he was on a hot seat since his team didn't win the pennant.

While Cooper was extremely proud of winning the MVP award, he gave much of the credit to his teammates, saying without them he would never have achieved it. Three of the first four in the race were either Cardinals or former Redbirds. Johnny Mize finished fourth and the only non-former or current Cardinal was number three—that great New York Giant—Mel Ott.

Voting for the Hall of Fame was to take place in January 1943. The odds on favorite for the Hall was Lefty Grove, who owned a 300–141 career mark and if he had not been held back by Jack Dunn, owner of the Baltimore team in the 1920s, he would have had an excellent chance to win 400. Dunn kept him on the team for five years, when he could have been in the majors. He did this because Baltimore was a minor league powerhouse and Grove the kingpin. He posted a 108–38 mark during that time.[6] Others under consideration for the Hall were Ed Delahanty, Dan Brouthers and Hugh Duffy.

Rickey contended that the Cardinals had made $150,000 to $200,000 during the past season and could sell $100,000 (a high figure in those days) of talent and still compete. There was that much talent in the system. Breadon told Rickey the door was still open, but the question was how wide. Breadon stated that Rickey would probably earn a $40,000 bonus for the 1942 season.

Cooper had just completed a three year contract that graduated his scale to a final pay of $8,000 per season for 1942. He was certainly in for a big boost for 1943 and ensuing seasons, and while unknown at the time this would be the beginning of contract problems with the Cooper brothers, a la the Deans in the 1930s. It was estimated Cooper could bring $100,000-$150,000 on the open market. Many other Cardinals were also in line for nice pay increases after a highly successful season. Breadon reminded everyone that the Cardinals had a number of bright prospects that could be brought to the major team. This was an effort to try and hold the paychecks in line.

Rickey was named general manager and president of the Brooklyn Dodgers at $65,000 per season. They had to beg him to take the job. He said, "We must measure our team by the Cardinals."[7] The St. Louis Browns had wanted Rickey and badly needed him, however his demands exceeded their budget, thus in the end he signed with Brooklyn. Rickey was a great theorist, but also a practical person. He was not successful as a manger because he could never get his players to understand what he was talking about. They shouldn't have felt bad, as most sportswriters didn't either.

Rickey kept his lip buttoned on Leo "the Lip" Durocher. He wouldn't say if he would stay as manager, as many called for his scalp when the Cardinals overtook the Dodgers. Another concern about Durocher was his draft status. He had a call up scheduled for June 1, 1943, and this could have kept him from getting the manager's position. Rickey didn't have to worry about managerial help, as 2,000,000 Brooklyn fans were ready to assist him. They wanted their Dodgers back in the World Series.

The Cardinals' farm system was greatly reduced for the 1943 season. It was not by choice, but rather necessity. Many of the lower leagues couldn't field complete teams as hundreds of players were drafted. Remember, most of these players were in the 18–21 age bracket, which had the highest draft potential. There just wasn't enough talent available to be able to compete in many leagues.

On the major team there were several developments regarding the military. Slaughter was still waiting for his call up, but brilliant rookie Beazley enlisted in Army Aviation saying, "I'm through with baseball and will make the Army my career." Everyone hoped he was joking. You just don't find a 22 year old rookie pitcher every day that goes 21–6 in his rookie season (not even in the Cardinals' rich farm system).

New rules permitted major league teams to draft more than one player from the minor league clubs. This would help the weaker teams, but can hurt the stronger ones (Cardinals, Yankees, Dodgers) as they had far more talent to lose. St. Louis had 23 farm teams, 13 more than any other rival National League club. Breadon settled into the plow seat ready to make his crop match the war needs. He did not intend to curtail the farm system any more than the exigencies of war made it necessary. Breadon said there would be a tremendous shortage of talent, especially with the new law drafting 18 and 19 year olds. He didn't see them being replaced by 16 and 17 year olds at the minor league level.

The Cardinals started the 1942 season with 14 clubs owned outright and had working agreements with nine others. Due to the draft and the closing of some leagues the Cardinals finished the season with one less team in each category. The Cardinals supplied money and players to all 23 teams, which was the only way they could stay solvent. A few years earlier St. Louis had over 30 teams. As Breadon said, they had always been the leader in that area. The war had a profound effect on all teams, including the Cardinals.

Breadon believed his club would be fortunate for 1943 if they could field a roster of 25 players. They might have to settle for less, maybe 23. Breadon was opposed to more than 14 night games. During 1941 the team drew more in the seven allotted games than in the first 11 night games of 1942. It was only in September when the team was making its mad rush for the pennant that attendance at night games improved. They played one against Cincinnati and two against Brooklyn.

Breadon believed attendance would be hurt further in 1943 by the war, as many people would now be employed in defense work and not readily available for ballgame attendance. Another factor that contributed to slacking attendance was gasoline rationing, as people had to conserve their use of a car for true emergencies. While public transportation was available and good, not all people readily availed themselves of this mode of travel.

The biggest challenge the team faced for 1943 was replacing Beazley. It just wasn't that simple to replace a 21–6 record. The team had Pollet and White on the squad, but both also were in the draft vulnerability category. As the team searched the minors for pitching help they found Harry Brecheen (18–9), George Munger (16–13), Ted Wilks (13–8) and Elwin "Preacher" Roe (6–11). The latter was once a bright prospect, but had fallen on hard times. Other prospects included Blix Donnelly (21–10), although he was 27. Max Surkont was not in the plans as he had left for the service.

While the team probably would be able to put together a quality pitching staff, there was great concern over the outfield. Slaughter and Moore would be extremely difficult to replace. Slaughter was the team's leading hitter and Moore the best center fielder in the game. Hopp and Walker were candidates, but truthfully neither could play center in the manner of Moore nor hit like Slaughter. The latter had both average and power. If Sanders didn't make it at first then Hopp would become a candidate for that position. Thus while the team had a lot of talent, there were some problems. When compared to the rest of the league that paled, however, as the Cardinals still had the deepest strength both at the majors and in their farm system.

Breadon called St. Louis the best baseball city in the country. Based on a 50 mile radius, St. Louis had the lowest population of all major league cities. While St. Louis itself was larger than some major league cities, Cincinnati and Pittsburgh, they didn't have any large cities in that 50 mile radius to add significantly to their population. All other cities had large towns in their drawing radius. Cincinnati had both Dayton and Columbus (each well over 100,000 population). St. Louis area had a population of 2,000,000 and drew 600,000, almost 30 percent. This was the best relationship of attendance to fans drawn of any major league city.

The Dodgers had problems of their own, as manager Durocher faced potentially being drafted. If he was this would be a real blow to the team. For all of his idiosyncrasies he was considered one of the best managers in baseball. He had the drive, fire and spirit of the old Gas House Gang and tried to instill it in the Dodgers. Without Durocher that would be lacking and they wouldn't be the same competitive, combative team.

President Ed Barrows of the New York Yankees wanted to increase the squad during the season from 25 men to 30. His position was simple. With the draft likely to take many players, including stars, it was better to be prepared than not. It was his feeling this was not the time to cheapen the game, when it was so important to the morale of the servicemen and the country.

Mathes was in daily conference with Breadon, as he would probably be his next right hand man. Mathes had been part of the Cardinals organization for 15 years and had performed in many jobs, duties and functions. However, Breadon was going to be in charge and be his own man. One of his first acts was to drop Frank Rickey, brother of Branch, as a scout. There was concern on this issue from many quarters as this could be a fatal mistake. Frank had found players such as Mize, Slaughter, White, Lanier and Marty Marion. Not a bad job, they told Breadon. He replied that they had other scouts of the same caliber. Closed subject as far as Breadon was concerned.[8]

Breadon said the Cardinals couldn't assist other teams with talent, as they would be fortunate to have enough to fill their own major roster and supply all their farm teams. He predicted the situation would get worse before it got better and that wouldn't happen until the war ended, as eventually there would be over 5,000 men from the majors and minors in the military. For now Breadon's main concern was working agreements with New Orleans and Mobile, Alabama; Springfield, Ohio; Williamson, West Virginia; Union City, Tennessee; Washington, Pennsylvania; La Crosse, Wisconsin; and Duluth, Minnesota. This was a major bill to fill, the Cardinals had concluded.

The Cardinals continued to search for replacements for Moore, Slaughter and Beazley. While others would also be lost to the military, this was the key priority for the present as Breadon viewed it. Erv Dusak batted just .268 in the minors, but did have 18 home runs; however, he informed the team that he would be leaving for the service shortly. Another possibility was Buster Adams, who batted .311 with 28 home runs in the minors in 1942. The team also faced the possibility of losing Musial to the military. If that happened only Hopp, Walker and Triplett remained and none of them could play center like Moore. The Cardinals organization had given 69 men to the service since the end of the 1942 season and that brought their total to 205 players from their system that now belonged to Uncle Sam.

The major league plans for 1943 were streamlined to be in sync with the war effort. They agreed to a 40 percent reduction in miles traveled. This was handled in various ways, including longer road trips and more games in each city per visit, thus reducing the trips to each town. Baseball voted on providing various types of service aid in the forms of uniforms and equipment as well as exhibition games for servicemen, whenever possible. Free admittance to all games was granted to military personnel. For the minor leagues loans were authorized to help keep them in a stable financial position, fees were dropped for the duration, while the territories of disbanded clubs and leagues were frozen for the duration. Teams where leagues folded were permitted to join another league.

Thirty-two year old Frank DeMaree was picked up by the Cardinals as outfield insurance. He had been a free agent. DeMaree batted just .225 in 64 games in 1942, but had been a past all star. DeMaree had batted over .300 five times between 1935 and 1940, with a high of .350 in 1936. He also had 115 RBIs in 1937 and 96 in 1936. While he was past his prime, given the current military situation, DeMaree represented a body that could play the outfield from time to time.[9] The Cardinals had just learned that Adams could go into the service which was another factor in picking up DeMaree. It was possible he could stage a comeback with a team like the Cardinals, that a fire might be lit underneath him. At least this was what Breadon and Southworth were hoping.

The dividends from the World Series were paid to the players 90 percent by check and the balance in war bonds. This amounted to about $42,000 in bonds. Meanwhile the Cardinals declared a $2 per share stock dividend; this would total $20,000 as most of the stock was owned by Breadon. This was the smallest dividend in several years. The farm losses had cut deep into the dividend that was available for distribution. It had been $12 in 1938, $10 in 1939, $10 in 1940 and $7 in 1941. The trend was downward, but much of it could be explained through farm system expansion until the losses suffered in 1942.

New fielding records were set in the major leagues in 1942 by two National League players. Philadelphia Phillies outfielder Danny Litwhiler played in 151 games and handled 327 chances without an error, becoming the first outfielder in major league history to play over 150 games and not make an error. Cincinnati's shortstop, Eddie Miler, set a new major league percentage fielding record for shortstops with a .983 mark. He handled 735 chances and made just 13 errors.

The Cardinals' fans thought that Slaughter should have been awarded the batting title in 1942. Officially it was given to Cincinnati's Ernie Lombardi (the slow footed catcher, perhaps the slowest man in baseball), as he batted .330 to Slaughter's .318. The fans shouted "compare the numbers." Lombardi had 309 at-bats in 105 games, made 102 hits for 149 total bases, scored 32 runs and drove in 46. Meanwhile Slaughter had 591 at-bats (almost 300 more) in 152 games, made 188 hits for 292 total bases, and scored 100 runs driving home 98. No doubt a far better performance. However, the criteria at that time was that a player had to appear in 100 games to qualify for the batting crown and Lombardi reached that mark. A similar situation occurred in 1940 when Deb Garms appeared in just 103 games, but won the title with a .355 mark. The ruling would later be changed that a player had to make 3.1 plate appearances for each game his team played. Under those rules Slaughter would have won the batting title.[10, 11]

Other honors that the Cardinals received included Southworth being named manager of the year for the second consecutive season and Rickey general manager of the year. He had also received the award in 1938. Thus the Cardinals copped the MVP award, as well as manager of the year and general manager of the year. This was a tribute to the job done by the men in key positions.

During the first full year of the war the minor leagues sent 1,439 men to the military service. This number would eventually approach 5,000. The Cardinals had contributed almost one-seventh of this number, although there were 16 major league teams. In fairness to the other clubs it must be remembered that St. Louis had the largest chain by far. Billy Southworth Jr. became a war ace and war hero. He would wear his redbird cap on bombing raids and never received a scratch. Among his biggest targets were the German U-boat hideouts in France.

The major leagues decide to seek training bases closer to home to help cut expenses, travel time and aid the war effort. Some baseball analysts feared that northern training would be injurious to older ballplayers as the cold weather was not conducive to getting into shape. The St. Louis Cardinals and Browns agreed to a seven game spring series before the start of the regular season. The Cardinals trained in Cairo, Illinois, about 110 miles southeast of St. Louis. Cairo was normally 13 to 15 degrees warmer than St. Louis.

Despite having a shortened right arm due to childhood injuries, Whitey Kurowksi received his draft notice. Should the Cardinals lose Kurowski to the draft that would create another hole in the lineup. One of the options was to play veteran Deb Garms at third or move Lou Klein to that position and search for another second baseman.

Night baseball was king to the Cardinals in 1942 as they were 16–4. Cooper was 7–0, while Beazley posted a 6–0 record. Slaughter was the top hitter in night baseball at .372.

Musial and Walker were both holdouts. They were offered identical contracts for 1943, giving them increases over 1942. Dickson hadn't reported to camp and his whereabouts was unknown. Reserve catcher Ken O'Dea was with his family because of a major illness. The Cardinals now faced the possible loss of Bobby Brown and Howard Krist to the service. If they lost Brown, then young Lou Klein would take over at second. Southworth was grooming him for the job. George Fallon was a good defensive player, but hit just .240 in the minors last season.

Southworth said the pitching was going to depend on how well some of the rookies performed. His top three pitchers for the year would be Cooper, Lanier and Pollet. Lanier could be the best left hander in the league. Donnelly had been impressive in his spring appearances.

Musial and Walker report and this relieved Southworth, as this represented two-thirds of his outfield. He now planned to use Musial in left and Walker in right with Adams in center field. Hopp would also be in the outfield picture if Sanders could make the grade at first base.

Breadon called the idea of James T. Gallagher, general manager of the Chicago Cubs, hairbrained. Gallagher's idea was to pool the talent of the teams and then as teams lost players they could draw from the talent pool. This would make for better balance in the league. Breadon said it would kill player incentive and destroy the game.[12]

Another idea suggested was to sign a player for one year and then each player negotiate with whoever he wanted to at the end of the year. That would destroy fan loyalty. You would never know who played for whom from season to season. Little did Breadon think this would come to pass over 40 years later.[13]

Breadon said it was different with professional football where they drafted college players. They didn't have the expense in searching out and then developing these players for several seasons. There was little expense on the part of the professional football team in player development. A major league team had scouts, coaches, training, player development, farm teams and stadiums to maintain. There was a huge investment in a player before he was brought to the majors and then only a small percentage of them made it to stay.

Breadon said, "We need to train the youth now to save the game for post war." He supported training camps around the country for youth and developing them into major league players through the normal apprenticeship in the minors. The difference was they would start as youths in training camps and then be selected for the next level when they were old enough to qualify.[14]

The Redbirds got their wings clipped as Marion had an appendectomy and could be lost to the team for six weeks. Klein would take over at shortstop until Marion returned. There was also concern about Cooper, the ace of the staff, as he fell off a ladder at home and injured his back. The report was that he would be ready for the season. The Cardinals sent Clay and Donnelly to Rochester. Wilks, Roe, George Dockins and Beckman were sent to Columbus on 24 hour recall.

St. Louis was picked to repeat with Brooklyn second in a guess packed race. There were too many unknowns with all the personnel lost to the military. The Cardinals had speed, a great manager and a reservoir of talent in the minors. They would win despite the losses to the service, with more expected to come. The infield looked great and when Marion returned Klein might prove to be a very valuable reserve. He wouldn't play second as well as Brown, but did a very capable job.

The major leagues got all balled up on the new baseball. There was a flurry of low hit, low run games in both leagues. A test of the new ball showed there was a 26 percent drop in vitality of the ball from 1942. It was called the balata ball. It had a dead sound when the bat hit it. In the first four games with Cincinnati the two teams each won two. The Cardinals made 18 hits and Cincinnati 20 as each team scored just three runs. Some of the teams thought it was unfair some have the baseballs from last year while they had to use this balata ball. Once all teams were allowed to use the same type of baseball as last year the scoring would improve.

In game one Johnny Vander Meer defeated Cooper 1–0 in 11 innings when Cooper was late covering first base. The next day Ray Starr defeated Ernie White 1–0 in 10 innings. Finally in the third game the Cardinals scored their first runs of the season. Musial stole home as Ray Mueller dropped the ball while tagging him. That was St. Louis' first run of the season. The second was scored on a passed ball as Gumbert won 2–1 with Krist saving the game. The last game was another 1–0, with St. Louis the winner as Pollet applied the whitewash. Cooper tripled and scored on Adams' squeeze play for the only run of the game. Klein was hitless in the four games, but did a good job defensively.

An ailing elbow forced Cooper out of the first game of a double-header on May 2 with Cincinnati. He had a two hit shutout and was leading 4–0 when forced to leave. The Cardinals eventually won the game, but Cooper didn't get credit for the victory. Of greater concern was how long he would be lost to the team. If he was out for any length of time it could mean real trouble for St. Louis. Pollet won the second game 6–3 and he looked like he would take up the slack left by Beazley's departure.

Klein had hit .367 at Columbus in 1941, but fell to .249 in 1942. The problem was his vision in one eye was 20–40. Eddie Dyer, manager at Columbus, said he needed professional help and got the team to send him to St. Louis to Dr. Alvin G. Mueller. He had worked with these types of problems before. He was able to help Klein and it produced a marked improvement in his batting. Mueller was the brother of former Giants, Braves and Cardinals outfielder Clarence "Heinie" Mueller.

For awhile the Cardinals' injury list reminded everyone of 1941. Cooper was out with a sore arm. Brother Walker had an injured ankle. Hopp was left at home because of back problems. Brown was also in St. Louis, nursing a finger he broke in camp. However by May 9 Marion was back at short and Klein at second and both Coopers were ready for duty. Mort won game one 8–1 and it looked like another big year for him. St. Louis trailed Brooklyn by two games after two and one-half weeks of play.

Cooper defeated Philadelphia in the series opener on May 15 and when Krist took the second game 4–3 it marked his 13th win against Philadelphia and just one loss. Krist had a major league mark of 28–4 at this point, with almost half of his wins against Philadelphia. Gumbert lost the second game of the double-header, 2–1. Philadelphia was 42–109 in 1942, but were an improved ball club over last season, as they would finish 64–90, a 22 game improvement. Musial led the team with a .323 mark while Pollet was 2–0 and Cooper 2–1. In the early going St. Louis was third, three and one-half games behind Brooklyn. Were they going to have to make another stretch drive to catch the Dodgers?

The Cardinals completed a strong eastern trip at 11–6. They split four with Brooklyn, but finished by taking two double-headers from New York.

Kurowski had a 22 game hitting streak and Klein a 15 game streak. The two had been the hottest hitters on the team. Brown was well and ready to play, but Klein had played so well Southworth was reluctant to take him out of the lineup.

The Cardinals pitching had been bolstered by strong relief pitching from Brecheen and Dickson. White injured his shoulder in the 7th inning of game two at Brooklyn. Brecheen came in and stopped a rally and won the game. The next day Lanier got into trouble. Brecheen came back and allowed no runs and no hits for three innings to protect a Cardinals victory. At the Polo Grounds Dickson replaced Lanier in the first game of a May 23 double-header and pitched 7⅔ innings with no runs and just two hits for the victory. With relief pitching like that the opinion was that the boys would repeat.

Musial continued to lead the team at .330 with Walker at .320 and Klein at .300. The Cardinals were now second, two and one-half games behind Brooklyn. The thinking was that Brooklyn would wilt when the sun heated up. Kurowski's 22 game hitting streak stopped on May 26 versus Boston, while Klein's was stopped at 21 in the first game of a double-header on May 31 with Brooklyn. Musial now had a 17 game hitting streak. He was the sweet note in the Cardinals' attack. He was a daredevil on the bases, in part to compensate for the loss of Slaughter and Moore. He knew it was his responsibility to pick up the mantle left by those two and he had been doing an excellent job.[15] Brown couldn't get into the lineup as Klein was going so well.

Lanier had been pitching terrific baseball, but had trouble gaining victories. The team hadn't hit behind him. He finally got his third win on May 28 versus Boston, a 2–1 game in 10 innings. It marked his third extra inning game of the month. He had lost the first two. He lost in 14 innings on May 3 to the Cubs and to Boston on May 14 in 10 innings.

Cooper had lost a win earlier against Cincinnati when he was forced out with a 4–0 lead by a sore elbow. He got even by picking up two wins in three days. On May 29 he pitched 1⅓ innings of relief of Krist and got a victory over the Giants. Two days later he pitched a one hit shutout against the Dodgers. The only hit was a bloop double down the foul line by Billy Herman. He now had five victories with two shutouts.

Brecheen made his first start in the nightcap and lost 1–0. It was the first run scored off him in 18⅔ innings. This would be just the first of many times during his career that the little left hander would suffer tough luck losses.

The highlights of the first week of June included Cooper pitching two one-hitters, Musial hitting in 22 straight games, 28,748 seeing a night game in St. Louis, the team is being in first place for the first time that season and the Cardinals acquiring Danny Litwhiler from Philadelphia. The Cardinals were supposed to send some farm hands to the Phillies after the season.

Litwhiler was the most sought after player in Philadelphia. He now gave the Cardinals the best outfield in the league. Litwhiler would be in left, Walker in center and Musial in right. They gave up Coaker Triplett and Dain Clay (who had been playing at Rochester) and Adams. The Cardinals also got outfielder Earl Naylor, who was sent to Rochester.

Fans are asking, "How did Sam pull off this trade?" He got a $50,000 player, who with a team of prominence and dash like the Cardinals could be a $100,000 player. One suggestion was that Breadon might give up a couple of fair pitchers at the end of the season. Philadelphia could have traded with the Dodgers, Giants or Reds, but they didn't have the players the Phillies wanted, said Bill Cox, president of the team. Once again the Cardinals' rich farm system paid dividends.

Litwhiler was an excellent hitter and outfielder. He played the entire 1942 season without making an error. In his first game on June 2 he injured his wrist crashing into the left field wall trying to catch a long foul ball. He missed the rest of the series. Two days later Cooper had a no hitter for seven innings when Jimmy Wasdell led off the eighth inning with a single for the only hit.

His feat of two successive one hitters was exceeded only by Vander Meer's successive no-hitters in 1938 and Howard Ehmke's successive no hitter and one hitter for the Red Sox in 1923. Cooper had pitched no hit ball for 11 consecutive innings. He was now 6–3 with three shutouts and was definitely fully recovered from his early season injury.

The Cardinals took over first place on June 5 when Krist pitched eight innings of shutout ball against the Phillies. Musial's hitting streak ended the next day when rain washed out a double-header with Philadelphia. Play reverted to the fifth inning and it was a tie game and Stan was hitless at the time. He was now a candidate for the batting title with his .359 average. The current leader was Babe Dahlgren (a strange name for this category). A sore shoulder forced him to shorten his swing which had increased his average.

Walker hit his first career home run on June 1 in the 12th inning as St. Louis defeated Brooklyn, 11–9. The team now had a two and one-half game bulge on the Dodgers and slowly started building that margin. Dickson, Brecheen, White and Lanier all had won three games each, while Pollet had four victories. Dickson and Brecheen were both undefeated at this point in the season.

It was a dull day, week or month when the Cardinals weren't involved in some kind of streak, either individually or collectively. Last week they had 21 consecutive scoreless innings against Pittsburgh. Cooper pitched the last three in game one, which was followed by shutouts from Lanier and Pollet. Walker was up to .350 with his 21 game hitting streak and was now runner-up to Dahlgren. He had served notice he would fight for the batting title. He was the latest in the fad of the Cardinals—individual hitting streaks—as he followed Kurowski, Klein and Musial.

On June 14 Cooper picked up his eighth victory. If the team had a weakness it was lack of a good right hand starter behind Cooper. Dickson and Gumbert seem to perform better in relief and Krist was at his best when his spots were picked for him. Currently they had the three of the best left handers in the league in Lanier, Pollet and White. If Pollet didn't get drafted he could win at least 15 games. Concern for White centered around his tender arm, which hadn't been the same since his 17–7 1941 season.

Breadon nixed the "Mr. Brain" idea as the Redbirds soared without Rickey. Breadon said, "I'd be damned dumb if I didn't know how to run the club now." The Cardinals were better in some ways than in 1942. The public wasn't interested in Breadon; the fans wanted to read about the Cardinals. Any publicity, give it to the team, but leave him out, he declared. No man was indispensable on a ball club, whether he was an executive, manager, scout, coach or player.[16]

It was the organization that got the job done. Some might be missed more than others, but you carry on. In the last ten years with Rickey all deals had to have Breadon's approval. It was a different atmosphere with Rickey gone. The players could come and see Breadon anytime they wanted to. He was one of the boys. He might own 70 percent of the Cardinals' stock, but he had an open door policy.

A quick analysis of the team showed that Klein had improved the infield and Kurowski was a better player than in 1942. Musial was vastly improved, as both hitter and fielder, as was Walker. Litwhiler had also made a big difference in the outfield. The pitching was the best in baseball. The Cardinals held a three game edge on Brooklyn, but six games on the loss side.

Brecheen was rapidly becoming the latest Cardinals pitching star. He was 69–32 from 1939–42 before his call to the majors. The rap on Brecheen was that he was too small, standing just 5' 10" and weighing 160 pounds. He would prove them wrong, spending 11 full seasons in the majors, 10 with the Cardinals. He compiled a 128–79 mark for a .631 winning percentage as a Redbird. That included six seasons of 14 wins or more, with one at 20–7.

The Cardinals hit a little tailspin as the team went into a hitting slump. They ended their homestand with a split with the Cubs. Then they traveled to Cincinnati where they took two of three but lost two straight in Chicago and got just eight hits in two games. The Cardinals bounced back to take a double-header from the Cubs as Litwhiler hit two home runs to win the first game 3–2. When Hiram Bithorn defeated St. Louis in the first game of the series it marked the fourth time this season he had defeated them. This time he allowed just two hits, a single by Hopp and a double by Litwhiler.

An interesting comparison between the Dodgers (considered a group of old codgers) and the Cardinals, the speedsters of the league. The Redbirds were last in steals, but used their speed to take the extra base and for daring base running. The Dodgers had twice as many steals as the Cardinals. So far the expected runaway hadn't developed. Perhaps that would happen when the mercury climbed.

It looked like the Cardinals would be losing some of their personnel to the military. Brown was told to report on June 26 to Jefferson Barracks. Pollet, reclassified 1A, enlisted in Army aviation. He would be told when to report.

The race remained tight as Brooklyn went on a 9–2 spree while St. Louis was just 6–5. The Cardinals had built the lead to six and one-half games, but it now was just three and one-half. One of the main problems was the Cardinals' inability to handle Chicago so far. They were just 7–7 with that team.

The Cardinals placed a record eight players on the All Star team. They were Musial, Marion, Kurowski, Walker, Lanier, Pollet and the Cooper brothers. The only regulars not selected were Sanders, Klein and Litwhiler.

The team got hot in the East as they took two of three from New York and swept Brooklyn in a three game series. Pollet pitched two shutouts, one over New York and then three hit Brooklyn in a 10 inning 2–0 victory. Cooper lost a game in relief in New York, but came back to get victory number 10 in Brooklyn.

The Cardinals began to forge ahead much to the chagrin of Dodgers manager Leo Durocher. As the Redbirds won five in a row Brooklyn lost the same number. St. Louis now had a seven game lead and the Dodgers had played eight more games than the Cardinals.

The Cardinals continue to surge and were 48–24 with a five and one-half game bulge on Brooklyn who was 47–34. The Cardinals had played nine games less than Brooklyn, who were 10 back on the loss side. The team was now geared to a runaway. The Cardinals were notoriously slow starters. This was explained partly by the fact that they were a young team and they didn't get rolling until the season was well along. Last year the team was seven and one-half games out at this point. It was 10½ by early August. It was youth versus age and the hot weather stagnancy.

During their 11–2 Eastern trip the Cardinals' pitching really shined, featured by four consecutive shutouts. Two were by Gumbert and one each came from Cooper and Pollet. However, the team suffered a severe blow when Pollet was ordered to report to the Army on July 22. He was 8–4 with 12 complete games, five shutouts and a 1.75 ERA. He could just as easily have been 11–1. He had pitched that well. Pollet had three straight shutouts and 28 consecutive scoreless innings when ordered to report. He was the hottest pitcher in the league.

The Cardinals misdealt in Pittsburgh by losing four straight. In the second game of a July 18 double-header they were leading 6–5 in the seventh inning when the game was called. Cooper ended the slump with a 7–4 victory. Brooklyn had been able to cut the led to three and one-half games and seven on the loss side because of the Redbirds' slide.

To strengthen the southpaw side of the staff Breadon acquired Al Brazle from the Sacramento farm team. He had been in the minors for eight years. He was just 8–13 at Houston in 1942, but was 11–7 for a weak hitting Sacramento club. He was 28 years old. The left hand corps had been depleted. Pollet was inducted on July 22 while Brecheen had been order to report for draft induction on July 26. White was sent home for treatment of a bursitis condition in his pitching arm. Then Lanier (the only available left hander) lost to Pittsburgh. Krist was then stung for five runs the next day and the team followed that with a double-header loss. So there were jitters. They finished the trip at 16–9.

When the homestand started there was a lot of gloom. Pollet was in the army and Lanier, White and Gumbert were complaining of sore arms. Then the team started an eight game winning streak, their longest of the season thus far, to open an eight and one-half game lead on Brooklyn. Last year they were behind by seven and one-half games.

The Cardinals were also soaring at the gate as their attendance was up by 30,000 over last season. This made everyone happy, especially Breadon. He not only had a pennant winning team, but attendance was booming.

During that winning streak Munger made his first start and beat New York. Gumbert, his arm better, pitched six scoreless innings and Krist completed the shutout. Brazle made his major league debut with a 5–1 victory over Boston and Munger got his second win of the week in the nightcap. Cooper, en route to another 20 plus win season, gained his 13th victory, beating the Giants 6–2, while Lanier showed his arm was okay by pitching a shutout over Boston on July 24.

Musial now led the league with a .342 mark and Billy Herman was second at .334, followed by Stan Hack at .323. Cooper had 37 RBIs in 63 games (a 100 per season pace, but he wouldn't be in enough games to reach that goal). Litwhiler, Walker, Kurowski and Klein continue to hit steadily for the team.

Breadon was elated for several reasons. First, the Cardinals were in first place. Secondly, their expenses were $100,000 less than last season. It showed you can win a pennant without extravagance. Players all got increases. The savings came not from cutting salaries, but from saving Rickey's $50,000 salary and a reduction in farm operations.

Attendance both at home and on the road was up, so income continued to roll in. All players from the 1942 team still with the club got an increase. Last year's payroll was $180,000, while this season's was slightly less because of the loss of stars to the service. Newcomers and replacements didn't earn what departing stars did. It was also pleasing to Breadon because he could direct the club on a successful basis without Rickey. Breadon had it all. He cut expenses, kept players happy with salary increases and had his team on the way to another pennant.

The Cardinals ran their current winning streak (the longest in the majors this year) to 11 before it was snapped by Philadelphia on July 28. During that six game series Philadelphia won three. The Cardinals then moved into Brooklyn and took the first three games. The series was highlighted by a fight between Walker Cooper and Mickey Owen. Both were banished from the game.

As the temperature heated up so did the Redbirds. Their lead was now 11 games and second place had a new occupant. It was Pittsburgh. Brooklyn was now 12½ games back. The warm weather had caught up with the team as nine of the 12 most used players were 31 or older and four of the first eight pitchers were 35 or older. Whit Wyatt, now 35, winner of 41 games the last two years, developed a sore arm and would see limited duty, finishing at 14–5. He was unable to pitch the full season. Their other ace pitcher, Kirby Higbe, who won 38 games the last two seasons, would finish at 13–10.

Musial continued to lead the league in batting and now had a 14 point lead on Billy Herman. However, it was the pitching that continued to carry the Redbirds. Cooper was 14–5, while Gumbert was 8–4 and Krist 7–3. Dickson, used mostly in relief, was 5–1 and Lanier was only 6–5, despite an ERA around two runs per game. Munger, Brecheen and White had combined for 10 victories. It was a well balanced pitching staff.

Pittsburgh's Rip Sewell came into the game with a 17–2 mark and a personal 11 game winning streak. The Redbirds flattened his famous "eephus" pitch or blooper ball. Sanders had a bases clearing double in the first and then later drove in two more with a triple, while Musial had four hits to take a 22 point lead on Herman in the batting race.

Southworth received the award as manager of the year for 1942. He had also won the award for 1941. Cooper received a watch for his MVP award. Both got their awards on the same night. Southworth would be selected manager of the year again. The Cardinals had two leading candidates for MVP, Cooper and Musial.[17]

National League president Ford Frick said, "The majors will play baseball in 1944." There had been some concern over whether the game would be played. However, there was such a clamor for it from servicemen and defense workers that the game would continue. Connie Mack suggested that the squads be cut to 20 players for next year. No action was taken on his recommendation.[18]

Breadon was happy as the Cardinals drew 83,213 for a four game series with Brooklyn. They drew 29,599 for a double-header and 29,648 and 23,678 for successive night games. Brooklyn fans had developed a chant, "Rickey ruined the Dodgers, we want MacPhail." However, in time they came to adore Rickey as his strategies helped bring them six pennants in ten years, many of which probably belonged to St. Louis. The Redbirds had now built their lead to 13 games. The runaway was on. The question now was not who was going to win, but by how much would the Cardinals win?

In order to reduce travel time it was suggested there be a one way World Series. It would open with three games in the American League city and then finish in the National League city. It would save some transportation cost. It would be a disadvantage to the National League team. However, the prevailing concern was travel time, making the railroad available for military and urgent government business.[19]

The Cardinals express was slowed slightly by a split in New York and then the loss of two of three games in Brooklyn, with Cooper suffering one of the defeats. He was hoping to improve on his 22–7 record of last season. Southworth believed the team would win, but wouldn't let them get overconfident. "We have a young team. I remind them of what we did last year. Somebody could do it to us," he said.

Walker's hitting streak had reached 27 games. Musial had more confidence this season. He said that he didn't lift the ball as much as some long hitters. So many of his were line drives that went between the outfielders. With his great speed he got a lot of doubles and triples. He currently had 16 triples, six more than anyone in either league.

Due to their slight slump the Cardinal lead was cut to 11½ games. There was a new team in second place; this time it was Cincinnati. We were starting to play musical chairs with that position. Cincinnati was 13 back on the lost side. The Cardinals were 69–36, a great pace, but they would do even better the rest of the way. The club would finish with a flourish at 36–13.

Musial was pulling away from all challengers and now led with a .349 mark. Cooper was well above .300 at .312 and had 52 RBIs in 82 games. Cooper was at 16–6 on his march to another 20 win season. Krist for the first time in his career had lost three in a row and was 7–4. He had lost as many games this season as his total from prior years. He was 26–4 entering 1943.

The champion Redbirds flew high in their Sunday best. One of the outstanding qualities of the 1942 club was its ability to play its best before large crowds. Even with the change in team personnel, the large crowds still inspired them. On weekdays they often looked like any other team. Come Sunday, watch out. For the season they were 26–5–3 on Sundays. The closest the team came to losing a Sunday double-header was on June 13. They lost game one to Pittsburgh and battled to a 12 inning tie in the nightcap.

In doubleheaders the team was 10–0–4. In single games on Sunday they were 2–1–1. On the last nine Sundays the Cardinals were 17–1. There was no great concern about Cincinnati, as they were not the type of club to put on the finish in August and September like St. Louis did in 1942, or for that matter in 1939, 1940 and 1941.

The team slowed down a little last week, going just 5–4. However, their closest pursuer, Cincinnati, posted the same mark. Individual accomplishments of the week included Cooper winning his 17th and Lanier now at 9–5. They had finally started to hit for him. Munger and Brecheen, both used primarily in relief and as occasional starters, each had five wins. The only bad news of the week was Walker's hitting streak was stopped at 29 games by Al Gerheauser of Philadelphia in the second game of the August 18 double-header.

When the Redbirds came home in September their only remaining road games would be in Chicago September 10 through the 12. The team helped Cincinnati set an attendance record during the four game series there last week. If the team just played at a .500 pace the rest of the way, the title was theirs.

One of the reasons there wasn't a tight race was that the Cardinals were 16–2 against Boston, including the last 15 in a row. They took five of five from them on their last visit to Boston. As August ended St. Louis was 79–43 while Cincinnati was 68–53, 10½ games back. No one was thinking of St. Louis matching last season's record, as it would take a 27–5 spurt to accomplish that. The Cardinals would go 26–6 to finish at 105–49.

Musial strengthened his candidacy for the MVP by holding his average at a league leading .351. Cooper, Walker, Kurowski and Klein also had contributed strong seasons. Cooper with 18 wins was only two away from his coveted goal of 20. The victories had been well spread with Lanier, Krist, Gumbert, Brecheen, Dickson and Munger sharing 45.

The Yankees favored a one way World Series. They would even be willing to let the first three games be played in the National League city. There would be more money for the players if the first three were played in New York, as they had a much larger stadium. The players' World Series share was drawn from the receipts for the first four games.

The players told Southworth they would get 106 victories to match last season. On Labor Day Kurowski hit a home run for a 1–0 victory over Cincinnati, as Cooper got his 19th win and sixth shutout of the season. Southworth's goal was 100 wins, but Walker Cooper says, "We'll make it 106 for you Billy, same as last year." They almost do it, missing by one.

In 1942 the team registered a league high 18 shutouts, led by Cooper's 10. This season they hoped to beat that mark, although Cooper wouldn't get 10 this time, but had a chance to lead the league in that category again. His main competition was Bithorn. It looked like the Cardinals were home free as they were 87–44, 14½ games up on Cincinnati (72–58). Another factor contributing to the big margin was their ability to win one run games. They already had 26 of them on the right side of the ledger. With great pitching you usually win the one and two run games.

Southworth's old tutor, John McGraw, had two axioms. First, pick on the tail enders. Second, have a good bench. The Cardinals had followed those rules. They were 16–2 versus sixth place Boston and 14–4 against last place New York. The Cardinals had to play with a patched up team and took 13 of 15 from Cincinnati, Chicago and Pittsburgh. In some games only one regular was in the infield and he (Klein) was out of position.

Marion was given permission to visit his mother in South Carolina, who was gravely ill. Hopp was at first base, Fallon at second, Garms at third. Sanders had been hit by a hard grounder on the ear on Labor Day. It was recommended that he stay out for a week. He got back into the lineup on September 11. Kurowski had been working his way back in when he injured his right groin again in Chicago. He was in severe pain.

Garms had to be brought in from the outfield to play third base. Walker was nursing a sore arm, but had to go to center field. As soon as Sanders was back for duty, then Hopp moved to center. The team had to get well for the series; they couldn't have a long hospital list heading into the World Series. Dickson had passed his army physical exam at Fort Leavenworth, Kansas. He was back with the team on a leave of absence. His length of stay was uncertain.

Brooklyn by mid–September had crept back into second place, but 15½ games out of first. The rain did something no one else could do and that was stop the Cardinals in Chicago on September 12. They had won 12 of 13 prior to that game. The way Southworth had been handling the staff it looked like he might use left handers in the series. In their recent five game winning streak, Brazle won twice and Lanier and Brecheen each picked up a win.

The Cardinals clinched the pennant on September 18 with 14 days to go. Only three National clubs had won titles earlier. Pittsburgh did it on September 16, 1902, with 19 days to go; Cincinnati did it on September 16, 1919, with 12 days to go and the 1931 Cardinals did it on September 16 with 11 days to go.

It puzzled fans that the Yankees were the favorites in the World Series, as they lost to the Cardinals in 1942. Both teams had lost key players to the war effort. The biggest Yankees losses were Joe DiMaggio and surprisingly 39 year old Charles "Red" Ruffing was taken. His early years with the Boston Red Sox (when they were last each year from 1925–29) and now this late call up prevented him from winning 300 games. Ruffing finished his career with 273 victories.

Southworth was worried about his staff for the World Series, as he had only six pitchers available. Dickson had been given orders for a military call up. The easiest of all Cardinals pennants was dampened by this saddening news. The six pitchers he had available were Cooper, Lanier, Brecheen, Brazle, Krist and Munger.

Though the team was young and full of vigor, they lacked the fervor of last season's pennant winning team. This group on clinching enjoyed themselves, but not in the same flamboyant manner as in 1942. Evidently the circumstances surrounding the winning of the pennant had much to do with the type and manner in which the team celebrated.

Southworth was only the second Cardinals manager to win consecutive pennants. Charles "Gabby" Street had accomplished the feat in 1930–31.

Southworth deserved considerable credit for this team's triumph. They lost more players to the service than any other team in the league, but still won going away. The wealth of talent in the Cardinals' farm system and Southworth's handling of the men were key in the victory.

During the season he had to contend with numerous injuries, but always found the right replacement at the correct time. During the year Sanders, Kurowski, Marion, Walker and Litwhiler were all injured at various times. White had a sore arm for most of the season, appearing in just 14 games, and now Gumbert had joined him on that list.

Southworth kept up team morale and they hustled all season. He picked spots for those available. He reminded the team throughout the season that Brooklyn had blown a big lead in 1942 and didn't want to see his boys let down and have that feat duplicated. Other key factors were great years from catcher Cooper and the MVP batting title season from Musial, who established himself as the premier hitter of the league, a position he would hold for most of the next two decades. Klein came through marvelously at second base, playing in 154 games. It was a team effort, as all players contributed.

When asked who would start the World Series Southworth responded by saying he didn't know. The only answer he would give was that he was working six pitchers in rotation and whoever's turn it was would start the first game. Lanier had pitched the pennant clincher by beating Chicago 2–1 and then in the nightcap Cooper gained his 20th victory. It would probably be one of these men.

The Cardinals' two year record of 211–97 was the best since the Chicago Cubs of 1906–07, 223–81. Their margin of 18 games was also the largest margin since Chicago won in 1906 by 20 games. Great seasons were enjoyed by many players. Besides Musial's first of three MVP awards and first of seven batting titles, several others enjoyed key seasons. Cooper batted .318 with 81 RBIs in 122 games (a 100 per year pace), Kurowski hit .287 with 70 RBIs and Sanders had 73 RBIs while hitting .280. Klein batted .287 with 91 runs and second best total of 14 triples. Had there been a Rookie of the Year award Klein would have easily won.

Cooper completed his second consecutive 20 win season with a 21–8 mark that included six shutouts and a 2.30 ERA. Lanier was 15–7 with a 1.90 ERA. He and Cooper were second and third in the league ERA chase, which was won by Pollet at 1.75. Krist finished at 11–5, giving him a three year record of 34–8.

To save transportation costs and travel time it had been decided to play the first three games in New York and then finish in St. Louis, whatever number of games would be required. This would also give the players the best possible share of World Series money.

Game one opened before 68,676 on October fifth and featured a pitching duel between Lanier and Spud Chandler, who posted an excellent 20–4,

1.64 ERA mark for the season. Chandler was victorious, 4–2. The Cardinals scored first in the second when Cooper singled, Kurowski sacrificed, Litwhiler walked. Marion then doubled to score Cooper, but St. Louis got a bad break when the ball hit the tarpaulin and stopped dead and Litwhiler was out at home on the relay. That would prove to be a crucial turning point for the Yankees.

In the New York fourth Frankie Crosetti was safe on Lanier's error, stole second and took third on Billy Johnson's infield hit and scored as Charlie Keller grounded into a double play. Joe Gordon then followed with a home run for a 2–1 Yankee lead. The Cardinals tied it in the fifth on a single by Sanders, Nick Etten's wild throw, Litwhiler's long fly and a single by Lanier. However, the Yankees won it in the sixth when Crosetti and Johnson singled and the former scored from second on a wild pitch by Lanier. Bill Dickey then singled Johnson home.

Game two the next day had an almost identical crowd, as 66,578 attended. Cooper and the Cardinals won 4–3. This was a very dramatic victory for Cooper. He had learned of his father's death only hours before the game, but went out and pitched his heart out to defeat the Yankees. Marion homered in the third for the first Cardinals run. In the fourth Musial singled, Cooper sacrificed and Kurowski's hit scored Musial and then Sanders hit a two run home run.[20]

The Yankees got a run back in the fourth when Crosetti got a pop bunt hit over Sanders' head. Bud Metheny flew out, but Johnson singled and Keller's fly ball scored Crosetti. Cooper then held them scoreless until the ninth when a Johnson double and Keller triple and Etten ground out scored two runs, but Gordon popped out to end the game.

With the series tied at a game apiece it was reminiscent of 1942. The Yankees had won the first and then the Cardinals tied it and would win three more for the championship. However, the roles would reverse this year. The pitching opponents were Brazle and Hank Borowy. The latter would triumph 6–2. The Cardinals jumped to a 2–0 lead in the third when Musial singled, Kurowski doubled and Sanders was intentionally passed. Then Litwhiler singled to score two runs.

On the throw home Sanders and Litwhiler took second and third. Marion was then intentionally passed, but Brazle popped out and Klein grounded out. Thus the Cardinals' chance to break the game open was lost. They would score no more the rest of the game.

The Yankees got an unearned run in the sixth on Borowy's double and Kurowski's error on Johnson's ground ball. The Yankees then blew the game open with a five run eighth. Johnny Lindell singled and went to third when Walker fumbled the ball. Snuffy Stirnweiss (pinch-hitting for Borowy) bunted and Sanders threw to third and they had Lindell out, but Kurowski dropped the ball as Lindell crashed into him. Tuck Stainback hit a short fly to Litwhiler, but

Lindell couldn't score, and Stirnweiss took second on the throw home. Crosetti was intentionally walked and then Johnson tripled scoring three runs.

After Keller walked, Krist relieved and Gordon singled, scoring Johnson. In came Brecheen and he gave a hit to Dickey when his batted ball hit Gordon on the leg. Etten then got a clean single scoring Keller, but Dickey was out at third. This game had the largest crowd of the series, 69,990.

The World Series moved to St. Louis and though down two games to one, fans and players alike were certain of a Cardinals comeback. On October 10 36,196 showed up for game four and were treated to an old fashioned pitchers' duel between Marius Russo and Lanier. The Yankees broke on top with two out in the fourth when Gordon doubled and Dickey's single drove him home.

The Cardinals evened matters in the seventh. With two outs Crosetti dropped Sanders' pop fly. Litwhiler doubled, sending Sanders to third. Marion was intentionally walked and Sanders scored when Johnson booted Demaree's (pinch-hitting for Lanier) ground ball. Klein, for the second time in the series, grounded out with the bases loaded. They just couldn't get the hit needed in the clutch, unlike 1942.

Brecheen took over the pitching duties and the Yankees won it in the eighth. Russo doubled, Stainback sacrificed and Crosetti's fly ball scored Russo with the winning run. Lanier had pitched great in both starts and finished with a 1.76 ERA, but was 0–1 for the series.

The final game was played the next day before 33,872 and Chandler drew Cooper as an opponent. Chandler defeated big Coop, 2–0. The Yankees scored twice in the sixth when with two out Keller singled and Dickey hit a home run. The Yankees had their revenge for 1942. The Cardinals would have to wait until 1964 to gain their revenge on the Yankees.

Neither team hit during the series. The Yankees batted .220 and St. Louis hit .224. New York's ERA was 1.40 and St. Louis posted a 2.51 ERA. Chandler was the pitching hero with a 2–0 mark and 0.50 ERA. Marion led the Cardinals in hitting with .357 and Johnson hit .300 to pace the Yankees. The busts for St. Louis were Walker at .167 and Klein at .136 (which included the two aforementioned ground outs with the bases loaded).

The Cardinals would win next season's pennant race even easier than in 1943. They would again win 105 games, giving them a three year total of 316 victories. No other National League team ever won 100 or more three consecutive seasons. The 1929–31 Philadelphia Athletics won 104, 102 and 107 for a three year total of 313.

Not even the great Yankees ever won 100 or more three seasons in a row. Twice they won 100 or more in three of four years. They won from 1936–39 102, 102, 99 and 106. Then from 1939–42 they had 106, 88, 101 and 103.

For over three quarters of the season it looked like the Cardinals would surpass the Chicago Cubs' 1906 total of 106 victories or beat the Pittsburgh

Pirates' margin of 27½ games in 1902. Key injuries to Musial, a sore arm by Lanier and a late season hitting slump cost them the opportunity.

Musial finished second in batting at .347. For his career he would win seven batting titles, finish second three times, third four times and fourth twice. Not only did he win three MVP awards, but was second in the voting four times. No other player had ever matched that record until the early 2000s. The Cardinals had the MVP winner for a third consecutive season when it was given to their great shortstop, Marion.

Other great seasons were had by Sanders with 102 RBIs while hitting .295, Kurowski had 20 home runs and 87 RBIs and Litwhiler had 15 home runs and 82 RBIs. Hopp, batting lead off, hit .336 and had 72 RBIs, while Cooper hit .317 with 72 RBIs in just 112 games (another 100 plus RBI pace).

The pitching was outstanding as Cooper was 22–7 with a 2.46 ERA and league best seven shutouts. This gave him a three year record of 65–22 with 23 shutouts. Lanier finished at 17–12 (a seven game losing streak cost him 20 or more wins), Wilks was 17–4 and Brecheen 16–5. Munger was 11–3 with a 1.34 ERA before being inducted into the service. They would play the St. Louis Browns in the World Series and win four games to two. It was the only time the Brownies won a pennant.

It was a great three year run and had it not been for the war, there was no telling how great the team would have been or how many championship flags would have flown over St. Louis. Players such as Slaughter and Moore lost three key years out of the middle of their careers. Others like Beazley, White, Krist and Grodzicki saw their careers lost to the military.

FIVE

1944

Almost a New Record

The 1943 World Series, which was won by the New York Yankees over the St. Louis Cardinals, featured Yankees pitching versus Cardinals pitching and speed. St. Louis was generous with their World Series shares as they gave each player in military service half shares. Recipients were Terry Moore, Enos Slaughter, Johnny Beazley and Frank Crespi, as each missed the entire season. Full shares were voted to Howard Pollet and Jimmy Brown, who left before the season ended.[1]

The Cardinals' 1942–43 record of 211–97 was the best since the Chicago Cubs of 1906–07, who went 223–83. The Cardinals were aiming for not only their third straight pennant in 1944, but wanted to become the first National League team to win over 100 games in three consecutive seasons. The New York Giants established an unenviable record with a team high 98 defeats.

Despite a runaway race the Cardinals home attendance was only 30,000 less than 1942 when the race went down to the last day of the season. The night attendance was 221,949 for 14 games while 321,424 attended 63 day games, making a total attendance of 543,373. The Cardinals made $100,000 in 1943 as expenses were reduced as the number of chain operated clubs was lowered to six because of loss of manpower to the military services.

Many teams were forced to utilize rejected 4F's, overage veterans or retreads for the upcoming season, as the war had cut deeply into the available talent pool. The Cardinals were fortunate in having a deep talent pool, although they too would have to utilize some of the 4F's, overage veterans or retreads. Major league teams returned to train in the same areas as in 1943. It had been hoped they could return to Florida or California, but due to travel restrictions that became impossible.

Stan Musial's feats got rave reviews in his hometown of Donora, Pennsylvania. He was currently classified 3S as he was married with one child. In the off-season he had a job at the Donora Zinc Works. When he was being honored Musial said he would rather face the toughest pitcher in baseball than make a speech. Musial won the MVP, while Morton Cooper finished second.

A losing share of $4,321.99 still looked awfully large to a Polish kid who was lucky not to be laboring in the mill or, at this time, toting a gun. He wanted to do something in the war effort and welcomed the chance to entertain American troops stationed in Alaska and the Aleutians. That winter, after putting in a stretch working in the mill, Stan made a six week tour for the government with Frank Frisch, Danny Litwhiler, Hank Borowy and Dixie Walker.[2]

Branch Rickey, now with the Brooklyn Dodgers, said he didn't see how any team could beat St. Louis in 1944. Even though their talent pool had dwindled it was still stronger by far than any team in the league. Rickey predicted St. Louis, which won by 18 games in 1943, could win by double that number in 1944.[3] He also predicted the Yankees would win in 1944, setting up a rematch between the two teams. Both were favored because of their deeper talent pools.

Joe Garagiola at 17 was the second string catcher for the Columbus Championship team. He started in organized baseball at age 16. He and Yogi Berra grew up together in the hill district (which was all Italian) in St. Louis. Garagiola was first spotted at age 13½ in 1939 while playing sandlot baseball. Later he was signed to a contract and began his professional career at Class C Springfield Western Association Club at just 16 years of age. In his first at-bat he hit a home run and Rickey predicted he would reach the majors by the time he was 20.

Sportswriters and scribes asked Breadon his greatest baseball thrills, as he had been owner of the team for almost 25 years. He called his four greatest thrills Pete Alexander's strikeout of Tony Lazzeri in game seven of the 1926 World Series, the great series of 1931 when St. Louis defeated the world champion Philadelphia Athletics four games to three, the 1934 World Champion Gas House Gang and of course the great 1942 Cardinal team that defeated the Yankees four games to one.[4]

Many changes were made in the minor league arrangements, rules and regulations. Under the new proposals AA leagues would have voting power over lower leagues by a 10–1 margin. AA leagues would have 10 votes, A-1 leagues would have 8 votes, A leagues would qualify for 6 votes, B leagues got four votes, C leagues would have just two votes and D leagues only one vote. Also there would be an increase in team player limits and tougher territory protection for all leagues, but higher leagues would be allowed higher player limits.[5]

The Cardinals' record under Southworth had been outstanding. During the 1941–43 seasons they were 308–151 and had been 377–190 since he took over the team in early 1940, when they were about 15 games out of first place. To add to their problems for the coming season Al Brazle and Harry Walker both left for the Army. Fortunately they had a deep pool of talent.

Meanwhile postwar plans were waiting for action from the games' moguls. A way had to be found to reorganize leagues, and shifts could bring new cities into the fold. Key issues to be decided included policies on distribution of players returning from the service, park improvements, lighting uniformity and revisions of minor league agreements. Waiting until the war was over was too late, as plans had to be made immediately so that when the war was ended baseball could start anew with all the pieces in line.[6]

There were 70 cities with over 50,000 population without minor league teams and hundreds of towns between 25,000 to 50,000 all begging for clubs of their own. This was truly virgin territory. These areas along with the inclusion of revived towns that lost teams due to the war should be the first objective. Only 63 cities operated teams last season in the minors as 152 cities were forced to cease operation with the war as the key factor. There were over 188 cities of over 25,000 population that had never had a team.[7]

No National League team had ever won 100 games or more three consecutive seasons and the Cardinals would be trying to become the first team to achieve that goal in 1944. Despite losing Brazle, Walker and Murray Dickson to the military since the end of the season, they still had an excellent team. The Cardinals could also lose Walker Cooper to the military as soon as his trigger finger healed. He broke it on a foul tip of the bat off Frankie Crosetti in the final game of the 1943 World Series.

The Cardinals planned on bringing outfielder Augie Bergamo up from Columbus, where he had batted .303 and .324 the last two seasons. They also had planned to take a look at Columbus second baseman Emil Verban. From the Sacramento team of the Pacific Coast League they wanted to bring St. Louisian Bud Byerly. He didn't have a good won-lost record, but Sacramento had a weak hitting team. Byerly completed 27 of 31 starts, which encouraged Southworth to take a further look at him.

The owners meeting was confronted with new problems. Among the items were team player limits, schedules and night games. Many believed that the latter would be a big boon to teams after the war. They could foresee dramatically increased attendance and revenues for each club. National League president Ford Frick also addressed the issue of how to absorb returning veterans. He had stated they couldn't wait until the war was over; it must be addressed quickly.

Commissioner Landis continued his grueling hard faced attitude by personally scanning West Coast exhibition games to try and find any major league player who participated. Major league rules stated that no player could play baseball ten days after the end of the World Series.

Landis continued his watchdog attitude toward the game by banning from baseball thirty-four year old William D. Cox, the flamboyant owner of the Philadelphia Phillies, for gambling. Landis ruled he was ineligible to hold any position with any major league team. Cox had bet on baseball games and this led to his banishment. Cox resigned as president of the Phillies and sold his stock, worth an estimated $330,000. There had been no gambling scandal under Landis' regime, as he ruled with an iron hand. While he may have had his detractors, Landis was good for the game.

The Cardinals received more bad news regarding players to report for the military service. Walker Cooper's trigger finger had now healed and he took his physical on November 17 and was told to get ready to report for military training in the very near future. Meanwhile, star second baseman Lou Klein was reclassified as 1A and faced almost immediate draft.

In 1940 there were 43 minor leagues with 314 cities and in 1943 only nine leagues with 63 cities could operate. This forced the owners to begin serious thinking and debate about postwar plans. These plans included more leagues with more cities which would lead to greater competition. On the schedule there would be more night games and more players in the game. Plans were also considered for a third major league, with great consideration given to the Pacific Coast League. The airplane could be the future way of travel for baseball, especially if the Pacific Coast League were integrated into the majors.

The major leagues had a board of 11 to study the postwar problems and re-alignment. They appeared willing to give more autonomy to the minor leagues. Other issues under consideration included the "conduct detrimental to baseball" clause which was a stumbling block. Returning servicemen presented a major problem, as there were currently over 3,000 and the number was expected to reach over 5,000. Another question perplexing the owners was Washington's decision on the reserve clause, if it would be in effect after the one year deadline. Some major league stars thought they might be free agents and could bargain with any team. The majority of players didn't like this idea, as they said only the rich teams would win pennants and the poor teams would always be also rans. They wanted to maintain the reserve clause as their protection.[8]

Sam Breadon was getting quite upset over the continual loss of key and star players to the military. The latest to go was Klein, who enlisted in the Coast Guard. Breadon said if the team lost any more players they would have to dig deep into their Class AA teams. He did point out that they were better off than the competition with the talent the club had available. There was also consideration of bringing 17 year old Joe Garagiola up to the parent club.

Paul Robeson, a black singer and actor, became involved in the first movement to recognize black athletes in major league baseball. He had waited outside the major league meeting rooms to present a plea for all Negro players to be given consideration to be in organized baseball. Robeson, who had communist leanings, eventually left the United States. His political activities did not endear him to the country and his career was eventually ruined.[9]

The Cardinals would have 21 night games for the 1944 season and 12 Sunday double-headers, leaving them only 32 potential weekday games. However, one had to figure on possibly as many as seven postponements and this would reduce that figure to 25, as more double-headers would be necessary to make up for the lost games. St. Louis and Cincinnati had the hottest, most humid summer months and therefore night games would help the players and the fans. However, Chicago, Pittsburgh, New York, Brooklyn and Cincinnati all opposed increasing the 1943 limit of 14 night games.

The Cardinals received more bad news as Mort Cooper reported on December 13 for his physical at Jefferson Barracks. His loss would be a real blow to the team, as he was 43–15 the past two seasons and the top pitcher in baseball. He won the MVP in 1942 and was second to Stan Musial in 1943. Ernie White had just been reclassified as 1A, even though he had been married ten years with a five year old son. Cooper had a six year old boy. Breadon said, "I will soon have a better team in the service than Southworth can put on the field. They aren't taking my second stringers, but my first line players."

A big chain boom was seen after the war as with the influx of players there would be many more leagues and teams. Individual ownership of minor league teams with a working agreement with a major league club was ideal, but economic conditions no longer prevailed to make it possible. It seemed the only feasible answer was ownership by major league teams and an expansion of the chain system. This was how growth had to take place. Landis finally acquiesced and said he would stop fighting the chain store operation, stating if minors were to grow they must have major league financial support.

Both the St. Louis Browns and the St. Louis Cardinals called St. Louis a one team city. It just couldn't support two teams. Breadon said it could no more support two teams than Kansas City could support one. St. Louis didn't have the "large" small towns in a 100 mile radius to draw from and support two teams like New York, Philadelphia, Chicago, Boston, Detroit and Cincinnati. The latter two cities had only one team each, despite their large drawing potential.

Owner Donald Barnes of the Browns eyed Los Angeles as a new spot for his team after the war. He had viewed this as far back as 1940, when he saw his team couldn't compete with the Cardinals. Barnes faced opposition from the Pacific Coast League as they were looking for major league status. Los Angeles was the breadwinner of that league and Wrigley Field there was owned by Chicago Cubs owner Phil Wrigley. In addition, the PCL was trying to get new legislation passed that would prohibit major league teams from moving into their territory. It made for a very complex situation. Major league owners might agree with Barnes, but the move would be hard to make. Travel could become a major problem as it was all done by train.[10]

The Cardinals finally received some good news regarding the military as Morton Cooper was classified 4F after taking his physical. He was not told why, but thought it was due to an old knee injury. His brother, Walker, had passed his physical, but no date had been set for his induction. On the downside, shortstop Marty Marion was reclassified as 1A, even though he was married and had a three year old daughter. Al "Red" Schoendienst was ruled 4F. He led the International League at .336 and could be brought to the parent team to replace Klein.

The Cardinals saw a long run of hit parade dominance by Musial. They expected him to rival Rogers Hornsby in his length of dominance in batting prowess. In 1943 Musial led the league in average, hits, doubles, triples, total bases and was second in runs. He was currently operating under a three year contract that ran through 1946. He became the sixth Cardinal to win a batting title. The previous winners were Jesse Burkett (1911), Chick Hafey (1931), Rogers Hornsby (1920–25), Joe Medwick (1937) and Johnny Mize (1939).

It wasn't just the hitting that dominated the 1943 team as the Cardinals also had the first three men in the ERA race. Howard Pollet had a 1.75 ERA and was 8–4 and should have been 11–1 or 12–0, as he also completed 12 of 14 starts. Second was Max Lanier at 1.90, while posting a 15–7 mark. Cooper was third with a 2.30 and a 21–8 record.

President Clarence "Pants" Rowland of the Los Angeles Angels said the West Coast was ready for the big league baseball. He said they were ready to buy or transfer a team to the West Coast. The problem of travel would be solved by using the airlines for West Coast trips. He further pointed out there were 3,000,000 people in a 25 mile radius of Los Angeles, thus more than adequate potential for a huge attendance. Furthermore, Wrigley Field in Los Angeles made most major league parks look ancient.

The Cardinals were now considering Verban as the potential second baseman for 1944. He was 26 years old and had eight seasons in organized baseball. He was the American Association outstanding second baseman in 1943. Verban was considered an excellent fielder with great speed. Even though he hit only .257 with little power, his speed enabled him to stretch singles into doubles. Due to a punctured eardrum he was classified 4F.

Breadon told the press that eliminating the farm system would mean utter chaos. In doing this only the rich clubs would prosper. Most minor league teams would fold. He strongly believed that the postwar plans must include a thriving, growing farm system, as this was at the heart of the game. What Breadon saw was a precursor of the ill fated decision to eliminate the reserve clause in the 1970s. Breadon said teams combed the sticks and woods to find players and train them. Then they hired managers to bring the kids along and if they won a pennant in the minors that was fine, but the real object was to get them ready to play major league baseball.

The Service Act would have little impact on major league baseball. However, the national conscription, as proposed by President Roosevelt, would send all men into off-season war jobs. However, their draft status would not be affected. The president was asking for a national conscription law that placed all females 18–50 and all males 18–65 under federal control. Baseball owners said this would mean year-round work for the players. They would be granted furloughs to play baseball and when the season ended they would return to their war jobs. Major league owners regarded with disdain the small portion of players who refused to take war jobs in the off-season.[11]

Unless the Cardinals lost more players they should win their third straight pennant, especially since Morton Cooper would now be with the club. While Breadon and Branch Rickey had disagreed on many things, they were in total agreement on the farm system, now and after the war. Rickey was the father of the farm system and wanted it continued, as did Breadon.

Landis was in a power struggle at the owners meeting in New York. Landis' term and the major league agreement that established his authority would expire on January 12, 1946, and this was the number one topic. It was potentially the TNT that would spark postwar fights and agreements during the New York meeting. No change could be made to the pact that ran counter to the major-minor league agreement. Any change had to have the consent of both the majors and minors.

Also Landis' contract and agreement were set to expire the same date. Landis had been asked to define the "detrimental clause." He refused to limit sweeping terms voluntarily. If changes were made they had to be made to the major agreement as well as the major-minor agreement. If the clause was stricken Landis might resign, as he had threatened to do so in the past. At this meeting the owners could only recommend action, but nothing could officially take place until late 1945.[12]

A poll of servicemen showed that next to mail from home, baseball was the most important thing to them. So far as the White House was concerned baseball had to solve its own manpower problem. The green light given January 15, 1942, by President Roosevelt wasn't good today as the world situation had completely changed.

More fuel to the fire on the farm system situation was added by Detroit general manager Jack Zeller. He wanted all farms abolished by 1947. He contended that the farm system was strangling individual teams. Ed Burrow, Breadon and Rickey said that Zeller's plan was idiotic. It would destroy the minor leagues. All three contended that the system and the reserve clause was what made baseball sound and strong. Most players agreed and had no objection to the system and clause as they were.

Breadon said it was not the time for salary battles. With a war raging that should be a secondary issue and if necessary it should be settled privately and not in the newspapers. Breadon said with all that was happening, the war, farm problems, and player limits, the salary issue should be handled privately and discreetly. Breadon had offered Morton Cooper $12,000 and he asked for $17,500. His brother, Walker, also wanted a substantial increase.

The Cardinals lost another key player to the military as Howard Krist, who had been a swing man for the Cardinals, left for the service. Krist posted a 34–8 mark during 1941–43. Pitching help looked to be on the way as Al Jurisch was released by the Navy and would join the team. Also in the infield mix was infielder Mickey Burnet from Sacramento, where he hit .278 and stole 35 bases in 1943. Pepper Martin, 40, returned as a Cardinal and could play infield or outfield. Frank DeMaree would be granted his unconditional release as soon as Martin could be signed. Marion was accepted for limited duty, but not given a call up date.

To date the minor leagues had sent 3,044 players to the service. The breakdown by league was as follows: AA (726), A-1 (302), A (265), B (703), C (394) and D (654). With no end in sight for the war no one knew how many more would be taken.

Many major leaguers had delayed signing their contracts because of doubt over what happened when they quit their war jobs to play baseball. As long as they were in a war job they were deferred, but as soon as they left to play baseball they became 1-A and could be drafted. The players wanted their status clarified.

Washington paid high tribute to the major league teams for their northern training. Washington realized the inconvenience to the players and the teams, but it helped tremendously on travel savings and for this they were very grateful. Voluntary action by Landis had done more than any other one thing to protect the interests of organized baseball, a government official declared. There was a dispute over part-time players. They would work five days a week at a war job and play ball two days per week. Some owners agreed and others didn't. The Yankees didn't like it while the Browns and the A's did. The players were classified as 2-B.

President Bob Quinn of the Boston Braves stated the postwar jobs of returning athletes depended on the farm system. He antedated Rickey as a chain store operator, and asserted independent teams could absorb all returning servicemen. The farm system was needed.

There were 83 National League and 74 American League players rejected by the military. A classy all star team would be possible for both leagues from this group. It certainly promised to help many clubs field more competitive teams. The entire St. Louis Browns infield was classified 4-F. The debate raged—if they can play baseball, wasn't there some job they could do in the service? A very good question. Your author does not believe in the 4-F category except in rare cases of mental or physical deficiencies. Most could be trained to do some clerical, supply or necessary support service, freeing others for front line duty.

Morton Cooper still had not signed as spring training neared, but he and Breadon were much closer. His brother finally signed his contract. On the classification front, both Musial and Johnny Hopp were classified 1-A. Marion's status was still uncertain. The key question in the Cardinals camp was, "How are they going to beat us?" It may sound cocky or conceited, but they had virtually the same team as in 1943 and won by 18 games. It was possible to lose Walker Cooper, Marion, Danny Litwhiler and Musial (although he had a high draft number).

The Cardinals' pitching staff looked strong. It was led by Cooper and Lanier. Then there were Harry Brecheen, George "Red" Munger, Byerly, Blix Donnelly, Harry Gumbert, Jurisch and Fred Schmidt. No team in the majors could claim a better pitching staff. The Cardinals' starting lineup would be Hopp in center or right field with Musial in the other and Litwhiler in left field. Kurowski was at third base, Marion at shortstop, Sanders at first and Cooper catching. The only new player was Verban at second base.

Servicemen clamored for baseball games and officers offered endorsements that baseball was a great morale builder. The use of part-time players was approved. No special permission was needed for part-time players, Landis stated.

Major General Lewis B. Hershey of the Selective Service said the over-26 draft stoppage would help the majors. All teams had players in that category. The draft ended at age 26 unless a man was in a non-essential job. Baseball was not considered an essential job per se, but it had been recognized as a tremendous morale builder for both the military and the people at home. Therefore the draft rule of 26 would apply, unless the situation became even more critical.

The Cardinals were the odds on favorite to win their third consecutive pennant. They had a stronger starting team than anyone in the league and even if they lost players, they had the deepest talent pool. Another runaway was predicted with Pittsburgh second, Chicago third and Brooklyn fourth. Shortly before opening day Musial was moved to right field and Hopp to center field.

The 4F players were expected to play a key role in the pennant races in both leagues. The St. Louis Browns had 18, the New York Giants 16 and the Cardinals 10. Sanders had a heart which occasionally skipped beats while Verban had a perforated eardrum. Kurowski had the shortened right arm and Morton Cooper a bad knee. Others in the 4F category were mostly pitchers: Brecheen, Donnelly, Wilks and O'Dea (the back up catcher).

With draft news, plans for after the war and spring training behind them, the Cardinals were now eager to open their season in quest of a third consecutive title. They didn't disappoint their fans by winning their first five games, two by shutouts and Lanier copping two of the victories. The question was by how much St. Louis would win the pennant. They had won by 18 in 1943 and some were now predicting they would win by 30 games this year. The only dark cloud was that the entire starting outfield could be in the service by July. This would mean that 35 year old Deb Garms, 40 year old Martin and rookie Augie Bergamo would patrol the outfield.

Fans voted for night baseball by a two to one margin. The main reason was that many had war plant jobs and couldn't see day games. They now had money to spend and wanted to see their beloved Cardinals.

The team then lost a double-header to Cincinnati, 10–3 and 1–0 with young Al Jurisch taking the loss in game two in 13 innings. The Cards had been coming up with good young pitchers for several years. In 1941 it was Ernie White, then Johnny Beazley in 1942 and Al "Cotton" Brazle in 1943. The latter was given special permission to play with the team after several had been drafted. He was 8–2 with eight complete games in nine starts in 1943. He also made four relief appearances.[13]

Hopp didn't make the trip to Pittsburgh as he took his physical on May 2 at Jefferson Barracks. Musial had asked that his papers be transferred to Jefferson Barracks in St. Louis and was expected to take his physical on May 16. In the meantime Southworth sent Byerly to Rochester and Sam Narron to Columbus and neither were happy. Both returned to St. Louis to discuss the subject with Breadon. Byerly asked if he could be sent to Columbus and Narron stated that with the shortage of catchers in the majors there should be a spot for him somewhere. When no job was forthcoming he retired to his tobacco farm in Middlesex, North Carolina.

The Cardinals rebounded from that double-header defeat by winning four in a row and now stood at 9–2 with New York at 7–3, Cincinnati at 7–4 and Philadelphia at 6–4. Martin still showed that same dash, daring and flaming Gas House spirit of the 1930s and it was passed on to his teammates. Lanier grabbed his third consecutive victory and his third complete game, two of them shutouts.

Due to the war and manpower shortages and players' draft status often being uncertain teams were permitted to carry 30 players until June 15. This gave them a 60 day grace period from the start of the season instead of the normal 30 days. This change applied to the 1944 season only. Also the length of time a player remained on the voluntary retired list was reduced from 60 to 30 days. Clubs did receive good news regarding the over 26 age draft as the goal would be reached from the pool of 1,700,000 under 26. The final team limit was still 25. This however had no effect on the June 15 trade deadline. That remained unchanged.

Cooper was off to a slow start, but rookie Jurisch was picking him up. Unfortunately he wasn't winning, but it wasn't his fault. The team didn't hit when he pitched. In his first 30 innings, the opposition scored just four runs, but he was just 1–2. Southworth said as long as he continued pitching like that he would win a lot of games. One of his defeats was the 1–0 loss to Cincinnati which was won on Frank McCormick's 13th inning home run, making it at the time the longest 1–0 game in history to be won by a home run.

On May 6 the Cardinals lost first place for a day as Bucky Walters pitched a shutout against them for the second time in the young season. They righted their ship the next day by winning a double-header and moved back into first place to stay. Musial had started with a 14 game hitting streak and then was cooled off in the Cincinnati series. At this juncture the team was 12–5 with Musial hitting .429, but trailing Brooklyn's Dixie Walker who was at .442. Litwhiler, O'Dea and Hopp were all over .300. Besides Lanier, Brecheen, Wilks and Munger were all undefeated at 2–0 each. Only Cooper (the ace of the staff) was struggling. Rarely did the team get a poorly pitched game.

The new draft policy would benefit the game, as it would slow draft calls for those over 26. The final decision however rested with the local draft board. The ruling though would help make team rosters more stable.

The early Redbird pace showed that there were no real challengers. Pittsburgh manager Frankie Frisch and Cincinnati coach Jimmie Wilson said the Cardinals were stronger than in 1943. Branch Rickey said the team would win by 36 games, double their 1943 margin. They were that good. Things were really looking up for the home nine as Cooper was now pitching effective winning baseball. In addition Gumbert seemed to have recovered from his arm injury of last summer, but now at 34 had just taken his physical and his fate was in the hands of the Houston, Texas, draft board.

Two more Cardinals had taken their physicals. Young outfielder George Fallon took his on May 16 and George Munger one week later. The Cardinals took three of four from Brooklyn and on May 24 cooled off the once hot Philadelphia team. Pittsburgh (picked to finish second) continued to be heroes one day and bums the next. They defeated the Giants in a double-header, but the three previous games they allowed weak sister Boston 53 hits in losing all three games. The Chicago Cubs set a new team record for frustration by losing 13 in a row. They finally broke the string by defeating Philadelphia 5–3 and the club stood at 3–17.

The Cardinals had built a four game lead over Cincinnati and Philadelphia by the middle of May with an 18–6 record and the other two at 13–9. The team was on a pace to threaten the major league record of 116 victories set by the Chicago Cubs of 1906. They finished 116–36. The only dark cloud was the hitting was almost 25 points below 1943, when they batted .278. The current team was hitting just .254. Only Musial (.369) and Litwhiler (.353) were hitting. The pitching was carrying the team.

The major leagues also participated in programs to help support the troops and provide additional amenities for them. They were extremely liberal with free passes to all servicemen. The cities placed no limit on the admittance and were extremely generous with the supply of tickets set aside for the military.

Most of the news was good for the Cardinals, although there was a sprinkling of bad news. The Cardinals hit pay dirt again with Sanders, who was normally a slow starter. Ray had found his stride in the 1943 World Series and it carried over into the 1944 season. Sanders had his eye on a .300 batting mark for the season. He followed a long line of nifty, classy, hard hitting first basemen developed in the Cardinals' organization. Preceding him were Jim Bottomley, Rip Collins and Johnny Mize. He had been a slow starter in 1942, finishing at .252 with five home runs and 39 RBIs in 282 at-bats. His improvement was quite distinct in 1943, as he finished at .280 in 144 games and 478 at-bats. This included 69 runs scored, 21 doubles, five triples, 11 home runs and 73 RBIs. Sanders also drew 77 free passes while fanning just 33 times.[14]

The Navy accepted Musial and he expected to report in about six weeks, as he was just 23 and would fall under the under 26 rule. Fallon was turned down, thus he would be available for outfield duty, but certainly was a far cry from Musial as a hitter. The other bad news was that Cooper was on the shelf and had just a 2–3 record. The club needed his strong right arm. The team was 9–4 on their eastern swing, losing only to Boston, whom they defeated 19 of 22 times in 1943. The team's percentage had dipped slightly as they were at .700 with a 21–9 record.

After a slow start and the Boston debacle, Pittsburgh went 7–1 with one more defeat looming. They were trailing Philadelphia, 9–4 when the Sunday blue law stopped the game after eight innings. The game would be completed in Pittsburgh. They were starting to look like the team that was picked for second place and give the Cardinals the most competition.

Walker had widened his batting lead considerably as he was hitting .408, while Musial had fallen into a slump and dropped to .344. Litwhiler was at the same mark, but the rest of the squad was not hitting as expected, although the team average had moved to .267. The Cardinals needed more punch from Cooper, Hopp and Sanders.

At this point Lanier was 5–0, Wilks 2–0, Brecheen and Munger each 3–1 and Gumbert 2–1. Breadon responded to the critics' fire. He took time out from his busy schedule to write lengthy letters to contact the public through the press and radio. He said he may have made a mistake in not starting an abbreviated night game before 8:30 on May 10 versus the Philadelphia team. It had been announced before the start of the game that no inning would start after 10:15 to enable Philadelphia to catch the 11:15 train.

Many fans complained they were shortchanged out of two innings. If the game had started an hour or so earlier they could have seen the entire game. There also had been previous criticism about charges for concessions being too high. However, the main complaint was the raising of scorecard prices from a nickel to a dime. Many fans complained this was like charging for a menu at a restaurant. Breadon countered that increased costs had made these changes necessary.[15]

Invasion day (D-Day) was to be marked by all leagues (major and minor) having a silent prayer for all troops involved in this action to free Europe from the heel of Hitler. The playing of the national anthem was suggested for the majors. Landis had said when news of the invasion came all games would be stopped for a few moments of silent prayer followed by the national anthem.

St. Louis had a frustrating week as they had two idle days, two rain outs and got only one game played. This was a victory over Brooklyn. Munger was accepted by the Army and his induction date was very soon. Cooper had rebounded from his slump with a shutout and evened his record at 3–3. At the one-quarter juncture the team enjoyed a four game lead, but most thought it should have been at least double that mark. The Chicago Cubs went on a seven game winning streak as they climbed out of the basement. They were now 11–20, after starting 3–17. The team would finish in fourth place with a 75–79 mark, considered quite respectable from where they started.

As of June 1 St. Louis was 24–10, followed by Pittsburgh at 18–12 and Cincinnati at 19–14. No other team was over .500. Walker continued his heavy hitting and was at .424 while Musial, although hitting .364, trailed by 60 points. Medwick had forced his way into the race for the title with a .350 average. The Cardinals were showing improved hitting as Litwhiler was at .310, Sanders .308 and Kurowski up to .307. The pitching continued to carry the team as Lanier was 6–0, Wilks 3–0, Munger 4–1, and Brecheen 3–1.

On their recent East Coast trip the team was just 7–7 and Southworth had been trying to impress on the club the need to pile up victories now as they would lose Musial, Litwhiler, Munger and Gumbert before the season was over. They needed to win as many as they could now, Southworth told his players. Just as Cooper regained his effectiveness, Lanier lost his. Freddy Schmidt lost a heartbreaking 1–0 game. Only Pittsburgh and Cincinnati continued to cling to the Cardinals' heels. All others were far behind.

It had been hinted that night ball might be used for the World Series. With many involved in war plant jobs this would have given them a chance to see a game. The night games had been turning the major league turnstiles and this was another factor under consideration. The Cardinals and Browns (if they won) would consider playing an all night World Series. This would be the first in history.

The Cardinals had averaged 11,779 per night game while the Browns drew 7,720 for their games under the lights. Pittsburgh was worried about a St. Louis runaway, especially after Rip Sewell (8–2) hurt his arm in a 2–1 win over Curt Davis and the Dodgers. The team had been carried by the pitching, as their hitting had been woefully weak, especially against right handed pitchers.

There were no games scheduled in the American League on D-Day, June 6. The only game scheduled in the National League was between Brooklyn and Pittsburgh and that game was called off. Six of the minor leagues also played no games that day. This was all done out of respect for our brave troops in Europe.

The Redbirds were securely atop the league as they returned from an 11–6 trip through the east and Cincinnati. When they came home in June to open a long homestand it was expected this would put the team out of reach of the rest of the league. They had played 11 consecutive games without an error, while Cooper had won three games in row, two by shutout. Munger, still waiting his call up date, was 7–1. Litwhiler had been reclassified as 2A.

On June 10 St. Louis defeated Cincinnati 18–0. This was the largest whitewashing since the Chicago Cubs beat the New York Giants 19–0 in 1906. In the Cardinal game 15 year old Joe Nuxhall became the youngest player to appear in a baseball game. He hurled two-thirds of an inning and gave up five walks and two hits. Your author was an 11 year old boy who saw this game.[16]

That day they also tied a major league record by leaving 18 men on base. The Cardinals turned nine double plays in the double-header, two over the former National League record and one shy of the Washington Senators' record against the Chicago White Sox on August 18, 1943.

In the second game of the double-header, Cooper, Kurowski and Litwhiler hit consecutive home runs on six pitches off former Cardinal Clyde Shoun. This marked the 17th time the feat had been achieved in baseball history. At this juncture in the season only Boston had an edge on St. Louis, four games to three.

By the middle of June St. Louis was 32–15 and Pittsburgh was 25–19, five and one-half games back. Cincinnati had dropped to 23–22, eight and one-half games out of first place. Walker widened his lead over Musial, as the latter slipped to .346, while Walker was at .421. At this point it didn't bode well for Musial repeating as batting champ. Lanier, Munger, Brecheen, Wilks and Cooper were a combined 25–7. The pitching rich Cardinals sold Gumbert for $25,000 to Cincinnati. He was 4–2 and would go 10–8 for the Reds, finishing with a 14–10 mark. His two losses this year had been 2–1 and 1–0. His tour of duty with St. Louis showed a 34–17 mark. Gumbert had been accepted by the Army but as a 34 year old father hadn't been called.

The sale of Gumbert was no real shock to the fans as the Cardinals' long standing policy had been to move a player while he still had some value. The farm system built by Rickey had such a reserve of talent that older players had to be moved out to make room for younger prospects. Many top notch players had preceded Gumbert. Among them were Bottomley, Hafey, Collins,

Mize, Medwick, et al. Only Martin and Jesse Haines got old in Cardinals uniforms. This trade would give young hurlers like Wilks, Schmidt and Jurisch a chance to show what they could do. Immediately after the sale the Cardinals achieved their best year-to-date two-date attendance. In a Saturday, June 16, and Sunday, June 17, double-header against Pittsburgh they drew 18,645.

The Cardinals had a good week, winning two from Chicago, who hadn't defeated them this season, and two of three from Pittsburgh. Their only two challengers (Pittsburgh and Cincinnati) were both light on hitting. With one-third of the season gone St. Louis was 36–16 (a pace for 108 victories), Pittsburgh 28–22 (seven games back), New York 28–23 and Cincinnati at 26–25 (now nine and one-half out). Musial climbed to .353, still 60 points behind Walker at .413. Hitting had picked up considerably as Kurowski was .322, Cooper .300, Sanders and Litwhiler at .294 and Hopp at .285. In reserve roles Fallon was .300 and Martin .308. Munger was 7–1, Lanier 7–2, Brecheen 4–1, Wilks 3–1 and Cooper 5–3. Other leading pitchers in the league were Bucky Walters at 10–3 and Sewell at 8–2.

The Cardinals had built a nine and one-half game lead and it looked like Southworth and his charges had no worries. Then Munger dropped a bombshell. He advised he was to report for military duty on June 24. Munger's home was in Houston and he had requested that his induction be transferred to Jefferson Barracks, as this would give him a couple of more starts. Munger had been the most consistent hurler since opening day, going 10–1. Schmidt, who was from Asheville, North Carolina, and considered as a potential replacement for Munger, had been requested to take his pre-induction physical on July 5. Schmidt had requested that his papers be transferred to St. Louis.

As far as inductions were concerned Southworth did receive some good news, as Musial might not be called for a month or two, even though he was 23. Musial however was a father and they weren't calling them until all single men had been taken. Musial had been accepted by the Navy and was just waiting for a call up date.

Since returning from the east the Cardinals were flying high as they were 13–2 against the supposedly stronger western clubs (Chicago, Cincinnati and Pittsburgh). There were also two 5–5 ties with Pittsburgh that had to be replayed. The players in the first division, except for Pittsburgh which remained in second, kept changing. There was a constant shuffle between New York, Brooklyn and Cincinnati. At the end of June St. Louis was 41–16, Pittsburgh checked in at 31–25, New York was 32–29, Brooklyn was 33–30 and Cincinnati was 31–30. Walker had slipped to .385 and led Musial by only 20 points, who had climbed to .365. His chances of repeating were improving. Hopp was at .313 and Kurowski at .312 while Sanders, Litwhiler and Cooper ranged between .280 and .288. Lanier was 7–3, but the loser in three of the last four decisions, while Cooper had improved to 6–3 with his fourth consecutive victory. Other leading pitchers in the league were Walters at 11–3 and Sewell at 9–2.

The All Star game would be played at Forbes Field in Pittsburgh and St. Louis dominated the squad by placing six men on the team. They were Musial, Kurowski, Marion, Lanier, Munger and Cooper.

The renewal of the major league agreement that created the commissioners' office was to be considered by the owners. It was originally designed in 1921 to last 25 years and currently was set to expire on January 1, 1946. Renewal of the pact that created Landis' role was the reason for reviewing it at the present time. It would give Landis a chance to accept or decline. If Landis were to decline then the owners would have to find a new commissioner. However, it was highly unlikely that Landis would willingly step down from a role he created and immensely enjoyed. Despite his idiosyncrasies, he had been a bulwark for the game and straightened it out following the infamous Black Sox scandal.

The Cardinals' chance at tying or breaking the major league win mark of 116 was derailed by three straight losses to Philadelphia. Two of them were shutouts by former Cardinals' farmhands Bill Lee and Ken Raffensberger. Cooper picked up his sixth consecutive victory on June 30 with relief help in an 8–4 victory over Philadelphia. With the team at 43–19 and a 9½ game bulge over Pittsburgh, the team still had an excellent chance to be the first National League team to win 100 or more games three consecutive seasons.

There was almost a dead heat for the batting title with Walker at .378 and Musial at .374. Hopp was the only other Cardinal over .300, although several were in the .280s. Munger led the staff with a 10–2 mark, having just lost a 1–0 heartbreaker to Bill Lee of Philadelphia. Cooper was now at 7–3, but Lanier continued to have his problems as his record slipped to 7–5. After a 6–0 start, he had won only one of his next five decisions. He was complaining of a sore arm, which he didn't have when he ran off his six game winning streaks. Walters continued his pursuit for 20 or more victories with a 12–3 mark. Sewell at 9–4 was trying for his second consecutive 20 win season.

It looked like a clear track for the trolley (street car) series based on the old theory that the team in first place on Independence Day wins the pennant. Both St. Louis teams were in first place and should the Browns win the American League Title, it would mark their first pennant. They had come close in 1922, but fell one game short of the New York Yankees. Many consider that the best St. Louis Browns team.

The Cardinals were 10–5 against the eastern teams on their current homestand. Munger at 11–3, 1.34 ERA left for the military on July 11, the same day Schmidt took his physical. Munger, with a break, could have been 13–1 or even 14–0. He didn't pitch a bad game all season. Munger's call up and Lanier's slump gave hope to the other teams; however, they had a very substantial deficit to make up.

Brooklyn lost its 13th consecutive game on its western tour and when game two of a double-header with Pittsburgh was completed and if the score held (Pittsburgh 9 and Brooklyn 7) it would go into the record books as the 14th consecutive loss, tying the team record set in 1937. This was the same team that won 100 games in 1941 and 104 in 1942, although there were some different personnel on the current club. This losing streak dropped Brooklyn to 33–43, 20½ games out of first place and just one-half game ahead of Chicago (29–40), who had been 26–23 after that dismal 3–17 beginning. The losing streak reached 15 before it ended in the second game of a double-header against Boston.

As the first half neared its end the Cardinals were 51–21 with Pittsburgh (39–30) and Cincinnati (42–33) both 10½ games out of first. The Cardinals were on pace to win 110 games. They needed to step it up a little to tie the Chicago Cubs' record of 116 wins. Musial just pushed ahead of Walker in the batting title race, .373 to .372, while Hopp had climbed to .327. Cooper was now 9–3 and Lanier 8–5, while Brecheen was 6–1 and Wilks 4–1. Jurisch (Munger's replacement) was just 5–5. Walters (13–3), Bill Voiselle (11–9) and Sewell (9–6) were all shooting for that coveted 20 victory mark.

The subject of night baseball led to a hot fight at the owners meeting. There was a hot diatribe by the New York Giants in trying to curtail the number of night games. Other National League foes failed to stop the expansion of night games. Several teams hoped and were fighting to return to seven night games after the war had ended. They had agreed to the increase during the war to accommodate war workers, but after the war they wanted to return to a maximum of seven night games per team.

Marion had a tryout as a 17 year old, but wasn't sure he wanted to be a ballplayer. He was going to technical school, studying to be a draftsman and then had hoped to go to college. A friend of his, Johnny Echols, heard the Cardinals were having tryout camp at Rome, Georgia, which is about 60 miles from Atlanta. He talked Marion into going. The team wanted him to sign a contract, but he wouldn't do it without his parents' permission.

Marion went back home and didn't think much about it. He continued going to technical school, and made plans to go to college. Later that summer he and his friend both got wires to come to St. Louis at the Cardinals' expense. He still didn't sign a contract at that time. This was 1935 (the year the Cubs stole the pennant from St. Louis with a 21 game winning streak). Finally in early 1936 Rickey sent his brother Frank to Atlanta and he signed Marion. That was how the rumor started that he signed Marion after seeing him in a few high school games. Marion said if that was true he never knew it.[17]

It seemed strange that it took so much persuasion to sign a 17 year old to a major league baseball contract. Marion was modest to a fault. He let others speak for him. He had truly earned the sobriquet, "Mr. Shortstop."

Spurred by Southworth's "fight talk," the National League outclassed the American League in all areas in a 7–1 triumph on July 11. This was the most lopsided win to date in all star history.

As the first half ended St. Louis at 54–23 held an 11½ game lead. If they were to duplicate this in the second half the club would finish with 108 victories. However, this looked like it would be hard to do with Munger in the service. Southworth was hoping that Jurisch could pitch against other teams the way he had dominated the Cincinnati Reds. If so, they could achieve or surpass that 108 win total. The record looked like a stretch at this point in the season.

The race now was for second place. Pittsburgh (41–33) and Cincinnati (44–36) were vying for that title. Musial had jumped to a 14 point bulge over Walker at .366 to .352. Medwick had crept to .332 while Hopp was at .323. Cooper was the other Cardinal currently over .300 at .308. Cooper led the pitchers with a 10–3 mark and Brecheen had moved to 7–1 while Wilks was 5–1. Walters (14–3), Sewell (10–6) and Voiselle (11–10) were all on a pace to win 20.

The Cardinals' new front four were Cooper, Lanier, Brecheen and Wilks. Schmidt and Jurisch would alternate for the fifth spot. When Litwhiler took a nose dive in his hitting, Bergamo was platooned with him, facing right hand pitching. Although not a power hitter, he did respond with a .286 mark.

One of the strange and unexplainable happenings of the start of the second half was Walters. He was riding high with a 15–3 mark and seemed headed for 25 or more victories. All of a sudden the bottom dropped out. He was knocked out three straight games, but his relief took the loss. He gave up five to six runs each game and this was a pitcher with a 2.40 ERA. This was the most runs he had given up all season. Sewell also fell into a slump as he was now only three games over .500 at 10–7. This was from an 8–2 mark and he hadn't won a game since July 5.

By the end of July St. Louis was at 61–24 with a 13½ game lead over Cincinnati (48–38) and 14 over Pittsburgh (46–37). No other team was over .500. The batting race now was a one point advantage for Musial (.357) over Walker (.356). The Cardinals had two more over .300 with Cooper at .321 and Hopp at .318. The rest of the team was in the 270s and 280s, except for Verban who was in the .250s. However, he was a slick fielder and had teamed with Marion to give the Cardinals another great double play combination. They had Marion and Frank Crespi in 1941, Marion and Brown in 1942, Marion and Klein in 1943 and Marion and Verban in 1944. Each year they had been blessed with good fielding double play combinations. Crespi, Brown and Klein were all good hitters.

Some players considered a guild or group to represent them. Most opposed the thought, as they believed they could negotiate better with the owner on their own. However, the majority of players didn't want to see

Landis retire as he had been the ballplayers' best friend. Both the owners and the players wanted the reserve clause kept and protected. Their fear was without it, the rich teams would buy up all the talent and most would never have a chance to get into the World Series. However, if we look at who had won pennants in the past 20 years it was the teams with the best and largest farm systems, however, not always the richest clubs. The Cardinals didn't rank as a rich team, but this pennant would be their eighth in 19 years, while the Red Sox had not won since 1918, despite multi-millionaire Tom Yawkey buying all stars since the early 1930s. In the final analysis the players wanted the reserve clause to stay in place, as they felt it also gave them some protection.

It looked like a street car series—an all St. Louis World Series. This would be the first time. The Browns had a four and one-half game lead, but the Cardinals were coasting (or perhaps we should say flying high) on a 15½ game lead. Speculation again arose as to the chance of the Cardinals tying or breaking the total win mark. They had won 14 of 16 on a swing through the east, which included a nine game winning streak. To keep that pace with just two veteran pitchers (Cooper and Lanier) was a lot to ask. However, Brecheen (second season) and Wilks (rookie) had pitched tremendous baseball. Maybe they would be able to maintain that pace. They could win 110 games which would tie them with the 1909 Pirates and the 1927 Yankees.

The Cardinals had to play three double-headers in four days and that put a tremendous strain on the pitching staff. Though they were well extended during those games in Brooklyn and Philadelphia, they came away winners. Southworth called up Byerly to help, but he arrived in poor shape and then hit his knee in batting practice and had to be sent back to St. Louis for Dr. Hyland to examine. Credit must be given to Billy Southworth and his pitching staff for what they had accomplished. With Munger gone the Cardinals relied on eight pitchers. They were Cooper, Lanier, Brecheen, Wilks, Donnelly, Jurisch, Schmidt and Byerly (the latter got into only nine games after his call up).

When Cooper pitched his fifth shutout it was the 17th for St. Louis. During the 1942–44 seasons St. Louis hurled 65 shutouts and Cooper had 23 of them, leading the league in 1942 and again in 1944. By the first week of August St. Louis was 68–26 (a pace good for "only" 111 victories) with a 15½ game lead on Cincinnati (53–42) and 16 over Pittsburgh (50–40). Walker and Musial had both cooled down and the latter led by a .351 to .348 margin. Hopp at .320 and Cooper at .318 continued to help carry the attack. Cooper was 12–4, Wilks (seven wins in a row) 9–1, Brecheen at 8–2 and Lanier 10–5. Jurisch won to make his mark 7–6, but did not win another game for the year. Walters (15–4) seemed a cinch for 20, but time seemed to have faded for Sewell (10–8) and Voiselle (12–11).

Lanier became a left handed pitcher when he broke his right arm twice as a youngster. St. Louis finished their road trip at 18–4 to give them a 16½ game lead on Cincinnati and 18½ games ahead of Pittsburgh. The club would be home until the end of August. Wilks (10–1) was hit in the head by a line drive off the bat of Cincinnati's Steve Mesner. He was rushed to Cincinnati Memorial Hospital, but the x-rays were negative. St. Louis was 72–27 when they returned home. Cooper was now 14–5, Lanier (with a five game winning streak) was 12–5, Brecheen 10–2 and the aforementioned Wilks rounded out the top four. Walters defeated St. Louis 5–3 for his 16th victory and fifth over the Cardinals. He had been 0–2 and three no decisions in his five previous starts.

Southworth got a two year contract and became the first Cardinals manager since Rickey to receive longer than a one year contract. Rickey had a multiple year contract in the early 1920s. The Cardinals and Breadon had been noted for changing managers almost as rapidly as someone changed their garments. From 1926 to 1930 Breadon had five managers in five seasons even though they won three pennants and finished second (1927) and almost won that one.

The Cardinals' lead was now 18½ games, larger than at the end of 1943. It looked like Rickey's prediction might come true, or at least close to it. Hopp was enjoying the greatest season of his career as he was batting .346. If Southworth had played more of a running game, his name would be at the top of the stolen base list.

When asked to define his greatest baseball thrills Southworth said, "That was easy, as they all were related to the 1942 World Series triumph over the Yankees. My two biggest thrills were Kurowski's game winning and Series winning home run off Red Ruffing in the ninth in game five. Second was Moore's diving catch of DiMaggio's line drive in game three won by White and the Cardinals, 2–0." Musial fell to the ground to avoid collision and if Moore hadn't made the catch it would have been an inside the park home run as Slaughter was too far away and Moore and Musial were both on the ground. Southworth was also thrilled in game four when Slaughter climbed the screen in right field to take a home run away from Charlie Keller.[18]

The Cardinals were now at 78–28, driving hard to try and reach that 116 victory mark. Lanier won three games in one week and this ran his winning streak to eight and tied him with Cooper for the team lead with 15 victories. Wilks and Brecheen were both 10 game winners, with the former charged with one loss and the latter with two. Musial held a two point edge on Walker, .358 to .356.

Breadon said the major leagues were educating kids in the proper playing of baseball. He cited the baseball camps, the Muny leagues, sandlot play and American Legion play. Each was giving the youth of America the opportunity to play baseball. It not only taught them the skills of the game, but it helped mold their character and make them better adults and citizens.

St. Louis was still striving to tie or exceed the Chicago Cubs' victory record. Bill Brandt, National League publicity chief, sent a wire to St. Louis sportswriters that on August 16 the Cardinals became the earliest team to achieve victory number 80. It now looked like 116 wins or better was a distinct possibility. Schmidt had pitched a five hit shutout over the Giants for the victory. The previous best was by the 1942 Dodgers who accomplished the goal on August 18. Unfortunately it hadn't helped attendance, as fans lost interest in a runaway race. They knew the outcome and that the team was headed for the World Series. Tight races like 1941 and 1942 had the pressure, tension, mystery and drama which drew the fans. Breadon had learned the same lesson Connie Mack learned with his great Philadelphia Athletics teams of the 1910–1914 era.

Pittsburgh, trying to take over second, won 11 of 12, but failed to gain any ground on St. Louis as they matched their record. In a weekend series against New York Cooper had eight hits in 10 at-bats, including three doubles and three home runs for a total of 20 bases. Brooklyn was eliminated from pennant race, 41½ games out of first in last place with a 45–73 record. How the mighty had fallen. All that was left for Dodgers fans to root for was Walker defeating Musial in the race for the batting title.

St. Louis now stood 84–29, an unbelievable pace, but still somewhat shy of the pace needed to pass or tie the major league record of 116 victories in one season. They were on a pace to win 114 or 115 games. They would have to improve a little to tie or surpass the record. They had won almost three of four games and now were being asked to win four of five. That was quite a goal to achieve. They also wanted to surpass the Pittsburgh margin of 27½ games set in 1902. Their current pace would give them a 25 game lead.[19] Walker edged ahead of Musial, .357 to .356, giving Dodgers fans something to cheer about. Hopp moved into the batting race with his .346 mark, besides playing a great center field. Cooper and Sanders were both at .299 with the latter at 82 RBIs and on pace for 100.

The Cardinals' homestand was completed at 16–3–1. When Pittsburgh came to St. Louis they had been on a 19–2 tear, but the best they could do was win one, lose and tie one, thus gaining no ground. At the end of August St. Louis was 90–30 and had four goals. First was to win the pennant (almost a foregone conclusion). Second, break the Chicago Cubs' mark of 116 victories. Third, beat the 1902 Pittsburgh margin of 27½ games. Last, but not least, set a new early clinching date. They already held the record at September 16, set by the 1931 Cardinals.[20]

At this point Cooper was 18–5; Lanier, riding a 10 game winning streak, was 17–5 with Brecheen at 13–2 and Wilks with an eleven game winning streak at 12–1. What a mighty foursome. Jurisch was below .500 and Schmidt a couple of games over. One had to wonder what the team record would have been had Munger still been with the club. Walker crept ahead of Musial, .358

to .355. Hopp was at .344, Cooper at .331 and Sanders at .304 with 90 RBIs. Musial had 85 RBIs and both looked like a cinch for 100 or more. They would be the first Cardinals since 1941 to have 100 RBIs, when Mize drove in that exact number. Walters (18–6) seemed like a shoo-in for 20 victories, with Sewell (14–10) and Voiselle (15–14) still having a chance.

The Cardinals increased their record to 92–30 for a winning percentage of .754. If they continued that pace they would tie and possibly set a new record for wins in a season. A 24–8 mark would tie it, while a 25–7 mark would give them 117 victories. Then the seemingly inconceivable happened. A team that had played the greatest sustained baseball of any team since the 1906 Chicago Cubs hit an unbelievable slump. The Pittsburgh Pirates dumped them four straight, a team the Cardinals had an edge on, 10–3 for the season. That reduced their lead to 16½ games, the lowest in over a month. Their hopes for 116 wins were dented, but certainly not destroyed.

Wilks had turned out to be the best of a fine rookie crop of pitchers. Early in the season Southworth used him primarily in relief and picked spot starts for him. Now he was a regular starter, just another great Cardinals pitcher in a long line of talent. His 11 game victory streak was snapped, but he bounced back quickly and was now 15–2. If the baseball that hit him in the head had been an inch lower, it would have been fatal. Wilks was a husky man and just 5' 9½", but was a workhorse. He needed to keep his weight down to 175 and therefore liked to have a lot of work.

Cooper was now at 19–5 and looked like a cinch for his third consecutive 20 plus win season. The last pitcher to do this was Dizzy Dean, when he won 20 or more from 1933–36 and then a premature injury basically ended his career at age 27. During those four seasons Dean won 102 games. What a pitcher! Lanier's ten game winning streak was snapped and he dropped to 17–6. Schmidt moved to 5–2 and replaced Jurisch (7–9) in the rotation. Musial trailed Walker, .356 to .352. It was a see saw race for the bat title.

In the first week of September the Cardinals began taking requests for World Series tickets. The requests exceeded last season's and one reason was that it looked like the possibility of an all St. Louis World Series. Requests were limited to the St. Louis area until they officially clinched the title, as the team was in its first slump of the season. They had lost seven of 11 games as of September 11. Their chances for three of the four goals or new records were greatly diminished.

After defeating the Cubs in 14 consecutive games, they finally lost as Chicago pinned the third loss on Wilks. Cooper won the nightcap to pick up his 21st victory, tying his 1943 mark. Lanier was again complaining of a sore arm, as he dropped his fourth consecutive game and his chance for 20 wins was fading. It was strange as he had no sore arm when he was 6–0, but then had a sore arm when he dropped five of six. When he won 10 in a row his sore arm disappeared, but now it had reappeared as he dropped four straight games.

Musial was hurt in a collision with Garms in early September and this cost him the batting title and a chance for 100 or more RBIs, as he finished with 94. He later said he returned to the lineup too soon. He had returned because St. Louis was losing. There wasn't a danger of losing the pennant, but you don't want to go into the World Series with a losing streak, as you have lost your momentum and that could lead to defeat. On September 17 the Cardinals dropped a double-header to Chicago and they also lost their last nine games to Pittsburgh and lost the season series 12–10. This was the first time since 1940 any team won the season series from St. Louis.

The club dropped 15 of 20 games before the slide could be stopped. Their record went from 92–30 to 96–45. Injuries played a major part in this slump. Not only did Musial get hurt in the collision with Garms, he returned to the lineup too early. Then he was called to Donora, Pennsylvania, as his father was extremely ill and Stan missed a total of 10 days. Kurowski was sent back to St. Louis with an eye ulcer. This had affected his batting in recent weeks. Thus two key players were out of the lineup in the late going.

The Cardinals' lead had shrunk to 12½ games as they were 96–45 while Pittsburgh was 82–56. St. Louis had already clinched the pennant, doing that on September 21 with a victory in the first game of a double-header with Boston. The team righted its ship and won nine of their last 13 games, while Pittsburgh was just 8–7 and the Cardinals finished with a 14½ game bulge. However, this was far from what they had imagined just a month earlier. Injuries, perhaps a little overconfidence looking toward the World Series, all played a part in the slump. Hopefully the slump was behind them and they were ready for the World Series.

Walters, Sewell and Voiselle all made the 20 win circle, with Walters at 23, Sewell and Voiselle at 21 each. Cooper finished with 22 victories, achieved in the club's 100th victory in a 16 inning duel with Raffensberger. When Wilks got his 17th victory on September 24 it also marked the team's 25th shutout, the best in baseball. Musial lost the batting title to Walker, .357 to .347, and his injury played a major part. Hopp ended at .336 and Cooper at .313 and tied the team record for home runs by a catcher at 13. Despite his eye problems, Kurowski hit .270 with 20 home runs (team best) and 87 RBIs. Sanders finished at .295 with a team high 102 RBIs. Cooper was 22–7 (matching his 1942 record), Lanier 17–12, Wilks 17–4 and Brecheen 16–5. The Cardinals captured their eighth titles in 18 seasons and with a few breaks it could have been four or five more.

This was a typical Cardinals team, as only two players (Litwhiler and Garms) did not come through the Cardinals' system. The other 20 Cardinals players had a total of 96 minor league seasons behind them, once again showing the method of St. Louis grooming and how it paid off. The Cardinals didn't believe in bringing a man to the majors until he was thoroughly trained and schooled. They didn't want to rush a player to the majors and not have him ready to step in and perform everyday duty.

The Cardinals led the league in runs scored (772), hits (1507), doubles (274), home runs (100), RBIs (720), team average (2.75) and slugging percentage (.402). They also captured the pitching statistics, leading with a 2.67 ERA and 26 shutouts and second with 89 complete games, as Cincinnati won the latter with 93. The Browns trailed in all the statistics, as they batted just .253, hit only 72 home runs and had a 3.17 ERA. The Cardinals had made just 106 errors in the season compared to the Browns' 161.

The Browns clinched the pennant on the last day of the season and this would be their first World Series appearance. This also marked the first time the World Series would be played in the same ballpark since the 1921 and 1922 series was played in the Polo Grounds between the Giants and the Yankees. The Browns were the underdogs, but the sentimental favorites. It was fury versus the world champions.

The Cardinals entered the World Series confident, but not cocky. The Series turned out to be a pitchers' delight as the Cardinals batted just .240 to the Browns' anemic .183. The Cardinals made just one error in the six games, while the Browns made 10. Had their fielding been better, the outcome might have been different. Early in the series the Cardinals were lethargic and looked like the team in early and mid–September. After game three they looked like the dynamo that had swept through the National League for the first 122 games.

In game one Cooper tossed a two hitter, but lost to Denny Galehouse 2–1 when Gene Moore singled and McQuinn hit a two run homer in the fourth inning. Game two saw a great relief job by Blix Donnelly. He had relieved in the eighth inning after Mike Kreevich had doubled with no outs. Donnelly then fanned Chet Laabs, Vernon Stephens and Mark Christman. In the 11th inning McQuinn opened with a double, but great fielding by Donnelly on Christman's bunt got McQuinn at third base.

Instead of having runners on first and third and no outs, the Browns had a runner on first and one out. That was considered the crucial play of the World Series. Had the Browns won that game, they would have had a two game to none lead and since they won game three they would have been up three games to none, an almost insurmountable lead. The Browns made four errors as the Cardinals won the game 3–2, with two of the runs being unearned. They scored the winning run in the 11th when Sanders singled, Kurowski sacrificed and Marion was intentionally walked. Ken O'Dea pinch-hit for Verban and hit a sacrifice fly to score Sanders with the winning run.[21]

In game three, Jack Kramer beat the Cardinals 6–2 as the Browns kayoed Wilks with five singles and four runs in the third inning. Schmidt was unscored upon in three and one-third innings. The Browns added two off Jurisch in the seventh on a walk and doubles by McQuinn, who hit .438 for the Series, and former Cardinals farm hand Don Gutteridge. The Cardinals got seven hits, while Kramer fanned 10 in the defeat.

The Cardinals evened the Series behind Brecheen 5–1 as Musial had a single, a double and a two run homer. Game five was a rematch of Cooper and Galehouse, but this time the edge went to Cooper. He allowed just seven hits and fanned 12 while Sanders and Litwhiler hit solo home runs to give the Cardinals a 2–0 victory. In game six Southworth handed the ball to Lanier and he was touched for a home run by Laabs, but that was all the Browns' scoring for the day. With one out in the sixth he walked Laabs and McQuinn and then wild pitched them to third. Southworth brought in Wilks and he got Christman to ground to Kurowski who threw out Laabs at home. Ray Hayworth flied out to Hopp to end the threat. Wilks retired all 11 men he faced. Thus the Cardinals were once again world champions, this for the fifth time.

A new World Series strikeout record was set as the Browns fanned 49 times and the Cardinals 43. The Cardinals had the edge in hitting as Verban led them with a .412 mark. After going just two for his first 12 and being lifted for a pinch hitter in each of the first three games, he finished with a five for seven flourish. Sanders had one hit in each game and batted .286, while Cooper hit .318 and Musial .304. The real edge was in the fielding and here the Cardinals made just one error, while the Browns made 10, including three by Stephens, while Marion fielded brilliantly.

Marion won the MVP in the National League making it three consecutive seasons a Cardinal took the honor. Marion, formerly the "all American out," had become a very respectable hitter. But it was his fielding that won the raves and made him "Mr. Shortstop" and he became the first player to win the MVP because of his defense.

The 1944 Cardinals, while slumping cost them a chance at a new victory total record, were only the fifth team in baseball history to lead the league in runs, batting, fielding and ERA. They would shoot for their fourth straight title in 1945, despite the loss of Litwhiler, Walker Cooper, Schmidt and the biggest of all, Musial, to the service. It was felt they still had enough talent left to take a fourth straight title, perhaps not a new record, but another 100 plus wins. The club looked stronger and deeper than any other in the league. The drive and hunger was still there despite three straight titles.

SIX

1945

Cubbyholed

The Cardinals had just completed finishing off the St. Louis Browns in the first and only all St. Louis World Series. Never again would the two teams meet in the Fall Classic. While the Cardinals would enjoy many more seasons in the sunshine, the Browns would be sold and transferred to Baltimore by 1954. This marked the Cardinals' fifth world title, tying them with the Boston Red Sox and the Philadelphia Athletics for second place behind the New York Yankees. The Cardinals simply outpitched, outhit and outfielded the Browns.

Marion won the MVP for 1944 as he was simply the best shortstop in baseball. He became the first player to win it because of his defensive abilities. This paved the way for future athletes to win awards based on their defensive wizardry. He was called "Slats," or the "Octopus," but the name baseball best remembered him by was "Mr. Shortstop."[1]

Pittsburgh, after their heady finish, averred that it was pennant or nothing for them in 1945. Nothing less would satisfy fans and team. They believed they could overtake St. Louis and win it all. Their star pitcher, Treutt "Rip" Sewell, kicked around the minors for years before he finally got a chance in the big leagues in 1938 at age 31 with Pittsburgh and it looked like he wouldn't make it as he was 0–1 in 17 games. He had appeared in five games for Detroit in 1932 and then it was back to the minors for seven more seasons. However, this time he stayed and from 1939 through 1944 he won, 10, 16, 14, 17, 21 and 21. He was here to stay and would anchor the hopeful pennant bound Pirates.

International League head Frank Shaughnessy said, "Class AA is closer to the majors than in years." This was because of the war and all the quality players taken by the military. He stated that the "Class AA was closer to the majors than to the lower leagues. We are not quite ready for big league status but want a new classification that puts them closer and separates them from the lower leagues." Meanwhile President Clarence Rowland of the Pacific Coast League said, "After the war we want status as the third major league." Shaughnessy said, "If Pacific Coast League rates that so does the International."[2]

St. Louis Browns president Donald Barnes may have helped contribute to his team's defeat in the World Series by getting Cardinals second baseman Emil Verban riled up. After three games and the Browns up two games to one and Verban's wife had a poor seat behind a post he went to Barnes and asked for a better seat for his wife. Barnes, in a cocky mood because his Browns were winning the series, made a joke of it. This made the Yugoslav seething mad.

During the season, while a defensive whiz, he batted just .257 with only 14 doubles, two triples, no home runs and 43 RBIs. In many games Ken O'Dea or somebody pinch-hitted for him in the late innings. During the first three games he was lifted for a pinch hitter. However, after Barnes' slur Verban got red hot and finished the series at .412, and was a key factor in the Cardinals winning the last three games. After Ted Wilks fanned Mike Chartak to end the series Verban told Barnes, "Now you get behind the post, you fathead." He swore he did not use any foul language, although accused of it.[3]

Augie Bargamo, who batted .286, and Wilks (17–4) were voted to the all rookie team for 1944. After the season surgery had to be performed on four Cardinals. Bergamo had a balky knee, as did Bud Byerly (who was of little value after July). Max Lanier had his appendix removed while Walker Cooper had bone chips in his arm and would have an operation similar to brother Mort's in 1941. The surgeons cut a growth off his arm.

The next president (Franklin Delano Roosevelt or Thomas E. Dewey) might have chosen the game's next commissioner if the majors had failed to agree on Judge Landis' replacement. His illness again raised the question of his retirement. A clause in the agreement said if they failed in three months to appoint a successor then the United States president had the authority to appoint someone. This was in the original agreement which was dated January 12, 1921.

Leslie O'Connor was said to be Landis' choice. He had been his secretary and treasurer since the job of commissioner was created in 1921. However, many believed that a more colorful and exciting figure was needed, perhaps not with the same firm hand as Landis, but someone with public appeal. Those suggested were Dwight Eisenhower, Douglas MacArthur or Eddie Rickenbacker (World War I flying ace). Landis turned 78 in November and had been in poor health. He missed his first World Series this year since becoming commissioner in 1921 and sent O'Connor as his representative.

There were several feelings hurt on the split up of the World Series money. Traveling secretary Leo Ward received just a one-half share, while clubhouse man Butch Yatkeman got a one-quarter share, the same as Byerly. For years the practice of pennant winners had been to give the traveling secretary a full share. Even the third string catcher (age 34) who got in one game and caught just two pitches got a full share. Neither manager nor coaches participated in the decision making. All decisions were made by the players.

Rumors continued that both the Browns and Cardinals could be moving to other cities. It was rumored that the Browns would be moved to Los Angeles while Breadon would move his team to Detroit. Breadon averred the latter was not true. Baseball people said only New York and Chicago could support two teams. Not even Philadelphia and Boston could afford to support two clubs, this being borne out by the attendance at the games. A Cardinals move to Detroit would have to be approved by the other National League owners (they would make more money as Briggs Stadium had twice the seating capacity of Sportsman Park). However, it would also require the approval of all eight American League owners, who would vote thumbs down.[4]

A huge problem faced baseball after the end of the war. The game had to find jobs for over 4,000 returning veterans. This was a huge problem faced under the Preference Act (a returning veteran got first opportunity at a prior job). The National Defense List of Players continued to increase and under the Preference Act an individual had to be given the same or an equivalent job to the one he gave up when he entered the military. The major leagues had 438 on the service roles. All employers in the country were faced with the same problem—they had to give an equal job to a returning veteran. Initially the act only guaranteed a job to a person drafted, but now it was open to all that served in the military.[5]

A training site in Hawaii was proposed for major league teams, as this locale was a huge operation for the military with tens of thousands stationed in the Islands. The military believed it would be a tremendous morale booster for the men and the services would like to see it take place. Hawaii had ideal weather for training; it was a great tourist locale and a rest and relaxation post for the military. However Commissioner Landis had not relaxed his rule of team training close to home and saving transportation costs in line with what the Office of Transportation desired. If the Department of Defense requested the major league teams to train in Hawaii then Landis could hardly refuse.

Branch Rickey wanted night baseball held to seven games per team. He showed that the figures didn't justify an expansion of night baseball. An unrestricted schedule in Washington and St. Louis did not generate the revenues the owners stated would be there.

Rickey further related that for some time all clubs would be under the heel of the St. Louis Cardinals. They had the longest and deepest pitching staff in baseball. Currently the club had 13 major league pitchers in the military with seven coming up from the minors. No other team in the major leagues could match that pitching strength.

Breadon's headache was after the war, although it was a blessing in disguise. He would have 14 hurlers (all proven winners) when the pitchers came marching home. He would also face the problem of who to retain in the outfield as he had Terry Moore, Enos Slaughter and Harry Walker returning plus what the team currently had, although Stan Musial and Danny Litwhiler would soon be leaving for the military. This would give the Cardinals five everyday outfielders. The question was who to keep and who to trade. A nice problem to have.

The Cardinals would be forced to dispose of some players, but Breadon would not take any action without first discussing it with Southworth. The team would have three second basemen besides Verban. Returning were Lou Klein, Jimmy Brown and Frank Crespi. The pitchers were Mort Cooper, Max Lanier, Ted Wilks, Harry Brecheen, Freddy Schmidt, Blix Donnelly and Al Jurisch. Returning from the service the team had Johnny Beazley, Ernie White, Howard Krist, Howard Pollet, Al Brazle, George "Red" Munger and Murray Dickson. You could make three starting staffs from those two groups.

Manager Billy Southworth was nicknamed "Billy the Kid" and batted .301 for ten seasons in the majors. He had been a failure at Cleveland, but made the grade with Pittsburgh Pirates, New York Giants and Boston Braves. He played on the 1926 team, batting .317 (coming in a trade from the New York Giants) and hit .301 the next season. He didn't play in 1928, but managed the team in 1929 and used himself sparingly as a pinch hitter and reserve outfielder. The Cardinals got him in a trade in early 1926 with the Giants as he clashed with dictatorial John McGraw. He helped solidify the team and was a key cog in the championship club.

All major league teams would be faced with the returning veteran problem. There would be major stars that had large salaries which would lead to increased costs. All clubs would have excess personnel and this could make for more equality if teams like the Cardinals and Yankees were forced to sell their excess talent.

Washington Senators owner and president Clark Griffith defied Rickey on night baseball. He told him "he had no authority to dictate to other teams. What he did with the Dodgers was his business, but that was where it ended." Griffith stated that "some clubs need night baseball to survive and Washington was one of them." He rather related it helped second division teams to stay alive and allowed workers and others too busy to see day games enjoy baseball.[6]

Breadon announced plans for the Cardinals to build an ultra modern baseball field after the war at Grand and Chouteau where he owned 13 acres. Currently the biggest attraction was the annual circus and carnival that lasted about three weeks. Breadon told the press that when the labor and materials were available then construction would begin. Currently there were six years to run on the lease with the St. Louis Browns on Sportsman's Park. Only Briggs Stadium in Detroit and Cleveland's Municipal Stadium would compete with the Cardinals' new park. Capacity was expected to be around 40,000 and Breadon vowed there would be at least a 25 percent increase in attendance.[7]

In 1944 the Cardinals set a record with 17 double-header victories. They were 9–2–7 at home and 8–3–5 on the road. This gave them a composite 17–5–12 for a double-header record of 51–22. No wonder they were so unbeatable during the season.

Landis had to decide on extending his term to 1953 when he would be 86–87. The major league joint committee recommended re-election with a voice confidence vote in his administration. It was now up to Judge Landis to determine if his health would permit him to perform the duties of his office. Before a final decision could be made Landis died on November 25, 1944, of coronary thrombosis. He had been the only baseball commissioner in the history of the game, as there had not been a commissioner prior to 1921.

A temporary council was appointed to run operations until a new commissioner could be appointed. American League president Will Harridge, National League president Ford Frick and O'Connor formed a triumuirate to supervise the majors in the absence of a commissioner. If they couldn't agree on a new appointment then either league had the right to ask President Roosevelt (elected to his fourth term) to appoint a commissioner. This would be temporary until the current pact expired on January 12, 1946.[8]

Everyone agreed that the new agreement needed to fit the needs and the current times. There were only two of the original pact signers left and they agreed that times had changed since 1921 and the new pact should reflect those changes. The new commissioner should not be all encompassing or powerful, but the dignity of the office must not be destroyed. There was a long list of candidates available. Landis ran the office as an iron man with an iron hand and was an absolute ruler for 24 years. He was re-elected three times by owners to whom he dictated. He was named as the supreme authority after the infamous Black Sox Scandal of 1919. He became a national figure as a stern, but just ruler. He wanted no funeral, no flowers, just cremation.

The saga of Litwhiler continued as he was rejected for military service due to a knee injury from 1944. His classification had gone from 1A to 2A back to 1A and now he was rejected. However, he could be re-evaluated at a later date and the Cardinals could still lose him to the service.

It was voted to lift the player limit for war veterans. This would apply between the period of September 1 of one year and May 13 of the next year. The off-season roster limit would be raised from 40 to 50 to accommodate returning veterans. Boosts were also recommended for playing periods and the number of options on a player. It was further agreed that five players could also be added during the playing season, raising team limits to 30. Also approved was the number of players a team could control, raising it from 240 to 320 and each could be optioned out at least three times.[9]

Breadon donned earmuffs and stuffed cotton in his ears to trade talks. He was in the driver's seat and didn't intend to let anyone else at the wheel. He scoffed at reports of giving up Brecheen. Schmidt was inducted into the army on December 8, 1944, and was the ninth pitcher the Cardinals lost to the military. Breadon said after the war ended there would probably be a lot available for the marketplace, but not at the current time.

The major leagues re-affirmed the one man pact policy for the commissioner, but the job would be restyled to fit current needs and conditions. Also the new commissioner would not have an iron fist and would have to rule with more flexibility. He would still be in control, but not a one man iron rule.

The election of Landis into the Hall of Fame on December 10 was the one to honor men who distinguished themselves before the 20th century. As many as 10 could be chosen for the list, but final selection required unanimous approval. The committee consisted of Stephen C. Clark, head of the National Baseball Museum at Cooperstown, who was chairman, Connie Mack, Ed Barrow, Bob Quinn and two veteran sportswriters. They were Sid Mercer of the *New York Journal-American* and Mel Webb of the *Boston Globe*. These groups had permanent members and operated continuously. Players, coaches and managers from the 19th century had to be elected unanimously. When the book closed then they would vote only on 20th century players and they needed 75 percent approval.[10]

The Cardinals decided to play 30 night games. They would limit the number of Saturday night games, especially when followed by a Sunday double-header. The playing of three games in less than 24 hours was pretty strenuous, especially on players of Marion's stature and physic.

Another change took place regarding baseball players and their draft status. The new change affected over one-third of all major league players. All 4Fs were to be given new tests. This would also apply to athletes recently given medical discharges. The reason for the change was that they proved they could perform some remarkable feats on a baseball field (the same was also true of football players); then why not like 16,000,000 other men shouldn't they be in military service?[11]

The Cardinals set a new major league mark with the fewest errors at 112 and the highest ever fielding percentage at .982. The 1944 Cardinals had the equivalent of what would be today gold glove players, but no such award existed at that time. Ray Sanders, first base; Marion, shortstop; George "Whitey" Kurowski, third base; and Johnny Hopp, centerfield: each of these individuals was deemed the best at his position.

War mobilization director James Byrnes said the "government had no intention of curtailing or stopping major league baseball. It would go on as planned. They only wanted to review the 4Fs and see if any could be put into military service." Baseball would miss receiving the same fate as all dog and horse tracks, which were closed for the duration. Byrnes couldn't or wouldn't say what percentage of 4Fs might go into war work during their off hours from the baseball field.[12]

The Cooper brothers were high on the talent scale and had performed at exceptional levels in the past. There wasn't any foreseeable reason why they shouldn't continue into the future, barring injury or draft. Mort was classified 4F and Walker was classified for limited duty. Mort would be 32 on March 2 and Walker 30 on January 8. Reclassification might not have any effect on them.

Lanier advised that he passed his physical and was told to get ready to leave anytime. During 1944 only Dixie Walker (.357), Musial (.347) and Joe Medwick (.337) were ahead of Hopp's .336, who was also the top defensive outfielder in the league. The team was advised that they would lose Musial to the Navy by the end of January. Chances for a fourth straight flag were dimmed. The key question was what type of lineup the team would have without Musial. The loss of Musial and Lanier narrowed the gap between St. Louis and the rest of the league.

To illustrate the dominance of the Cardinals and the depth of talent one only has to look at the major league all star team for 1944. The Cardinals landed five of the 11 positions. They had Musial, Sanders, Marion and the Cooper brothers. Detroit placed three players, thus no other team had more than one. The National League took seven of the 11 positions.

The major leagues would whittle the "conduct unbecoming rule." The new baseball pact would be ready by February 3 for approval. Still no candidates had been considered for the commissioner's job. Players' rights were presented and protected.

The election of the new commissioner was scheduled for February 3. Ford Frick seemed to be the leading candidate. This happened when Warren Giles and Larry MacPhail were running ahead of others as Frick's replacement as National League president. It now looked like it would be after February third to find a new commissioner as the boom for Frick had subsided. Byrnes stated he was not interested in the job.

Albert "Red" Schoendienst was classified 4F because of a major eye injury caused by a plant accident. This brought him an early release from the Army. He then went to the minor leagues and became a standout shortstop. He would be going to spring training, but would have to try another position, as Marion owned the shortstop job. He would get the job only if Marion were called to the service. He would probably be tried at second base or in the outfield.

Bob Feller landed at Seattle after 18 months at sea. He saw action and won eight battle stars. He said to keep the games going as the men wanted it. They lived for baseball. It was a tremendous morale booster.

The current census showed 260 4Fs in the major league with a high water mark of 281. Nationally there were 3,900,740 men classified as 4F. Many believed this number too high. Certainly there was some duty that the vast majority could have performed, duty that would release more qualified men for the battlefield. Businessmen thought it was about time to let up on the 4Fs.

The saga of Litwhiler's draft status continued. The draft board couldn't decide what category he belonged in. He was reclassified again—this time as 4F. His case now went to the office of the surgeon general in Washington D.C. The Cardinals were hopeful they would have him, as that would give them two-thirds of a starting outfield with Hopp. Only time would tell the final outcome of the situation. Litwhiler was also employed in a war plant in St. Louis during the off-season.

J. Edgar Hoover, head of the FBI, backed the game of baseball 100 percent. He stated there was no doubt about the wartime value it brought to the military as well as the home public. The game was going to ask priority to avoid the "slacker" tag that some had applied to those classified as 4F or other deferment. New legislation recently passed was heartily hailed by organized baseball because those playing the game would now have the official government stamp of approval.

The wounded veterans, both overseas and those that returned home, wanted the game continued. They along with most veterans and servicemen called the game necessary to the youth of our country. There was strong G. I. support for the game. A strong ear was given by the government to the wishes and desires of the military troops. They had listened to them all, in the air, on the seas, on the land, in hospitals and prison camps and the word was, "let the game go on." The major league presidents went to Washington hoping to get final official approval of the game. The right to use 4F players was not needed, but approval was sought by organized baseball.[13]

Major Billy Southworth Jr. was killed in air crash in Hudson Bay, New York. He had flown 25 combat missions and never received a scratch and then was killed in a routine flight. He had won several medals in combat and he was flying a B-29 when it crashed. Southworth had been the first professional ballplayer to enlist. He was to be promoted to lieutenant colonel when the crash happened. One engine had conked out and he had to make an emergency landing on a short runway for the B-29 (which was the new Superfortress). He was unable to bank on one side because of a disabled engine and couldn't bank on the other side because of the air tower. All that left was to land straight ahead and with a shortened runway the B-29 skidded into the icy waters of Flushing Bay, killing Southworth and his crew.

Mort Cooper was officially declared 4F and so was O'Dea by his draft board, but his was not final until boards of appeals agreed. The Army did okay Walker Cooper for military duty and he would probably be included in the March 26 quota. It looked like teams might have to go with a 22 man limit, instead of the normal 25. This would include 4Fs.

St. Louis had a smaller squad than in 1944 at this time. To compound their problem was the uncertainty of the 4F situation. On teams that won pennants, their players usually expected increases, but in St. Louis' situation it was a little difficult as attendance had fallen off the last two seasons. The reason was simple. The attendance was great in 1941–42 when the race was to the wire, but the last two seasons the Cardinals made a shambles of the league and many peoples' attitude was, "Why go to the game? They are probably going to win anyway. Plus they are already 15 games or so in front." The enthusiasm wasn't there as in earlier seasons. The Cardinals also delayed starting spring training until March 13, the latest ever.

No decision had yet been made on a commissioner. The minor leagues reserved the right to approve the selection of the new commissioner. The revision committee recommended that the new commissioner be given the same broad, wide, sweeping powers that Landis had. The minor leagues also wanted greater protection from invasion from the majors as well as higher draft prices for their players.

The latest census, dated March 8, 1945, listed 509 major leaguers in uniform and 3,576 minor leaguers in the military, for a total of 4,085. There was a strong possibility that each club might be asked to send 10 percent of its personnel to do war work. This percentage would not be taken from players alone. It would include groundskeepers, administration personnel, ticket takes, ushers, hucksters and management personnel. The problem of how to equalize their pay had to be worked out. They had to make certain war work pay was equal to baseball pay, regardless of the job. Another problem was lack of uniformity in how draft boards handled 4Fs. Some said okay play ball, while some said do war work. It would be hard to work eight hours in a war plant and then play baseball. The players wouldn't have the proper training and conditioning and would be too tired to perform at their peak.

The Cardinals finally started spring training on March 19 and Southworth might be late in getting there due to the death of his son. Breadon told the press more players were under contract now than a year ago. The Cardinals called up 28 year old Ken Burkhart from Columbus, where he went 15–9 in 1944. They needed him to bolster their staff with the expected loss of Lanier. The Cardinals would play 42 night games, 12 Sunday double-headers, a Decoration Day double-header and a Labor Day double-header, leaving only seven weekday games. What a change from just a few years ago.

Other major league teams were bringing war wounded discharged veterans to their training camps. The Washington Senators would give one-legged Bert Shepard a trial. He had been a bright pitching prospect prior to the war, during which he lost a leg. The Philadelphia Athletics would also give wounded veteran Lou Brissie a chance. He wore a brace on his leg from wounds received in combat. While he looked good in spring training the concern was the major leaguers would bunt him off the mound. Only time would tell.

For the third time Morton Cooper was classified 4F and now the Cardinals would be able to keep him on the squad. This was a giant step forward for St. Louis as Big Coop was 65–22 the last three seasons for the best record in baseball. His goal was another 22 win season (accomplished in 1942 and 1944). His brother, Walker, and Lanier would stay with the team until called by their draft boards. Including the Coopers and Lanier the Cardinals had only 17 players on hand to start spring training. It certainly didn't look promising with less than a full squad. They also had Byerly, Donnelly and Bill Trotter from last season and rookie pitchers Jack Creel, Burkhart, Stan Partheimer and Henry Koch. In addition they had Sanders, Kurowski, Verban and Schoendienst, and outfielders Deb Garms and Jim Mallory. The bad news was that Hopp was reclassified from 4F to 1A.

The Cardinals and Pittsburgh were featured as co-favorites for the title. This was a comedown for St. Louis, who had been the favorite the past four seasons. The losses in personnel suffered by this club had a long way to go in setting this forecast. For the past three seasons the team had been able to withstand losses to the military because of their wealth of talent in the minors. Breadon told the press the barrel had run dry.

The team had lost its star player, Musial, to the Navy. Fortunately Hopp and Litwhiler had been reclassified and the latter was now 4F. Then overnight Litwhiler was reclassified again as 1A and overnight inducted into the Army. Thus two-thirds of last season's outfield disappeared. The team also stood to lose Hopp, who was 1A. Southworth and Breadon shook their heads, wondering who would play the outfield if Hopp was taken.

To further compound their problems O'Dea (Cooper's replacement) hadn't shown up for spring training and Wilks, Marion and Brecheen were unsigned and not in camp. Schoendienst had a stiff right arm (which was injured in a late 1944 Army game). Currently he was limited to throwing underhanded, thus his status was undetermined. Added to that was the flooding at their training camp in Cairo, Illinois, which lasted a week. This was not a good time for Smiling Sam, who had become Sad Sam.

Marion signed for $12,500 and reported to camp, while Schoendienst, normally a shortstop, would probably play the outfield once his arm was okay. Southworth wanted him there as this was currently the Cardinals' weakest spot. There was some sore tissue in his arm, but no bone or ligament damage. Wilks signed and reported, but Brecheen and Hopp were still holdouts. The latter's failure to show was tied to his demand for more money and not his 1A classification.

The Negro in organized baseball was an evolution and not a revolution, Rickey told the press. Two Negroes insisted on tryouts with the Dodgers, while the Yankees and Giants would also be asked to give tryouts to Negro players. Several newspapers promoted pitcher Terrance McDuffie and first baseman Dave "Showboat" Thomas into appearances at the Dodgers' camp. Their tryouts were not requested, but demanded. They further advised they would take their players to New York for tryouts with the Yankees and the Giants.

The trio sponsoring them was Nat Law, sports editor of the Communist Party's *Daily Worker*; Joe Bostic, Negro sports editor of the Harlem *People's Voice*; and Jim Smith, Negro sports editor of the *Pittsburgh Courier*. New York clubs were picked because of the passage of the Quinn-Ives bill which made those who barred Negroes liable to prosecution. The Brooklyn team was targeted because they finished seventh in 1944 and needed help. Rickey said, "McDuffie at 32 is definitely not big league material and Thomas at 34 is not big league material because he couldn't hit a curveball with a bull fiddle." Rickey said, "I wouldn't take him if he was 24."[14]

Bostic issued a statement that this tryout was the first official recognition that Negro players were potentially big league material. Rickey countered that was not his interpretation and that force would not get the job done. The Negro acceptance at the major league level must come through regular channels (the minor league system), just like all white ballplayers had done for decades. Rickey further stated that "an evolutionary process, not a revolutionary action will decide the fate of the Negro ballplayer. Force or revolutionary action will only delay the cause of the Negro player and delay their entrance into the game."[15]

Rickey related that one time Brooklyn had 97 men at tryout, but all were invited. If they came indiscriminately there would have been utter chaos. Rickey compared the entrance of the Negro into organized baseball to Prohibition; it required education. He told the trio they were defeating their own purpose by their action.

The final forecasts still showed St. Louis as favorites, but not by an overwhelming margin as in the last two seasons. They were followed by Pittsburgh, Cincinnati and Chicago. If you recall, Chicago started 3–17 in 1944 and finished at 75–79, a very good turnaround. Their prospects depended on the condition of their outfield and how their new pitchers respond. Their leading pitchers were Claude Passeau, Hank Wyse and Paul Derringer. Passeau had won 98 games in the prior six seasons, never below .500 and had a 19 and 20 win season included. The other two were question marks. Wyse had been 9–7 and 16–15 in 1943–44, while Derringer, winner of 207 games, was only 27–38 for the past three years—a far cry from his salad years of 1938–40 when he won 66 games. At 38½ it was questionable how much value he would be.

Kentucky senator Albert B. "Happy" Chandler was named the new commissioner of baseball. He would lead as well as police the game. Chandler saw his job as the vigorous promotion of baseball. He opposed draft discrimination against players and believed 4Fs should be spared to play the sport. Chandler told the press he would be an active leader, traveling and talking for the game. He was a direct opposite of Landis. He was friendly, charming and outgoing. His smiles hid a determination that nobody could push "Happy" around.

The Cooper flare-up happened again. Mort staged a sit down strike and failed to accompany the team on April 24 to Cincinnati. He arrived a day later saying he stayed for his brother's farewell party. His lawyer, Leo Havener, went along for the ride to Cincinnati. Just the day before Havener had issued a statement saying that Cooper was still dissatisfied but would join the team. Cooper didn't want a long delay in settling his dispute, but was playing under protest. Not a good omen for the club or someone bent on equaling his 1942–44 record of victories.

Ten old time (19th century) stars were inducted into Baseball's Hall of Fame. They were Roger Bresnaham, Hughie Jennings, Mike Kelly, Wilbert Robinson, Hugh Duffy, James O'Rourke, Ed Delahanty, Dan Brouthers, Jimmy Collins and Fred Clarke. With these entered into the Hall all future voting would be addressed to 20th century players.

V-E Day (Victory in Europe) was May 8 and that eased the player shortage situation. Fewer call ups were anticipated. The order for capital review of 4Fs was rescinded. Baseball took a back seat to the announcement the war in Europe had ended. A decision was made to release 2,000,000 men and ship 6,000,000 to the South Pacific to fight and defeat the Japanese. There would be a slackening of the draft. The main effect was on players over 28 with 1A status awaiting calls who could now expect not to be called.

Unfortunately this came too late for the Cardinals and Walker Cooper, as he had already been drafted. The case of Litwhiler, previously classified 4F, was marked on papers to his draft board that he couldn't be considered to fill the quota for the Army or Navy as he didn't meet minimum military requirements. There were others in similar situations. Now the concern would be for present players and whether they could keep their jobs when the veterans returned. Just last week it was whether 4Fs would be able to play.

The Cardinals started slowly and after two weeks were just 5–4 while New York led the pack at 8–4. Despite losing Cooper to the Navy and Litwhiler to the Army plus a series of infield accidents the Cards intended to make a drive for their fourth straight pennant. The team suffered under the handicap of having limited spring training and losing more talent than any club in the league. Up until May 5 no Cardinal had hit a home run and Schoendienst had the only triple. On that day Hopp broke the ice with the first Cardinals home run of the season.

The next day in game one of a double-header Hopp hit another home run, which was duplicated by Kurowski in the nightcap. In that same game

Verban got the Cardinals' second triple of the season. The home run production was bound to fall as Musial, Litwhiler and Cooper hit 40 of the team's 100 home runs and 24 of their 59 triples. All three were now in the military. Marion and Schoendienst both hurt and Kurowski had an ailing arm, but all were back in a few days. For the second consecutive Sunday Cooper and Lanier won a double-header, with Cooper getting his first complete game of the year. It looked like he was back in form. If only the service didn't take Lanier.

After three weeks the standings showed a surprising New York team at 12–4, Brooklyn 9–6, St. Louis at 8–6 and Chicago at 7–6. While Sanders at .317 was the only Cardinal over .300, the pitching was rounding into shape. Brecheen, Burkhart and Cooper were all 2–0 and Lanier was at 2–1. It looked like the team was molding into shape.

The major leagues were not too alarmed by the comment by the Department of Transportation that the World Series might be cancelled because of transportation needs. Baseball believed with the relaxation on 4Fs and discharging 2,000,000 men this didn't square. They were confident there would be a revision of thought. One comment made was all the games would be played in one city, i. e., if New York and St. Louis won, one city would be chosen for all the games.

Just when it looked like all the pieces were coming together the Cardinals stumbled, dropping four of five to New York and Brooklyn, falling to 9–10 compared to pace setting New York at 17–5. The Cardinals after a month of play had fallen 6½ games behind. Some were wondering about another classic Cardinal come from behind. Southworth stated, "If we lose the pennant, I'll be the fall guy, all the writers had dropped the title in my lap." If we win, he said, "Anybody could win with that team."

What was forgotten was what happened to the talent wealth of the team. At one time the Cardinals had the deepest talent in baseball and could lose or trade a player and just call up another one, like nothing had happened. Those days had temporarily ended. The barrel was dry. A team can't lose Musial, Walker Cooper and Litwhiler and not feel the hurt. Then Marion and Schoendienst were injured and George Fallon proved unsatisfactory as a replacement.

Desperate for help, especially in the outfield, the Cardinals got Buster Adams (a former farmhand who had tryouts in 1939) from Philadelphia, where he had been traded in 1943 in the Litwhiler trade. The Cardinals sent two reserve infielders, Johnny Antonelli and Glenn Crawford, to Philadelphia in the trade. Bergamo was in the dog house for several days when he lost a fatal fly ball in the first Brooklyn game because he failed to wear his sunglasses. Then, as if the team didn't have enough problems, Wilks, Brecheen and Donnelly all had sore arms. The first two could be attributed to the lack of spring training and their holdout. No wonder the team was struggling. It looked like they would have to do as they did in 1939, 1940, 1941 and 1942—a great August and September. The only bright spot at this point seemed to be the hitting of Hopp (.333), Sanders (.283) and Kurowski (.356).

It looked like a combination of bad effects had finally caught up with St. Louis. The Cooper revolt, the amazing pace and spurt of New York and Brooklyn, injuries to key players and then the loss of star players to the military. Another factor was perhaps some complacency had set in after winning three straight pennants and 316 games in three years. Wilks, Brecheen and Dockins were all nursing sore arms while Marion was playing on and off with a bad ankle. Lanier was 5–0 last year at this time and now was in South Carolina waiting to be drafted. No wonder the team was at 12–12 versus 18–6 just one year ago.

The rough ride St. Louis had experienced left the door open for their rivals. The Giants were setting a blistering pace at 21–5. No National League team had started like this since the Giants did at 25–5 in 1907. On the bright side it looked like the Department of Transportation overreacted and gave an unnecessary scare regarding the World Series. It now looked like it would go on as usual.

Organized baseball was now in a conflict over the new Negro League. The United Negro League had the blessing of Rickey (Griffith said Rickey was trying to be its czar). This new league was in opposition to the Negro American and National Leagues. There were several new teams with strong identities in the new league. The key question to Chandler was would their league and teams get recognition from and become members of the National Association of Professional Baseball Players? Chandler said he would give it due concern. Griffith claimed Rickey was trying to be a dictator and destroy the integrity of the Negro American and National Leagues, that he wanted to force them into the new league for his own glorification.[16]

Cooper left the team on May 16 when scheduled to pitch in a double-header. In prior years his only headlines had been victories. Now he was the Dizzy Dean of the 1940s, referring to Dean's antics in the mid–1930s. The Cards were in dire straits with their pitching staff as George Dockins and Brecheen were sent back to St. Louis to have their sore arms checked. Wilks and Donnelly were with the team, but had sore arms and Lanier was in South Carolina being drafted. Normally mild mannered Southworth was riled and exploded, "Fine time to leave team, suspended him indefinitely and fined him $500." Cooper was now willing to settle for a three year contract at $13,500 per season with a clause that the contract would be nullified if he were sold or traded, but it looked like a safe bet he would pitch elsewhere afterwards.

By the third week of May (22nd) New York still was setting a blistering pace at 21–7 with surprising Brooklyn second at 17–10. St. Louis and Pittsburgh, pre-season favorites, were 14–13 and 12–14 respectively with Chicago (12–13) sandwiched in between them. Tommy Holmes continued to lead the league in batting at .400 and Kurowski was the only Cardinal over .300 at .369. The Giants and Brooklyn had ten players between them at .300 or more. The question became what happened when these hitters tapered off to their normal pace? On the pitching side New York's Bill Voiselle was 7–0 and the Cardinals' Burkhart and Cooper were 2–0, while Brecheen was 2–1, making the rest of the staff a less than mediocre 8–12.

The new question was who would have the last laugh as Cooper was traded to Boston for $60,000 and Charles "Red" Barrett. Players sold or traded in the past ten years had brought St. Louis $850,000 ($15,000,000-$20,000,000 in 2006 dollars) plus disposing of Cooper (the premier pitcher in baseball at 65–22 the prior three years) for a losing pitcher (Barrett, 2–3 on the current season and 26–37 career). Breadon had stuck to character.

The trend started with Rogers Hornsby after the Cardinals won the 1926 World Series. He wanted $50,000 per season for three years, but Breadon, peeved over the events of 1926, offered only one year. Later he traded Hornsby to New York for Frankie Frisch. At the time it was a very unpopular trade, but fans came to love the fighting Irishman. He played, led or managed the Cardinals to four pennants and two World Series titles.

The biggest deal was for Dizzy and his sore arm to the Chicago Cubs for $185,000 and two good pitchers (Clyde Shoun and Curt Davis) plus outfielder Tuck Stainback prior to the 1938 season. When the latter three were eventually traded (although Davis was a 22 game winner in 1939) they brought the team another $50,000. Breadon was quite a horse trader.

Barrett won his first start for the Cardinals. Although the Cardinals had won pennants that lacked the color of the Gas House Gang, they got it in chubby, jolly Charles "Red" Barrett. It was not just the color of his red hair and while he didn't drink or smoke Barrett was quite a character. He told teammates that he had sung with most big bands and when asked in what voice, Barrett's response, "I'm a bass at 8 AM, 3PM I became a baritone and by 8PM I am a tenor." At midnight still a tenor and after that he became a light soprano. His favorite pastime was sitting around the clubhouse drinking his Coke and warbling with the bands. Southworth liked his attitude. He wasn't fast, but he didn't give players good pitches to hit. Barrett was willing to start today and relieve tomorrow.

Although Barrett totaled only nine wins in 1944, seven of them came at the expense of first division teams. It showed he could pitch winning baseball against the better clubs. He defeated St. Louis three times by the identical score of 5–1 and the only runs were home runs, two by Walker Cooper. Barrett was 30 years old, born February 14, 1915.

By the end of May, New York continued to hang onto first place with a 21–8 record, but Pittsburgh and Chicago had now moved into a second place tie at 17–14, while Brooklyn was right behind in fourth at 18–15. St. Louis was close with a 17–16 mark, as they couldn't seem to get any type of winning streak in place. The injuries to the pitching staff had greatly slowed the team. It looked like the team would have to pull off another hot August and September, a la 1930, 1934, 1939, 1940, 1941 and 1942. Holmes continued to set a torrid pace in the batting race at .426 while Kurowski was up to .396. Voiselle led all hurlers at 8–0 while Burkhart had improved to 3–0.

The returning veterans were blazing to major league stardom in their return. They came back in top shape. Fans were thrilled with the pitching and playing of players such as Dave "Boo" Ferris, Al Benton and other returnees. Ferris in his first 64 innings had hurled 59 scoreless frames. What a way for a rookie to break into the major leagues. Besides his excellent pitching Ferris was a first class hitter, made in the mode of Red Ruffing, Wes Ferrell, George Uhle or Red Lucas.

New York, Chicago and Pittsburgh all chaffed at Breadon for snubbing them and not giving them the opportunity to make a trade for Cooper. They collectively accused Breadon's actions by saying, "We sold Cooper to Boston because they didn't have a chance to stop the Cardinals." Breadon denied this was the reason for the trade to Boston. He said it was the best deal he could make.

The Cardinals concluded a homestand against the eastern teams with a 9–5 mark (which was good when you consider three of the four teams were in the running for the pennant). This moved the club into third place. Wilks got a complete game victory over New York in the second game of a doubleheader on June 3. He then picked up his third win of the campaign against four losses a few days later. Last season he lost only four games all year, while winning 17. There were two big differences. He didn't have a sore arm in 1944 and he had a much better team behind him that season.

Donnelly was slowly working the soreness out of his arm and Brecheen was getting close to pitching again. Even though his arm was sore Dockins volunteered for relief duty, telling Southworth that he believed he could hold them for a few innings. Southworth liked that kind of spirit in his players. Barrett won a night game on May 29 and relieved the next day. Burkhart and Jack Creel had both moved into the starting rotation due to the rash of sore arms.

After the first week in June New York hung onto first place with a 27–14 record (just 6–9 in the most recent 15 games), while Pittsburgh took over second at 22–16 and St. Louis was third with 23–18, trailed by 21–19 Brooklyn and Chicago at 19–18. Barrett had won his first three starts for St. Louis and improved his overall record to 5–3. Holmes still led the league with .392, followed by Kurowski at .380. Adams had started hitting for St. Louis and was at .287 with 23 RBIs in 36 games (a pace of 100 or more for the season). Voiselle after winning his first eight decisions had now lost two in a row. For the Cardinals Burkhart was 4–1 while Brecheen (pitching for the first time in almost a month) improved his record to 3–1.

Southworth had stated that when New York and Brooklyn were setting a torrid pace the club he worried the most about was Pittsburgh. He related that to win a fourth straight pennant the Cards had to beat the Pirates. If you recall they defeated the Cardinals the last nine times they met in 1944 to erase a 10 to three games deficit and take the season's series 12 to 10. They were also one of the factors that the Cardinals didn't come closer to challenging the Cubs' record of 116 victories. It looked like Southworth's prediction might come true as the Cardinals lost three of four to Pittsburgh at home, including a Sunday double-header.

The injury jinx continued to haunt the Redbirds. It gave nightmares to Southworth as he could recall what happened to his team in 1941 and why they lost that pennant (due to a string of unbelievable injuries). In the prior week Kurowski could play only two games and had no power in his right arm, thus affecting both his hitting and his throwing. Hopp was out with a foot injury from fouling off a ball that hit his foot, but was forced to take over first base when Sanders injured his finger sliding into second base. Wilks was still having sore arm problems, while Brecheen was trying to pitch the soreness out of his. Certainly looked like shades of 1941 to Southworth.

As the middle of June approached it found six teams over the .500 mark. New York remained entrenched in first at 29–18 (just 8–13 for the last 21 contests), Pittsburgh (26–20) just edged ahead of Brooklyn (25–20). St. Louis at 26–21 rounded out the first division (only three games from first), while Chicago was at 23–19 and Boston in 6th place had a 22–21 mark. Holmes continued to lead the league with a .390 mark, followed by Kurowski at .378. Garms was playing the outfield and relieving the injured Kurowski at third, batting .333. Unfortunately he lacked power.

Commissioner Chandler supported a proposal that the Baseball Hall of Fame pay tribute to the late President Franklin Delano Roosevelt. Ed Barrow and Bob Quinn also supported the approval letter display by making it a permanent exhibition of historic proportions. Included would be the famous "Green Light" letter written to Landis in early 1942 paving the way for the continuation of major league baseball during the war emergency.[17]

Barrett and Burkhart both give credit to the Cardinals' brilliant double play combination of Marion and Verban in making them winning pitchers. Both said the two turned what on many teams were hits to the outfield or infield singles into outs and double plays. Their play had made consistent winners of the two pitchers.[18]

The Chicago Cubs were fattening up on the Cincinnati Reds as they had defeated them eight straight games. This put them over .500 on June 19 as opposed to 1944 when they were mired in the cellar at that time. However, then they lost three straight to Pittsburgh, which put the latter in first place. Pittsburgh, however, had become the Reds' patsy, as they couldn't defeat them consistently. It was kind of a ring a round the rosy with these three teams.

The Cardinals completed their recent homestand at just 12–9, which while a winning mark was far below their success rate of 1941–44. They started off losing game one in Pittsburgh then won three straight (June 17–18). They banged out 45 hits in three games with Kurowski hitting two home runs. Hopp had two triples, while Schoendienst had a triple, double, three singles and two stolen bases. The bats had come to life. The Cardinals received some good news as Burkhart failed his Army physical and returned to the team, while utility outfield Fallon passed his and would leave shortly for the Army. Kurowski and Sanders both were back from the injury list and in the every-day lineup.

By the third week in June the torrid pennant race hadn't let up, only the positions of the players had changed. Brooklyn had regained first place with a 31–21 mark, while Pittsburgh held second by a nose with 30–23 over 29–23 St. Louis. New York rounded out the first division at 30–24 (remember they started the season 21–5). Chicago at 26–22 was closing in and Boston was still at .500 with a 25–25 record. Poor Philadelphia was last with a 14–42 record. Since 1933 Philadelphia had finished seventh or eight every season. The had finished seventh five times, eighth seven times (losing 100 or more games six times, including five in a row, 1938–42). The last time they were over .500 was 1932 at 78–76.[19]

Holmes continued to lead the league in batting at .392 while Kurowski, though slipping, still held second at .355. Garms in a reserve role was at .333. Adams was at .289 with 32 RBIs in 48 games. Only he and Kurowski were batting higher than rookie Schoendienst. Burkhart was proving to be a winning pitcher as a starter, giving a large helping hand to Barrett. Dockins was pitching well, but Brecheen still couldn't pitch consistently because of a sore arm. Burkhart was 5–3 and Barrett was at 6–4. Hopp was beaned on June 24 (another injury) by Chicago's Ray Prim and while there was no fracture, it was a very serious concussion which would keep him out of the lineup for several days.

Cooper had been paying big dividends in Boston as he was currently 6–0 (2–0 with St. Louis and undefeated also with Boston). Voiselle after his 8–0 start was now just 8–5. Sewell had moved into a tie with Voiselle with the identical record. He had started slowly, but was now winning and so were the Pirates. It looked like Cooper had a sore arm as he was forced out of his last two starts. On June 22 he lasted just two innings and then his previous start he was down 7–3 after six innings.

By the end of June Brooklyn (the surprise team of the league) had strengthened their hold on first place with a 37–22 record and a three and one-half game bulge on the Cardinals (33–25). It looked like it was going to be another St. Louis—Brooklyn battle for the pennant, a la 1941–42. Pittsburgh was third at 33–26 and New York, continuing to fade was 32–26, followed closely by Chicago at 29–25. Holmes continued to pace the league with a .381 average, while Kurowski was second at .352, but a new player had entered the race. Phil Cavaretta of the Cubs was third at .351. Garms continued performing well in a substitute and pinch-hitting role, batting .333. Adams was at .288 with 35 RBIs in 53 games. He and Kurowski were on a pace to hit 20 home runs and drive in 100 or more runs each. Unfortunately the pitching wasn't keeping pace. Only Burkhart was still winning at 6–3, while Brecheen was 3–2 and sidelined with a sore arm. Barrett after a quick start had slumped and was now 6–6. Voiselle was winless in over a month and had fallen to 8–6 as had Sewell.

It looked like St. Louis was ready to make their move as they started their road trip with a 10–4 mark, taking three of four in Chicago. They were 1–1 at Cincinnati and then 6–2 versus Pittsburgh and Philadelphia. From there the club went to Boston, who had been their favorite patsy in 1944, with a 19–3 record. However, Boston got its revenge. Southworth had his staff going smoothly with Barrett, Burkhart, Wilks and Donnelly, but in Boston the starting trio got ripped for 22 runs in a three game loss. This was a major blow to the Cardinals. There was some good news as Hopp was out of the hospital and would join the team in New York on July 1. Del Rice moved into the number two catching slot and showed good defense, while batting around .260. So there was good news to go with the bitter defeats the team suffered in Boston.

Brooklyn looked like the team to take it all as by the end of the first week of July they were solidly in first at 41–25, with a three and one-half game bulge on St. Louis (38–29). It was beginning to look like St. Louis would have to stage another rousing August-September, as they did each year from 1939–1942. New York took over third at 37–31 (just 16–26 since their hot start) and Chicago rounded out the first division with a 33–28 record. Pittsburgh was 34–31 and Boston, thanks to the three game sweep of St. Louis climbed back over .500 at 32–31. Philadelphia continued lounging in the cellar at 19–52. Holmes was at .394, but Cavaretta was moving up at .363, while Kurowski was at .350 with 47 RBIs in 57 games, having missed 10 games due to injuries. Adams was at .295 with 45 RBIs in 61 games and Burkhart now led the staff with an 8–3 mark, while Barrett climbed back over .500 at 7–6.

Voiselle finally broke his long drought and tied for the league lead in victories with nine and was now 9–6, as was Sewell. Hal Gregg of the Dodgers also had nine wins, with just four defeats, as he was pacing the Dodgers' pitching staff and their drive to the pennant.

Even though the 1945 All Star Game was cancelled players were still chosen for the game that might have been. The Cardinals placed seven on the hypothetical team. They were Kurowski, Marion, Donnelly, Adams, Verban, Barrett and O'Dea. A number of these would not have made the team in prior seasons, when the more talented players were available. However, they were the best at this time. Only Kurowski and Marion ever made the All Star team in any other season.

Cooper was now nursing a lame arm and had a 7–1 record. He left the club for a physical examination. It looked like maybe St. Louis didn't make such a bad trade after all. Cooper could pitch about three innings, but had nothing on his pitches. He would see the Cardinals physician, Dr. Hyland. He was the same one that operated on him in 1941 and turned Cooper into a 20 game winner. He was hoping for a repeat performance from Dr. Hyland.

After their three game loss in Boston, St. Louis took three out of four from the Giants at the Polo Grounds and did the same thing to the Dodgers at Ebbets Field. Finishing the trip with a 16–9 mark and a long homestand coming up the team looked like they were ready to make their annual pennant drive; they expected to be in first place by the time it ended. Then a surprise hit. Chicago went on a nine game winning streak and vaulted over St. Louis and Brooklyn into first place with a 42–28 record. Brooklyn, losers of six in their last eight, were second, one game out at 43–31 and St. Louis just one-half behind them at 42–31. Southworth now saw it coming down to a three team dogfight.

Holmes, intent on winning the batting title, climbed back to .400. Could he be the first National League player to bat .400 since Bill Terry hit .401 in 1930? Cavaretta continued his hot hitting and moved to .367, while injuries had slowed Kurowski to .334. Adams was at .309, while Garms in his reserve role climbed to .347. Second year man Augie Bergamo, filling in for the injured Hopp, was batting .301. On the pitching side Barrett had won three in a row and stood at 9–6, while Burkhart was 8–4. Rookie Creel was a surprising 5–3, but unfortunately would not win another game during the season.

The Cubs now thought they could beat anyone and could breeze home. They were on a roll and defeating all teams, except St. Louis against whom they had a losing record. The irony was that while St. Louis was roughing up the Cubs they had trouble winning against the sixth and seventh place teams (Boston and Cincinnati). To illustrate what was happening the Cubs won a double-header on July 15 from New York (whom they once trailed by 11½ games) while St. Louis dropped a double-header against their 1944 patsies, Boston. This was a telling defeat and disaster.

The Cubs, after losing six of their first seven to St. Louis, defeat them two of three games and stretch their streak to 15 wins in 16 games, which included a 10 game winning streak. Shades of 1935 and the Chicago 21 game winning streak in September which over took the Cardinals. The team had done it with tremendous hitting paced by Cavaretta, third baseman Stan Hack and outfielders Bill Nicholson, Andy Pafko and Harry "Peanuts" Lowery and superlative pitching from Wyse, Derringer and Passeau.

Patchwork pitching, mainly due to injuries, had hurt the Cardinals. Only Barrett and Burkhart had been constant and dependable pitchers. This had been a far cry from once was considered the pitching rich Cardinals, who were the envy of all of baseball. Barrett had 12 complete games and Burkhart could win when they got him three or four runs. The staff had been hampered by the sore arms of Wilks, Brecheen and Dockins. If the first two had been okay and pitching as they did in 1944, the Cardinals would have been five to 10 games ahead of the pack instead of trailing. All had been in and out. Donnelly's history for the season had been good game, bad game. Lack of consistency.

The Cubs had a winning trio in Wyse, Passeau and Derringer, whereas St. Louis had trouble matching that group. To further compound problems had been their inability to defeat Boston, to whom they had dropped five consecutive games. St. Louis, once an excellent home team, was just 18–14 at Sportsman's Park, while they were 26–20 on the road. Winning double-headers on Sundays at home used to be almost a sure thing for St. Louis, but not this season. They had won two (Chicago and New York), divided with the Reds and lost to Pittsburgh, Boston and the lowly Philadelphia club. Many injuries and sore arms had slowed down the Redbird express. Southworth told the press there was still plenty of time to right the ship and make one of their patented pennant drives.

By the middle of July Chicago (48–29) had widened its lead over St. Louis (45–34) to four games with Brooklyn four and one-half behind, followed by Pittsburgh eight out and New York now 42–41, nine behind. Remember, they once led the Cubs by 11½ games. Thus the Cubs had made up over 20 games on the Giants. This thought gave new hope to the Cardinals. Holmes continued to lead at .394, but Cavaretta had closed the gap with his .374. Kurowski was at .330 with 53 RBIs, while Adams at .300 had 60 RBIs. The Cubs three leading pitchers were Passeau (10–3), Wyse (11–5) and Derringer (9–6), while the Cardinals had Barrett at 10–6 and Burkhart at 9–4. Unfortunately they couldn't come up with a consistent third starter, due to injuries or inconsistency.

The Department of Transportation lifted all objections to the playing of the World Series. Commissioner Chandler had thought of going to the Pacific with the teams and the servicemen could see the World Series. Both the Army and the Navy wanted to see the World Series teams. Admiral Nimitz's plan was for the World Series winner to play the United States Navy team.

The Dodgers no longer viewed the Cardinals as the team to beat and took aim for the Cubs. Durocher believed their home park advantage was their big edge over the Chicago Cubs. The Cardinals lost a home double-header on July 22 to the Dodgers as Kurowski missed the series with a sore arm. His absence from the lineup had hurt in several key games.

Brecheen had pitched a shutout against Boston on July 16 and it was his first start since June 26 and his first complete game since May 2. Just when everyone thought he was back on track Brecheen went only five innings in his next outing on July 21. The hope was that warm weather would bring his arm around. So far it hadn't responded. Schoendienst, although playing, was sub par as he also had an ailing arm. Meanwhile Creel joined the sore arm brigade of Wilks, Brecheen and Dockins. To help out the situation the Cardinals called up 29 year old Glenn Gardner (who was 8–7 with a mediocre Rochester team) and he had already made three relief appearances.

As July moved to a close it found St. Louis and Brooklyn deadlocked for second place at 49–38, four and one-half games behind front running Chicago (52–32). Pittsburgh completed the first division at 47–42, seven and one-half games back. Holmes was now at .369 and Cavaretta at .354. Kurowski, despite injuries, was still hitting .320 with 61 RBIs. Barrett was riding a six game winning streak at 12–6, while Burkhart was 9–5.

It was a strange story how the Chicago Cubs landed Hank Borowy of the New York Yankees from the waiver list. Several teams said they didn't see his name on the list. Neither Washington, Brooklyn nor St. Louis would have passed on him. He had to get by seven American League and seven National League teams. Something didn't look right about the transaction. There was much dispute over how Borowy got to the Cubs. One scribe said, "It was a you scratch my back and I'll scratch yours." Landis had tried to plug the hole in the waiver loop in 1922. June 15 is only a theoretical bar. Griffith wanted the rule tightened.[20]

Southworth responded with, "Well we have 12 games with the Cubs and we currently hold a 7–3 edge. So we will take our chances for the pennant by beating them." The Cardinals took the final game from the Dodgers and then defeated Pittsburgh four of five. After a four game set with the Reds they would be on the road until August 31. Thus if they were going to make up ground they would have to do it on foreign soil.

By the end of the month Chicago (58–32) had stretched its lead to six games over St. Louis (53–39) and Brooklyn (54–40). Pittsburgh, after the four game loss to the Cardinals, was all but out of it at 49–46, 11½ games back. Adams continued to push toward the 100 RBI mark with 71 while batting .293. Barrett's six game win streak was stopped as he dropped to 12–7, while Burkhart was 10–5. Brecheen was back in the rotation and was now 5–2. It was hoped that he could start the rest of the way. That would give them a trio to match Chicago's, but they now had a quartet with the addition of Borowy. Passeau, Wyse and Derringer were a composite 34–15.

Another factor, besides injuries, that haunted St. Louis this season was the inability to win against the sixth, seventh and last place teams. Southworth said you defeat the second division teams and break even with the contending teams and that was how you won pennants. That was also the message McGraw always gave his players and it helped him win ten pennants. The Cardinals were just 22–21 versus Boston, Cincinnati and Philadelphia, but 37–19 against Chicago, Brooklyn, Pittsburgh and New York. The Cubs had followed the old McGraw theory and were 38–8 against the last three teams, but only 25–26 against the other four contending clubs. The Cardinals were 8–7 against Cincinnati, while Chicago was a whopping 17–1 and there lay the reason Chicago was first and St. Louis second.

It seems the Cardinals couldn't keep a totally healthy squad. Shades of 1941? Just when Brecheen, Wilks and Kurowski were back, the team lost Schoendienst and Hopp. Schoendienst was out with an arm ailment. He couldn't throw, while Hopp was having back problems.

Rickey bought the Dodgers for $750,000 for 50 percent of the stock. He and a group of associates acquired 50 percent of the estate owned by Charles Ebbetts. Rickey would now be in the driver's seat and run the team the way he wanted and build for a run of championships as he did with the Cardinals.

Cubs' fans were now ecstatic and said 93 victories would give them the title. The Redbirds, despite hobbling on one leg, weren't ready to concede anything. Injuries continued to dominate the team as Kurowski was again forced out with an ailing arm and Marion was out with a bad back. Southworth said there hadn't been a game this season that he could put his entire regular team on the field. No sooner did one player get well than another went down with an injury. There hadn't been a game in which four or five players hadn't been hurt or ailing. Wilks was back, but couldn't start; he just did occasional relief duty. Creel was still out and Schoendienst, while playing, couldn't throw properly. Yet the team fought on with that Cardinal do or die spirit for which they had become famous over the past two decades.

By mid–August the Cubs had built a six and one-half game lead on St. Louis and eight and one-half on Brooklyn. In Chicago they no longer called St. Louis the Redbirds, but the dead birds. The Cubbies were rooting and having their fun. The Cubs planned on the K.O. punch for the August 24 visit at Wrigley Field. The team had been in first since July 8 and had been waiting for St. Louis to come to town. The Cardinals had been 13–6 on their road trip, but the Cubs had done even better. The standings on August 23 showed Chicago at 74–39, six and one-half games ahead of St. Louis, who were 69–47. Brooklyn had faded at 63–51 to 11½ back and Durocher, after his boast, was extremely quiet.

Holmes still led in the batting race over Cavaretta .371 to .363. Wyse was now 18–7, Passeau at 13–4. The Cardinals had picked up as Brecheen, now in the rotation, was 8–2 while Barrett at 17–8 was headed for the 20 win circle. No matter who played on the Cardinals they were imbued with that winning spirit and never conceded defeat to the other side. It was the do or die nature of the Redbirds. It's that contagious and analogous to the Notre Dame do or die fighting spirit.

This had been Southworth's greatest managing job. He didn't have the talent of the 1941–44 teams, but had made do with what he had and struggled through a rash of injuries and the team fought on. When you consider all the personnel losses and injuries it was extremely surprising to find the Cardinals challenging for the pennant as much as they did.

Chicago planned on the coup d'etat in Chicago, but instead got swept as Burkhart, Brecheen and Barrett held the league's highest batting average team to two runs in three games. The Cubs were up seven and one-half games and seemingly had it won. Then they lost five in a row while the Cardinals won six and all of a sudden it was a race again. The Cardinals were just two behind and anything could happen. The situation was similar to 1942 when they trailed the Dodgers by 10 games on August 6 and went on to win it all. The Cardinals were now 10–3 versus Chicago for the season and now the Cubs were singing the St. Louis Blues.

As August ended Chicago was 74–43, two and one-half games ahead of onrushing St. Louis, who were now 73–47 and playing their best ball of the season. Brooklyn, New York and Pittsburgh, while not mathematically eliminated, were too far down the list. As the final month approached Adams had 96 RBIs and a .290 average while Kurowski had 75 RBIs and a .322 average. Barrett was 18–9, Burkhart 14–7 and Brecheen was 8–3. The Cubs had Wyse at 18–8, Passeau (14–5), and Derringer at 14–7. Borowy was 4–1 and had made the difference. Remove his record and you have a tie for first place. The slippery way the Cubs received Borowy now loomed large.

The largest crowd (36,701) to see a Sunday game since 1939 saw the Redbirds drop a double-header to Cincinnati and they now trailed them 9–8 on season play. Chicago was 21–1 against the same team. The Cardinals were just 27–26 versus Cincinnati, Philadelphia and Boston. St. Louis rebounded and took three of four from Chicago when they came to town. They could have taken all four except for a great throw by Lowrey that cut down Adams at home plate with the game tied 1–1 in bottom of the ninth. The Cubs then won it in the 10th 4–1 on a three run double by pinch hitter Pat Secory. Lou Klein returned from the service and Southworth hoped he would show his 1943 form in time to help down the stretch drive.

Larry McPhail asserted that Pacific Coast major league baseball was at least 10 years in the future. One of the main problems was transportation as airline equipment had not reached the level of standard travel fare. Also, except for major league style ballparks in Los Angeles and San Francisco, the rest of the league would not be in a competitive mode. McPhail asserted that thinking of major league status for the West Coast was a little premature. It would also wreck a great top of the line minor league when you took out the two key cities.

As the first week of September ended the Cardinals found themselves once again trailing the Cubs by four games. The rest of the pack was at least eight games behind. In fact, New York, which was 71–56, would finish the season just two games over .500 at 78–76. The Cardinals squared off with a thin and patchwork pitching staff while Chicago had four solid starters, although Passeau and Derringer were showing signs of age and tiring. They were 36 and 38 respectively.

The Cardinals then dropped two to the Pirates, but bounced back by taking three of four from Boston and finished with a 12–10 edge. While this in itself was not scintillating, when you consider they lost the first five games to the Braves, it was a nice turnaround. The Cardinals had five games left with the Cubs over whom they held a 13–4 edge on the season, so all was not lost. Another blow to the Cardinals as they discovered Wilks had bone chips in his right elbow and would need surgery and would probably be out for the balance of the season.

By the middle of September St. Louis had whittled the deficit to two and one-half games, as they were 82–53 and the Cubs were 84–50. It didn't look like 93 victories would do it for Chicago, as St. Louis was on a pace to win at least 94. Meanwhile in the batting race Cavaretta had inched ahead of Holmes, .361 to .357. Wyse was 18–9, Passeau 15–6 and Derringer was 15–8. The real helper had been Borowy, who was 7–2. The Cardinals had the league's first 20 game winner in Barrett at 20–10 (18–7 as a Cardinal), while Burkhart was 15–7 and Brecheen, now pitching regularly, was 11–3. The team sure missed his left arm in the first half of the season. That would have made the difference and the standings would be reversed.

The Cardinals were tripped up by the Dodgers in their drive for the pennant. Much of the blame can be laid at their own doorstep. On the night of September 14, which was a cold, damp, rainy night, the Cardinals insisted on playing a double-header. This so greatly angered and aroused the Dodgers that they swept St. Louis. The temperature at game time was 50 degrees. Those two games would come back to haunt the club. Their only chance now was to sweep the Cubs in their final five meetings. Meanwhile Chicago had split a double-header with Philadelphia and the Cardinals trailed Chicago by three games. Hal Gregg and Vic Lombardi defeated Barrett and Burkhart in the double-header. Despite all their problems the team had gotten this close and maybe blew it by forcing Brooklyn to play a double-header on a cold, rainy night. There was five inches of rain in 36 hours.

As the third week of September ended Chicago held a three game edge on St. Louis via a 90–53 mark versus 87–56. Cavaretta now held a 10 point edge on Holmes, .360 to .350. He had led the league for three-fourths of the season. Kurowski's average (due to injuries) had fallen to .310, but he also had 86 RBIs. Adams had also slumped and was at .281, but 106 RBIs. Barrett was 21–11, Burkhart 16–7 and Brecheen 13–3. Not a bad trio. Wyse was 19–10, Passeau 16–6 (he would be 1–3 in his final four decisions), Derringer was 15–9 (he would be 1–2 in his last three games) and Borowy (the life saver) at 8–2.

The history of the Cardinals for the past 20 years had been that they were often in the chase until the last week of the season. This also made for great attendance as this was the fans' dessert. St. Louis would make their final bid on the road. They started with a two game set in Chicago on September 25, over whom they held a 15–5 edge. They then had a postponed game with Pittsburgh and three with Cincinnati. The Cards dropped one of the games to Chicago 4–1 in 10 innings after leading 1–0 in the bottom of the 9th. Chicago scored and tied the game on a Kurowski error and a Pafko single. Erase that defeat and we had a different race.

When the series ended Chicago was 92–55 and St. Louis back one and one-half games with a 91–57 mark. The season would finish with Chicago at 98–56 and St. Louis, with a gallant effort riding a worn out injured horse, at 95–59. In the World Series Chicago had the pitching and batting edge, but lost the series to Detroit four games to three. Borowy won two for Chicago, but also lost two in the World Series.

Cavaretta captured the batting crown at .355 with 94 runs scored and 97 RBIs, as he was awarded the MVP title. In this writer's opinion it belonged to Holmes, who batted .352 with 125 runs scored, a league best 47 doubles, a league high 28 home runs and 117 RBIs. He also drew 70 walks while fanning just nine times. In other words, he hit over three times as many home runs as he struck out. Unfortunately he played for Boston (mired in sixth place with a 67–85 record).

Wyse led the pitchers with 22–10, Passeau (17–9) and Derringer (16–11), both weakened down the stretch. The savior was Borowy at 11–2, a 2.14 ERA (league best), 11 complete games in 14 starts and one save in his only relief appearance. His complete game totals dispute the rationale given by McPhail for his being put on waivers. It had been stated that while he was 10–5, he had just seven complete games in 18 starts and hadn't gone the distance in over a month and could no longer pitch complete games consistently. As stated earlier the entire process by which Chicago acquired Borowy smelled like a barrel of week old fish.

Another factor that Chicago greatly escaped was the injury jinx. None of their leading pitchers were sidelined and their outfield of Pafko (110 RBIs in 144 games), Nicholson (88 RBIs in 151 games) and Lowrey (89 RBIs in 143 games) missed just a composite of 27 games. The Cardinals' outfield of Adams (140 games with St. Louis and 14 with Philadelphia), Hopp (104 games in the outfield) and Schoendienst (110 games in the outfield) missed 96 games. Also both Schoendienst and Hopp were forced to relieve Marion and Sanders in the infield when they were out with injuries. The injury list of the Cardinals' pitchers has been well detailed. Just to use one example this could have and probably would have made the difference—Brecheen. When he was finally able to pitch on a regular basis he started 18 games, completed 13 and finished the season at 15–4 with a 2.52 ERA. Give him an additional 15 starts for the first half and the reader can see another 10–12 Cardinals victories and another World Series appearance. Now the team would have to wait for the returning war veterans.

SEVEN

1946

When Johnny Comes Marching Home

As the 1945 baseball season drew to a close, fans, owners and players alike were waiting with bated breath for the return of the veterans from the military service. They all knew it would be a new game again. Many of the current players realized that their sojourn in the majors would undoubtedly end, as their positions would be taken by the returning veterans.

A bombshell tossed at Commissioner Chandler turned out to be a dud. There was a rumor that at the annual joint major-minor league meeting in December he would be offered a buyout of his seven year pact at $50,000 per season. President Will Harridge of the American League and President Ford Frick of the National League called an emergency meeting and 13 club owners attended. Harridge and Frick had prepared statements that denied the rumor and Chandler related he knew nothing about it and would read the story in the papers. The statement was handed to Chandler on October 8 just before the start of game six of the World Series. The rift supposedly was tied to Chandler wanting to raise the umpires' salaries for the Series from $2500 to $4000. The decision was not to buy out Chandler as it would have made the owners look bad in that they would have picked the wrong man.[1]

Breadon saw three Chicago defeats and the only time he was happy was when Chicago won game six, 8–7. He said, "We seem to be the only club that has held up the National League in World Series play, as we had won five of eight series. That was a far better average than that of other clubs in our league who had been in a number of World Series."[2]

With the return of the veterans the biggest trading in 30 years was expected. Player turnover was expected to be the largest since the old Federal League folded after the 1915 season. The path was being cleared for returning war veterans and stars and many current players knew their jobs would disappear and the only future for them would be in the minor leagues, at least for the foreseeable future.

For the first time since 1928 St. Louis exceeded 1,000,000 in attendance as the Cardinals drew 595,000 while the St. Louis Browns drew 482,986 for a total of 1,078,206. The 1928 attendance was 1,117,646 with the Cardinals drawing their all time high of 778,147 and the Browns drawing 339,497. The 1945 attendance was the Cardinals' sixth best and the Browns' fourth best. The Cardinals drew better in 1945 than they had in 1942–44 and it was their best since 644,978 saw them play in 1941. The Cardinals' road attendance for 1945 was 870,542.

The Cardinals and Chicago Cubs played to 424,961 with 169,053 in St. Louis while 225,908 went through the turnstiles at Wrigley Field. Breadon said he didn't want to start hiring business managers for the minor league teams until he saw how many and what players were returning from the service and where they would be assigned. The Cardinals received good news in that Max Lanier was discharged and Walker Cooper was transferred from Great Lakes Naval Training Station in Illinois to Lambert Field in St. Louis and was expecting a quick discharge. The veterans were coming home.

Larry McPhail said what led to Borowy's downfall and his trade to Chicago was a game against Detroit on July 15. With one out in the fourth inning Doc Cramer singled, Rudy York walked and then Bob Meier flied out. Then pitcher Zeb Eaton pinch-hit for Detroit pitcher Al Benton and Borowy got two quick strikes on him and then he grooved a pitch and Eaton hit a three run homer into the left field upper deck. It was the longest home run hit in Yankee Stadium that season. McPhail said, "Borowy was through around here." He was given one more chance against the Chicago White Sox a week later and muffed that one. That did it. He had been knocked out in five consecutive starts and his last complete game had been on June 24 in a 13–5 victory over Philadelphia, who touched him for 11 hits that day. McPhail was convinced he lacked the stamina to be a winner after mid-season and thus sent him packing. He would be 11–2 for the Cubs with a 2.10 ERA and 12 complete games in 14 starts. He also won two World Series games. He was the reason the Cubs defeated the Cardinals for the pennant. Take away his record and they finish second.[3]

The anti-discrimination law became effective July 1, 1945, in New York state and the Negro player issue was headed for a showdown. The recently passed New York state statute was cited by Branch Rickey. However, Jackie Robinson was signed by Montreal and would not be playing for the Dodgers in 1946. It was quite conceivable the story had more attention than it truly deserved. John McGraw had a Negro player at Baltimore many years ago and after a short while was forced to let him go. In this situation Robinson had not been signed by Brooklyn, but Montreal, a Brooklyn farm team.

Rickey told New York writer Dan Daniels, "Robinson was not now major league caliber material and there was not a single Negro player in the country who would qualify for National or American League status." Robinson said, "I found on my arrival at Brooklyn that Negro teams had played in Ebbetts Field and believed something should be done to give them an opportunity to display their talents or skills."

When asked about hotel, restaurant, and train reservations, Robinson replied, "If I'm not wanted I won't stay." Most players, managers and owners said it wouldn't work. Whites and blacks could not play and live together six months out of the year. They also argued it would break up the Negro leagues. The Yankees were currently receiving $100,000 annually from Negro ball clubs in New York, Newark, Kansas City and Norfolk. Robinson was quoted as saying, "Guess I'm a guinea pig." Owners, general managers and managers said returning veterans should be given a chance before anyone else was considered.[4]

It looked like the Cardinals' keystone bag would be a bit overcrowded come spring camp. They had Lou Klein returning from the service and he had played second in 1943 and had a standout season. Jimmy Brown could play all three infield positions and had played regularly for the team from 1937–1943 and was a star in the 1942 World Series triumph. Emil Verban held the job during 1944–45 and was the best fielder, but the weakest hitter of the three. Breadon said he was like the old lady who lived in a shoe as he would have so many Redbirds he wouldn't know what to do.

Muddy Ruel was named top assistant to Chandler. His role would be to assist players in having a greater voice in the game. He had a very distinguished background, as he was a lawyer, former player, coach and understood the needs, wants and problems of the players. This action would also help forestall any attempt at a players union, which was being attempted in the Pacific Coast League. The players' representation would be heard at the highest level. It had long been recommended, but was fought off by the late Judge Landis.[5]

Southworth, even though he had one season to go on his contract, had asked permission to talk with the Boston Braves who were very interested in him. Breadon consented, saying, "If he can better himself elsewhere, so be it." Southworth was the most successful Cardinals manager in their history. For five and three-fourths seasons his record was a gaudy 578–300, almost a .667 winning percentage. From 1941–45 his teams won 508 games, an average of almost 102 games per year. He was offered a three year contract by Boston and Breadon wouldn't match it. Southworth was extremely popular with fans and players alike. He would be sorely missed. Eddie Dyer would pilot the team in 1946. Southworth would be reunited with Morton Cooper, his pitching ace of 1942–44. Meanwhile the Cardinals had to rebuild their two top farm teams (Rochester and Columbus) which finished last in 1945.

Dyer would stress youth and inside baseball. Many of the current or returning veterans played for him in the minor leagues and he had their respect. He won numerous flags for various Cardinals minor league teams. All Dyer asked of a ballplayer was to stay in shape and play winning baseball. He planned on coaching at third base. His major league career was mediocre as he was 15–15 as a pitcher and .223 as a hitter. Howard Pollet, Ted Wilks, Harry Brecheen, Ernie White, Johnny Grodzicki, Howard Krist, Al Brazle, Murray Dickson, Ken Burkhart, Freddy Martin, George "Red" Munger, Enos Slaughter, Augie Bergamo, Johnny Hopp, Walt Sessi, Walker Cooper, Erv Dusak, Klein and Brown all played at various times for Dyer in the minors. This team in and of itself was quite impressive and of championship caliber.

Breadon already had Southworth under contract and had no thought of him not managing the team in 1946. However, when Lou Perini, owner of the Boston Braves, offered Southworth a huge contract ($35,000 per season), guaranteed through 1948, Breadon wouldn't stand in his way. Breadon then went to Dyer, who didn't want to leave his oil business. After several tension filled days he finally told Breadon he would accept the job. Now things looked bright for the future as with the returning veterans, more good youngsters in the minors, everything boded well for the next several years. Breadon saw several more pennants and World Series titles in the Cardinals' crystal ball.

Chandler was extremely specific in outlining the rights of the returning veterans. They would receive the same salary they had when they left, receive a fair trial for a position and guaranteed 15 days' pay if they were let go before the start of the season. If a player was brought up from the minors to a higher minor league or to the majors, he was guaranteed a 25 percent pay increase. If a player was sent down to the minors or a lower level, the club had to ask waivers on him and pay the difference between contract figures. No player could be sent to the minors without staying 30 days in training camp or 15 days after the start of the season.

Basically St. Louis fans accepted Southworth's departure in good stride. They had become used to managers coming and going over the years. So this was really nothing new, even though he had been the most successful. Although he was extremely successful and popular many believed he made a mistake, considering the talent of the two teams. However, only time would tell the full story. The question one might ask is what would Southworth have done with the Cardinals teams of 1946–49? An interesting subject and question.

A committee appointed by New York City, Mayor Fiorello La Guardia investigated organized baseball's color ban, but to the surprise of many, issued a report that was in part an indictment of the Negro Leagues. Mayor La Guardia said the "only reason for qualifications for the major leagues should be skill. However, before Negro players can join the major leagues, the Negro leagues must clean up their own problems. They had loose and non-binding contracts, players jumping from one team to another, close decisions and players' misbehavior are often overlooked by authorities because they dared not challenge management as owners were often also president of the leagues." Negroes had fared well in track, boxing, football and basketball. Why not baseball?[6]

There were two key reasons why Breadon was not making any trades. First, he was not sure what veterans would be back by spring. Secondly, 1946 tax reductions, especially on profits, would be a factor. It would be to his advantage to wait until after January 1, 1946, when the new tax law took effect. There would be an excess of talent and some would have to be sold, but not until after spring training.

Slaughter would be back in time for the season, as he had been in the service since early 1943. However, there was uncertainty as to when Stan Musial, Danny Litwhiler and Walker Cooper would be released from military duty as they entered the service late in the war.

More than 30 leagues would answer the 1946 roll call in the minors. Ten were reactivated and nine new ones were added. The minor leagues were told to clean up the gambling at their ballparks. However, there were no players or umpires involved; it was strictly fans or gamblers. The minor leagues were also cautioned on reckless spending as inflation rose and signing bonuses had to be kept to a minimum.

The Cardinals, who previously favored day games, had now switched positions and wanted more night games. The 1945 figures showed that attendance at night games was much higher than in the daytime. Breadon said you couldn't judge St. Louis by other cities. They needed the night games for better attendance. The Cardinals were prepared to fight any attempt to reduce the number of night games they would be able to schedule. The Cardinals announced they would have 39 players on the active list and 33 from the National Defense List.

Now that the war had ended and peace had returned to the country, the Pacific Coast League began a war of its own. They had not forgotten their prewar ambitions of a third major league and once more began agitating for that status. However, most baseball pundits viewed major league status for the Pacific Coast as premature, citing numerous reasons. Half of the parks were inadequate, namely Sacramento, Portland, Oakland and San Diego. There would be other obstacles to face such as increased salaries for the players, coaches and managers, as well as increased overhead and ticket prices. Those in power wanted to table the program for now.[7]

The minor leagues (after years of restriction and domination by Judge

Landis) wanted more autonomy and less control from the commissioner's office. The minor leagues had also planned to eliminate bonus signing, as this would give them more freedom in their negotiations and activities. The commissioner could still overrule the minors, but must provide in writing a valid reason to the teams and leagues involved. No longer would it just be an arbitrary decision by the commissioner's office. The Pacific Coast League, American Association and International League were all made AAA leagues. This would at least temporarily take the steam out of the drive for major league status. The other two leagues thought they deserved major league status if it was granted to the PCL.

Deals spurted after January 1, 1946, due to the new tax laws that benefited corporate profits. Breadon was in the driver's seat with his surplus of talent. Many teams coveted Cardinals players and were anxiously waiting to make trades and purchases. The rumor mill had Brown going to Pittsburgh and Martin was coveted by Brooklyn. Then Breadon hit the Cardinals with a surprise when he sold Walker Cooper to the New York Giants for $175,000. He had been dissatisfied with the Cooper brothers since their squabble over salaries in 1944. Many players were shocked and dismayed by that action. Cooper had three superlative seasons before going to the military and his right hand bat would compliment the left hand bats of Musial and Slaughter. Adding Cooper with Kurowski to the lineup would have given St. Louis the most potent lineup in the league, if not in baseball. Many thought Singing Sam let his emotions and feelings get in the way of a good baseball decision when he sold Cooper.[8]

Major league baseball was back and Chandler was the authority over the game. Restrictions proposed by the minors were thrown out. The major league owners spiked the move to take the promotion program from the committee and rejected the bonus plan. This same group also turned down the Pacific Coast League's request for major league status. The owners agreed to allow bonus signing for AA classification and up, but not below. Unrestricted night baseball was allowed everywhere except Sundays and holidays in the minors. The Pacific Coast League said it would be back, but not with hat in hand. Next time they would be fully prepared, they vowed.

It was beginning to look like several big deals were on the horizon for the Redbirds. The Cardinals expected four or five trades to be coming their way. It now looked like Brown was targeted for Pittsburgh. Breadon now told fans, scribes and players, "We wanted Cooper only if he wanted to play in St. Louis and was satisfied." Many didn't believe or accept that story. Brooklyn now had 17 farm teams and wanted more. They were second only to St. Louis's 24.

The 1946 season promised to be a watershed year. A big season was in the offing. There was the return of the veterans from the war coupled with a huge expansion of the farm system by all teams. Then there was the continued fight over night baseball and strong consideration and care had to be utilized in the handling of the returning veterans. Baseball was facing a new era. It was a different game from the one many left after the 1941 season.

The Cardinals began trimming their roster by cutting utility infielder-outfielder Deb Garms and veteran pitcher Bill Crouch. The veterans planned on being in camp 10–14 days early for extra training and conditioning. While many had played service ball, it still wasn't the same as major league competition. Some had been away from the game for four years. It was a long time.

The Cardinals had been rated the overwhelming favorites to win the 1946 pennant. With the store of wealth and rich pitching system, no one saw any team that could touch the Cardinals. Many were predicting a runaway similar to 1943 or 1944. Some were saying if it was like 1944, the Cardinals wouldn't stumble at the end this time. The Cardinals, with surplus talent, were ready to sell, trade or bargain for the best deal. Breadon knew the Cards were stacked in his favor.

Two hundred and two writers were voting on 21 potential Hall of Fame candidates. These were men who had played from 1900 to 1943. Nominees would need 152 votes or 75 percent to win selection to the Hall. The 202 writers could nominate collectively 150 players, but the number would be narrowed to 21 and then on January 19, 1946, the balloting would take place. From that group only those receiving 152 votes would go into the Hall of Fame.

The Cardinals wanted their final 1946 game to be played at home just in case they won the pennant. Then they would be all set to host the American League opponent in the World Series opener. Most experts had handed the pennant to the Cardinals. This made Dyer uneasy; he reminded fans and players alike that the game was played and won on the field, not on paper.

Frank Crespi, star second baseman of the 1941 team and in the service since 1942, faced another operation. He had broken his leg playing baseball at Ft. Riley, Kansas, and then while in the hospital recuperating he broke it again in a wheelchair race. He had already had several operations and needed one more. It was quite questionable whether he would play baseball again. When his playing days were over, Crespi's goal was to manage in the Cardinals system.

Brown was sold to Pittsburgh for $30,000. The reasons given for his sale were that the Cardinals were overstocked on second basemen, he had been gone since the end of 1943 and that he was now 36 years old. Still he would have made a valuable reserve, even if he could no longer play every day. Cooper and Brown were the last two team captains and both were sold. The rumor mill now had Hopp and Lanier on the trading block. The Giants assumed all risk in the sale of Cooper since he was still in the service. It now was being rumored that Dusak would be traded. While the team certainly had excess talent, there was concern that Breadon was acting too hastily. A few injuries and the club could miss those traded. It was expected all the deals could total

$700,000 for St. Louis. Breadon quickly pointed out Brecheen would not be traded or sold. Brecheen was the kind of pitcher that Breadon wanted for his club.

Hopp was in a precarious position as he was the fifth outfielder behind Musial, Slaughter, Moore and Walker. Hopp's Gas House style of play and high salary made him trade bait. The Braves had also been in the running for Cooper as they wanted to reunite the Cooper brothers. Philadelphia and Brooklyn both made overtures for George "Whitey" Kurowski, but Breadon said no sale. Brooklyn was willing to pay $100,000 for the third baseman, but now with Cooper gone he was the biggest right hand power threat.

A potential $100,000 deal was in the making involving Lanier and Hopp with the Giants. If Breadon wasn't careful he could load up his opponents with talent that would come back to haunt St. Louis. Cash was only good in the bank. It couldn't play on the field. Cooper's decision to accept the trade was heightened when Dyer took over management of the team. He had played for Dyer in Houston and the two did not get along. The Cardinals didn't seem concerned because they had young catchers in Joe Garagiola, Del Rice and Del Wilber and veteran catcher Ken O'Dea. They felt well covered in that department.

All 21 Hall of Fame nominees failed to be elected. Frank Chase was the closest with 150 votes. He was just two votes shy.

The Cardinals received their first piece of bad news when they found out Krist had received a broken jaw in an automobile accident on January 18, 1946. Krist, a mainstay of the bullpen from 1941–43 when he was a composite 34–8, had been counted on as an anchor with Dickson in the bullpen. The severity and longevity of the injury would determine how the pitching staff and team would be affected. In a surprise move all 15 major league teams passed on waivers on Augie Bergamo (who batted .286 and .316 for the Cardinals as a reserve outfielder in 1944 and 1945). With a surplus of outfielders the Cardinals didn't feel they needed him. The surprise was no one picked up a 28 year old outfielder with a career mark of .304 in 496 at-bats. The rap was he lacked power. Still a speedy outfielder that could hit .300 or better would fit into someone's lineup at the top, one would think.

White and Beazley expected to be discharged from the service soon and Dyer would be glad to see them. He envisioned a repeat of White's 17–7 1941 season and Beazley's 21–6 1942 year. Those two would make that pennant look a lot easier. He then had the likes of Brecheen, Lanier, Pollet, Wilks, Brazle and Dickson to fall back on, a pretty strong looking staff. This didn't even count Munger, as no one knew when he would be discharged.

There were 15 players returning from the service that would receive between $20,000 and $60,000 per season. Detroit's Hank Greenberg was the highest paid at $60,000, followed by Bob Feller at $45,000. Joe DiMaggio was at $42,500 and Ted Williams was number four at $40,000. The highest paid in the National League was the New York Giants' Mel Ott at $35,000. Ott, now 37, was only a part-time player, but the full time manager of the team.

Under new rules a returning veteran had to report to his team as soon as he was released from the service. If a player was ordered to report on February 16 and never reported his 30 days were up on March 15 and he received no pay. Under the old rules he could report at his leisure and still receive 15 days' pay. The player's option under Chandler's new rule was removed and therefore players would be reporting quickly.

A feud was broiling between the Dodgers and the Cardinals. Basically it was between Rickey and Breadon, with the latter claiming he discovered the Coopers. Breadon said he got Mort for $75 and agreed to give his brother a tryout. He then got great seasons from the two (including three pennants, two world titles and three second place finishes) and then sold them for $235,000 and 23 game winner Charley "Red" Barrett. Rickey said he discovered the Coopers and Breadon didn't know who they were.

The Cardinals were still smarting from the double-header loss to Brooklyn on a damp, cold September evening which virtually killed their pennant chances. Brooklyn didn't want to play the two games because of the weather, but since it was in St. Louis and the Cardinals were the home team they could force the issue and did. This infuriated the Dodgers so that they proceeded to defeat St. Louis in the double-header and this basically cost them a fourth straight pennant. Had they won those two games they would have been in first place and put the pressure on the Cubs. This, added to the Borowy deal, did them in. However, in retrospect one could almost say the Cardinals did themselves in by insisting on playing those two games that night. They could have been scheduled for another day.

St. Louis now had Slaughter, Moore and Walker back for outfield duty, Musial was still in the service, but said he would be there by opening day. Litwhiler's status of return was uncertain. The big question was who would be the outfielders. The team still had Buster Adams (who hit .292 with 20 home runs and 101 RBIs in 140 games for St. Louis) and Hopp (who batted .336 and .289 in the past two years). Hopp could play first base. There was also concern over the condition of Moore's legs at age 34, thus Hopp would be a valuable asset to have.

The Cardinals were hoping that Dick Sisler (son of Hall of Famer and former St. Louis Browns star George Sisler) would hit similar to his father. Sisler had played winter league ball for Mike Gonzales, the canny Cuban. He said, "If he played every day he hit 30 home runs—ceench." Sisler hit a total of 55 in his career. His only relationship to George Sisler was that he was his son. Yes, Hopp would be a valuable asset to have on the team.[9]

Meanwhile the Cardinals continued selling their excess talent (feeling they had an endless surplus of talent in the farm system). Everyone was hoping that the well wouldn't run dry. Breadon said, "It hasn't in 25 years and look at the record we have put up. Eight pennants, five World Championships, six second place finishes." All that had happened in the past 20 seasons. Breadon sold pitcher Al Jurisch (who never did develop the way he was expected to) and outfielder Johnny Wyrostek to the Phillies. Also rumored on the trade block were pitchers George Dockins and Fred Schmidt.

Dyer said, "Our system was so full of good players we had to sell some of them. It didn't mean we were wrecking clubs. We only have one objective and that was to regain the National League Championship and the World Title. We can't have over 25 men on the team so some had to go."[10] Concern was growing however that St. Louis was acting too hastily in disposing of so many fine players. The fans were saying Breadon was looking only at the dollar signs. They thought the team needed to keep some of those players in case of injuries or if some of the returning veterans didn't perform the way everyone believed.[11]

Major league salaries reached new highs for the 1946 season as they topped the $5,000,000 mark. The Yankees and the Tigers led the American League while Brooklyn led the National League. Not too many years past the total for the National League had been just $700,000. There were some owners claiming inflation and that it was running away with itself. They cautioned restraint in increasing salaries and ticket prices as it could become a vicious cycle. The Yankees' payroll was $360,000.

The Cardinals were faced with holdouts in Kurowski and Marion with the latter wanting $15,000. Certainly as the best shortstop in the league that request didn't seem out of line. Kurowski had just come off his best season and thus a decent raise didn't seem unreasonable. Lanier was also asking for a $1,500 increase (which seemed minimal when you consider he won 17 games in 1944, his last full season in the majors).

Senor Don Jorge Pasquel, president of the Mexican League, said that their seeking major league players was just payback for what the National and American leagues had been doing for years by raiding the Mexican League. He called it just retribution for the major leagues taking Mexican players, such as Luis Olmo. Pasquel said they had $30,000,000 available to make the Mexican League better than the major leagues. They were willing to offer big contracts to Joe Medwick (who was past 34, but they said he could still hit) and Babe Ruth for a managerial position. Pasquel stated, "We believe money talks loud; they were offering three and five year deals, which was security. Salaries were tax free and we would also pay living expenses." Thus it became intriguing to many players to consider.[12]

One thousand major league players would battle for 400 jobs this season. The Cardinals had Sanders and Sisler battling for first base while Klein and Verban slugged it out for second. Moore (age 34 and gone for three years) had to battle Walker to regain or hold his center field position. He also had gimpy legs with which to contend. Schoendienst was also in the hunt for a job, either in the infield or outfield. Dyer initially was not impressed with him, as he batted just .278 against wartime pitching. Dyer said there was no room in the outfield for Schoendienst and the infield was sewed up.

Barrett got a pay boost and the redhead was elated. He told anyone who would listen that with bigger Cards bats (Musial and Slaughter) he expected to have as good a year if not better than in 1945. Remember he was 21–9 with St. Louis and 23–12 overall. His toughest loss in 1945 (and costly in the pennant race) was 1–0 in 13 innings to lowly Cincinnati, whom he had held hitless until the ninth inning. It makes one shrink when you can see how easily the Cardinals could have won in 1945. Dyer continued to be amazed at the pitching talent. His main concern now was how to start seven or eight pitchers. He couldn't get enough work for them. What a dilemma for a manager to have. Most don't have enough pitching. He had too much.

Another Gas House Gang was Dyer's goal. He promised the fans they would see a team with both speed and courage. He was shaping his team for big innings and he then appointed Moore as team captain, believing Moore would provide the fighting spirit to win 16 of 22 games against teams like Chicago as they did in 1945. The only thing they had to do was defeat the tail-enders more consistently. His big inning philosophy was based on the bats of Moore, Musial, Slaughter, Kurowski and Sisler.[13]

More good news came as Wilks looked like the pitcher of 1944 when he was 17–4. Dyer had a difficult job of trimming his team to 11 or probably 10 pitchers. He had so much talent available. Since Walker was six days late he was officially listed as a holdout. Since every team was bidding and asking for Cardinals players, Dyer thought he would also play the same game. He said he would like to have the Dodgers' Pete Reiser. Someone asked him where Reiser would play and he said, "I'll figure it out when I get him. At least he wouldn't be playing against me."[14]

Rickey asked for a ban on all players that jumped to the Mexican League. He wanted Chandler to issue an edict banning them from organized baseball if they jumped to the Mexican League. He said the situation could be very serious and detrimental to baseball. The latest to jump was pitcher Alex Carrasquel of the Chicago White Sox. The total population of the eight teams in the Mexican League was about 1,100,000 while New York City alone had over 8,000,000 and a drawing area of 15,000,000. Players returning from Mexico would have to pay income tax on their earnings. Pasquel charged organized baseball was like a slave market because of the reserve clause which bound a player to his team. Pasquel said, "We treat players right here, not like slaves. U. S. players are bought and sold like so much cattle and have no control over the decision."[15]

Musial was discharged from the Navy and Breadon told him that he could skip the second year of his three year contract (which had a substantial increase). Year one had been 1944 and year two would have been 1945, but Musial was in the Navy. Breadon could have made year two 1946, but chose to make it the third year. Perhaps Pasquel had put some fear into Breadon.

During spring training the Cardinals had some injuries. There was soreness in Moore's right calf. X-rays showed a pronounced curvature in his spine and this made his right leg a fraction of an inch shorter than the left one. This caused muscle soreness produced by an unnatural running position. One possible remedy was building up Moore's right shoe by ³⁄₁₆ of an inch. There was also alarm over a knotty spot at the rear of Beazley's pitching arm near the shoulder, but x-rays showed that it could possibly be cured by diathermy and x-ray treatment. He had yet to throw his first pitch during the initial two weeks in camp.

Chandler warned Mexican League jumpers that they faced a five year ban from organized baseball. He held the door open for those who jumped and wanted to return to the United States. He told the players they could still return, but once the season began it would be too late. The Mexican League was scheduled to start on March 14, but had been delayed until at least March 21 because U. S. manufacturers wouldn't sell them bats or baseballs for fear of antagonizing U. S. organized baseball.

Marion received an increase to $16,000 and was now in camp, while Walker, recipient of a Purple Heart, came to terms and joined the club in spring training. Kurowski was now the lone holdout and concern was expressed that he would not be in condition when the season began. He already had the problem with his short right arm and now missing training and conditioning could set him back further. Dyer was not concerned as he believed he had enough talent to play without Kurowski until he was ready to sign. His team was ready as he had a veteran ball club. Pollet, Martin and Max Surkont pitched seven shutout innings against the Yankees.

There were four key question marks on the pitching staff. Beazley and White both had sore arms while Grodzicki, due to injuries received in the war, couldn't be counted on at this time. He was one of the most promising pitchers in the Cardinals' system prior to the war. He was wounded in the buttocks area which severed a nerve and produced a dropped left foot, which was the push off foot for a right handed pitcher. The injury threatened to be career ending. The other concern was Munger, as no word had been received as to when he would join the team. He had been counted on to be one of the key starters, based on his half season performance in 1944 when he was 11–3 with a 1.34 ERA.

Meanwhile the war of words continued between Mexico and United States over baseball. The Mexican officials disputed the U. S. population count of the Mexican League at 1,109,162. They said it really was 2,016,079 for 1940, but closer to 3,000,000 for 1946 with 2,000,000 in Mexico City, which had two teams. However this was still a far distance from New York City and its 8,000,000 people and 15,000,000 drawing area.

While battling for positions was great for baseball, it did have a downside. The competition had really increased with all the returning veterans. One problem that developed was the overeagerness of the veterans in trying too hard to reestablish themselves. The concern was that serious and perhaps permanent injury could occur. One prime example was outfielder Hoot Evers of the Detroit Tigers who would be out indefinitely with a broken leg and fractured thumb from his overeagerness to regain a starting position. Some questioned whether Beazley and White had hurt their arms in the same manner. It could be safely stated that since Beazley hadn't thrown a ball, his dated to a service connected injury.

The two best outfields in baseball belonged to the St. Louis Cardinals and the New York Yankees. The Cardinals had Musial, Moore and Slaughter while the Yankees had DiMaggio, Charley "King Kong" Keller and Tommy Henrich. They faced each other in the 1942 World Series, except for Henrich, who had been called to the service before the season ended. In game three of the 1942 World Series (won by St. Louis behind White, 2–0) successive great catches won for St. Louis. Musial took a home run away from Joe Gordon and Slaughter robbed Keller. The Yankees trio cost $57,000 plus five mediocre players versus the Cardinals' cost of $2,000 for their trio.

As spring training drew to a close only Musial, Slaughter and Marion were certain of their starting positions. Injuries had held Moore back so Walker was a strong candidate for the center field position. First base remained a battle between Sisler and Sanders, while Verban had a slight edge on Klein (the better hitter) at second because of his defense. Third base had become an enigma with Kurowski being a holdout. The battle was now between Schoendienst, Dusak and Jeff Cross. Catching (with the departure of Cooper, which may have been premature) had become a problem. O'Dea was unable to catch for three weeks and neither Wilber nor Rice had been impressive. There was some good news when Beazley in his first outing allowed just two hits in four innings.

In most major league camps the returning veterans had been winning the vast majority of the jobs. There were many who weren't certain whether the ballplayers after a two to four year layoff could regain their form and win the jobs. However, in most instances the veterans had defeated the young hopefuls, who either went to the bench or back to the minors to wait a call up for a later time.

Of all managers in baseball Dyer was on the hottest spot. He not only inherited a team that had won three pennants, two seconds and two World Series titles in five years, he also replaced one of the most popular and likeable managers the team ever had. They won it all in 1942 and 1944, lost to the Yankees in the 1943 World Series and except for injuries would have won the pennant in 1941 and 1945. They were in the race until the last day of the season. With a break they could have won five straight pennants. Finishing second was not an option for Dyer.

Pasquel told organized baseball that the player raids had just begun. Mickey Owen was the latest to jump to the Mexican League as he would catch and manage the Torreon club. Pasquel was ready to wager $5,000,000 the league would not fold. Vernon Stephens, the St. Louis Browns' hard hitting shortstop, reportedly signed a five year contract to play in Mexico. Needless to say the Browns were quite upset. The New York Giants lost three more players. Gone were pitcher Sal Maglie, second baseman George Hausmann and first baseman Ray Zimmerman.

The Cardinals seemed to be well padded and protected at all positions except in the catching department. With an uncertain future for O'Dea a tremendous burden was placed on Rice and Wilber. The catching department consisted of O'Dea with a chronic sciatic nerve condition, sophomore Rice and untested Wilber. Sure could have used Cooper, some were thinking. With Kurowski in the fold, but not ready for everyday action, Schoendienst was scheduled to open at third base. Meanwhile Sisler seemed to have grabbed the inside track for first base. White had been unimpressive and was sent to St. Louis to have work done on five infected teeth, which may have caused him some problems in his pitching rhythm. Dyer said soon he had to make some drastic cuts in the pitching staff, as he had too many pitchers.

The Browns received good news when they learned that Stephens left Mexico. He told the press, "It was a mistake on my part and I have made peace with my team." Since he returned before the season began he would not be barred from the game. He signed his 1946 contract with the Browns and everyone was happy. Stephens said he got out of Mexico "by an almost spy espionage arrangement." He was aided in leaving Mexico by his father and scout Jack Fournier who drove him to Laredo, Texas, where he walked across the border to the United States. He was happy to be home. He warned U. S. players against going there, that it was not as it had been portrayed. The fields (other than Mexico City) were terrible. Owen also refused to jump and came home. Then he changed his mind and jumped back to the Mexican League. Rickey said he could stay there and rot.[16]

Chandler told the players that jumpers still had time to return as the season had not started. Once it had it would be too late. Player raids showed the bush league facilities of the Mexican League. Many parks lacked clubhouses and the stands had rough boards on which the fans had to sit and view the game. Players fraternized with the opposition and also smoked and drank beer in the dugout. A total lack of discipline and control. Umpires often were targets for angry spectators. Pasquel promised changes and improvements. His goal was to force U. S. teams to double or triple their current salaries.

Kurowski signed for $13,500, but they had to battle for his job as Schoendienst was hitting over .300 and playing a fine defensive third base. Then when Marion got hurt he moved to shortstop and Kurowski took over his old position at third base. Meanwhile Klein took over second base, batting .328 to Verban's .206. Sisler won the first base job over Sanders, batting .412 to his .192 in spring training. Dyer's biggest job was reducing his 22 man staff to 10. His starting five would be Pollet, Lanier, Brecheen, Martin and Barrett. On the eve of the start of the season the Cardinals sold Surkont and Sanders to Boston, which soon would be called the Cape Cod Cardinals, as they had 10 ex-Cardinals on the team.

Martin was a rookie at 30 after spending 11 seasons in the minors. His last four years had been spent in the army. While this was old for a rookie, his credentials were such that he warranted the opportunity. His last full season (1941) before he went to the Army he was 23–6 with a 1.52 ERA at Houston. This was not only old for a rookie, but for the opportunity to make money. However, he was very impressive in spring training and therefore would be in the starting five. Had Beazley or White not encountered arm trouble, the best he probably could have expected would have been a relief role.[17]

Rickey saw a danger of Cardinals runaway, but Dyer was still very much on the spot. While Brooklyn had a rebuilding job, the Cardinals were a set ball club. Rickey saw it as a dog eat dog fight below the Cardinals. Dyer said he was in a strange position because the comments would be, "If he wins they would say Joe Doakes could have done it with that team and if he didn't how could he lose with that ball club." It became almost a no win situation for Dyer.

Dyer continued to be disturbed by the Cardinals' super duper ratings. He said too many things could go wrong. You win on the field, not on paper. The team had lost six of its first seven spring games, then went 23–5 to finish at 24–11 for the spring training period. It looked like outfielder Adams would be traded. He had been told by Dyer when he reported to camp he wouldn't be playing regularly, even though he had an excellent 1945 season. Adams felt he never had a fair chance under Dyer. It would have been different with Southworth. Dyer didn't know what to expect from Beazley, White or Grodzicki and had concerns about Barrett, who had been hit hard all spring. Also he still didn't know when Munger would be out of the Army and what would be his condition.

The American Baseball Guild was formed as an independent labor union by Robert Murphy of Boston, a former examiner for the National Labor Relations Board. He said he couldn't name names, but he had a majority of players on some teams. He was asking for a minimum wage and said in the old days there had been no law behind them. Now players had the NLRAB. Many previous attempts had failed as the players were in a profession and not a trade. No two players had the same ability and each had to be judged by his own performance on the field. Teams could not set a maximum based on performance, perhaps a minimum, but until now all previous attempts had failed.

Murphy also wanted a player to get part of the sale price if and when he was sold to another team. Most thought this type of arrangement and thinking could destroy baseball. Calvin Griffith, owner of the Washington Senators, said this would destroy the reserve clause, which was the foundation of baseball. The guild wouldn't help high salary players. At this time most players felt protected by the reserve clause. They also believed the richest teams would wind up with most of the top talent if there was no reserve clause and the rest would toil for very little in the bottom of the league. They saw the reserve clause as a shield for them.[18]

Sisler started the season on the spot since he was the son of an all time great and Hall of Fame player. Few sons of previous stars had shined. He had a great reputation to live up to. It was hoped that the pressure would not be too much for him. He seemingly had the talent, and the big question was whether it could be brought out and shine in the major leagues.

The Cardinals dropped their opening game to Pittsburgh, then won three in a row over Chicago and Pittsburgh. They won in come from behind fashion on Sunday with a 7–6 victory over Chicago. Kurowski looked shoddy in the game and was replaced by Schoendienst. It was evident that he was not yet in top shape after his long holdout. Rumors persisted that he would be traded, but the Cardinals continued to deny them. During the first week Pollet, Lanier and Brecheen allowed just two runs in three games as they ended week one tied with Brooklyn for first at 5–1. Some were already asking, "Is this another 1941–42 two horse race?" Schoendienst was selected as player of the week on his seven for 20 performance.

There were 90 former Cardinals players in the big leagues. Boston, Brooklyn, Cincinnati and Philadelphia each had 10. There are also four former Cardinals that were managers. They were Frankie Frisch at Pittsburgh, Leo Durocher at Brooklyn, Billy Southworth at Boston and Bill McKechnie at Cincinnati. Sixty-two of the players were with National League teams while the American League had the other 28. The reason the Dodgers had so many was Rickey as he had originally found and signed many of the players and then when he joined Brooklyn he reacquired them.

The Cardinals rushed to a 9–2 pace and then slumped as the mound corps started to show cracks. The biggest disappointment had been Barrett. On April 28 the Cardinals dropped a double-header at Sportsman's Park to their favorite pets, the Chicago Cubs. Prior to this double loss the Cardinals had won 19 of the previous 25, including the first three this season. Lanier and Martin had both pitched good ball, while Pollet and Brecheen had been in and out. One good game, one bad game. Beazley hadn't pitched since opening day, while Dickson and Donnelly had been inconsistent. After the first two weeks of the season Barrett was without a victory. There had also been problems outside the pitching arena. Marion was hit by a Claude Passeau pitch on the right foot and forced out of the game. Schoendienst took over at shortstop and Kurowski came in to play third. Walker was off to a very slow start, just one for his first 17 at-bats.

The end of April showed the first division as Brooklyn (9–3), St. Louis (9–4), Boston (7–4) and Chicago (6–5). The top five hitters were Elbie Fletcher (Pittsburgh) .407, Pete Reiser (Brooklyn) .400, Frank McCormick (Philadelphia) .379, Musial also .379 and Mickey Witek (New York) .379.

Adams (who Dyer said wouldn't play much) was the only other Cardinal over .300 at .357. With Moore nursing an injured leg and Walker not hitting, Adams was given an opportunity and he produced. Pollet and Lanier were each 2–0 with the latter having two complete games in two starts.

Larry McPhail asked for a court order to restrain raids by Pasquel and his members after offers were tendered to Phil Rizzuto and Snuffy Stirnweiss. Pasquel was totally undaunted and not a bit concerned. The hearing was set for May 6, but a temporary restraining order was put in place, pending the final hearing. Meanwhile, Reiser turned down a $100,000 five year deal.

The Cardinals were active in the trade market as they sold Verban to Philadelphia. Kurowski rejected the third Mexican League offer. He said he fought for all the money he could get, but once he signed a contract, that was it. There was no turning back and he honored all agreements he had made. The supposedly runaway Redbirds were slowed to a walk; between rain and hill problems the Cardinals had just one victory for the week ending May 5.

A bright spot had been Lanier, who had won all four starts with complete games and had an ERA below two runs per game. Martin had been consistent both as a starter and in a relief role. Pollet won his first two starts and then was knocked out his next two starts (both on a Sunday). Brecheen pitched a six hit shutout over the Cubs after being routed by Pittsburgh and the Giants. He had pitched eight solid innings against New York and then was hit by four runs in the ninth inning and charged with the loss. Continuing to nurse a sore arm, Beazley hadn't pitched since opening day. Walker was still not hitting as he was just three for 28. The Cardinals picked up veteran catcher Clyde Klutz from the Giants. It was hoped that O'Dea could resume his catching duties shortly. Dyer's pessimism seemed to have come true. You didn't know what was going to happen, who was going to be hurt or not produce. You win on the field, not on paper.

At the end of the first week of May, St. Louis and Brooklyn were tied for first at 10–6, as the latter had dropped four of five games. Boston was third at 8–5 while Chicago and Pittsburgh tied for fourth at 9–9. Musial was the player of the week with a 12 for 20 mark that included four doubles and two triples. The man had returned and was leading the league with a .415 mark. The question surfaced: would he hit .400 for the season? Musial answered the number one goal was winning the pennant and the World Series, adding that hitting .400 would be nice. On the latter only time would tell. He had batted .357 and .347 in 1943 and 1944 against wartime pitching, but there was better pitching in the league now and he would have to hit 50 points higher. However, he added, he was also a better hitter than before he left for the Navy.

Dyer still thought he had a good team, but forecasters that gave him the pennant on a silver platter had caused him unnecessary anguish, worry and headaches. He said that he knew before the season started there were problems with the team, even thought it was a good ball club. Dyer said it was silly making them overwhelming favorites, as they had problems that the critics didn't see or refused to acknowledge.

There were too many question marks on the team. Moore's legs, Beazley's and White's arms, and could Barrett be a winner against the returning veterans as opposed to the players he defeated in 1945? Dyer had difficulty in finding a dependable right hand starting pitcher. Barrett won 23 in 1945, but had no victories thus far in 1946. Beazley hadn't pitched since opening day and he was using Dickson in the bullpen. Dyer contended he might have to move Dickson into a starting position, although he preferred him in relief. Moore was still used sparingly due to leg problems and Walker hadn't hit. Kurowski's long holdout hadn't helped as he was slow rounding into playing condition.

From 1942 through 1944 the Cardinals were virtually unbeatable at home for Sunday double-headers. It had been a different story so far this season as they had only one victory in six Sunday games. They lost double-headers to Chicago and Cincinnati and their only victory was in a split with Boston. To further complicate problems Dyer had to move Musial to first when Sisler was out with a spike injury.

Brooklyn won five of six games to forge ahead with a 15–7 mark by the middle of May, while St. Louis marked time with a 2–2 record and landed in second place at 12–8. Boston was 12–10 while Chicago and Cincinnati were tied for fourth at 11–10. It was proving to be a heated batting race with Musial leading the way at .403 followed closely by Pee Wee Reese at .400, Holmes at .388, last year's batting champion, Phil Cavaretta, at .377 and former Cardinal Wyrostek at .371. Several Cardinals had come alive with Schoendienst at .333, Kurowski now hitting at .310 and Slaughter was at .304. Thus the bats came alive, but the arms seemed to die. Holmes led the league with 16 RBIs and Musial and Cavaretta were second with 15 each.

A New York justice called attempts to lure players malicious acts and denounced Pasquel in handing down his decision. The Yankees were granted a temporary injunction prohibiting Pasquel from approaching their players. May 28 was now set as the date for determining if the injunction should be permanent. Charges of monopoly by Pasquel against organized baseball were proven to be unfounded.[19]

Klutz, who started as a Cardinals farmhand, was back in the fold. He had been regained in a roundabout deal with three clubs on one day. On May 1, New York manager Ott said he had been traded to the doormat of the league, Philadelphia, and Klutz responded with the comment, "At least I'll catch every day." Before he could leave the Chase Hotel in St. Louis the Phillies traded him to St. Louis for Verban. This all happened in the span of less than 24 hours. Klutz was happy as he was now with a pennant contender and had a chance to play in a World Series. He had been a Cardinals farmhand since 1938 and since that time had been with Boston and New York in the National League.

The Cardinals took five of six in Brooklyn, Boston and Philadelphia as Lanier, Pollet and Brecheen showed the way with victories. At this point most wins were coming from the port side of the pitching staff. With this spurt St. Louis edged back into first at 17–9, trailed closely by Brooklyn at 17–10. It certainly looked like 1941–42 all over with many of the same cast, although some new members for both clubs.

Musial led the Dodgers' Dixie Walker .375 to .370. Kurowski had moved his average to .312 and Schoendienst (now injured) was still at .333 and Slaughter had moved up to .312. On the downside Sisler had fallen to .270, while Adams slumped to .267 and continued to slide downward and be in Dyer's doghouse. Lanier remained perfect at 5–0 with five complete games in five starts and his ERA remained below two runs a game. He was headed for 20 to 25 victories. Pollet was number two with a 3–1 record.

Murphy continued to push the union issue and wanted to expand it to include the minor leagues. He claimed to have the majority of players on six teams, but was vague about certain issues and features. He had no affiliation with the AFofL or CIO. Bill Werber, a former major league infielder, said, "Union security was not suited to the game of baseball." Werber was known as a hard negotiator in his time, but did not believe baseball should have a union. Seniority was the cornerstone of a union and it did not and could not apply to baseball. If it did then a manager would be forced to play an aging veteran over a bright, hot, young prospect. Werber added, "Baseball players were highly individualistic performers and there were only 400 of them in the major leagues. No other profession had such a small cadre of performers. With a union baseball would wither and die on the vine," Werber contended.[20]

The Cardinals' pennant hopes were dealt a mighty blow as Lanier (6–0, six complete games in six starts, 1.92 ERA), Martin (2–1) and Klein jumped to the Mexican League. Lanier had a 21–7 career mark against Brooklyn and this would be another blow to the team, losing the pitcher who could defeat the Dodgers in three of four tries. As bad as this situation was, it could have been worse as all three Cardinals outfielders (Musial, Moore and Slaughter) were offered lucrative contracts to jump to the Mexican League.

All three turned down the offers. Musial turned down a $50,000 cash offer that had been put on his kitchen table at his southwest St. Louis home. He said the offer was mighty tempting, but his integrity and the game meant too much to him to accept the money. He added, "What would I tell my son in later years when he said, 'Dad, why did you accept the money and desert your team and ruin your good name?'"

Lanier said he could make more down there in a few seasons than in a lifetime playing major league baseball. He was supposedly offered a $50,000 signing bonus and $30,000 per season for five years. This was not a shock to Breadon as he expected it. He and Dyer had discussed the situation in great detail with all three players before they made their decisions. This was truly a great blow, especially the loss of Lanier, as the pitching on the field wasn't as good as on paper.

Barrett wasn't winning and White had been dispatched to Boston and would never win another major league game, going 0–3 over the seasons 1946–48. Krist never fully recovered from his injury and would be only 0–2 for the season and his career would be ended. Thus three pitchers counted on heavily had produced zero results for St. Louis and now their best pitcher was south of the border. The question now was—did the pennant also go south of the border?

Amid all the gloom and despair there came a bright and cheery note. Beazley got his first complete game and pitched a four hitter against New York on May 23. Maybe he was going to round into form and be the pitcher of 1942. He was just 28, when the supposed prime years of a pitcher began. Then in his next start he lasted just two innings and left for Nashville, Tennessee, to have his arm examined. Joe Garagiola, the highly touted St. Louisianan, was discharged from the Army and joined the team and caught Burkhart in his first game. The Cardinals tried five catchers for the year and eventually Rice and Garagiola would do the bulk of the catching. Oh, for Walker Cooper!

Brooklyn ended May in first place at 23–11 with a two game bulge over St. Louis at 21–13. With Chicago at 16–16 and Cincinnati at 15–15 it was beginning to look like a two horse race. Philadelphia, who had been the doormats for the past almost 15 years, were there once again at 6–24. However, they would come to life and go 63–61 to finish in fifth at 69–85. Musial (.374) and Walker (.369) continued battling for the title, while Slaughter and Holmes were tied for the lead in RBIs at 26. With Lanier gone Pollet now took over the mantle of ace of the staff and moved his record to 4–1.

The Dodgers' suit to halt the Mexican raids was dismissed. Also there was no evidence that a *St. Louis Star Times* sportswriter conspired to support Mexican parties in an effort to lure U. S. players to the Mexican League. A court ruled, "He was just inspired by the zeal for a scoop." It was further reported by columnist Drew Pearson that Jorge and Bernardo Pasquel were on the U. S. blacklist in 1941 for trading with the enemy (Germany).[21]

The Cardinals were now scraping the bottom of the barrel for pitching. Their pitching staff, once the envy of baseball, was now in deep trouble. Between holdover pitchers Barrett, Burkhart, Brecheen and Wilks and returning veterans Beazley, Brazle, White, Krist, Lanier, Dickson and Martin it looked like the biggest problem was finding enough work for all the pitchers. Such was not the current situation. Pollet and Brecheen were pitching effectively, although the latter wasn't winning because they weren't scoring runs when he pitched. Dyer's number one problem now was to find a pair of good starting right hand pitchers. Burkhart had pitched a few strong games, but Barrett had done nothing and Wilks did well in relief then hit hard when he started and Beazley still had a sore arm. Also there was no word as to when Munger would be available.

As the first week of June ended Brooklyn (28–14) had increased their lead to three and one-half games over St. Louis (24–17) and fans were now wondering were the Cards going to have to have another hot August and September to win it all. To add to the woes Musial had gone into a slump and fell to .340, while Walker had zoomed to a 39 point lead at .379. Schoendienst was at .359 while Kurowski was at .327 and Slaughter was hitting .304 and led the league with 30 RBIs.

Pasquel continued to hound Musial and tried to wear him down and lure him to Mexico. He had offered him a five year deal worth $130,000 which included a $50,000 signing bonus. Musial had told him he needed a day or two to think it over and then turned it down. Musial said he was young and should be able to make a lot of money for a long time in the U. S. Also, he didn't want to leave St. Louis. Breadon was quite satisfied with his decision. He said Stan would be a Cardinal forever. Meanwhile the New York Yankees suit was tabled until October 18, 1946. The Internal Revenue Service said the jumpers would pay income tax when they returned to the U. S.

A baseball strike was averted, but the guild stayed active in trying to solicit members. Pittsburgh players had voted against refusing to play night game on June 7 with New York. However, they were still guildsmen, but they did not intend to pursue a striking course anymore this season. They went into the meting at 6 PM and a heated debate lasted until 7:15 PM. They decided not to strike and the vote was 20–16 in favor of the strike. However, prior to the meeting it had been agreed it would take a three-fourths majority to strike. They then completely dissipated any rumors of dissension with a 10 run (tying season high) 15 hit victory over New York, 10–5.

Murphy was barred from the meeting by manager Frisch when he went to hold a meeting with the team prior to the start of the game. Rip Sewell and Brown were avowed anti-guild and they led the opposition. Lee Handley, Pittsburgh third baseman, said club president Bill Benswanger's talk with them persuaded them not to strike. He had always been fair with the players. Many didn't believe the strike or the guild to their benefit. They also cited family reasons. Benswanger said, "Players could come to him individually anytime they had a problem and Murphy didn't like that." The Pittsburgh players had a lot of respect for Benswanger. Most fans were glad there was no strike. Out of all of this would probably come a minimum salary and most players believed the union was not to their benefit.[23]

The Redbirds were finally chirping as Barrett picked up his first win of the season with a one hitter in a near perfect game on June 6 against Philadelphia. Dyer was hoping this was just the first of many more victories to come and maybe he had found his right hand starter. Most prognosticators believed if Beazley didn't have arm problems and that Lanier and Martin hadn't jumped then Barrett would probably have been gone by now. Del Ennis' one out single in the 8th inning was the only base runner against Barrett. The Cardinals sold Litwhiler to Philadelphia for $15,000, where they got him from in 1943.

Just when it looked like Brooklyn would pull a runaway and open some daylight they slumped and lost five of six and only one game separated the two teams. Walker continued to lead the league with .376, while Hopp had moved into contention at .342 and Musial was third at .340 and Schoendienst next at .338 with Kurowski at .313 and Slaughter at .295, but with a league best 35 RBIs. Many fans were saying they sure could use Hopp in that lineup now. With Walker and Adams both below .200, his .342 mark would have helped win several more games and had the team in first by three or four. Pitching problems continued as Pollet (the new ace) was just 4–3. Brecheen pitched effectively, but the team didn't score for him. Beazley was 2–1, but couldn't pitch.

Garagiola was spotted as a 14 year old playing sandlot ball in the hill district in south St. Louis. He played in the minors for two seasons before going into the service. He remembered being eight years old and watching Schoolboy Rowe pitching against the Cardinals in the 1934 World Series. Now he was going to face him as a 20 year old rookie in 1946. Breadon believed that after two or three years in the league Garagiola would have Cooper's hitting and catching skills and a much better disposition.

After his brilliant one hitter Barrett's next two appearances were busts. He was pounded hard in relief by the Dodgers on June 12 and then lasted just one and one-third innings against Philadelphia in his next start. Thus Dyer was back to searching for at least one dependable right hand starter. Even though Sisler's hand was better Musial continued at first base. The hitting that was supposed to be so robust hadn't materialized, except with Musial, Slaughter, Kurowski and Schoendienst. Then the pitching, which was supposed to be the best in baseball, hadn't been what it was from 1941–45. Pollet, who was expected to pick up the slack with Lanier's departure, was winless in over two weeks.

Breadon made a trip to Mexico and visited Pasquel. He called it a peace trip. He said the trip was only for himself, but he would report the results to the joint major league committee. He denied rumors that the Cardinals were for sale. He said he was not trying to sell the club to the Pasquel brothers. Then Singing Sam added, "Of course if someone offered me five times their value I would have to think about it." A sly old fox was Breadon.

The court ruled any player returning from the service to his club was protected by the Selective Service Act and couldn't be fired by his club without being paid one year's salary. Organized baseball was legally and morally bound by this agreement. This had far reaching effects regarding the decision in the case involving the Seattle Pacific Coast League team in the Al Niemec case. The court ordered the team to reinstate the infielder as he was entitled to one year of employment under the act. This opened the door for claims by many ex–GIs. The act and decision affected 143 major league players and an undetermined number of minor leaguers as this decision was upheld.[23]

The Cardinals placed six men on the all star team. They were Musial, Slaughter, Marion, Kurowski, Pollet and Brecheen. In addition four former Cardinals were also on the team. They were Mize, Hopp and the Cooper brothers. Fans asked how far in front would St. Louis be if Hopp was in the outfield with Musial and Slaughter, Mize at first, Cooper behind the plate and Cooper pitching? Perhaps 10 games or more. Shades of 1943–44?

As June neared its end Brooklyn had moved three games ahead of St. Louis, 38–23 versus 35–26. At this juncture St. Louis was baseball's biggest disappointment. They were expected to be way ahead of the pack, but instead they trailed by three games. However, who could have foreseen the jumping of players to the Mexican League, sore arm pitchers and players batting less than .200? Everything considered they still weren't in bad shape. Another disappointment continued to be their Sunday double-header performances. They were just 6–12 with one win, four losses and one split. Not like 1942–44.

Dyer said if they were no worse than five games out by July 4 they could still win the pennant. Many thought his team would be 10–15 games ahead. On the morning of July 3 they were seven and one-half games behind Brooklyn, who was 45–23 while St. Louis was 37–30 and being pushed by Chicago at 36–30. This was a swing of 17 to 22 games over what most forecasters had predicted.

What went wrong? Start with the pitching. Sore arms, players jumped to Mexico and pitchers not performing as expected. Add to that Moore's injury and Sisler's failure to perform as expected. Perhaps he was overrated. The problems included catching deficiencies, Barrett's one win, Beazley's one complete game and now he had a sore arm, Brazle and Burkart were inconsistent, Adams at .183, Walkert at .180 and O'Dea at .123. Hopp's .350 would help. Pollet, after a shaky spell, had pitched well and with Dickson they were the only currently dependable pitchers. Brecheen had pitched well, but the team hadn't hit behind him. A lot of well-pitched games were lost.

A company union plan was likely to offset the guild. MacPhail made a proposal that would set a minimum starting salary for ball players. He had helped form an advisory council, which would include representatives from the players. There would be a panel of three to settle salary disputes, but the reserve clause would remain in place.[24]

The All Star Game was a romp for the American League as they demolished the National League 12–0. Williams hit two home runs and added two singles. He accounted for seven of the runs. He was now hitting .500 in all star play. He scored four runs and drove in five, both new records. He also had 10 total bases for a new record. Williams' home run off Sewell's blooper ball was the first hit off it. The prior longest hit had been Musial's triple.

The Cardinals unloaded more unwanted players. In this case these were not ones that would haunt them for the next several seasons. They sold O'Dea to Boston and Blix Donnelly to Philadelphia, both for the waiver price. O'Dea had expected to be the number one catcher with Garagiola the backup, but his back let him down and he was hitting .100 when sold. Garagiola and Rice would now split the catching duties. Donnelly had performed well in the 1944 World Series and was one of the heroes. He had a good curve, but also arm trouble.

The Cardinals' turnstiles and fortunes both took an upturn before the All Star break. The team won seven of eight including their first double-header win at home (against Pittsburgh on July 7). The Cardinals were inching toward the 500,000 mark and expected to break the season record (1928) of 778,147. The first half ended with Brooklyn at 48–27 and St. Louis at 43–32, five games out. Dyer said there was still plenty of time. Remember 1942.

Pittsburgh currently had 24 players in the guild and a decision would soon be made whether it was legal. The decision was to be made on July 18 and the program was aimed at breaking up the guild. This was the reason management was willing to permit players to participate in drawing up a new contract and helping set other player guidelines.

Meanwhile, back in the baseball wars, the Cardinals were using their old flag system of slapping down their chief opponent as they had defeated Brooklyn in nine of the first 12 games. The Cardinals had drawn 87,047 for a Sunday double-header (July 14) and night games on the 15 and 16 as they played the Dodgers in a four game set. Thus far the Dodgers had won just one of seven games played in St. Louis, while they were tied at two wins each in Ebbetts Field.

John McGraw used to say the way to win a pennant was to break even with the contenders or go 12–10 and then beat up on the second division teams. This was the system he had used successfully to capture 10 National League pennants as the manager of the New York Giants. It had worked well for him and he was a strong believer in the philosophy. It seemed in many seasons the Cardinals beat up on the contenders and played just over .500 ball against the second division teams, although they might have a patsy or two in that group.

Musial was not only hitting for a high average with power and driving in runs in addition to playing an excellent defensive first base. He was already a stand out outfielder and with his natural skills the switch to first base proved no difficulty. Slaughter had broken his slump and raised his average 30 points in the past two weeks. The Cardinals had won the double-header on home runs by Musial and Slaughter. They took game one 5–3 and game two 2–1 in 12 innings. Game three was a runaway 10–4 victory while game four saw Dusak hit a three run pinch-hit home run in the bottom of the ninth to win the game 5–4. However, the pitching remained spotty and Dyer said they sure needed Munger, but there was no word when he would be released from the service and join the team. This sweep had put St. Louis (50–34) in first place, one-half game ahead of Brooklyn (49–34). Pittsburgh was last at 34–48 raising the question, was this due to guild or union activity which led to dissension on the team?

Meanwhile labor issues continued to surface and National League president Frick said salaries less than $5,000 per year were wrong. The players made several new proposals to the owners. Among them were:

• Minimum salary of $5,000 per season
• Establishment of a pension plan
• No reduction in salary if a player is sent to the minors
• Abolish the 10 day notice of the release clause
• Improve clubhouse and dugout conditions.

The players had no opposition to the reserve clause. The owners asked each club to have a player representative and the clubs would name three delegates for the league. There was scheduled a joint meeting on August 20 to adopt a new contract and make changes in the system. Some of the items that would be agreed to included no reduction in pay during the life of a contract if a player was sent to the minors. There would be an expense money allotment of $35.00 to $50.00 per player per week during spring training.

For the pension plan each player would contribute $50.00 per month to be matched by the owners. Also it was agreed that a player would receive part of the sale price, but no figures or percentages had been agreed. It was agreed to abolish playing double-headers after night games, except in the case of a double-header necessitated by a rainout of a prior game. Management also agreed to improved clubhouse and dugout conditions. At this time only 29 players in the league made less than the minimum.[25]

The Cardinals' drive was aided by the pitching of former relief expert Dickson, who was now a starting pitcher. He had defeated the Dodgers in 12 innings on July 14 and then on the 18 he relieved Brazle and allowed two hits in four innings and got the win in a 5–4 game. Then he defeated Johnny Sain, on his way to a 20 win season, 3–1 in 10 innings. In 26 innings Dickson had allowed just two runs, pitched two complete games and was 3–0. For the season Dickson would appear in 47 games, starting 19 and completing 12 during a 15–6, 2.89 ERA season. He had ice water in his veins and a rubber arm.

Prior to the Cardinals' sweep of the Dodgers, Durocher opened his mouth again and inserted his foot. He said the Cardinals were not the team to beat, but the Cubs were the team they had to watch. He said the Dodgers would have to lose eight of nine in the west before anyone would hear of the Cardinals. Evidently he didn't expect the Cardinals to sweep his team. This was reminiscent of Bill Terry and the New York Giants when he inquired whether the Dodgers were still in the league. They showed Terry and the Giants by helping to knock them out of the pennant race in 1930, letting the Cardinals take it all.

The Cardinals completed their homestand with a 16–6 record, including taking four Sunday double-headers. Early in the season the team was just 14–16 at home and had trouble winning Sunday double-headers. In July this was all reversed. Their road record had kept them in the league. They played .641 ball on the road and with their July homestand boosted their home record to .583. They started their eastern road trip one and one-half games out of first as they were 54–36, while the Dodgers were 55–34. Brooklyn had won six in a row after the St. Louis debacle, while the Cardinals went 4–2.

In the batting race Hopp had forged ahead with a .383 mark, Walker was second at .373 and Musial third at .361. Fans were still dreaming of what the team would have been like had Hopp remained a Cardinal. This was especially critical when one realized that Walker and Adams were below .200 and Moore was sidelined with bad knees and legs. The Cardinals were paced on the mound by Pollet (12–4), Dickson (8–3) and Wilks (6–0—all in relief).

The owners said full acceptance of the players' demands seemed reasonable and saw no problems. The concept of dismissed "for cause" would likely replace the 10 days' notice. A resolution committee for settling disputes, cause for dismissal, etc., would be established. The guild was dead with these changes. The new contracts would be ready by September 1 and the goal was to sign as many players as possible by season's end. Ninety-nine percent of the players favored retention of the reserve clause.

This would also help ward off future raids by Pasquel. Thus these new contracts and policies served a two fold purpose. Moore and Marion were appointed as delegates for the Cardinals and the latter was working on the pension plan. He would spearhead this program and later players owed much credit for the effort Marion exerted in this area. The pension plan would pay a player $100.00 per month (if retired) at age 45 to 50.[26]

Meanwhile the Cardinals didn't find their trip to the east to their liking. They dropped five of seven games and scored just 10 runs on 34 hits in those contests. Hitting disappeared during this stretch. Marion was zero for 23 and some of the blame was placed on his work on the pension plan as it was taking all his time and energies. The team did right itself by taking the last two from Brooklyn. In game one they scored 10 runs on 15 hits, including four triples and two doubles. Game two was won on a home run by Slaughter. There was some good news on the pitching front as Beazley looked like he had regained his form, even though he lost both starts. He was defeated 3–1 by Boston and 2–1 by New York. Some hitting would have turned those defeats into victories.

By the first of August Brooklyn was still in first place at 58–37, one and one-half game ahead of St. Louis who was 57–39. Chicago, Durocher's choice for the top contender, was eight games out at 53–48. Walker had taken over the batting lead at .378 to Hopp's .374. Musial was still third at .357 and Mize had joined the hunt with his .345 batting mark. Schoendienst had fallen to .299 and showed considerable signs of wear and fatigue. This showed had sorely Klein was missed, as he could have replaced Schoendienst and given him a rest. Kurowski was at .294 and while Slaughter had dropped to .287 he led the league with 80 RBIs. Moore and Sisler were both at .262 and not playing regularly. Moore was out because of injuries and so was Sisler as he had not produced the potent bat expected.

Pasquel had taken the passports of all American players, making it very difficult for them to leave the country. Owen kept his and fled the country by air, concealing his identity. It was like a cloak and dagger mystery for many of the players. Olmo was fighting to come back, contending he was not under contract with the Dodgers when he jumped. Both wanted to be reinstated. As of now Chandler said that the ban would remain in place.

Only St. Louis had been removed from any further raids by Pasquel because of Breadon's trip to Mexico. Pasquel said he had a letter from Musial, saying he was ready to go south. Musial denied it, stating that Pasquel lied. Owen told the Dodgers he would play for his pre-war salary of $14,500. When asked if he was traded Owen said he would play anywhere. He just wanted back in organized baseball. Stephens said let them stew in their mess. They took the money.

St. Louis fans were wondering if 1946 would be a repeat of 1945 when St. Louis lost the pennant by going just 38–28 against the three bottom teams while Chicago was 53–13, a 15 game swing. St. Louis had a 16–6 edge on the Cubs, but that was not enough to erase the disparity with the last three teams in the league. The Cards had played 41–25 versus the third, fourth and fifth place teams and that same record against the last three would have tied them for first place. This season the Cardinals were 11–5 versus Brooklyn, but 6–10 against the last place Giants and 9–7 versus the fifth place Philadelphia team.

Dyer said this season he had Pollet, Brecheen and Dickson ready for the

Dodgers and Cubs and then had to get by with what he could for everyone else. He could not afford a let down against the other clubs. Last season the Cardinals had Barrett, Burkhart and Brecheen to go against Chicago and Brooklyn and the balance of the staff against the rest of the league. St. Louis would return home on August 15 for a three week homestand and that could determine who would win the pennant. Munger was expected to be ready to pitch by then. The Dodgers and Cardinals had played to 178,432 in Brooklyn for eight games and 177,000 in St. Louis for seven games.

By the second week of August Brooklyn continued to set the pace at 63–40, while St. Louis was 60–41, now two games out. When we review Cardinals history we find that their teams of 1926, 28, 30, 34, 39, 40, 41 and 42 all caught fire and tore up the league in August and September. Fans were waiting for the Redbird express of 1946 to gain momentum. Musial went on a hitting binge with 20 for 30 and Slaughter continued to pace the league in RBIs. Pitching had also improved as from July 20 to August 14 the Cardinals changed pitchers only six times in 23 games, and several of those were for pinch hitters.

Through August 12 the team had eight consecutive complete games. Pollet (14–6) and Dickson (11–3) were still leading the team, but were receiving help from other areas. Brecheen was now pitching winning ball, as the team was getting him some runs. Brazle had consecutive shutouts (a two hitter versus Boston and a three hitter versus Chicago) and even Beazley was showing his 1942 form, although he dropped well-pitched games. By the time St. Louis returned home Brooklyn remained in first at 68–41, while the Cardinals were two back at 65–42. Chicago now looked finished at 57–51, 10½ games out of first place.

Musial (after a .643 clip) raised his average to a league best .374, followed by Hopp at .366 and Walker at .365. Mize was at .337, but out with a broken hand, which would also cost him the home run title. Slaughter had climbed back to .300 and continued to lead the league with 88 RBIs. Kurowski had fallen to .271 with 57 RBIs. Injuries had slowed him considerably. Sisler moved up to .270, but he still was not driving in runs or hitting with power.

Dyer was predicting a photo finish in the race. He told fans that the Cardinals had a rough road to hoe. They went east in September while Brooklyn was at home. In the last nine days of the season the Cardinals would play the Cubs six times, while the Dodgers would have Boston and Philadelphia, which had been easy pickings for them thus far that season.

Through August 13 the Cardinals had been shut out just twice and then on successive days they got whitewashed. Johnny Schmitz and the Chicago Cubs defeated Brecheen 1–0 (they had trouble scoring for "The Cat" again) and the following day Ken Heintzleman and the Pirates defeated Dickson 3–0. Sisler's bat temporarily came to life and at a fortunate time as Musial went into a slight slump with just two for 16. Kurowski was out again with arm trouble and Dusak did a good job filling in for him. The Cardinals found out Munger would be ready to pitch for the team by the end of August. Dyer said they sure needed him.

The guild was about as dead as Pittsburgh (mired in seventh place). Led by the very vocal Sewell they voted it down 15–3 with 12 players abstaining. Then they went out and defeated Brooklyn to try and prove there was no dissension on the team.

McPhail outlined new plans for baseball, which incorporated changes for the players. All National League teams were willing to accept 30 day dismissal notices to players. Only three American League teams were opposed. McPhail had become the powerful management operator in baseball and thus people gave allegiance to him. One other new proposal was a 168 game schedule which would allow each team to play 24 games against their opponents. The reason for this was to help defer some of the costs of the new benefits to players.

Several objections were raised. The players would be playing an additional 14 games or over a 9 percent increase on the season for the same pay. Another argument against the increase was what it would do to all the records, as now a player would have 14 more games to surpass single season totals in doubles, hits, home runs, etc. Player representatives also said they were never appraised of the proposal for a longer season. This would also mean fewer open dates for the teams. It was proposed that the 1947 season would open April 15 and close September 28. The executive council was composed of one player from each team, Chandler, McPhail, Giles, Frick and Harridge plus four representatives from the minor leagues (two would be players). The players would only vote on management-player relationships.[27]

As the season edged into its final month the Cardinals held a two and one-half game bulge on the Dodgers as they were 76–47 versus Brooklyn's 72–48. This edge had been built up around the Cardinals' 13–6 margin over the Dodgers, of which 8–3 was at home. They were also 5–3 at Ebbetts Field. After the sweep of the Dodgers in July at home, Brooklyn bounced back and was able to split the four game set with St. Louis at Sportsman's Park in August.

At that point the Dodgers left tied for the lead and the schedule favored them. The Dodgers attendance in St. Louis for the season was 269,682 and on August 28 the Cardinals set a new home team record attendance at 782,943. World Series hoopla erupted in St. Louis on August 28 when St. Louis snatched a double-header win at home from the Giants while Chicago was defeating Brooklyn in a single game to put St. Louis ahead by one and one-half games. The Cardinals added another game to the lead before the month ended.

Dickson was a gutsy guy and pitcher and had come out of the bullpen and posted 12 victories. He had a rubber arm as he could start and relieve.

He was also a good hitting pitcher, batting around .275. Walker was show-ing signs of his age and his batting mark had fallen to .344 and he was about out of the race. Hopp still hung in there at .364, trailing Musial by just seven points. Slaughter was just under .300 at .294, but had a league and career high 99 RBIs with 31 games to play. Pollet continued to lead the staff with a 17–4 mark while Dickson was 12–4. Brecheen had inched up to .500 at 12–12, despite his ERA around 2.50. The team had not been able to score for him all season, as he could easily have been approaching 20 victories. Wilks was 8–0 coming out of the bullpen, but had just one save to his credit. Pollet led the team with five, followed by Brecheen with three.

There was considerable opposition from the players to the expansion of the season to 168 games. The issues included salary, fewer open dates and records that would become meaningless. After considerable player disgruntle-ment over the proposed expansion the owners acquiesced and abandoned the idea and said the season would remain at 154 games.

The key question for Brooklyn for the 1947 season was where Robinson would play if he made the team. Eddie Stanky was fantastic at second in addi-tion to being a superb leadoff hitter. Reese was second to Marion among shortstops in the league. Third base seem to be the only place open, but Robinson had never played there but was willing to give it a try. He had orig-inally been a shortstop but hurt his arm when Clyde Sukeforth and other Dodgers scouts came to see him play. He was switched to second and won over three other candidates. At Montreal he was leading the league with a .353 mark with one week left in the season. Robinson was an excellent bunter and base runner, but lacked home run power.[28]

A whiff of series cabbage had the Cardinals stirring. Many on the 1946 team had never played in a World Series. Four ex-GIs missed the wartime classics. Veteran newsmen were surprised by the Cardinals' enthusiasm, since they acted like a team that had never been to the fall classic. The sportswrit-ers pointed out that the Cardinals won in 1942–44, almost made it in 1941 and 1945 and therefore this should be an old story for them, but that was not the St. Louis spirit that had been instilled in the Cardinals.

The team went berserk when Dusak and Sessi hit game winning home runs against the Dodgers and Giants. Sessi (a highly prized rookie prior to the war) appeared in only 15 games and had two hits in 14 at-bats, but one was a two out, two strike home run in bottom of ninth for a game winning two run homer off the Giants' Bill Voiselle. Even Breadon went wild as the 70 year old owner leaped over the rail of his box and embraced his players after Sessi's home run. Sessi's career covered just 1941 and 1946 and he appeared in only 20 games with two hits in 27 at-bats, but one was the biggest of his career. He had been a prized rookie, but then spent four years in the Army and was not the same talent when he returned.

Schoendienst, Sisler, Rice, Garagiola, Klutz, Sessi, Adams, Barrett,

Burkhart and others had never appeared in a World Series. Moore, Slaughter, Pollet and Beazley last were there in 1942, spending 1943–45 in the military. Meanwhile Munger picked up his first win of the season. Slaughter hit three home runs on Labor Day to help the Cardinals take three of five from Pittsburgh and Cincinnati on a short road trip. The team had hoped to leave for the east with a five game bulge, but it was just two games by the second week of September. They now figured they had to take two of three from Brooklyn at Ebbets Field on September 12–14.

St. Louis was 82–48 to Brooklyn's 81–51 with just over three weeks left in the season. It now looked like Musial would win the batting crown as he was at .367, while Hopp had fallen to .351 and Walker was at .331. Pollet was closing in on 20 wins at 18–7 and Dickson was 13–5. Slaughter was at an even .300 and had crossed the 100 RBI barrier for the first time in his career and was at a league best 106. Kurowski was on the rise at .286 and had 70 RBIs and looked like he would finish with close to 90.

Pollet and Dickson staggered slightly and Brecheen hadn't won like he did in 1944–45 (31–9), but had pitched as well. The team just didn't score many runs when he was pitching. His record stood at .500, as did Brazle's. Brecheen was 13–13 and Brazle 10–10, thus the addition of Munger looked to be a key down the stretch drive. Dickson had been kayoed four straight games and Pollet was ill with a 102 temperature. He had come back to pitch and gave up six runs to Pittsburgh in four and one-third innings after hurling 12 consecutive complete games. On the bright side Munger picked up his second win just as the team was heading into Brooklyn. They were 46–26 at home and 40–24 on the road.

The Cardinals dropped two of the three in Brooklyn, losing the second game 4–3 when Cross was out stealing second to end the game with Slaughter and Kurowski on deck. Kurowski had been hot and pushed his average to .300 and RBIs at 81, despite missing over 14 games, while Slaughter led the league with 116 RBIs. Many thought it was a bad move by Cross. The next day Branca shut out the Cardinals 5–0. It had looked like St. Louis was home free when they had taken the opening game, but Brooklyn was not to be denied. They didn't roll over and play dead.

It was also here that Musial earned the sobriquet "The Man." Bob Broeg, St. Louis Hall of Fame sportswriter, said it came about when Brooklyn fans started shouting when Musial came to the plate, "Oh, no. Here comes that man again." Broeg liked the name and it was picked up and from this point forward Musial became known as Stan "The Man" or Stan "The Man" Musial. He enjoyed the title, besides hitting in Brooklyn.[29]

Pollet was called the left handed Christy Mathewson as he had poise and skill. Pollet rarely got hit hard and was always a poised and dependable starter and when needed could be brought in to save a game, which he did on numerous occasions in 1946. He had a knack for pitching his best against the toughest pitchers and teams in the league. He became the first southpaw to win 20 games in a season since Carl Hubbell won 22 and Cliff Melton 20 for the New York Giants in 1937. Pollet was a regular fellow in the clubhouse, but like Mathewson had innate refinement, culture and breeding. He had class both on and off the field.

Beazley was not satisfied with his pitching and said he would retire at the end of the season. A once promising career was cut short. His was a casualty of the war. Also casualties of the war were White and Krist. Beazley was just one of many ballplayers that weren't the same on their return. The years away from the game had dulled their skills, while others suffered injuries or wounds that proved to be career ending.

The Cardinals had won eight pennants since 1926, but only three were easy. In 1931, 43 and 44 they steam rolled the opposition. The Cardinals had been in 10 pennant races since 1926 that went down to the wire. Several of them weren't decided until the last or next to last day of the season. They won by two game margins in 1926, 28, 30, 34 and 42. They missed by 1½ games to Pittsburgh in 1927; 1 in 1935 when it took a 21 game winning streak to overtake St. Louis in the final days of the season; 4½ games to Cincinnati in 1939 and this wasn't settled until a few days before the season ended; 2½ to Brooklyn in 1941 settled on the next to last day of the season and three to the Cubs settled in the final weekend of the season. In all but a few seasons the Cardinals were always in the thick of the pennant chase.

The Cardinals had been 6–10 versus the Giants, destined to finish last, but swept the last two series to finish 12–10 against them. They won three in St. Louis in August and swept three at the Polo Grounds in September. At this juncture it looked like Musial would be the batting king, as Walker and Hopp had cooled considerably and Slaughter would be the RBI champ. Kurowski continued his fine hitting at .302 with 86 RBIs. Injuries prevented him from reaching the coveted 100 RBI level.

Some said the Cardinals were aging, but Dyer said they were like fine wine, "They just got better with age." The Cardinals' future was to win with seasoned veterans like Musial, Kurowski, Slaughter and Marion, while working in promising young players like Schoendienst, Dusak and Garagiola. There had been trade rumors about Moore, but the team planned to keep him and hopefully with winter surgery he would regain his old form and give him several more stellar seasons. The Cardinals had been in every race since 1938 (except for 1940 when a terribly slow start doomed them) and the question was what is ahead for 1947?

It was a well known fact that the Cardinals' triple AAA and double AA teams didn't have the same caliber and quality of players that existed before the war and this made many concerned about the Cardinals' future. This was especially true when one considers all the talent traded away (the Coopers, Mize, and Hopp just to name a few) and then the Mexican loss of Lanier,

Martin and Klein. When we add the disappointment of returning veterans such as Krist, White and Beazley there was great concern. The once rich pitching Cardinals could be in for some rough days. On the bright side was that Walker came on strong near the end and finished at .237, plus the team would have Munger for the entire season. Beazley might also change his mind and not retire. The team set new attendance records for the road (1,487,054) and home (1,036,000).

St. Louis and Brooklyn each had opportunities in the final week of the season to win the pennant, but neither seemed to be able to cash in their chips Entering the final day of the season each team had a 96–57 record. Brooklyn was playing at home against Boston while St. Louis was hosting Chicago. The Brooklyn game ended first as former Redbird ace Cooper shut out the Dodgers 4–0. Now all that was needed was a Cardinals triumph and they would have their ninth pennant.

Munger drew the starting assignment and Musial hit a home run that gave him a 1–0 lead, but the big redhead couldn't stand prosperity and was belted out in a five run sixth inning and the Cardinals lost the game, 8–3, setting up the first playoff in baseball history. It was also determined that all records would count as part of the season. Commissioner Chandler decided a coin toss would decide where the playoffs would begin. St. Louis won so the first game was in St. Louis. However, this meant if it went three games, Brooklyn would host two of them. St. Louis wasn't concerned about the Dodgers as they had a 14–8 record on the season and were extremely confident they could take the series.

In game one Pollet pitched brilliantly and defeated the Dodgers behind Musial's 20th triple of the season, three hits and two RBIs from rookie Garagiola and three hits from the laughing Irishman, Moore. Game two looked like a cakewalk as Dickson carried an 8–1 lead into the bottom of the ninth. Then Brooklyn erupted for three runs and had the bases loaded and Brecheen was now in the ballgame. He fanned Stanky, who rarely struck out and then slipped a curve by Howie Schultz, pinch-hitting for Dick Whitman and St. Louis was once again the National League champions.

As if the World Series wasn't enough excitement, news hit the papers that two groups were angling to buy the Cardinals. Louis B. Mayer of MGM wanted to buy the team and move it to Los Angeles, while Mark Strinberg, director of the team and an investment broker, wanted to buy the club and keep it in St. Louis. With the World Series approaching Breadon was deaf to all offers.

Both teams had rich World Series histories, as Boston had been in five and won them all, while St. Louis was appearing in their ninth and had five victories going into this series. For the Cardinals that included a 2–2 split with the mighty Yankees and a 1–1 split with the powerhouse teams of Connie Mack's Philadelphia Athletics in 1930–31. Boston had won 104 games with a margin of 12 games ahead of Detroit. Featuring a batting order of Ted Williams, Bobby Doerr, Rudy York and Johnny Pesky and pitching aces Ferris (25–6), Tex Hughson (20–11) and Mickey Harris (17–9) they were installed as 7–20 favorites. The real battle would pitch hitting star Musial against Williams.

In game one St. Louis held a 2–1 lead in the top of the ninth inning when Boston rallied to tie the game. With one out Mike Higgins' grounder skidded through normally reliable Marion for a cheap hit and then Rip Russell singled him to third base. Roy Partee batting for Hughson struck out. Dyer, calling signals from the bench as rookie Garagiola was catching, called for a fast ball to right hand hitting Tommy O'Brien. When the pitch was relayed to Pollet from Garagiola, Pollet shook it off. Dyer called for the same pitch again and it was waived off by Pollet. Dyer relented and called for a curve and O'Brien got a seeing eye hit past Kurowski to tie the game. Then in the top of the 10th inning York hit a home run against the hot dog stand in the left field bleachers and the Cardinals lost 3–2.[30]

Game two was pitched brilliantly by Brecheen as he shut out Harris and Boston 3–0. He also drove in one of the runs. Game three was all Boston as Ferris blanked the Redbirds 4–0 before a screaming crowd at Fenway Park. The big blow was a three run home run by York off Dickson. He had been the key man in the first two Boston victories. In game three Munger took the mound against Hughson and the press box cynics wondered if St. Louis could score enough for the big, squeaky voiced guy who wasn't nearly as tough as the king sized wad of chewing tobacco in his jaw.

Munger didn't have to be brilliant, but he held Boston to three runs, while St. Louis set a World Series record banging out 20 hits in a 12–3 victory. Slaughter, Kurowski and Garagiola each had four hits. Frustrated by his failure to hit more than by the unorthodox defense, Williams bunted for a hit toward third base. The headlines in the Boston papers read: "TED BUNTS."

In game three Pollet lasted only a third of an inning and was charged with three runs in a 6–3 loss to Chuck Dobson. Pollet's back gave him severe problems and he would not be able to pitch again in the Series. Dobson also hit Slaughter on the elbow, apparently sidelining him for the Series. Dr. Hyland recommended Slaughter not play, noting the movement or flaking of the blood clot could be fatal. Slaughter, in typical Gas House Gang style, responded that "he would play and the life was his." All the way back to St. Louis Hyland alternated cold and hot compresses on Slaughter's elbow. The Redbirds returned to St. Louis down three games to two.[31]

In game six Brecheen again took Harris's measure, this time 4–1. Slaughter had a hit, an RBI and a scintillating catch. Moore also made a couple of fine catches, including one off the bat of Williams. It all came down to game seven with Dickson matched against Ferris. Dickson gave up a first inning run, but then the Cardinals kayoed Ferris with a three run fourth and the runs were driven in by Walker, Dickson and Schoendienst. It looked like another Cardinals World Series triumph entering the eighth inning as they led 3–1.

Dickson couldn't stand prosperity. Russell and George Metkovich delivered a single and double that put Dickson's lead in jeopardy. With left hand hitters coming up Dyer sent Brecheen into the ball game. He fanned tough Wally Moses, but Pesky lined to short right to Slaughter, too short and too shallow to try the magnificent crippled throwing arm. Then Dominic (Joe's younger brother) doubled home the tying runs, but in the process he sprained an ankle and Leon Culberson ran for him and took over centerfield in the ninth inning. Williams had popped out to end the inning, making him just one for 11 against Brecheen.

Slaughter led off with a single, but Kurowski attempted to bunt him over and popped out. Garagiola, having been injured on a foul tip from Williams' bat in the top of the eighth, had been replaced by Rice. He was a less dangerous hitter and he was easily retired. Slaughter rested on first, frustrated and 270 feet from home plate. Walker, although a bust during the season, batted .412 with six RBIs in the Series, and was the next hitter. He hit an arching fly ball into medium deep left center and Slaughter was off at the crack of the bat and never stopped running. When Culberson fielded the ball, DiMaggio might have caught it; he threw accurately but not strongly to Pesky.

Neither Pesky nor Higgins thought Slaughter would try to score and both were startled when he kept on running. Pesky held the ball momentarily, but long enough for Slaughter to make his famous dash for home and score the run that would prove to be the game winner. Walker was credited with a single, although it was later ruled a double, which took some of the romance out of a great play. In reality the batted ball was only worth a single.

The Red Sox didn't go away easily in the ninth as York and Doerr both singled. When Higgins tried to sacrifice Kurowski played it smart and threw to Marion, covering second, forcing Doerr instead of getting Partee at first. This kept the lead and potential winning run at first base. Partee's grounder failed to score the second out and then Shoendienst trapped McBride's grounder and threw him out to end the game and St. Louis was once again the world champions.

Brecheen had become the first left hander to win three games in a World Series. His best friend, Dickson, had already left the clubhouse and gone home, hearing the end of the game on the radio. Dickson, Brecheen's closest friend, was angered at Dyer for pulling him in the eighth inning and that was why he was not around for the gala festivities.

The expected hitting duel between Musial and Williams never developed. For the season Williams had batted .342 with 37 doubles, 38 home runs and 123 RBIs, but in the Series he was just five for 25, all singles including a bunt, two runs scored and one RBI. Musial, although he was just six for 27, did have four doubles, one triple, three runs scored and four RBIs. Musial and Williams each won their league's MVP award. Musial led the league in at-bats (624), runs (124), hits (228), doubles (50), triples (20), batting (.365), and slugging percentage (.587). He also had 16 home runs and 103 RBIs. The Cardinals could now rest over the winter and prepare to defend their crown in 1947.

EIGHT

1947

Injuries and Illness

Several Cardinals needed surgery in the off-season to be able to perform at the necessary level in 1947. Whitey Kurowski had surgery on his right arm to remove bone chips, while Moore had knee surgery hoping it would allow him to perform at his pre-war peak. Moore had torn cartilage in his right knee. Marty Marion rested his ailing back over the winter so he could play 140 or more games.

Leo Durocher and Branch Rickey had criticized the Cardinals during the 1946 campaign. Durocher had said in midseason that the only team he feared was the Chicago Cubs and he didn't think too much of the Cardinals, who had the last laugh. If Howard Pollet hadn't had back problems at the end of the season and was knocked out two straight starts by the Cubs there wouldn't have been a playoff as St. Louis would have won the title outright.

One of the unsung heroes of the season was Walt Sessi, who had only two hits in 14 at-bats, but one was a game winning two run home run in the bottom of the ninth against the New York Giants on August 28. For his career he was just two for 27, but he hit one that would never be forgotten. Sessi had been a great prospect prior to the war, but after four years of military service his skills had been greatly decreased and Dyer had been criticized for keeping him on the team, but it turned out to be a fortunate move.

When asked if he would sell the Cardinals Breadon said his asking price was $3,000,000. During the World Series he had been approached, but no agreement had been reached. In that Series the Cardinals used the Boudreau shift on Williams and he was held to five hits in 25 at-bats. Dyer saw the Cardinals as repeaters in 1947. Musial had changed his stance while in the

191

Navy, using a closer stance. He said he was now ready for a long and brilliant career. He had enjoyed his greatest season and became equally adept at first base.

Clarence Rowland, president of the Pacific Coast League, renewed his bid for major league status. He was to be the host of the winter baseball meetings for organized baseball. The National Association met during December 4 through the 6 while major league baseball met from December 5 to the 7. The Pacific Coast League had played 44 consecutive seasons and only in 1918 did they play as few as 100 games (curtailed by World War I). Their 1946 attendance was 3,720,000 and Rowland said if they had had major league status it would have been much larger. Los Angeles was the cream of the crop. He was pushing hard for major league status for his league.[1]

For the season just ended there was a new attendance record in the minors which was close to 20,000,000 as 42 loops finished the season. This was two more than in 1941. The National League took 10 of the 11 rookie positions and all were war veterans. The group was Warren Spahn, Ewell Blackwell, Eddie Waitkus, Billy Cox, Joe Hatten, Grady Hatton, Ralph Kiner, Buddy Blattner, Del Ennis, Hoot Evers and Bruce Edwards.

Breadon was asked if the Cardinals' run of dominance had ended. He said, "No, as we are just starting a new chirp." Pitching would be stronger than before. The team would have Red Munger for all season and players in new positions would improve Musial at first base. Red Schoendienst would be back at second and Moore would be improved after his operation as would Kurowski. Harry Walker would be an improved player and regain his prewar form. Johnny Beazley was expected to return to his 1941 winning ways and Murray Dickson would now be a full time starter. In addition young Joe Garagiola (one of the heroes of the World Series) would be an improved catcher and become one of the future stars of the game.[2]

Slaughter said that his elbow was still sore and he would have it examined by a doctor in the off-season. Otherwise he contended he was fine. His legs were in good condition, he still had his speed and they would have to rip his uniform off him before he would quit the game. His goal was to be a Cardinal for as long as he played the game of baseball.

Harry Carey was voted the top National League broadcaster, although he did both the Cardinals' and Browns' home games. He was teamed with Charles "Gabby" Street, who managed the pennant winning Cardinals of 1930 and their World Championship team of 1931. Carey had a unique, fascinating, exciting style of broadcasting.

There were many subjects to be discussed at the major league owners meetings. Among them were players' bonuses, pension plans and limits on night games. The owners had to make some key decisions on these issues.

Many of the Cardinals wanted pay hikes for 1947 as this was the usual result of a world championship season. Breadon had lots of fun seeing the

Cardinals defeat Brooklyn in the playoffs and then upset the Red Sox in the World Series. Now the time had come for him to pay the piper. Musial wanted a two or three year contract, with the latter being worth $100,000. All the key players were looking for substantial raises. This included, but was not limited to, Slaughter, Kurowski, Pollet, Dickson, Brecheen, Marion and Schoendienst.

For 1947 new rules would be put into effect on the waiver system. Currently a player could be waived three times. For 1947 they wanted to change it to twice, but it would eventually go back to three. Another change would limit the number of players on waiver for a single team at any one time to seven. There was to be a slight increase permitted in night games for the National League from 137 to 150. As of now St. Louis would have only one Sunday double-header at home, as this would help attendance by having more Saturday night games and single Sunday games. Of course postponements could change that scenario.

Many awards came to St. Louis following their highly successful season. Dyer was voted manager of the year for guiding his team to a World Series triumph in his first year at the helm. Few managers win titles in their freshman season, but Dyer did by overcoming great adversity. In spring training he said he would only have to be a push button manager because of the nucleus of talent his team possessed.

Then came injuries and Mexican jumpers, but he pulled them together and moved players adroitly in achieving his goal. He took a brilliant outfielder (Musial) and moved him to first base, where he not only won the batting title, but became a very capable and adept fielder. He alternated three light hitting outfielders (Harry Walker, Erv Dusak and Buster Adams) and converted Schoendienst to second base, where he became the best in the league.

When his right hand starting corps didn't perform, he moved Dickson from the bullpen and made him a starter, and he finished with a 15–6 record. The Cardinals looked like a repeat for 1947 per the experts with the only concern being some aging veterans. Moore at 35 had gimpy knees, although surgery was to correct that problem, while Slaughter would be 31, but he played every game in 1946 and led the league with 130 RBIs. Musial, however, was expected to be the National League batting king again.

Musial was also voted the major league player of the year, edging out Boston's Ted Williams. Musial not only led the majors with a .365 average, he also took over a new position and developed into one of the game's best defensive first baseman. Musial was not just a five tool player, but a true team man, willing to do whatever would make the club a winner.

There was considerable challenge to the Pacific Coast League being allotted major league status at this time. The National and American Leagues both stated San Francisco and Los Angeles could make major league cities. This could be accomplished by transferring one of the weaker franchises to the West

Coast. Potential candidates were the St. Louis Browns, the Boston Braves or one of the Philadelphia teams. However, none of the balance of teams would be potential candidates for this move.

Lefty O'Doul, manager of the San Francisco Seals, asserted that "the Pacific Coast League was major league caliber now." They had 3,700,000 attendance last year and given one or two seasons it could reach 5,000,000. He argued that if Los Angeles and San Francisco became major league teams it would wreck the league and the other six cities. He was opposed to that route. O'Doul also pointed out that air travel from one coast to the other was seven hours and this would complicate scheduling and bring added expense.[3]

The Cardinals sold catcher Clyde Klutz to Pittsburgh, while rumors abounded the Cardinals might get Pete Reiser from the Brooklyn Dodgers in a trade. If this took place he would be back home, as he was a Cardinals farmhand set free by Judge Landis in 1938. He was one of 80 players that Landis set free that year and the Cardinals were prohibited from dealing with them for three years and that was how they lost Reiser to the Dodgers. Reiser then went on to star with the Dodgers and only injuries kept him from achieving his true greatness. If he was healthy he would shore up the outfield. The only question about him now was his throwing arm, which had once been one of the best in baseball. We would have to wait until spring for this decision.

The Cardinals led the National League in batting at .265, had the league's best ERA, 3.01, and the top fielding team with a .980 percentage. With a combination such as that it was pretty easy to see why they became world champs.

The debate over the merits and abilities of Jackie Robinson began and the question if he was ready for the major leagues. Lloyd McGowan, a sportswriter from Montreal, said, "Given an even chance Robinson was a cinch to make a major league team." He played an excellent second base at Montreal, hit .349, scored 113 runs and stole 40 bases in 119 games, but had just 66 RBIs. He also lacked power as he hit just three home runs.

The key question was where would Robinson play, as Brooklyn already had Eddie Stanky at second base. Cy Kritzer, Buffalo columnist, said, "Robinson lacked the physical equipment to make a major league team." Hopper, Montreal's manager, said, "Robinson played his best ball on Sunday when there were large crowds, but was just an ordinary ball player when the crowds were small."

Hopper didn't believe that Robinson had enough experience or ability to learn a new position, such as third base, where the Dodgers were weak. Hopper felt if he could play second base he might have a chance to make the grade. Many of Robinson's hits were due to the speed of his teammates as he was an excellent hit and run man. He was hitting second and therefore got a break when an infield position was left open and he could hit through it. Several hits would otherwise have been routine ground ball outs. It was believed that Robinson needed more seasoning before going to the major leagues.

The final decision on Robinson was passed by Rickey to Durocher. He said, "I don't want to force him on players, fans or the press." He and Durocher agreed that they would let the players see him in action and then decide for themselves whether he could be of value to the team. Time would tell, was their belief.[4]

The Cardinals planned to use Joe Garagiola and Del Rice in a platoon tandem at the catching position. If the Cardinals hadn't needed a left handed bat to complement Rice, Garagiola would have been sent out for another season in the minors. It had been felt O'Dea would have fit the bill, but he batted just .100 and then had back problems, thus they were forced to keep Garagiola for the entire season.

Pee Wee Reese of the Dodgers, Eddie Miller of the Cincinnati Reds and Buddy Kerr of the New York Giants were all excellent shortstops and challenging Marion for the title of Mr. Shortstop, but as good as they were they came up a little "short" when compared to the master. Marion's height and ability to get a quick jump allowed him to play in closer than others. His height also enabled him to get to ground balls that others couldn't reach.

Breadon made the decision to have Carey and Street broadcast the Cardinals' games exclusively over one system, the Griesedieck Beer Network. This put the frost on the window between the Cardinals and the Browns as the cold shoulder was given to Dizzy Dean and the Browns. This action further gave credence to the story that the Cardinals would break away from Sportsman's Park and build a new stadium as soon as possible.

The delay was due to the lack of materials and as soon as they were available and costs returned to normal the stadium would be built. Breadon told everyone, "I may not live to see it, but my nephew [Bill Walsingham, assistant president] would. Carey and Street would broadcast the Cardinal home games live and road games at Cincinnati and Chicago. The balance of the road games would be done via wire." Dean was shocked, but said he would still root for the Cardinals. Breadon wrote a letter to Dizzy explaining the situation.[5]

For 1947 the Cardinals would play 60 night games of which 41 would be at home. There would be more Saturday day games and fewer Sunday double-headers. Musial signed a three year contract (1947–49) and received a substantial raise. The first year would pay him $28,000, making him the highest paid Cardinal in history. Rogers Hornsby and Frankie Frisch had each earned $28,000. Garagiola also received a new contract with a nice increase.

Pollet was down to 160 pounds by the end of the season and had back problems, which forced him out of his second World Series start. He has been in therapy during the off-season and was up to 184 pounds and back in good condition. Kurowski signed early this year and therefore would not be a holdout and not be ready for the start of the season. Slaughter signed a two year contract with a very substantial raise.

Police would enforce the National League park blacklist. The league voted to bar all gamblers, touts, bookies and other undesirables from the stadiums. A staff of park detectives would have the responsibility for enforcing this operation. Other than writers, radio and other newsmen all visitors would be banned from the clubhouse. Any player receiving a bribe offer had to report it to the major league office. Failure to do so meant lifetime banishment from the game. The American League didn't vote to go along, stating it agreed with these rules but already had them in place.[6]

Baseball's pension plan was nearing completion. Players at age 50 could draw their money. A first year player would pay in $45.45 in year one; $50.90 in year two; and up to $454.75 in year 10. Once a player had paid in $2500 his annual contribution fell to $250 per year. Owners would pay in $250 per year for each player on the team and make other contributions. Owners would pay 80 percent of the cost of the program. To properly fund the pension plan they needed about $675,000 per season and were currently $200,000 short and were still working on this part of the problem. The seeds had been sown and it was only a matter of time until it would be finalized. If a player didn't stay in the major league for five years his payments would be returned to him. If he died before age 50 his beneficiary would receive his payment for 10 years.

Rickey planned to cut the stardom route in half from the current five years to approximately two and one-half. He said, "We should no longer spoon feed the player, but give them an extended crash training program and bring them along quicker. In this manner they can reach the major leagues sooner and have a longer career and make more money. The team would have a good player for a few extra seasons. Thus both the team and the player benefits." Rickey predicted the Dodgers would win the pennant in four of the next eight seasons.[7]

The Cardinals would bring 21 players to spring training on February 21. Hopes for a second consecutive pennant and fifth in six years were extremely high. The Dodgers said they were too young to compete with a veteran Cardinals team. The Cardinals planned on using three left hand starting pitchers (Pollet, Brecheen and Brazle). This would be the first time a team had three lefty starts since McGraw's Giants had three in 1917 (Ferdie Schopp, Harry "Slim" Sallee and Rube Benton).

The other two starters would be right handers Munger and Dickson. The team looked solid. Breadon said the Cardinals' "chain system" had worked for both the players and the team. They were tutored, trained, and guided along by knowing professionals until they were ready for the major leagues. Moore said he was a weak outfielder until he began in the minors and was taught how to chase down long fly balls. The results were history. Breadon said players had to be willing to concentrate and work long and hard hours to succeed.

The Williams versus Musial debate continued. Their hitting was about on a par. Williams hit more home runs, while Musial hit more doubles and triples. Williams had more flare, flash and color, but Stan was the better team man and fielder (note his switch from the outfield to first base without causing the team any problems). Williams held a .353 career average for his first five years, while Musial had a .349 for his first four seasons. Musial was the better base runner, fielder and team player.

All Cardinals spots were filled and the team looked solid and strong, but Dyer still worried. He saw that other teams had also improved and were stronger. Dyer said it would be a tough struggle all the way and every game counted. They had to win as many as they could early, because those they didn't would haunt them late in the season.

Dyer planned on giving young pitchers a full opportunity in spring training. He had hoped that Beazley would return to his 1941 form, as that would be a big blessing and pickup for the team. The only open position was left field and it was a battle between Walker, Dusak, Sisler and Adams. Vernal "Nippy" Jones was to be Musial's understudy, while Tommy Glaviano (who stole 64 bases in the California League and was also a good hitter) was planned to be the key infield reserve.

Team desertions had shaken the wobbly Mexican League. Nuevo Laredo and Torreon dropped out of the league. Two others were asking to resign and Jorge Pasquel told them no. The league would open with six teams, but was on shaky ground. Lou Klein led the league with a .330 average. The Cardinals could use him as a reserve.

Durocher said the only infield spot available for Robinson was first base. Thus Montreal planned to use him at first base and the Dodgers could get a look at him. If he performed satisfactorily then the Dodgers would give him a trial. Robinson said the Dodgers had a good ball club and it was going to take a lot for him to break into the lineup. He added another season at Montreal wouldn't hurt and could help him.

Young Bernie Creger, a returned war veteran from the Cardinals farm system, could be the backup for Marion. He was built along the same lines as Marion and was a great fielder. He would battle with Glaviano and others for a reserve infield position on the team.

Dyer had an array of key questions he wanted answers to: (1) Was Moore's knee okay? Could he play 130 games or more? (2) Had Slaughter fully recovered from the elbow injury he received in the World Series? (3) Would Marion's back stand up for 140 or more games for the season? (4) If it didn't could Creger hit enough to take over the shortstop position? (5) What about Kurowski's throwing arm? How did the removal of five bone chips from his arm affect his throwing and hitting abilities? (6) Would Beazley regain his

1941 form? (7) Could war wounded Johnny Grodzicki regain the prewar form and promise that he showed in 1941? (8) Had Pollet fully recovered from his back muscle injury late last season? (9) How soon would Del Rice recover from the shoulder injury he suffered March 3?

If there were pleasing answers to the majority of these questions then the pennant should be a breeze. If not then there would be a lot of trouble for St. Louis during 1947. At the present time Moore, Marion, Kurowski and Slaughter all seemed okay and ready to play a full season. Beazley was throwing harder than he did last year and that was an encouraging sign.

Grodzicki (25–5 in 1941) was the best pitcher in the minors before he went into the Army. He was wounded in the right leg but he had improved. This was the first time in three years he felt pain in his leg which meant the blood flow had improved. Pollet was throwing well and seemed fully recovered and ready to pick up where he left off in 1946. However, Rice was carrying his arm in a sling and it would be weeks before he could throw a baseball. He had suffered a shoulder joint separation when he fell.

Due to the massive influx of returning veterans a swift farm expansion had overpowered the minor leagues. The major leagues had control of 60 percent of the teams. Half of the 24 AAA teams were owned outright. There were 52 minor leagues with 388 teams and the Dodgers had 25 clubs, the Cubs had 21, the Yankees 20 and the Cardinals 19. At one time the Redbirds had over 30 minor league farm teams.

The major league teams owned or had working agreements with 18 of 24 AAA teams in three leagues; 13 of 18 AA teams in two leagues; 21 of 22 A teams in three leagues; 42 of 68 B teams in nine leagues; 57 of 105 C teams in 15 leagues; and 83 of 150 D teams in 22 leagues. The Cardinals still owned the most farm teams with 16, followed by Brooklyn with 13 and the Cubs with 10.

One of the problems that plagued St. Louis in 1946 was the lack of adequate relief help. When Pollet, Dickson or Brecheen ran into trouble it often wasn't available. Wilks posted an 8–0 mark with an acceptable 3.41 ERA, but only one save. He was not as dominating as he had been in his 17–4 1944 season. There was little other help available relief wise during 1946. This season the Cardinals had several hopeful candidates. They had Jim Hearn, Ken Johnson and while Grodzicki was not throwing with pre-war speed or his curve breaking like it should, he was showing better form and results than in 1946. Dyer was hoping he could make it for two reasons. First, it would benefit the team and secondly, it would be a real reward for what this man had suffered through.

On the downside Beazley had again developed arm trouble and was completely discouraged. He was so unhappy and disappointed that he called Breadon and asked for his unconditional release. However, he came back and was throwing again. Many thought his problem was that he started throwing too hard too soon and re-injured his arm.

Meanwhile Garagiola was on the hospital list as he had a broken bone in a cheek from a bunt by Slaughter, but was slowly recovering. The club was planning on him as the number one catcher and looking forward to a big season from the youngster. Among the new outfielders Chuck Diering was doing an exceptional job defensively in center field, but not hitting, although his track record in the minors showed he could. The other newcomer, Bill Howerton, had hit well and was quite impressive.

Robinson stated that he wouldn't play for Brooklyn if there was resentment on the team. However, the main reason he wanted to play in Montreal was that he could make more money. He was on a pennant winning and Junior World Series team and there was no friction or tension. If it existed in Brooklyn he would prefer to stay in Montreal. Rickey decided he would not poll the players regarding Robinson's status, but leave the decision in Durocher's hands as to how he wanted to handle the situation.

Dyer had to prove himself last season and he did by winning the World Series. He couldn't take chances he would have liked nor done much experimenting, although he did take a star outfielder and played him at first base. Here he was fortunate as when you have a five tool future Hall of Fame player such as Musial, the risk wasn't that great. This was especially true considering the lack of prima donna in the man.

During 1946 the players supported and helped Dyer over the rough spots, especially during the Mexican fiasco. Dyer felt more at ease this season and was ready to do more experimenting and take chances that he couldn't last year. He had some concern regarding Kurowski's arm as it was sore from throwing. The team needed his big bat in the lineup, as well as his skills at third base. No one else on the team could play that position as well.

The Cardinals' pitching staff had been quite impressive in spring training, especially the starters. The team had a surplus of outfielders thus Buster Adams was sold to Philadelphia. Adams was extremely sore at Dyer as he accused him of playing his pets. Adams claimed he was told when he reported for spring training in 1946 he wouldn't be a regular. With an outfield of Moore, Musial and Slaughter this was understandable, but when Musial went to first he still wasn't given a fair chance in his opinion. He believed based on his 1945 performance (even against weaker wartime pitching) he deserved a better opportunity. Adams had led the 1945 team in hits, runs, home runs and RBIs.

On the bright side Hearn was now the top rookie candidate in camp and could have a starting job, freeing Brazle for bullpen duty, where he was very effective. Diering was the number two prospect, especially if Moore's knees faltered and he could play center field on a regular basis.

The Cardinals were pinning their pennant hopes on pitching, speed, defense and spirit. The team did not posses great power. Musial, Slaughter and Kurowski were the lead hitters. The six leading candidates for starters were Pollet, Brecheen, Dickson, Munger, Brazle and Ken Burkhart with Wilks and Freddy Schmidt slated for bullpen duty. This left rookies Hearn and Wayne McLeland for the last two spots, although Hearn could step into a starting role. If Beazley and Grodzicki should recover their pre-war form, what a starting staff!

For the present the team would carry three catchers—Rice, Garagiola and Del Wilber. The starting outfield would be Moore in center, Slaughter in right with Dusak and Walker platooning in left. Diering would be the main reserve outfielder. Dick Sisler would provide outfield and first base back up support. The infield would be Kurowski, Marion, Schoendienst and Musial. Jones, Creger and Joffre Cross were to be the infield reserves. Barring any unforeseen accidents it should be another St. Louis pennant.

For the first time in 72 years the major leagues would have a black ballplayer as the Dodgers signed Robinson. Initial plans were to use him as a pinch hitter, pinch runner and reserve infielder. His new manager would decide his final role on the team. It was interesting to watch as this drama unfolded. How would teammates, opponents, fans and the media react and think? Could Robinson succeed? Did he not only have the talent, but also the temperament to overcome any racial bias, ridicule or harassment?[8]

Commissioner Chandler rolled up his sleeves for new swings. He believed his efforts to run the game with gentle hands had been misconstrued and he was forced to take the following actions: 1) Durocher had been judged guilty of conduct detrimental to the game and suspended for the entire 1947 season as the Dodgers' manager. 2) Colonel Larry McPhail had been fined $2,000 for allowing Durocher to use him in getting a better contract offer from Brooklyn and for airing a squabble that was injurious to baseball. 3) The Brooklyn club was fined $2,000 because its officials engaged in conduct harmful to the game. 4) Harold Pariote, secretary of Brooklyn, was fined $500 for having ghosted the *Brooklyn Eagle* article which helped to bar Durocher.[9]

The baseball writers made their selections for 1947 and in the National League the order of finish was expected to be St. Louis, Pittsburgh, Chicago, Boston and Brooklyn in fifth place. In the American League Boston was expected to repeat followed by Detroit, New York and Cleveland. It was anticipated it would be a much easier time for St. Louis this season and the team was extremely confident as opening day approached.

The finality was written to the players' major league pension plan. A player could begin drawing his benefits at age 50 and the amount would be between $50 to $100 per month, depending on his length of service. A player would also have between $5,300 to $10,000 insurance while on a major league roster. A player had to join the pension program within 60 days from the start of the season or lose credit for past service. It was the first step in a new benefit for the players and they enthusiastically embraced it.

The Cardinals began their season with the 1946 finishing coat. The club always looked better with Moore in the lineup. Dyer stated, "We'll rest Moore whenever necessary to get better results and more use from him over the course of the season." It was a different ball club with Moore on the field, although Diering was a capable replacement defensively. The team finished its spring training campaign with a 13–6 record against major league competition. That certainly was a pennant winning pace—one that would produce 105–106 victories. Shades of 1942–44.

The debut of Robinson was "just another game." He had done his thinking about the situation the night before. Robinson stated, "Brooklyn players have been swell." He said, "Give me five years in the major leagues so I can make enough money to get a place of my own and an education for my son." One Dodger (who wanted to remain anonymous) said as long as Robinson could help the team there was no problem with him on the club. Well wishers said to let him alone and see what he could do. Robinson knew he had to make it this season or there would be no second chance, no next year for him. Stanky said, "Robinson learns quick. You don't have to tell him something twice."[10]

The Cardinals began the season on the wrong foot, making just one run and three hits in a 3–1 loss to Ewell Blackwell and the Cincinnati Reds. There wasn't great concern as St. Louis had a tradition of losing more often than winning on opening day. In game two Eddie Erraut blanked the Cardinals for seven innings before they scored four runs in the eighth inning to win 4–1. The hitting was slow in coming around and the team was 1–2 after the first three games while Philadelphia, Brooklyn and Pittsburgh all began the season at 2–0 and Cincinnati at 2–1.

The Boston Braves, sometimes known as the Cape Cod Cardinals (they would eventually have 10 former Redbirds on the team), kept buying Cardinals players. Their latest acquisition was sore arm Beazley for $20,000, as the team had finally conceded he would never regain his 1941 form. The Cardinals had received $205,000 for the 10 players. They received $60,000 for Morton Cooper (who would never be the pitcher of 1942–44 again) and $40,000 each for Ray Sanders and Johnny Hopp. From 1946 through 1950 Hopp's ledger would include seasons of .340, .333 and .306 and the Cardinals could have used that bat several times.[11]

Marion, not a conceited or braggadocio individual, did like the monicker or title "Mr. Shortstop." Musial changed his batting stance on advice from Grodzicki and moved closer to the plate and found that he could hit better and with more power. The advice paid off in game two of the opening series when he went four for four with a home run. As April neared its end St. Louis was 2–5 while Pittsburgh was 6–2, Brooklyn (a surprise team so far) 5–2 and Boston 4–3. Only Kurowski was over .300 at .323. Munger was the lead pitcher at 1–0 in two games with one no decision. The team had lost three in a row.

This was the worst Cardinals record since the pre–Breadon area as the team was now 2–11 with nine consecutive defeats as of May 3. Six of the losses were at the hands of left hand pitchers. The team was neither hitting nor pitching. This was totally unexpected as they had been picked by 88 of the 96 writers to win the pennant. Munger had been kayoed in two of his three starts; Dickson (though pitching well) was 0–2 and to show how bad things were Brecheen was defeated by the Cubs for only the fourth time in 19 decisions in his career. Brazle was also kayoed in his only start.

During the nine game losing streak the team allowed an average of five runs and nine hits per game while they batted just .200 and scored 2.4 runs and made 6.4 hits per game. They also allowed 13 home runs, 51 walks (the latter was two per game last season). This in essence summed up the Cardinals' plight during this dark decline. Only Slaughter was over .300 at .350, but no home runs. Kurowski had the only other respectable average at .288.

The only other Cardinal over .200 was Marion at .231. Moore was at .333, but had only six at-bats with two hits, so he didn't really qualify. The rest were Sisler and Schoendienst (.188 each), Rice and Walker (.182 each) and Diering and Musial each at .146. Stan had gone hitless in 12 consecutive at-bats. Garagiola was 0 for 12 and Dusak was out with a painful charley horse. The team was in sad shape as the first week of May rolled around and found them at 2–11 and Brooklyn led with 10–3, while St. Louis looked up at them from the cellar (an unaccustomed place for this team).

Breadon said "the rumor was ridiculous that the Cardinals threatened to strike if the Dodgers used Robinson in lineup." The story had started because Breadon was concerned whether his players would play against a black ballplayer and over a few drinks mentioned it to *New York Herald* sportswriter Rud Rennie, who couldn't print it as it would be breaking a confidence. When National League president Frick heard about it he was upset and said he would fine and suspend the entire team if they refused to play against the Dodgers because there was a Negro in the lineup. The club had never said that and vehemently denied the story the club had taken a vote on the subject. No vote had ever been taken. It was simply a tempest in a teapot. Unfortunately the canard hung heavily over the Cardinals. Some didn't want to play against Robinson, but knew they would forfeit the game as well as pay. Thus Frick never did threaten the team and no vote was ever taken, but the Cardinals received a black eye.[12]

In fact there were many players in the league who did not want to play with or against a Negro and were far more vehement than any Cardinal. While it was limited on field, off field it was quite vocal, especially in the clubhouse. Musial said that, "I had played with a black in Donora and the man was now a college professor and I had no trouble playing with a Negro."[13]

After these incidents the Cardinals started perking up both on the field and in the trade market. Previously home runs surrendered and passed balls had been their bugaboo leading to the loss of a large number of one run games. The team needed a good catcher, defensively and offensively. Walker and Schmidt were traded to Philadelphia for outfield Ron Northey who hit home runs and had a rifle arm, but did have some defensive liabilities.

The concern about the catchers was not that they were not hitting, but someone needed to help the pitchers. Dyer wasn't certain that the young catchers Rice and Garagiola were up to the job. In the first 16 games the team had allowed 16 home runs while walking 70 men. Walker had hit just .237 last season after batting .314 in 1942 and was hitting just .200 this year. Northey hit 2 home runs in a 9–0 win that ended the nine game losing streak. The team had already lost five games by one run and last season were 34–19 in that category. Quite a turnaround.

Pollet won a 2–1 game, but had base runners all over the place as he allowed nine hits and walked eight in pitching a complete game win. The team was last in complete games, but one more than their opponents. Currently the team was 4–12 and seven behind Brooklyn. A bullpen of Wilks, Brazle, Burkhart and Grodzicki was not doing its collective job. On the other side the opposing relief pitchers had held the Cardinals to one run in 41 innings and none in 22 before Musial, slowly coming out of his slump, hit a three run home run off Boston's Glenn Elliott.

Chandler said, "the Robinson incident was to be kept under wraps." Chandler stated, "He will get a fair and equal chance and the rest was up to him. The game was open to all players, regardless of race, creed or color." In 1946 several Dodgers were opposed to playing with a black and the same happened again in early 1947, Not all the players involved were from south of the Mason-Dixon line. Some Dodgers said last year they would rather fight for the pennant without Robinson.

Many National League players wanted the Negro issue addressed when negotiating on pensions, minimum salary and other changes taking place. They wanted both leagues to bar the use of black players. There was the drinking cup incident in Cuba where white players refused to drink from the same cup as black players. The black players were urged to show sportsmanship and good conduct in order to help smooth the way for Jackie. Also many whites felt blacks should have to go through the same apprenticeship as white players. Most white players spent five to seven years in the minors and felt the same should be required of the Negro players. They did not want black players to be given an automatic free pass to the major leagues.[14]

President Warren Giles of Cincinnati said most stand pat championship teams seldom repeated. There had been few changes in the Cardinals from their 1946 team. Other clubs had improved, but the Cardinals were going with basically the same team and some players' skills could slip as they were a year older. However, he still thought they were the favorite and would repeat.

The situation didn't look bright as Pollet (the ace of the staff in 1946) lost for the fourth time in five starts as Dave Koslo of the Giants held the team to two singles. In a 13 game road trip the team was 4–8–1, winning just one series as they took two of three from Brooklyn and almost swept that series. Breadon said that last season the Cardinals led the league in everything; those fellows couldn't lose it all overnight. The team was still hitting only .200 and Breadon added that from the dire predictions it would sound like they were in the fifth month of the season and not the fifth week.

A story circulated that Musial was flown from New York because of injuries suffered in a beating administered by Slaughter was ridiculous. Musial and Slaughter were very close friends and had been teammates since 1941. He said he and Stan were buddies. Bob Broeg of the *St. Louis Post-Dispatch* saw a nude Musial in his hotel room and the doctor examined him. There were no bruises or cuts, but he was in much pain from his appendix. Dr. Hyland felt he could treat Musial without an operation. He spent three days at St. John's Hospital in St. Louis and several more at home. His appendix was frozen until the season over. With an operation he would have missed a month or more of the season.[15]

By the end of the second week of May Chicago had taken over first place with a 14–9 record followed by Boston at 14–10. Brooklyn had been just 3–8 in their last 11 games and fell to 12–11, closer to what was predicted for them in the spring. Meanwhile St. Louis continued to languish in last place at 7–13. Northey at .303 was the lone Cardinal over that sacred barrier, while Brecheen with a 3–1 record was the only winning pitcher.

Through May 20 Northey had raised his average to .296 (.255 for Philadelphia and .333 at St. Louis). Smiling Northey put a cheerful chirp on the Redbirds as he had a jovial way of helping players to relax under tension and pressure. The problem with the Cardinals was they weren't smiling and baseball had ceased to be fun for them. They had enjoyed the game so long and successfully as a team (1941–46) they were having a difficult time coping with this unusual situation presented to them. The last time this had happened was during the first seven weeks of 1940 when the team was 15–30, pre–Billy Southworth days. Northey liked the hot, humid weather of St. Louis, telling everyone he was a big guy and it helped him. As a heavy muscled fellow like a football player it took time for him to get loose. He was not happy in Philadelphia as he and manager Ben Chapman did not get along.

Adams' forecast of the Cardinals seemed to be coming true. There was still uncertainty in the catching department and Moore's gimpy knees gave him trouble, not allowing him to play every day. Kurowski's sore arm was bothering him and Diering (Moore's heir apparent) wasn't hitting. The team was last, holding up the rest of the league, and Adams had enough resentment in him, not for the players, but for Dyer, that he was glad to see it.

The team was 10–18 with 11 of the losses to left hand pitchers. They were just 4–11 against left handers and 6–7 versus right handers. Every team was now saving its left hand starters for the Cardinals. To show their futility the team and Brazle lost to Kenny Raffensberger and Philadelphia 1–0 in 12 innings. They had a chance to break the game open in the seventh, but couldn't get a key hit or even a fly ball. Kurowski and Slaughter had singled, Musial bunted for a hit (his first in 25 at-bats). The bases were loaded and no outs. Marion grounded into a force-out at home and Dusak popped up and Brazle grounded back to Raffensberger. Results—three hits—no runs. Total futility.

As May was rapidly drawing to a close St. Louis continued to languish in last place at 10–19, while just two games separated first place Chicago (17–12) from fifth place Pittsburgh (13–12). Sandwiched in between were New York (15–11), Boston (16–13) and Brooklyn (15–13).

On May 25 Joe Medwick pinch-hit in game one of a double-header in the fifth inning for Hearn and doubled to drive in Rice. The team was down 2–0 against Fritz Ostermueller who blanked them earlier in the season. He had a string of 22 consecutive scoreless innings against the Redbirds. Medwick received a bigger ovation than during his halcyon playing days of the 1930s. The fans loved him and his return. All had been forgiven as they were glad to see Ducky come home to finish out his career. He wouldn't play every day, but his bat would help against left hand pitching.

There was a suggestion to remove the right field screen in front of the pavilion as it would help the Cardinals more than the opposition because of the number of left handed hitters on the team. Dyer vetoed the idea even though Musial hit the screen an average of 15 to 20 times a season. Instead of having doubles or occasionally long singles they would all be home runs. Dyer said he couldn't do it even if he wanted to as the Browns owned the ballpark.

Finally the team started to come out of its doldrums and make a move. It had been almost a daily occurrence to use three or four pitchers as there were very few complete games. The hurlers started to pitch complete games and the club began its slow ascent toward the top, where they felt they belonged. Slaughter, Kurowski and Northey had been carrying the team with their hitting, but Musial was still mired deep below .200. Brecheen had seven complete games and was 5–2 in them while Munger got his second victory after being kayoed five consecutive starts. He then won his next start 2–0.

Musial was still well below .200 with only one extra base hit in his last 15 games. He was 10 pounds below his normal playing weight. He had no strength and had lost his bat speed. He said he just couldn't get his bat around on a pitch. His not hitting was greatly hurting the team and his own personal pride. Here was a player that had hit .357, .347 and .365 the last three seasons with two batting titles and one second place finish and couldn't even reach .200. The low mark would be .140.

As May ended two games still separated the first five teams. Leapfrog continued in the standings, except for St. Louis, as Brooklyn took over first at 19–14, while Pittsburgh was now fifth at 16–15. Chicago (17–15), New York (17–15) and Boston (16–14) were right behind the Dodgers. St. Louis was still last, but only six games out at 14–21. The encouraging factor was the team had played 12–10 for the past three weeks and it looked like the turnaround had come.

On June 2 the Cardinals finally broke the left handed jinx defeating and kayoing Joe Hatten of the Dodgers. It was only the third time this season he had been knocked out of the box. Then they handed Warren Spahn his first loss of the season after eight consecutive victories, which included two over St. Louis. Munger won the game 3–0 on Musial's two run home run.

That marked the seventh straight game in which he had hit and his average was now over .200 at .209, but still a long climb was in front of him. In the same inning that Musial hit his two run home run Schoendienst got his first hit in 22 at-bats, a triple. Just as things started looking bright, two Cardinals pitchers got injured. In the second game of the Memorial Day double-header Brazle was hit by a line drive above the groin and on June 1 Wilks was hit in the jaw by a line drive off the bat of Brooklyn pitcher Harry Taylor.

During the first game of that Memorial Day double-header Marion had to be relieved because his hip was bothering him. Young Creger relieved him and had a double in his only at-bat. Cross played in the second game. Marion was back in the lineup when the club opened its second eastern trip against Brooklyn.

The home attendance to date was 261,365, which was good considering the poor start, the team was in last place, one Brooklyn night game had been rained out and a Saturday night game versus Pittsburgh had been postponed. Cold weather had also been a factor. The last time St. Louis was in the cellar this late in the season was June 1925 and Rogers Hornsby replaced Rickey and the team finished fourth and won the World Series the next season. Perhaps this was an omen of things to come, but with a World Series title this year.

By the second week of June the race remained tight with Brooklyn (25–18) hanging onto a half game lead over New York and Chicago (both 24–18) and Boston (23–20) close behind. St. Louis was still last, but at 18–24 and were 16–13 since their 2–11 start. Slaughter was up among the batting leaders at .361 and paced the St. Louis attack on May 28 with two home runs to give them a 4–2 victory. He had a triple and double in game one of the Memorial Day double-header, but they were wasted. In game two he was three for three with a home run in a 7–3 victory.

After the first game loss to Brooklyn on the start of their eastern trip he helped Pollet defeat the Dodgers 5–4 in 10 innings with three hits, two runs scored and two RBIs. At this point he was a regular hitting machine. Slaughter was a throwback to the old style player (Fred Clarke or Larry Doyle).

McGraw would have loved to manage Slaughter. He was also a team player as he gave up right field to play the more spacious left field in Sportsman's Park so that Northey (more familiar with right field) could play there. Slaughter took position shifts, slumps, marriages, and divorces all in stride. He never stopped hustling or trying.[16]

Breadon stated the Cardinals were not for sale as he denied rumors he was trying to sell the team. Other unnamed sources also denied the same rumor. A West Coast group headed by Postmaster General Robert Hannegan and Edwin Pauley, a wealthy California oilman, wanted to buy the team and move it to Los Angeles and let it play in the Coliseum. Some rumors said that $3,000,000 was offered for the team, but Breadon refused any offer that didn't give the true value for the team and its farm system.[17]

All one had to do was look at ex-teammates to see what was ailing the Cardinals. Walker was batting .372 and leading the league while Hopp was at .329 and Verban at .300 (although the team didn't need another infielder). Walker Cooper was hitting over .300 and was on a pace to hit over 30 home runs and over 100 RBIs. How good the bats of Cooper and Hopp, even Walker, would have looked in the lineup.

The Cardinals' recent eastern road trip bore out two key factors. They were a better road club and could defeat left hand starters. However, just when it looked like the breaks were coming St. Louis' way Slaughter was forced out of the lineup for a week with an ankle injury. In the first 15 games started by right hand pitchers against St. Louis there was only one complete game while left handers completed 11 of 20 starts and were 13–5.

On their first eastern road trip they were 3–5 and 5–10 overall. This time they were 5–5 versus the eastern teams (where the stronger clubs were supposed to be). Slaughter had injured his ankle on June 6 trying to stretch a triple into an inside the park home run when he slid into Cooper at home plate. The team still was just 3–11 in one run games, but finally climbed out of the basement on June 10, the first time they had breathed fresher air since April 20. It had been a long, hard grind. Almost like a prisoner in solitary confinement.

By the middle of June the leapfrogging continued and New York (27–19) took over first with Brooklyn and Chicago tied for second at 27–21. Boston was close behind at 27–20. St. Louis was eight games out of first place at 20–29 and tied for seventh and eighth. The Cardinals used the Dodgers and the Phillies as stepping stones to go from last to sixth and then fifth.

Musial continued to show some life in his bat as he hits a bases loaded triple in the bottom of the ninth to defeat Philadelphia 7–6. It was his third hit of the game. Then they defeated Brooklyn four straight games (reminiscent of 1946 when St. Louis did that to the Dodgers in July and started the team on their way to the pennant and World Series title). Schoendienst had emerged from his slump with 16 hits in eight games and moved his average up 45 points.

Moore and Garagiola were hitting, but Dyer was greatly concerned about the latter's throwing and the large number of stolen bases he had allowed. The word had gotten around the league and all the teams took liberties with his arm. Dyer said his team was on the way as Munger, Brecheen and Brazle were all pitching well. Hard luck loser Dickson got his first victory of the season after starting 0–7. His ERA was just over three runs per game, thus his record should be far better than 1–7.

Despite a street car and bus strike which tied up St. Louis for a week the attendance was holding up very well. For the four game Brooklyn set 90,481 saw the Cardinals sweep the Dodgers while 12,509 showed up for a Monday night game with Philadelphia. Things were starting to look a little rosier.

Breadon's policy on managers had always been—win or else. July and November had always been dangerous months for Cardinals skippers. Only two of the 14 pilots under his regime had quit voluntarily. Breadon was always quick to act when a team lost. He replaced three in July and four in November, two in June and one each in September, October and December. The two who left voluntarily were Bill McKechnie (after a fourth place finish in 1929) and Southworth after the 1945 season.[18]

As the third week of June ended another new team was in first place and this time it was Boston (31–23), followed by New York (29–20), Brooklyn (25–20—the sweep by St. Louis knocked them from first) and Chicago (27–23). St. Louis was now in fifth place, just one game below .500 at 27–28 and four and one-half games out. It had been a long hard climb. The team was 25–16 (a pennant winning pace) for the past six weeks. Slaughter was leading the league with a .358 mark while Brecheen (8–3) and Munger (5–1) were the leading moundsmen for the club.

Organized baseball retained the rights to sign college players before they graduated from college. Coaches wanted them to complete their education before they began playing professional baseball. Fred Shaughnessey, president of the International League, said he paid for his college education by playing professional baseball. College coaches said the same rule that governed signing high school players by colleges before they graduated should apply to organized baseball. Signing college kids before they graduated, organized ball claimed, was a different situation. These were older and more mature men and often had to earn a living.[19]

The Cardinals' nine game winning streak was paced by Musial who hit .485 with 10 runs scored and 15 RBIs. He was hitting like the Musial of old. At this juncture Garagiola, Moore, Slaughter, Schoendienst, Marion, Medwick and Northey were all over .300. Only Rice, Dusak and Kurowski were below the magic number. The team was now in a contending position and the old saying, "As goes Musial so goes the Cardinals," was certainly holding true.

Through the end of June St. Louis was 17–4 at night, but just 13–26 at day games, making them 30–30 overall. This would give credence to more night games for St. Louis and a key reason they were not in first place. Brooklyn climbed back into first place at 35–26, while Boston was just one half game back at 34–26. Moore had moved to .318 and Slaughter had fallen to .341 while Brecheen (9–3) and Munger (6–1) paced the mound corps. Munger was beginning to look like the 1944 version. Slaughter, Musial, Marion, Munger and Brecheen all made the All Star team.

A 13–4 homestand lifted St. Louis from last place to fourth (34–32). Dyer said a .500 road trip and the next homestand would tell the story. On the road trip St. Louis played every team in the circuit, including five doubleheaders. The homestand began July 22 and Brooklyn, New York and Boston would be mostly at home while the Cardinals were on the road. The Dodgers were especially tough at Ebbetts Field.

Brecheen was left behind to get treatment for a sore shoulder and he would miss a few starts and that hurt as he was the team's leading pitcher. Dickson took his place, starting for the first time in 40 days and he was knocked out in the first inning. He was now 2–9, but overall had pitched better than his record showed.

Cleveland signed the first black for the American League when they inked Larry Doby to a contract. Owner Bill Veeck said, "Why wait? Let's get the best." Doby was a star for the Newark Eagle Stars. Rickey saw a complete erasing of the racial line, although everyone didn't agree with him. The Dodgers also had in the minors pitcher Don Newcombe and catcher Roy Campanella, as Brooklyn was in the forefront of signing black players. When Cleveland played 22 year old Doby at first base it stirred up criticism as Eddie Robinson (regular first baseman and a top Cleveland prospect and MVP of 1946 for the International League) was benched.[20]

Meanwhile in the minors everything was coming up roses. Fifty-two leagues would finish the season and a new attendance record would be set. Only two teams folded. Tight pennant races in many leagues boosted attendance. Things looked very bright and prosperous for the future. This was the minor leagues' biggest season ever and they were looking forward to even better days in the coming years.

Hearn finally got another starting chance and defeated Pittsburgh 2–1 and Cincinnati 3–0. Dickson also shut out Cincinnati 2–0. These two seemed to be the answer to Dyer's prayers as this gave him two good right hand pitchers to go with Munger and his two left handers (Brecheen and Brazle), as Pollet had been relegated to the bullpen.

In the early part of the season Dyer had been quick with the hook on Hearn, although he showed a tendency to run out of gas after five or six innings. He also lacked experience in how to pace himself to go nine innings. Concern arose about Brecheen as he lost his last two starts before the All Star

Game and had a sore shoulder. Pollet seemed able to beat only Brooklyn, as three of his four victories were over them. The situation seemed to deteriorate as Brazle was hot and cold while the Cardinals hitters cooled off. Even Musial was in a slump again, just 2 for his past 24.

Despite the foregoing problems the team was only five games from first place at 38–35. They had played at 36–23 since their terrible start and that was a pennant winning pace. Brooklyn had climbed back into the driver's seat at 44–31 with Boston (41–32) and New York (38–31) trailing. At midseason Slaughter was .330 with 47 RBIs, Moore at .312 and Medwick at .327 in a part-time and pinch-hitting role.

Other hitters at this point were Northey at .290, Dusak at .282, and Kurowski .270 with 42 RBIs; expected improved health in the second half should give him better numbers. Musial, with his slump, was back at .246 and struggling again. Garagiola was at .250, Schoendienst at .240 and Marion at .234. More help was needed from Musial, Kurowski, Schoendienst and Marion in the second half. Brecheen was 9–5, Munger 7–1, Brazle 8–5, Hearn 4–3 and Pollet 4–4. Wilks was 2–0, but his ERA was over five runs per game. Dickson was 2–10, but his ERA was just over three runs per game.

Musial's bat and Pollet's arm carried the Cardinals' hopes and prayers for the year. If they performed as in 1946 then the Redbirds would repeat. Otherwise.... A profitable homestand would help and the schedule for the balance of the season had them at home more than on the road. Thus they had the opportunity to be masters of their own destiny. Musial said he could still hit .300 and Pollet said he could win 15 games. Everyone hoped so.

Over a 30 game period Musial hit .347, despite a couple of slumps, and this raised his average to .265. Pollet pitched his best game of the season for victory number five when he defeated Philadelphia 3–2 in 10 innings. Munger took the first loss since April 30 by the same score to Philadelphia. The big redhead had won seven in a row. It should be remembered that he had been kayoed several times and someone else got the decision. The Cardinals also played three double-headers in three days and were 4–2. They beat the Giants at the Polo Grounds for the first time this year taking four of five, outscoring them 38–27. The only game they lost was a slugfest, 17–8.

As the season entered the final week of July Brooklyn (49–35) was in first followed by Boston (45–36), New York (43–35) and St. Louis (44–39) four and one half games out, but firmly entrenched in the first division. Brecheen at 10–5 and Munger at 8–2 continue to lead the pitching staff.

With attendance lagging the St. Louis Browns signed two Negro players, infielder Hank Thompson and outfielder Willard Brown. Bill DeWitt said "they would help the team, although there were a number of doubting Thomases." Veeck said "the best Negro players had been taken. However, I believe more blacks will now take up the game as they see more opportunity to play in organized baseball." Scouts were watching Negro players all over the country. However, currently there were less than half a dozen good prospects. The jury was still out.[21]

On the West Coast Los Angeles was shaping up a rousing campaign to entice a major league club to their city. The selling job was planned on a very large scale. The Chandler group, including Frick and Harridge, were to get royal treatment as the Los Angeles group presented its story. They would wine and dine Chandler and his party. Phil Wrigley said he wanted whatever was best for the game, while the American and National leagues clamored for teams in Los Angeles.

Pacific Coast League president Rowland would hold out for a third major league status. There were two separate groups seeking St. Louis teams. Emory C. Percy, a Chicagoan and close friend of Babe Ruth, was after the St. Louis Browns. He would rename Sportsman's Park "Ruth Stadium," making him honorary vice president until the team was transferred to Los Angeles. Meanwhile Pauley was still pursuing the Cardinals.[22]

On August 18 Ebbets Field would be packed for several reasons. First, it was the last Cardinals-Brooklyn game there this year. Secondly, a doubleheader would be played. But the most important reason was the replay of a disputed 3–2 Brooklyn victory on July 20. All records went into the book. Frick upheld Dyer's protest and Brooklyn did not take the opportunity to enter a counterprotest five days after the event happened. Time had expired on noon of July 25 and therefore Frick ruled it a 3–3 tie game.

What happened was Northey had been told he hit a home run by umpire Beans Reardon, so he leisurely trotted around the bases and was tagged out for the last out in the ninth. Frick ruled he hit a home run and thus Hugh Casey lost his seventh win and Dickson averted his 11th loss. Normally rules prevail over umpire ruling, but this was similar to an incident involving Brooklyn (who lost the game) in 1942 and it was ordered replayed. Pitcher Whit Wyatt had hit a home run and then was tagged out. Two other precedents supported Frick's decision.

Frick said "to replay from point where Northey hit home run would be unfair to Brooklyn as the Cardinals would have a 3–0 lead and two out." In the game St. Louis had a 2–0 lead as Northey's home run was wiped off the books at the time. Then in the bottom of the ninth Brooklyn scored three runs to win the game 3–2. Either way St. Louis was not treated fairly. The game should have been played from the 3–0 point as St. Louis might have scored more. Brooklyn argued they were entitled to their three runs, but that would be true only after St. Louis had three legitimate outs, which they didn't.[23]

The St. Louis feeling was that six games was nothing for them to make up, as they had done that several times over the years. The World Series had almost become an annual event in St. Louis and Dyer agreed with the ardent Cardinals fans. The team had a successful road trip at 12–8, but let too many get away, including that game in Brooklyn. Slaughter hit .280, but Moore, nursing a sore leg, batted just .167. The catchers batted poorly. Garagiola hit .133, Rice hit .225 and Wilber hit .057. "Dyer," Joe said wryly, "has one catcher who can't hit [Rice], one catcher who can't catch [Wilber] and one who can't throw [Garagiola]."[24]

The Cardinals' home attendance was 601,547 and road was 947,954. The team expected to have new records for both this year. Negro players had helped the Browns' attendance as it had brought out more black fans. However, many players (white) felt they should have been sent to AAA (like Robinson) to prove their worth. It was unfair to white players that had spent several seasons in the minors.

Frick proposed a third National League team in Chicago and believed it should be the Cardinals. It would make for a natural rivalry like Brooklyn and New York. It would also solve the St. Louis problem of trying to support two teams. However, Frick forgot a couple of items. One, there already was a strong rivalry with the Cubs and number two, the Cardinals were a highly successful franchise, why move them?

It wouldn't be a good move if the Browns kept losing as the city could end up with no team. Also why should you transfer the most successful team of the past two decades that the National League had? They had won nine pennants, six world championships, and seven second place finishes during that time. Breadon had sent a feeler to Walter Briggs, owner of the Detroit Tigers, saying that for $1,000,000 he would transfer his franchise to Detroit. Briggs and the American League came back with a resounding no. Supposedly Breadon was opposed to Donald Muckerman signing black players, but he wouldn't confirm that.[25]

In the minor leagues southern circuits were to remain on an all white basis. There would be no black players south of the Mason-Dixon Line. As a result Dixie expected to offer faster baseball. Use of blacks in the majors and northern minor leagues would make more whites available south of the Mason-Dixon Line. Most Negroes came from the south and to play ball they would have to go north. They now played ball on sand lots and for the National and American Negro leagues.

Few minor league teams could afford to buy black players from the Negro leagues. They needed major league backing to accomplish this objective. Negro fans in the south attended minor league games and had their own seating and cheering section. They rooted hard for their teams (which were all white). There had been no real trouble, only an occasional scuffle in the stands.[26]

The Cardinals kept their spirits and chins up recalling past great drives, especially those of 1930 and 1942. They also remembered how well they played in the second half of 1939, 40 and 41 and almost won the pennant in 1939 and 1941. Their hopes were about dashed as Brooklyn won 13 in a row including a three game sweep of the Cardinals. On July 30 St. Louis was down 10–0 and they scored four in the bottom of the 7th inning and six more in the ninth to tie the game at 10–10. They almost won the game in the bottom of the ninth when Pee Wee Reese threw out Garagiola by a whisker as Marion crossed the plate with what would have been the winning run. The ball Garagiola hit, a foot either way, and the Cards would have won the game. Brooklyn then scored in the top of the 10th to win 11–10 as Hearn took the loss. The big concern had been consistent pitching. Brecheen had hip and shoulder problems and had lost more than he won lately while Munger had been hit hard his last several starts, although not normally charged with the loss.

By August 1 it looked like lights out for everyone save Brooklyn (63–36) who had built a 10 game lead on New York (49–42) and St. Louis (51–44). The caskets were draped with a black flag and the Cardinals' obituary was written. On the other side of town the Browns were having a different sort of problem. Their two black players were not performing very well. Thompson was hitting .194 and Brown .178. Fuel fired by fans as they said it was unfair to white players, who had to go through the system. These two should at least been sent to AAA teams for experience. It had helped road attendance, but in the long run the home figures had not improved.

The Cardinals once again came alive and brought back memories of 1930 and 1942. They turned the flag wake into a coming out party. They rallied with a new winning spirit, pitching steadies and Musial continued his climb and assault toward .300. Following the Dodgers' sweep the Cardinals swept Chicago, Cincinnati and Philadelphia to cut the lead from 10 games to five. Breadon said if they pulled this one out 35 Dodgers fans would jump off the Brooklyn Bridge.

Kurowski with 16 home runs should pass his career high of 21 set in 1945. Now that his injuries were behind him he had fired up and had a strong second half. Kurowski had a 13 game hitting streak during which he batted .431 and made 22 hits, including 13 extra base hits and had 20 RBIs. Marion was also hot and was expected to surpass his career high of 63 RBIs set in 1944. Dusak was hitting in the .280s and Moore went to the bench for a rest and returned when a right hand hitting lineup was needed. Musial was now at .298, almost to that golden circle. Brecheen was back in form and Dickson after an 0–7 start was now 8–11. Home attendance for 52 games was 840,708.

After the first week of August Brooklyn was first at 64–42, but only four games ahead of St. Louis (58–44). Kurowski was now .305 with 74 RBIs, a pace for over 100, while Slaughter was at .304 with 64 RBIs. Brecheen was 13–6, but Munger was 8–3 and without a victory since July 16. The Cardinals moved up and down as Musial's fortune went the same way.

A St. Louis sportswriter said to an associate early in the season that Musial looked like a little boy out there. He wasn't doing them any good, but they would be even worse without him. On May 8 he flew to St. Louis to see Dr. Hyland and his future looked as dark as the cellar where St. Louis was.

In his first four years he had led them to four pennants and three World Series championships. Surgery was postponed and treatment and diet prescribed until the season was over. He didn't regain his old form and strength immediately. He missed five games. He had been hitless in 18 of his first 44 games and got only one hit in eight games. Then he went on a tear, hitting safely in 47 of the next 59 games. Twenty seven times he had more than one hit and 7 times he had three hits and three times he made four hits in a game. The Cardinals were 41–17 (.707) pace once Stan started hitting (.370) which proved the old adage, "as goes Musial so goes the Cardinals."

Musial claimed he didn't hit as well at night as in the daytime. He had played more night games (55) in 1946 than anyone in the league. This year he had batted .361 in 37 night games, while batting just .253 in 62 day games. So he actually was hitting better at night than during the day, even though he thought the opposite was true.

A quick look at Musial's record will bear out the old adage and how important he was to the Cardinals.

May 2	Musial .174	eighth place
May 16	Musial .164	eighth place
May 30	Musial .188	eighth place
June 13	Musial .202	seventh place
June 27	Musial .253	fifth place
July 11	Musial .253	fourth place
July 25	Musial .282	second place
August 10	Musial .302	second place

The Cardinals were now confident if they could play .500 ball on the next road trip it would mean the pennant for the team. The club had only seven road games after September 1. They had moved from last to third place in batting and were second in runs scored. Only the New York Giants had scored more runs. The team had six players over .300. Over the past 60 games the club had played at a .695 pace and .722 in their most recent 36 home games. It looked like another patent second half St. Louis finish. St. Louis had 19 of their last 26 games at home, while Brooklyn would play 19 of their final 23 on the road. Of course pennants had been won on the road, mostly by the Cardinals. Medwick, Dusak, Slaughter, Northey, Kurowski and Musial were all over .300.

Brecheen had 16 complete games in his first 21 starts. Munger, knocked out five straight times, returned after a week's layoff due to chronic appendicitis and pitched a three hit shutout victory over Pittsburgh, The team also had turned 130 double plays in 108 games, but on the down side they were a sub .500 team in one run games at 13–18.

By mid–August Brooklyn (68–44) hung onto first place with a four and one half game bulge on St. Louis (62–47), who had been 60–36 since their horrible start. Wilks was 4–0, but his ERA was over five runs a game. He was unbeaten in the past two seasons with a 12–0 mark, but had been more lucky than good. Munger finally won a game and was 9–3 while Brecheen had an outside chance for 20 wins with his 14–6 record.

The team had split a four game series with Brooklyn, which was to the Dodgers' benefit and not St. Louis,' who needed to take three of four. The split was actually thanks to Kurowski who was on base 14 of 18 plate appearances, the last 11 in succession. He hit three home runs and had a career high 22 for the season. He had been the best right hand batter the Cardinals had had since the glory days of Medwick and the best home run hitter since Johnny Mize. Brazle's first start since July 11 was an 11–3 win over Brooklyn, ending a personal five game losing streak to them.

As the final week of August approached Kurowski hit his 23rd home run for a new record for third basemen, breaking the mark of 22 set by Freddy Lindstrom of the New York Giants in 1930. In runs allowed, despite a poor start and at times erratic pitching, the Cardinals had been the stingiest in runs allowed per game at 3.97 while Brooklyn was fifth with 4.8. It's puzzling why Brooklyn was first and St. Louis second when they had allowed almost one run per game less and scored the same number as the Dodgers. This would be one to mull over the hot stove all winter if the Redbirds didn't pull this one out.

It could only be traced to their ineptness against the weak sisters of the league. They had played .571 versus the first division teams of Brooklyn, Boston and New York, while the Dodgers were just .500 versus St. Louis, New York and Boston. The difference was the Dodgers were .690 versus the second division teams while St. Louis was .567 or basically the same they had played against the first division teams. Brooklyn had used the old McGraw theory of break even with the contenders and stomp the second division teams and it had them in first place. The Cardinals lost the series for the year in Philadelphia, 6–5. They never won a series in Philadelphia as they split two and lost the third.

Musial hit his 17th home run, a new personal record for him, but his teammate Slaughter was out of the lineup due to dizzy spells. It had to be very serious to keep ol' Eno out of the ballgame. By the end of August Brooklyn had increased its lead to seven games as they were 76–46 while St. Louis was 70–54. Both Slaughter and Musial drop below .300, leaving only Kurowski as a regular over that mark at .305. Munger was pitching better and was now at 11–4, but Brecheen had fallen on hard times. His quest for 20 wins seemed to have gone the same direction as the Cardinals' pennant drive. He had lost his last three starts and was now 14–9.

The Pacific Coast League barred the door against major league invasion. It would not allow any team to set up shop unless the Pacific Coast League was given major league status as a third major league. An invading franchise would have to pay $15,000,000 in compensation and in addition to $1,000,000 or more for a franchise. There was some consideration for 10 teams in the National and American League each with the current owners of the team becoming a major league club. Those considered were Oakland, Los Angeles, Hollywood and San Francisco. There was no final commitment by either side and the meeting ended with the future to decide what would happen.[27]

The Cardinals were looking for a sweep of the Dodgers when they came to St. Louis September 9 through 11. This was their last big hope, otherwise it would be almost over. The Cardinals were hoping for another thrilling finish like 1930, '34 or '42. Games here had been all or nothing this year. The Dodgers won the only game in May (limited due to rainout). The Cardinals then swept them four in June and the Dodgers took all three in July.

Unfortunately Dyer didn't have the same quality pitching staff that carried his predecessors through a great September. The road trip just completed was most tiring on the team as they finished 10–9. Musial was worn down and both Marion and Schoendienst needed resting, but Cross was hitting only .143 and Dyer didn't want to play inexperienced Creger. The team didn't have the quality infield reserves of years past.

The week before the Brooklyn invasion found them six and one-half games ahead of St. Louis as they were 83–50 to the Cardinals' 75–55. The Redbirds needed a sweep of the Dodgers to have any chance at all. Musial was at .303 with Kurowski and Dusak both at .301. Munger was having an impressive season at 12–4, although he had had nine no decisions, while rookie Hearn was 10–5 and boded well for 1948.

The Sporting News named Robinson rookie of the year. He gained the award for his all around athletic ability. He was being called the "ebony" Ty Cobb on the base paths. He had proven to be a capable first baseman and provided adequate defense. He had also hit close to .300, was a team player and had a fighting winning spirit.

The Redbirds got a lift from Brazle's sinker as Dyer relied on him in the trip east. He would use Brazle down the stretch drive. Batters looked like they were trying to kill snakes when they swung at his pet pitch. The only other consistent and dependable pitcher on the trip had been Dickson. Brazle became a lifesaver as he saved or won four of five games during a critical weeklong period from August 17 to August 23. He had a rubber arm and could start or relieve. Brazle (11–6) looked forward to more work. The more he pitched the better his sinker worked.

An injury to Schoendienst pointed out a big Cardinals weakness and that was reliable infield reserves. Rookie Vernal "Nippy" Jones took over at second base when Schoendienst's right shoulder came out of its socket. The key question was could Jones (who was second in the International League at .333) hit in the majors? Dyer wanted to return Musial, who had become an excellent first baseman, to the outfield and play Jones at first.

If Jones could hit Musial would be ideal for right field as he was a left hand thrower. Also, neither aged Medwick or rotund Northey were good running outfielders and Slaughter's ankle injury had put a strain on Moore's tired legs. A young, fast and healthy Musial would be a plus in the outfield. Dusak had been a splendid surprise with his hitting and was a great defensive player with a strong arm.

Dyer's ideal was eight men playing 154 games or as many as possible and hitting both types of pitching. However a team did need reliable reserves to rest some players and to cover for injuries. The Cardinals did have several good prospects for next season.

As the middle of September drew near Brooklyn held a five and one half game bulge on the Cardinals and it would take a total collapse by Brooklyn plus an exceptional hot streak by St. Louis to win it all. Kurowski was at .308 with 97 RBIs and Musial was .306 with 83 RBIs. Munger was at 14–4 and looking like the 1944 Munger, which was a blessing for 1948, Brazle was 12–7 and Hearn was 10–6 with Brecheen at 15–9.

The Rickeyless Cardinals fell as the Dodgers' empire grew. The Redbirds had to attract a flow of new talent. He said he would have kept the Coopers and prevented the jumpers from going to Mexico. With Walker Cooper behind the plate, Lanier and Martin on the mound and Klein as a reserve the Cardinals would have won it all. Klein could have spelled Schoendienst and Marion.

Twenty-five years earlier Rickey began building what became known as the Cardinals Chain Gang. It produced nine pennant winners, six World Series titles, and seven second place finishes in 21 years. The Cardinals had unlimited talent and had the cream of the crop. History had shown they could have won another five or six pennants. The Cardinals kept the cream and sold the rest to other teams.

They could afford that strategy in those days as they always had someone available in the minors. In Rickey's day they brought up two or three pitchers in September; most of the veterans on the team came up via that route. It looked like the Dodgers were about to replace St. Louis as the ruling team of the National League. What a sad day for St. Louis and what a sad turn of events. Many believed Breadon's ego and pride got in the way and Rickey took his talent to Brooklyn and this cost them the pennant in 1945 and again this season.

The Dodgers took two of three in the crucial September series. In years past it was St. Louis doing that. The Cardinals lost due to poor fielding and poor pitching, but there was great hitting by both clubs. The Cardinals missed Schoendienst's range at second base. Jones had six hits in the series, but couldn't go to his right. He also made a glaring error in game one and Kurowski missed the series due to an injury. The team was short on strength from the bench.

The club set a new attendance record at 1,156,515. Dyer would tear his staff apart next season if he was still the manager. No one would have a job, except Munger if his arm was okay and Brecheen if his shoulder was all right. Otherwise it was Katy bar the gate. Dyer wanted a staff strong enough that Dickson and Brazle could do most of their work out of the bullpen. He could use them as occasional or spot starts, mainly in double-headers or when one of the regular starters needed a little additional rest.

With 13 games left the Cardinals had outscored last year's team 716–712, but had also given up 47 more runs than last season's team gave up in 158 games (592). Therein was the difference between 1946 and 1947. Pitchers expected to be tested were Clarence Beers and Al Papai of Houston, winners of 25 and 21 games respectively, Ray Yochim (14–4), Bill Reeder (4–4) at Rochester and Ken Johnson (6–3) at Omaha and young Harvey Haddix (17–4) from Winston-Salem. He had been nicknamed "The Kitten," as he was smaller than Brecheen, but similar in pitching style.

The Cardinals, with a three game loss to New York in September, lost the season series 13–9. Mize and Cooper had 58 hits and 43 runs against St. Louis; that was biting the hand that once fed you. If St. Louis had either one or both of them in the lineup all year, how different the season would have been. Mize had 12 singles, eight doubles, one triple and eight home runs while Cooper had 15 singles, five doubles, two triples and seven home runs.

Dyer said not to sell the Cardinals short in 1948 as this club wasn't collapsing. The Cardinals were 46–31 at home (49–29 at home and on the road in 1946), but this season they were just 43–34 on the road. What caused the Cardinals to finish second? Name them. A 2–11 start, Musial's illness which caused him to be below .200 until early June, Pollet's decline and numerous injuries to Kurowski, Schoendienst, Slaughter and Moore. Another key factor was inconsistency by Munger, especially in the first half and then Brecheen's shoulder problems in the second half as he went from 14–6 to 16–11.

Three times St. Louis got close to Brooklyn, within four games, but the Dodgers rose to the occasion and took seven of the last ten games. Give St. Louis just three more wins in those meetings and they finish at 92–62 and Brooklyn at 91–63. That's how close they came. Again credit must be given to the Dodgers for holding off St. Louis.

Were the Redbirds dead? Not even sick, said Breadon; with $1,500,000 in the till and Dyer back, the owner didn't make dire threats. He said the Cardinals had brought more players to the major leagues the last two decades than any other team. Simply because they didn't bring any new players up (except Jones in September) didn't mean the system was failing or had collapsed. Employing a stand pat policy last season was a mistake; bringing up no new players was contrary to the Cardinals' winning philosophy.

The final attendance was 1,248,031. Final standings had Brooklyn at

94–60 and St. Louis at 89–65; after a horrendous 2–11 start the team was 87–56, which would be 95–59 for the season. Brooklyn lost the World Series four games to three. It looked like St. Louis would have to win the pennant again to give the National League a championship. Since 1941 only St. Louis had brought the world title home for the National League.

Everything considered we look at the records of four players and that tells the 1947 story. Let us put behind us injuries, mishaps and the like. Musial (regardless of the reason) went from .365 to .312. Slaughter slipped from .301 to .290, but more important his RBIs decreased from a league high of 130 to 86. On the pitching side Pollet was 21–10, with a 2.10 ERA, 22 complete games in 32 starts and five saves in 1946. In 1947, again regardless of reason, he was 9–11 with a 4.35 ERA, nine complete games in 24 starts and two saves. Dickson was 15–6, 2.89 ERA with 12 complete games in 19 starts, and appeared in 47 games. In 1947 he had a respectable 3.06 ERA, again appeared in 47 games, had 11 complete games in 25 starts, but was just 13–16. He finished 13–9 after an 0–7 start. If we take Pollet and Dickson they went from a composite 36–16 in 1946 to 22–27 in 1947, a decline of 12½ games in the standings. This paragraph tells it all as far as your writer is concerned.

NINE

1948

The Great Season

Stan Musial, who was off stride due to his appendix problems, and George Munger, who had the same problem that affected his pitching (even though he finished 16–5), both had their appendixes removed in the off-season. They both were expected to be at full strength for 1948 and each predicted a banner season. Musial felt he would duplicate 1946, while Munger would pitch like he did in 1944.

The dinner banquet was off limits for Musial and Joe Garagiola during this off-season. It didn't help them in 1947, especially Joe. If Vernal "Nippy" Jones, Mike Natisin (Columbus) or Glenn Nelson (Lynchburg) could make the grade in 1948 then Musial could go back to the outfield, which he and Dyer both preferred that he played.

Max Lanier yearned to come back to the big leagues and was anxiously waiting to come back to St. Louis. He missed the team, the town, his former teammates and major league baseball. He frankly admitted that his failure to heed warnings of a Mexican boomerang was the biggest mistake of his life. It had cost him in many ways, especially his major league career, which was really blooming in 1946 as he seemed headed for the best season of his life.

Lanier said, "If I never do anything else I want to go back and pitch for the Cardinals. Maybe at the end of the five year ban period, but I want to do it." He had no tangible reason to expect leniency from Commissioner Chandler, just hoping. Big leaguers gave a great deal of credit to the Mexican exodus for the pension plan and other benefits. Lanier was keeping in shape, waiting to pitch for the St. Louis organization. Lanier said, "Financially I am okay, but missed the major leagues and there was nothing like pitching in the big time." He had quit the Mexican League in midseason after reporting late because of a salary dispute. His salary had been cut in half as were the salaries of many American ballplayers.[1]

The Cardinals, who originated the farm system, came up with a new idea of drafting players from other clubs. Faced with the necessity of filling holes the Cardinals developed the plan. Thirty-three of the 108 players in the 1946 draft were selected by St. Louis, of which six proved to be outstanding prospects. They were part of a group under the National Defense Service List that had to be kept by other clubs.

Since the St. Louis farm system seemed to be rebuilding they probably wouldn't draft as heavily this season, but wouldn't pass up any opportunity. Joe Medwick drew his release and hoped to finish out his days as a minor league owner. He was invited to spring training, but had no guarantee of a job. Medwick hit .311 in 148 at-bats appearing in 73 games during 1947. In addition to his appendectomy, bone chips were removed from Munger's arm and that had also affected his pitching motion the past season.

St. Louis was to pay a rousing tribute to Sam Breadon on January 13, 1948, in a testimonial dinner honoring his Cardinals accomplishments and feats. He was to receive a long delayed appreciation for what he had given to St. Louis with the Cardinals. Senior league officials, major league club owners, former Cardinals managers, and stage and screen luminaries would join St. Louis civic leaders in honoring Breadon for bringing prominence to St. Louis with championship baseball via the St. Louis Cardinals.

President Henry Rowland of the Pacific Coast League presented a request at the annual convention of minor leagues in Miami that the Pacific Coast League be granted dual status as a major-minor league. They would change the name to the Pacific Major League and be under the direct jurisdiction of the baseball commissioner and major league council. However, they would also remain amenable to certain minor league rules, regulations and designations.

This was a compromise between those owners who wanted to go to major league status and those that wanted to go "outlaw" (do it without the approval of the major leagues). This special major-minor league status would be created for five years (1–1–48 to 1–1–53), subject to cancellation if and when full major league status was granted.[2]

Based on one of the rookies making the team Musial would move back into the outfield, where he preferred and could better help the club, especially with aging and injury prone Terry Moore. The Cardinals would form an outfield of Erv Dusak in center field, Enos Slaughter in right field and Musial in left field. Moore would be used as a reserve outfielder since his legs and knees no longer allowed him everyday play.

The Cardinals also had a good prospect in 22 year old Larry Miggins, who batted .288 with 16 home runs. He was a right hand batter with power, which the team could use. Dyer figured he needed a little more seasoning, but should be ready in a couple of years to take an everyday position. The fates of Dick Sisler and Ron Northey would remain unknown until spring training. It had been decided that Bernie Creger would be somewhere else next year. The team had to keep him on the roster all season as he was a National Defense player.

Breadon stated he was not in the market for the St. Louis Browns owned Sportsman's Park as he was still planning to build a new stadium. There was three years to go on the current lease, but if the Browns were sold and moved elsewhere then Sportsman's Park would be offered to the Cardinals as their permanent home. Breadon owned property at the projected site at Grand and Chouteau and wanted to build a modern new park as a tribute to the Cardinals. He said it was a Cardinals policy to own parks where possible as they owned several in minor league cities. He had no problem with the high school rule that you couldn't sign a player until his class was graduated, but his policy was still to sign players as young as he could.

Musial, with a career .342 average (hurt by his .312 season in 1947), was a white chip to finish in the top 10 for his career, if not fifth or sixth. His career average had been .347 prior to 1947 and the devastating illness that he suffered. His goal for 1948 was to regain what he lost during the past year.

Breadon hatched $3,000,000 on a $200 bird nest egg. "I'll never be poor again," he vowed in jobless days. His $35 as a parade vendor in 1903 provided the stake that led to fame and fortune as the Cardinals owner. He was living on 15 cents a day in 1903 at age 27 while he looked for work. He parlayed that into a $3,650,000 sale of the team on November 25 to Robert E. Hannegan, former postmaster general of the United States. Hannegan and associates had put up $650,000 in cash and the rest was negotiated by a loan.

He had taken a $75 monthly job with Halsey Automobile in St. Louis, which was $50 per month less than he had been earning at a bank in New York City. He saw a future in the automobile industry and when Halseys learned he wanted to start his own garage he was fired. He had been sending $40 monthly to his mother and living in a $1 per week room, getting free lunches in saloons by buying nickel beer. When his money ran out, he borrowed $300 and lived on 15 cents per day so he could continue sending $40 per month home without telling his mother he had lost his job.

He made $35 by selling popcorn to people watching a parade for the coming world's fair. Marion Lambert backed him in starting the Western Auto Company by putting up $10,000. In the first week he sold two cars and made $300 profit. In 1904 he made $20,000 and sold the business in 1908 and joined the St. Louis Cardinals. When Cardinals stock was offered for sale in 1917 he bought $200 worth and then made a loan for $20,000. He was then made a director and finally president of the team.

Breadon then sold a run down ballpark to the board of education (to use the land to build Beaumont High School) for $200,000 and that put the Cardinals on sound footing. From there the rest became history. Teaming with Branch Rickey they developed the farm system idea, although most of the credit does belong to Rickey. Starting in 1926 the Cardinals would soon become the best team in the National League and only the New York Yankees had been more successful, but not by much. Breadon ran and helped develop the most lucrative and profitable farm system in baseball, which gave the city one of the two best baseball teams in the major leagues.[3]

Los Angeles and Baltimore were both bidding for the St. Louis Browns. Robert Rosenberg, owner of the Baltimore Colts, seemed to have the inside track. He would want to sell Sportsman's Park to the Cardinals and move the Browns to Baltimore. There were also groups in Chicago and Kansas City interested in the Browns. Fans in St. Louis were all agog at what was happening. First the Cardinals were sold, but would remain in St. Louis and now outside sources were bidding for the Browns and wanted to relocate the team.

For the present time the Cardinals would hold onto all their aces as there were no plans by the new owners for trading or selling any of the current stars. The only move the team would make would be for an experienced catcher or first baseman. Dyer insisted Musial would return to the outfield. When questioned why they lost the pennant in 1947, Dyer said, "I don't like to make excuses, but we had a lot of misfortune. There was Stan's illness, injuries to Slaughter, Marion's back problem, Munger's bone chips and appendix problems and sore arms of Dickson and Brecheen at various times during the season."

He didn't state that the complete collapse of Pollet was another factor in the team failing to win the pennant. All you have to do was look at his decline from 21 victories to nine and that in itself tells why the Redbirds didn't repeat. Dyer believed that Pollet's operation should return him to his 1946 form. He was looking forward to the new campaign with great enthusiasm, especially new pitchers Clarence Beers, Al Papai and Gerry Staley.[4]

The major leagues again turned down the Pacific Coast League bid for major league status. They had asked for dual status as AAA and major league, but organized baseball said no. In their opinion the Pacific Coast League was not ready for major league baseball status. They would still be considered as a minor league, although high quality. In most areas they were lacking good parks and many players, while good, were not of major league caliber and this would cheapen the product offered to the public. The Pacific Coast League was crushed by the turndown. The National League favored a 10 club league, but the American League wouldn't agree. The idea was to make San Francisco and Los Angeles major league teams. President Rowland shouted, "Over my dead body as this would wreck the Pacific Coast League."[5]

The Cardinals formed A and B squads for spring training to make certain all players got an equal and fair opportunity. This would allow for more innings pitched and more at-bats for all players. The A team would be composed of regulars, but could be dropped to B if an impressive or promising rookie was there. The Cardinals were interested in catchers Phil Masi of Boston, Ray Mueller of Cincinnati and Clyde McCullough of the Cubs. Another interesting prospect was Vernal "Nippy" Jones as he led the International League with a .337 mark, had 38 doubles, 12 triples, 10 home runs and 81 RBIs in 445 at-bats before his late season call up to the Cardinals in 1947.

Hannegan found other teams weren't willing to trade a quality catcher to St. Louis. They backed away from a trade whenever that was mentioned. They knew St. Louis' weakness and realized that a good catcher could give the club the 1948 pennant. Dyer remained confident that Garagiola could be the everyday catcher and perform at a major league level both offensively and defensively. For now the only changes would be bringing up players from the minor leagues.

Jackie Robinson's success started a new clamor and argument regarding the black ballplayer. Liberal thinkers who just a year ago said open the gates to Negroes now said organized baseball was ruining the black player. They argued when the major leagues started taking the star Negro players then the fans stopped supporting their local black owned team and started following Robinson and the Dodgers or Larry Doby and the Indians. They pointed out as an example the Cuban National All Stars won the championship but lost $20,000. It was estimated that the Negro League finished in the red by $100,000. It seemed you couldn't please everyone. It was almost like you couldn't win for losing.[6]

The Cardinals planned on having a 50 game spring training schedule, using the A and B team concept. Hannegan wanted a $250,000 loan for property at Spring and Chouteau (formerly owned by Breadon) to obtain a new park. The Cardinals considered renaming the team the St. Louis National Baseball Club, Inc.

Breadon said, "St. Louis can't support two clubs as they have the smallest drawing area in major league baseball. There are no large cities in a 100 mile radius of St. Louis. Boston and Philadelphia, which had two teams, also have cities of 100,000 or more within 100 miles of their home base. Cincinnati with only one team has cities such as Dayton, Columbus and Louisville, Kentucky, within a 100 mile radius."

He never would have made this admission while owner of the team. He also added that "without lights at Sportsman's Park one team would have trouble drawing sufficient fans." There had been only a few seasons where the attendance was equally divided so both teams could make a profit. The 1944 year was a good example, but these were few and far between. Championship teams needed 700,000 to break even and second division teams needed

350,000. Night baseball had boosted St. Louis attendance, while various interests where trying to develop forces and finances to keep the Browns in St. Louis and maintain the city as a two team town.[7]

Classy recruits at first base and in the pitching area looked to bolster the Cardinals for the 1948 season. With Jones at first base then Musial could return to the outfield. However, Jones didn't have a lock on the job as he had major competition from Natison and Nelson. Both were left hand batters. Natison was 31 and hit .311, scored 93 runs, had 106 RBIs, 35 doubles and 22 home runs at Columbus, while Nelson (only 23) hit .371 with 38 doubles, 11 triples, 11 home runs (no player hit 20 home runs in the league so this was an impressive number), scored 98 runs, had 105 RBIs and stole 20 bases at Lynchburg.

Dyer was also beaming about his bright pitching prospects. Beers was 25–8 with 2.40 ERA and had 27 complete games while Papai was 21–10 with a 2.45 ERA and 24 complete games. Each also won four games in the playoffs. No Cardinals pitcher had 20 complete games in 1947. Brecheen led the staff with 18 (he had 16 in his first 21 starts and then a sore shoulder limited him to two in his last seven when he went just 2–5), Munger had 13 and Dickson registered 11. Dyer was elated with the possibilities for the coming season.

The Cardinals were demanding at least the same number of night games (41) in 1948 as they had in 1947, but they realized the visiting team had to agree. They pointed out that it was advantageous to both parties as the attendance was much better at night games and since there was a 60/40 split on the revenue between home team and visiting team each team's take would be higher. The Cardinals also planned to discuss trade possibilities at the winter major league meeting in New York.

The Mexican League asked for peace as they were sending emissaries to visit Walter Mulbry, secretary to Chandler, on January 21–25. They wanted a major-minor league status and a provision for jumpers to receive amnesty and be able to return to the major leagues. They proposed that major leagues pay $25,000 for any player purchased from a Mexican team and that a Mexican team could buy any player below AAA. They would pay $7,000 for an AA player down to $1,950 for Class D player. All this was subject to approval by Chandler.[8]

Lou Perini, owner of the Boston Braves, predicted there would be 12 teams in each major league within the next five years. This would require a re-alignment of the minors to make this change possible. He included in the majors Milwaukee, San Francisco, Hollywood, and Los Angeles. They would be the four head cities and they could run two 10 team leagues and expand at a later date. His proposal was receiving lukewarm acceptance at best.[9]

Robert Murphy, who had attempted to unionize players, had a bill before the House in Massachusetts which would eliminate the reserve clause in the Commonwealth of Massachusetts. This drew the fire of major league ballplayers. Dixie Walker and Johnny Murphy, the representatives of the National and American Leagues respectively, attended the meeting to protest and state the players' interests and concerns. They were joined by catcher Birdie Tebbetts and they all blasted the bill and said baseball and players needed the reserve clause. It was protection for the team and player. It guaranteed the team their players and the players were guaranteed a job. Tebbetts said how "the game had given him an education, paid his debts and helped support his family." His eloquent presentation won over the representatives and Murphy's bill was defeated.[10]

Dyer said making the correct choices on his mound corps was the key to the Cardinals' pennant chances. Everyone wanted to know where Musial would play in 1948 and Dyer said he was a manager's delight. He would play wherever the team needed and wanted him. He was the best defensive first baseman in 1947, but he believed he could better preserve his strength playing in the outfield. However, he would do whatever the team needed and wanted. Dyer predicted a four team race between the Cardinals, Braves, Dodgers and Giants.

The National League opposed amnesty for the Mexican jumpers. Owners also opposed softening the suspension. The prevailing attitude was they made their choice, now let them pay for it. Also discussed at the winter meeting was the elimination of the March 1 starting date for spring training. Many teams wanted to start earlier, especially for pitchers and catchers, to be able to look at more players and give them additional training and conditioning time.

Dyer saw a very close race and said they couldn't risk weakening the team with a trade. They had to get more than they gave, otherwise the team would be better to stand pat. Mel Ott of the Giants and Dyer talked several trade possibilities, but came to no agreement. The days were gone when you could sell a good player for cash. Today you have to have a fair trade that benefited both parties. The Cardinals needed players of quality caliber before they could make a trade, was Dyer's position.

Hannegan, after a tour of the farm teams, was convinced of the club's outright ownership policy. He was also convinced farms benefit players (they got training, honing of their skills, moving them along as they improved and promoting when ready and as they were needed). Hannegan preferred ownership to working agreements. The farm system was the best opportunity for youngsters to make the major leagues. Outright ownership was also better for supervision without division of authority and it further allowed the farm team a better chance to make a profit.

Larry McPhail, former president of the New York Yankees, blasted Rickey over a vote taken in 1946 regarding Negro players. McPhail denied that only Brooklyn voted to allow Negroes to play. He said Rickey lied and also denied that clubs tried to stop Rickey from signing Robinson as he said

Rickey also lied about that. McPhail agreed they destroyed the letters written at the meeting, not because they contained anti–Negro remarks, but unkindly and cutting statements about Commissioner Chandler. It was agreed to destroy these letters and issue a revised report that did not contain negative comments about Chandler. There was nothing derogatory about blacks in either set of letters.[11]

Most Cardinals players are signed with only six unsigned and among them were Musial, Brecheen and Marion. Rookie pitcher Ray Yochim, outfielder Harold Rice and catcher Del Rice were also unsigned. Musial signed and returned his contract. Dyer said the Cardinals' pennant chances hinged on the arms of Pollet, Munger and Wilks. The Cardinals needed Pollet to pitch like 1946 and Munger to improve on his 1947 performance, despite a 16–5 record. The team also needed Wilks to be effective out of the bullpen and be the pitcher he was in 1944.

Marion and Moore had saved Dyer's job in 1947 when Breadon called them into the office and asked if they thought he was a detriment to the team. Both spoke heroically of Dyer and said "the fact the team was in last place wasn't his fault, but a series of circumstances currently beyond his control." That meeting saved Dyer's job. One word from either and Dyer would have been fired.[12]

The team had four catchers in camp. They were Del Rice, Garagiola, Del Wilber and rookie Johnny Bucha (who batted .361 in the minors in 1947). They needed one of them to prove they could be a steady, dependable everyday catcher and hit with some authority, certainly not like Cooper, but with a respectable bat. Dyer said the Cardinals needed more power and believed that Brooklyn was the team to beat. He was also concerned that Brecheen was still unsigned.

Among the musts for the season were improved catching and better infield reserves. When Marion and Schoendienst had injury problems or needed a rest, no capable fill in was available. Had one been there then both could have performed better given a day off every now and then. However, Dyer said selecting the right pitchers was still the key to success. In the early going Munger and Pollet had looked good as had rookies Beers and Papai. Musial was healthy, strong and ready for a big season. Dyer continued to have an interest in McCullough as well as the Cubs' outfielder Andy Pafko. He was right handed and batted .302 with power last season.

This year things were different as the Cardinals slump came before the season opened (which was good news). They dropped their first three exhibition games. In 1947 they breezed through spring training with the best record and everybody predicted they would win the pennant in a runaway. Then the season started and they couldn't win for losing. Munger said his arm felt light as a feather after the operation and he saw a big season in the making for himself. Pollet continued to impress and Sisler had injected himself into the battle for the first base job with some strong hitting. Tommy Glaviano could be one of the infield reserves, as he could play second, short or third and possessed fine speed.

The Cardinals decided to stand pat with their regulars, but would have new reserves. This meant that the regulars kept their jobs. New pitchers were expected to bolster the pitching staff, which despite its problems in 1947 had the league's best ERA. Dyer had high hopes that Pollet would pitch like 1946 and that young Ken Johnson could overcome his wildness and provide a valuable assist from the bullpen or as a spot starter. Dyer remained concerned about the catching situation. It looked like the infield reserves would be Don Lang and Glaviano, while Dusak, Diering and Northey would be the outfield back up.

For a while a black cloud hung over the Cardinals' training camp as Marion's trick knee gave him considerable problems and it looked like he could be out for the season. However, now it was okay and Marion was ready to start the year. Musial said he was happy and content to be a Cardinal. He had received a good contract and didn't ever want to play for any other team. Sisler continued his fine hitting, so either he or Jones would be at first or share the spot, and Musial could now definitely return to the outfield.

For now Dyer decided that Wilber would be the number one catcher as Garagiola was still having trouble with his throwing and it might be necessary to send him back to the minors for more schooling and seasoning. Rice would play against left hand pitchers and get some fair playing time. Dickson was scheduled to pitch six innings against the Yankees, but because he had held them hitless Dyer kept him in the game. He finished with a no hitter as they defeated New York 7–0. All the Cardinals' runs came in the first inning off Floyd Bevens.

The Cardinals would be strong with their first line on the field, but there was still concern that the reserves overall didn't measure up to the seasons of 1941–46. The outfield would be Slaughter, Moore and Musial with Kurowski, Marion and Schoendienst in the infield with Nelson and Jones platooning at first. He had planned to play Sisler at first base but he was traded on April 7 to Philadelphia for cash and infielder Ralph LaPointe, who would provide better back up reserve than the team had in 1947.

The catching job for now was Wilber number one, Rice number two and Garagiola could be number three, number two, number one or back to the minors. He needed badly to get his throwing problems straightened out. The nucleus of the staff consisted of seven pitches who were Pollet, Munger, Brecheen, Dickson, Brazle, Hearn and rookie Gerry Staley. The last three spots would be a battle between Wilks, Beers, Papai, Johnson, Yochim and Ken Burkhart. Johnny Grodzicki was still trying to make the team, but the war wounded veteran didn't seem to have much of a chance. What a shame. The war evidently ruined a potentially fine career. He was one of the brightest prospects in the Cardinals' system prior to World War II.

The reserves had weaknesses. Dusak was a fine outfielder, but there were questions about his hitting, although he did bat .284 in 328 at-bats last season. Northey was a good hitter, but other than a rifle arm was not a good outfielder. Diering was an excellent defensive outfielder, but a weak hitter. Infield reserves Lang and Glaviano were question marks and the latter might need more seasoning. Beers figured to be in the bullpen with Wilks and unless Papai could get better control of his knuckle ball, he would be back in the minors.

The writers and scribes picked the Yankees to win the American League pennant followed by Boston, Detroit and Cleveland. In the National League it was Boston, followed by St. Louis, New York and Brooklyn. However, others claimed Boston in the American League and St. Louis in the National League, setting up a repeat of the 1946 World Series.

The Cardinals' pitching was rated best in the league. The Cardinals had the best ERA in the National League every season from 1941 through 1947 except 1945 when they finished second. If Pollet and Musial returned to their 1946 form then the Cardinals would win the pennant. There were some weaknesses as the reserves weren't up to par and the team wasn't as fast as in prior seasons. Other questions involved Moore and at age 36 how many games could he play, especially if his knees and legs weren't back to full strength? Jones would be the first right hand hitting first baseman in 25 years. After their horrible start and the Cards were eight games under .500 on June 13 they played .657 ball the rest of the way, which was the best in the league.

Jones looked good at first base as the Cardinals won their first two games 4–0 and 5–2 over Cincinnati behind route going performances by Dickson and Munger. Jones was playing great defensive ball and had taken over for the man (Musial) who was the best defensive first baseman in 1947. Dusak looked ready to step in if one of the outfielders needed a rest. Musial began the season hitting with authority. LaPointe had looked good filling in for the injured Schoendienst on April 21 against Cincinnati. The Cardinals started off well as they were 2–1 with Philadelphia and Brooklyn as well. Last season at this time the team was 2–5.

There had risen quite a furor over the bonus rule. It was said it was unfair to players receiving the bonus and unfair to players in the minors. Player receiving the bonus needed experience but were forced to sit on a major league bench while a deserving minor leaguer couldn't move up to a major league team and earn the minimum $5,000 salary. It's akin to giving a youngster a scholarship to college and then telling him he couldn't go to classes. Also, giving a bonus to an unproven youngster was unfair to proven major leaguers, as they could be earning more money instead of it going to some unknown player.[13]

On April 22 Brecheen defeated John Schmitz and the Cubs 1–0. Then rookie Cliff Chambers defeated the Cardinals and Russ Meyer of the Cubs beat Dickson 3–1, holding St. Louis to one hit. Three Cincinnati pitchers held St. Louis to seven hits. At one stretch Dusak was 0 for 13 and Slaughter 0 for 15. As of April 30 New York took the lead with a 7–3 record, while St. Louis fell to 3–4 with four losses in five road games. Boston, the pre-season favorite, was 4–7 and in last place.

In 1947 after 12 games Musial was at .174, while this season he was at .373 for a gain of 199 points. He had four doubles, three triples and three home runs. He had kept St. Louis in the race despite slumps by Dusak, Slaughter and Jones. When rest of the team began hitting the Cardinals would be tough, but so would the rest of the league.

The team also faced numerous injuries, some minor and some serious. Kurowski's arm was bothering him again, affecting his throwing and hitting. Marion had a charley horse in his right leg while Moore, Dusak and Jones all had sore right shoulders. There were injuries throughout the league, some worse than St. Louis. The changeable weather was blamed for many of the problems, as it went from wet to dry to wet, warm to cold to warm.

Rice had taken over the number one catching job, although hitting in the .190s, but Wilber and Garagiola were barely over the .100 mark. Also Rice was the best defensive catcher in the group. Meanwhile the team had moved up on Stan's hitting as they were third with a 7–5 mark while Pittsburgh was first at 9–5 and New York 10–6. Brooklyn was in at 6–6 and Chicago was last at 5–9 as of the end of week one in May.

Frankie Gustine of Pittsburgh led the league at .434 while Brooklyn's Bruce Edwards was second at .423, followed by teammate Carl Furillo at .389. Cincinnati's Bert Haas was at .385 and Boston's Tommy Holmes was at .379 followed by Musial with .373. Brecheen 2–0 and Brazle 2–1 paced the Cardinals' pitching staff.

Another problem that had loomed for organized baseball was national television. This was seen as a major blow to the minor leagues. The power to protect territorial rights was involved. Owners saw a mixture of gold and shadows on the screen. They wondered what would the future be like for both the majors and minors with the advent of widespread television. Minor league teams near major league cities were being hurt attendancewise because of television and it had put the game on the spot.[14]

Brecheen pitched his third consecutive shutout, a one hitter versus Philadelphia in a 5–0 victory at Sportsman's Park. Your writer was a young teenager in attendance. Philadelphia's Johnny Blatnik beat out a slow hopping grounder to Kurowski on a bang bang play at first base for the only base runner of the game. Umpire Al Barlick called him safe on an extremely close play. There were two out in the top of the seventh when this happened and Jones thought Blatnik out as the ball hit his glove before Blatnik's foot hit the bag. Schoendienst, with a clear view, agreed as did Kurowski. In his first 27 innings Brecheen had allowed just 16 hits, no runs, walked two and fanned eight while winning all three complete game victories.[15]

Dyer wanted the team to have more night games as he pointed to the big crowds. The players agreed as this meant more revenue for the team and in turn translated into higher paychecks for them. For now the starting rotation was Brecheen, Munger, Dickson, Pollet and Hearn, and Dyer would use them in relief if necessary. He also would pitch his starters out of turn if they came against a team that did not fare well against a certain pitcher, even if it wasn't his turn to pitch.

Two Cardinals were hit and a third decked at Ebbetts Field on May 20. The results were twofold. First, it was like 1946 all over—the feuding and fussing of that season. Secondly, the Brooklyn fans gave the Dodgers and Durocher the bums rush. Some fans were leaving as early as the fifth inning as they were that disgusted with the play of the club.

Hugh Casey had come in relief during the sixth inning and hit Kurowski in the kidneys as the first man he faced. With the next pitch he decked Slaughter, who got up and doubled. Then in the 8th inning he faced Rice, who had previously doubled off him at bat, and he beaned him with two men off base. Dyer was tossed out of the game for heatedly condemning the umpires for allowing this to happen. He said it looked like a repeat of 1946 when Dodgers hurlers threw at Cardinals hitters. This made the Cardinals so mad they swept the three games between May 18 and 20 by scores of 4–3, 14–7 and 13–4.

The Cardinals' improvement was traced to Musial's hitting (around .400 and 22 RBIs) and Pollet's improved pitching. Until the explosion in Brooklyn the team hadn't been hitting. Brecheen had pitched four straight Saturdays and won them all. He finally surrendered three runs in an 8–3 victory over Pittsburgh. Dyer was asked if he was making Brecheen his Saturday pitcher and he replied no, but maybe it was not a bad idea since he was 4–0 on Saturdays. It was believed that Kurowski and Slaughter would soon break out of their slumps and with the way Musial was hitting they would have a potent 3–4–5 hitting team. Meanwhile Dusak had shined playing for the injured Moore and Jones found his batting eye.

As the third week of May ended St. Louis was in first place with a 16–7 record. It certainly was looking like the pundits were correct as all the pieces had seemed to come together. They were followed by New York (14–10), Pittsburgh (14–12), Boston (13–12) and Philadelphia (14–13). Musial went on a .517 tear (15 for 26) and climbed to .411, second to Gustine (who was a spring hitter) at .414. Brecheen and Pollet paced the Cardinals at 4–0 each.

Managers were picking the Yankees to win the American League pennant and St. Louis to take the National League crown. The players were choosing the same teams. If they were correct it would be the fifth time they had met in World Series play since 1926. The Cardinals' bench was stronger with Lang and LaPointe while Wilks was shining in relief, pitching like he did in 1944. Jones was playing a good first base, hitting consistently and driving in runs. LaPointe had been a key factor in the early going as he had filled in during 16 games for Marion or Schoendienst when out with injuries. Northey and Medwick provided the same roles as last season, pinch-hitting and some outfield duty, with most of the latter done by Northey.

As May ended it found St. Louis (20–10) still in first, though they had only been 3–4 in the past week. New York was second at 17–12 and Boston now third with 16–14. They were 12–7 since their poor start. Brooklyn had suffered through an eight game losing streak and was 13–19. Musial was at .405, but still trailed Gustine (.427) and Holmes was also at the .400 mark. Rookie Richie Ashburn of Philadelphia was hitting .348.

The Cardinals lost ground on their road trip and the rumor mill stated that Kurowski would be traded as the Cardinals were limping along. Hannegan said no deal was pending, although rumors persisted that Kurowski and Dusak would both be traded. He added he wouldn't say they wouldn't be traded, but there was no deal in the offering. All teams wanted Pollet, Brecheen or Dickson. Kurowski said damp weather bothered his shortened right arm and he couldn't get a proper swing. In his absence Lang had been playing third base while the Cardinals lost seven of eight on the road. The only well-pitched games came from Brecheen.

It seemed like Munger, Dickson and Pollet forgot how to pitch. The hitting had also cooled off. They started the road trip fine at 6–1, but then ended 1–7 for 7–8 overall. Dyer said a break here or there and they could have been 10–5. Jones, after a fine start (he once was tied with Musial and Kiner for the RBI lead at 27), had slumped. Dyer was accused of hanging onto veterans like Slaughter, Marion, Kurowski and Moore. He stated they won the pennant for the team in 1946 and helped the Cards finish second in 1947. Without them in 1948, he said, the team would finish in the second division. Until the system produced good young replacements Dyer would go with the veterans.

By early June New York was back in first at 21–15 with St. Louis second at 21–16, compliments of that 1–7 slide. Chicago was now last at 13–23. Musial took over the batting lead with .392 while Holmes was at .389 and Ashburn hitting .373. Pollet and Brecheen were the leading Cardinals pitchers at 4–1.

Schoendienst set a new record with eight doubles and one home run in three games on June 5 against Brooklyn in St. Louis and June 6 in a double-header against Philadelphia. He had three doubles and a single in four at-bats on June 5. In game one of the double-header he had three doubles and a home run when his string of six hits was halted by a ground out in the fourth inning. In the nightcap he had two doubles. His eight doubles in three games and seven extra base hits in two games set a new major league record. His six doubles in two consecutive games and five extra base hits in a double-header tied a major league record.

Munger stumbled, slowed the Redbirds' pace. He was shelled out of the box in five of seven starts while Wilks continued to shine in relief. Rumors continued to fly about trades, but Hannegan said nothing was in the works. He acknowledged that the team turned down cash offers for Pollet, Dickson and Brecheen. There were three or four players in the league the team would like to have and if the proper proposal came along the Cardinals would make a trade.

Munger was just 2–5 on the season compared to just five losses in all of 1947. The big redhead had been counted on for 15 or more victories. Dyer acknowledged the Cardinals needed another starter. Brecheen was finally hit hard, allowing five runs, eight hits, a walk, and he hit a batsman in five innings, but he won the game as Wilks pitched four shutout innings. The Cardinals were considering using Beers or Papai in a starting role.

As the middle of June approached St. Louis had slipped to third place with a 25–20 mark, just 5–10 in their past 15 games. The main reason for the decline was the failure of the pitching staff, except for Brecheen and Wilks. New York was first at 25–19, while Boston had taken over second with a 7–1 run and was now 24–19. Chicago remained last at 17–30. Holmes had edged past Musial, .379 to .376 while Brecheen led all pitchers with a 6–1 mark.

The Yankees retired Babe Ruth's uniform number 3. It was sent to the Hall of Fame. Babe was at the ceremony, but his illness would only allow him to walk slowly into clubhouse with a friend on each side. He was weak and pale. They helped him to undress and put on his uniform. This was his last appearance in uniform number three. Your writer had the opportunity to see him at Sportsman's Park that summer, but in a business suit and he slowly walked to the plate with a bat on his shoulder and took a feeble swing.[16]

Hannegan said the Redbirds would get hot in July and August (as was their tradition) after a perplexing slump at home. They would play in the latter months like they did in '39, '40, '41, '42, '45, '46 and '47. After the homestand that ended June 13 the team was only 6–8, certainly not a pennant winning pace.

Several factors had contributed to the problem. Kurowski, who hit .310 with 27 home runs and 104 RBIs in 1947, was in the very low .200s and had no home runs for the season and had been injured much of the time. Another failure had been the inability to hit in the clutch. The players realized that all teams in the league feared the Cardinals and they would get hot and win, said Hannegan. The Cardinals' trouble started May 26 in New York when they were leading the league by four and one-half games. They blew a lead in the eighth inning as the Giants scored eight runs and up to that point they had won six of seven on the road. The team certainly wasn't out of the race as they had some good talent in the minors, especially pitchers. There was Cloyd Boyer, Jack Crimian, and Harvey Haddix as well as infielders Eddie Kazak and Glavaiano.

By the middle of June Boston (30–22) was first with Pittsburgh (29–22) second and St. Louis (28–23) third. Musial had regained the batting lead with a .389 mark followed by Chicago's Harry Lowrey and Holmes at .355 each while Ashburn was .357 and Pittsburgh's Wally Westlake was at .348. Musial also led the league with 40 RBIs and Slaughter was second with 37. Brecheen was 6–2, Hearn 4–2 and Wilks 3–2 to pace the St. Louis staff.

The players were demanding a uniform arc lighting system. Some parks had good lighting, others were satisfactory and still other parks had very poor lighting, of which St. Louis qualified. The players were demanding uniformity throughout the league. It varied from park to park and made it very difficult fielding and hitting. They also wanted assurance of no double-header after a night game except in the situation of a make up game due to a rain out or tie game that had to be replayed.

Richard Muckerman said, "it was up to the fans whether the Browns remained in St. Louis. Failure to show up for games may doom the team and speed their departure from the city." This gave revived hope to the Pacific Coast League in acquiring a major league franchise, especially in San Francisco or Los Angeles. There was a strong possibility seen as a shift of the team to one of these two cities.

Arc lighting was especially under fire at St. Louis. The Cardinals were aware of the problem and were trying to work with the Browns to remedy the situation. It became financial as the Browns were strapped and much of the expense had to be borne by the Cardinals. There were good reasons for the Cardinals to have the problem corrected so they could continue night play as they played their best ball at night. They had a winning mark in 1946 (25–13, .658) and in 1947 (29–10, .720). The decision on the Browns was tabled until the end of the season.[17]

The old Gas House Gang days were still dear to Medwick. The Redbirds were still in the race, the beaten Braves acknowledged after the Cardinals swept them in Boston behind the pitching of Brazle, Brecheen and Pollet. This was the same trio that had lost to Boston in St. Louis. Thus it was perhaps poetic justice they would return the favor in Boston. The Cardinals had hit 42 home runs, but allowed 48.

Dickson had pitched the most innings (84), but allowed 15 home runs while Pollet and Munger had given up eight each. Dickson had also allowed the most hits (96) and runs (47), followed by Pollet who had given up 95 hits and 43 runs. In a 26 game stretch during which the team was 12–14 they had just six complete games. From June 6 to June 20 the team failed to complete any of 12 starts. Musial now led the team with 15 home runs and no else had over seven (Slaughter). Long recognized as a team that came from behind, especially in the late innings, the Cardinals had not won or lost one in the ninth inning. However, the bottom line was, for the Cardinals to win the pennant, the pitching had to improve. Brecheen and Wilks couldn't win it alone.

As they approached the last week of June the Cardinals (33–25) were only a half a game behind front running Boston (34–25) with Pittsburgh

(32–26) and New York (30–27) not far away. Musial continued to lead the league with .403 and now everyone was talking about him hitting .400. Stan simply said it was a long season and they were just barely a third of the way there. Brecheen led the Cardinals' staff with 8–2, followed by Hearn (4–2), Pollet (5–3) and Dickson (6–5).

The young kids (potential future stars, although many became busts) were striking gold on huge bonuses. Wealthy Boston clubs led the spending parade. Johnny Antonelli of the Braves received a $65,000 bonus. This caused bitterness among the major league veterans, especially perennial 20 game winner Johnny Sain of Boston. He told Perini "he would strike if he didn't get a raise." Perini came across. To avoid any problem with Musial, Hannegan gave him a $5,000 raise without Stan ever saying a word. Still the bonus issue was becoming a major problem in baseball. Why should these unproven kids get huge bonuses (more than many players made in six or eight seasons), while the veteran players had to fight for $1,000 and $2,000 raises?[18]

Los Angeles was ready to talk business with the Browns. Muckerman had opened the door. His rap at the crowd was tagged the laugh of the year. Why should the fans support a team that traded away its stars (Vernon Stephens, Bob Muncrief, Jack Kramer, Ellis Kinder and others) which netted the club $575,000? Muckerman argued the team needed the money to stay afloat. If that was true then maybe they should leave the city. Conversely if they had kept those players maybe they would be contending for a pennant and not worrying about attendance or leaving the city. Kramer finished the season 18–5 at Boston, Kinder was 10–7 while Stephens hit 29 home runs, scored 114 runs and had 137 RBIs. Granted there was a power hitting Boston team and a short left field fence, but they all turned in fine performances. It might have been a step lower in St. Louis, but the Browns probably wouldn't have finished at 59–94.

Fans were saying maybe attendance was slim, but Muckerman's pocketbook was fat from all the sales of players. Los Angeles County supervisor Leonard J. Rosch was especially interested in the Browns as he had campaigned for them two years ago. Since Muckerman had taken over the Browns they had been the American League's doormat, its worst team with a 195–268 record for a .421 winning percentage. The group in Los Angeles with money believed they could turn this around.[19]

Musial hit right or left hand pitchers with equal aplomb. He was the first player in the majors to reach 100 hits and his aim was to be the first National League batter to reach .400 since Bill Terry of the Giants batted .401 in 1930. Only Chicago had stopped him at .177 in five games at Wrigley Field and overall he was just .241 versus Chicago. He hated to hit against those white shirts in the background in the left field bleachers. If he failed to hit .400 the fiasco in Chicago could prove to be the main culprit.

As July rolled around Boston (38–27) had opened a two and one-half game bulge on St. Louis (35–29) and Pittsburgh was close at (34–29). Musial remained over .400 at .401, while Brecheen was 8–3 with Pollet at 6–3 and Brazle at 5–3 and Hearn 4–3. Both Munger and Dickson had losing records, with the latter on his way for setting a new major league record for home runs allowed.

The Dodgers signed another Negro, catcher Roy Campanella, and optioned him to St. Paul to give him the chance to play every day. He was behind Bruce Edwards, Gil Hodges and Bobby Bragan on the catching depth chart. The Dodgers believed he would be back to help the team by next season. At the same time Satchel Paige (age 39) was signed by the Cleveland Indians, thus giving them two blacks on the team. He would be used mostly in relief roles.

Brecheen allowed his first home run of the season to Hank Sauer in the ninth inning of the first game of a double-header on July 4. As of July 15 Musial was at .415 and his chances for hitting .400 looked better. Meanwhile Munger had been kayoed for the eighth consecutive game and he had also failed in three relief appearances. He was 0–6 during that stretch and just 2–7 for the season. His market value as well as his team value had been greatly diminished.

Future Cardinals stars were being groomed. They included pitcher Haddix, nicknamed "The Kitten" because of his similarity in style and size to Brecheen. There was also Glaviano, Miggins, Boyer, Diering, outfielder Bill Howerton and perhaps the most interesting, catcher Larry Ciaffone. Although it was at a low classification, he showed promise, if only because of the Cardinals' catching problems and situation.

As mid–July approached Boston had a firm grasp on first place at 43–31 with Pittsburgh second at 39–32 and St. Louis third at 38–34. The Cardinals' pitching was led by Brecheen (9–3), Pollet (6–4) Brazle (5–5) and Dickson (7–7). Jones was hitting .267, but had 54 RBIs while Kurowski was batting but .216 with zero home runs. This was a key factor why the Redbirds continued to lag behind, despite their pitching problems.

The question was being asked were the Cardinals tripping over their gray beards? The answer was no as the average age was 29. While some teams had a lower average age, others were higher. Six of Boston's regular starting eight were over 30 and their five most used starters averaged 29 years. Brooklyn had also brought Campanella up from St. Paul and installed him as the number one catcher, as Edwards developed a sore arm and would play some outfield and third base.

Individual failures had hurt the team the most. Johnson was recalled from Rochester and Papai optioned there. Beers had made one appearance and allowed one run, three hits and a walk in ⅔ of an inning in his only appearance. He was dispatched to the minors, never to return. The Cardinals had a disastrous homestand (7–10) up to the Brave series and were just 8–14 over the past three weeks.

Other problems included Kurowski and his injuries and not hitting. Schoendienst had been out for a long time, missing over 25 games while Munger had been a bust to date at 2–7. Dickson was on the way to a new home run record as he had already allowed 25 and had an ERA over five runs a game as did Munger. Pollet had a winning record (6–4) but his ERA was around 4.7. From June 29 to July 30 the Cardinals were 11–18 and had only 27 complete games for the season with Brecheen having one-third of them. You didn't win pennants with that type of pitching.

The team had allowed 75 home runs, one-third by Dickson, while Munger had given up 11 and Pollet nine. The team was just 11–13 in one run games and 8–11 in two run games. The Cardinals were starting a 23 game road trip with their eastern swing. They had played well in the east and were opening in Brooklyn, against whom they were 9–4 for the season. They promptly lost all three games at Ebbets Field. It was not a bright looking future for the Redbirds.

By the end of July Boston (55–37) had a five and one-half game edge on Brooklyn (48–41) with New York (47–42) just a game back. St. Louis was in danger of falling out of the first division as they were now just 46–44. Musial had fallen below .400 at .390, but continued to lead the league with 77 RBIs. A player the Cardinals wanted earlier, Pafko, was hitting .337 and was second in the league. Slaughter was at .300 with 55 RBIs. Brecheen continued to lead the team with 10–4, while Brazle was 7–5 and Pollet was 6–5.

Just when it looked like it was lights out for the Redbirds, someone turned them back on. The punchy Cardinals were pulled off the canvas by hitters and hurlers. The report of their demise had been greatly exaggerated. Munger and Dickson gave route going jobs. The bottom had been hit when the team lost three straight in Brooklyn and dropped three games in the ninth inning in the same week and were just one-half game from the second division. They won two of three at Boston making them 10–7 versus the Braves for the season.

Pollet was starting to pitch like the Pollet of old and Dyer thought with Brazle and Brecheen and Pollet coming to life his left hand pitching was set. Then Dickson went the distance in a 21–5 pasting of the Giants at the Polo Grounds in the biggest scoring win of the season. Munger went the route in a 7–2 win for his first complete game in 10 tries since May 19. The "Cat" pitched a two hitter for his fourth shutout and 12th victory. This, coupled with Braves defeats, pulled St. Louis within four games of first place.

Wilks continued to do a good job coming out of the bullpen and saving games. Musial was staying close to .400 and Slaughter had a 15 game hitting streak. Kurowski chipped in with his first home run of the season and Northey in a part-time role was batting .364. In the 21–5 victory Wilber, who hadn't played in 71 days, caught Dickson and drove in five runs on three hits. He had been hitting .071. The Cardinals tried to reacquire Emil Verban to replace the injured Schoendienst, but the Chicago Cubs beat them to the punch.

Perini again proposed two 12 team leagues. He wanted to take eight cities from the top minor leagues. His plan was to add teams from California, Texas and Canada. He would take Los Angeles, San Francisco, Oakland, Hollywood, Milwaukee, Montreal, Houston and Dallas. This proposal, like the others, received very little attention and soon died a quiet death.[20]

Loyalty to an under fire Dyer inspired the Cardinals to come back. The pilot's patience with the men in face of fan criticism inspired the team to a wining spurt. From the time they blew a four and one-half game lead in late May until the disastrous start of their eastern trip the team was just 27–36. He kept confidence in his disappointing pitchers and kept pitching Pollet, Munger and Dickson. The latter had an ERA of over five runs per game for the first half of the season, but was around 2.50 the second half based on tips from Brecheen.[21]

Then they started turning it around. Slaughter, after a four for 40 start, was now at .325 with 66 RBIs and St. Louis was 10–7 versus Boston, and 9–7 against New York and Brooklyn. However, they were just 12–15 against Cincinnati and Chicago while Boston was 20–10, Brooklyn 20–11 and New York 19–15. Therein lay the difference. That was a similar pattern the Cardinals had followed the past few seasons. They held an edge on first division teams and had losing marks against seventh and eighth place clubs. This cost them the pennant in 1945 and 1947 and threatened to do the same in 1948.

By mid–August Boston was 61–44 with Brooklyn 54–45 and St. Louis 56–47. Brecheen was now 13–4 and had a chance for his first 20 win season. He was in a similar situation in 1945 and 1947 and then went just 2–5 down the stretch. Pollet was now 9–5 and Musial had slipped to .383, but still led the league in hitting and RBIs (89).

Brooklyn started its swagger, but was keeping a close eye on St. Louis as they feared the Cardinals and knew how they could play down the stretch. Wilks' rubber arm put snap into the Cardinals' flag bid. Regardless of where they finished St. Louis would be two or three rungs lower without Wilks. His game saving ability kept the team in the race. He had allowed only 22 runs in almost 100 innings (99⅔) in 40 games with a 2.07 ERA, His 5–4 record was deceiving, as he lost some games he should have won. However, the Cardinals were jinxed in two cities, Pittsburgh and Chicago, where they were just 2–6 in each town. Remember 1945 and 1946 when the Cubs were the Cardinals' patsies?

Babe Ruth died at age 53. He died without ever learning cause of his fatal two year illness. He had cancer of the throat. He died at 7:01 PM EDT on August 16 in New York City Memorial Hospital Center for cancer and allied diseases. Without a doubt he was the greatest ballplayer of all time.[22]

He held 56 major league records at his death, including career home runs

(714), career RBIs (2209) and a lifetime .342 batting mark. But it was not just his prodigious hitting or his great pitching feats as he was 94–46 until he turned full time to the outfield. His value to the game was that he came along after the Black Sox scandal and restored the faith in the game. He was a hero to millions of kids and fans all over the country. Yankee Stadium became the house Ruth built. We could write about his accomplishments all day and sing his praises forever. There never was and never had been a ballplayer to equal the Babe. He stood head and shoulders above all others for all time. In fact he still does. One more statistic cinches the case for Ruth. During his career he outhomered 48 teams and tied two others. Twice he out-homered every team in the league. Enough said.

The Cardinals were gearing up for another great September drive as they were just two and one-half games behind Boston. The Cardinals were 65–53, while Boston was 68–51. Entrenched in third just one-half game behind St. Louis was Brooklyn at 62–51. It looked like a three team donnybrook to the end. Musial was at .384 with a league best 99 RBIs while Slaughter was giv-ing the team a one-two punch with his .323 and 71 RBIs. Oh, how the club could have used Kurowski's big bat. Brecheen was 15–5 while Pollet was 9–6.

With Slaughter's onslaught this gave the Cardinals a two man batting blitz. The veteran Slaughter had shown his true colors after a slow start. Win, lose or draw the Cardinals promised to make a race of it right down to the wire. Slaughter just plugged away; he didn't get the headlines of his illustri-ous partner, but he got the job done. He was a fierce competitor and after the Cardinals had lost successive double-headers to Brooklyn he hollered, "We're not beat by any stretch of the imagination. It would be dog eat dog between us from here on out."

Under ordinary circumstances few of the 67,334 Cardinals faithful who had just seen the Cardinals blow two straight double-headers to Brooklyn would not return to see them play the lowly Philadelphia team, but this was Enos Slaughter night and 20,998 showed up to pay homage to the man. He came into organized baseball and thought he would always be a Cardinal.[23]

On that night Munger shut out Philadelphia 5–0 and Slaughter beat the drum for Dyer. The Cardinals are not out of it yet, he told the fans. He said Dyer had managed the club through the toughest times the last two years and had taken all the abuse and never passed it on to the players or laid the blame at their doorstep, although that was where it belonged. Some of those on the team had let him down the past two seasons.

With those double-header wins and a Boston slump Brooklyn had climbed into first place by early September with a 69–54 mark. Boston was next at 71–56 and St. Louis right behind at 69–57. It promised to be a three team fight to the end. The Boston chant was "Spahn and Sain and then pray for rain." However, the team did have two other starters in Bill Voiselle, who picked up 13 wins for the season, and rookie Vern Bickford, who would finish with an 11–5 record.

However, the Dodgers' kids reeled under the rugged pace while Musial's punches were misaimed and the Cardinals fall flat on their face. Stan had his first real slump of the season. The Cardinals lost nine of 11 in Pittsburgh as Stan hit just .255 there and Pittsburgh led the season's series 12–7. Dyer said they had had their pitching disappointments, hitting hadn't been what it was supposed to be, their defense and speed were not what they used to be, but except for infield injuries (Kurowski, Marion and Schoendienst) the Cardinals would still be in first place. That was really how good this team was.

Kurowski missed 78 games for the season, Schoendienst missed 36 and Marion 11. Dickson was 0–4 versus Pittsburgh despite allowing only 14 runs, 10 earned in 45 innings. Brecheen tied his career high 16 wins (1944 and 1947) when he shut out Chicago on September 9 4–0.

By the second week of August the race still hung in balance with Boston (76–57) holding off Pittsburgh (71–58), Brooklyn (71–59) and St. Louis (71–62). Only five games separated the four clubs. Brecheen was 16–7, having lost three in a row before gaining win number 16. Pollet was 10–6 while Hearn was 8–6. Musial had "slipped" to .367 and his dreams of .400 had disappeared, but he still led the league with 110 RBIs. His partner, Slaughter, was at .330 with 79 RBIs.

Musial was named the top player of the year by *The Sporting News* and was cited for his batting feats as well as sparking the Cardinals in their pennant drive. Brecheen led the major leagues in strikeouts (a rare place for him to be) with 138 in 210 innings, averaging six per game. He was headed for his first 20 win season at age 34. Musial snapped out of his slump and was back at .375.

Puffed wrists shackled Musial's challenge for the slugging title. Stout Stan was injured pulling off circus catches. Slaughter was sidelined with a broken nose suffered in Boston. It looked like for the second straight season there would be no World Series excitement at Sportsman's Park. The only excitement left was Musial's challenge for the slugging title and the triple crown. Not since 1941 had St. Louis gone successive seasons without going to the World Series and not since 1940 had they finished lower than second.

This oft crippled and injured club had seemed hard pressed to finish second, but that was till their goal and objective. Slaughter was hit in the nose by a line drive off the bat of Jones as he was running the bases. He would miss the balance of the season and it would cost him a chance at 100 or more RBIs, as he finished the season at .321 with 90 RBIs. Musial tied Ty Cobb's 1922 record when he got five hits in a game for the fourth time that season.

This performance was even more outstanding as he had two swollen wrists. Stan got three singles, his 441st double and his 38th home run in this second five hit spree at Boston this season. Chuck Klein held the National

League record with 107 extra base hits and Hornsby had 450 total bases. With nine games left Musial needed nine extra base hits to set a new record and 40 total bases to surpass Hornsby.[24]

Musial's injury occurred in Brooklyn on September 17 when he made three brilliant catches, two of the somersault variety. The Cardinals in the off-season needed a third baseman, first baseman, center fielder and pitching help. They also needed a right handed power hitter as Kurowski would not be able to play again. Dickson allowed his 37th home run, a new record, and would finish the season 12–16 with a record 39 home runs allowed.

The players cheered the news that Dyer would stay. They knew that the team should have won the last two seasons and it was not their manager's fault. Dyer said he had a rebuilding job to do. Moore announced his retirement. The Cardinals' patsies for the season were Philadelphia (17–5) and New York (15–7) including the last 10 games. The Cardinals were 41–36 on the road and 44–33 at home as they did finish second by one game over Brooklyn. Brecheen finished 20–7, had the league's best ERA, 2.24, and led with seven shutouts. Munger was just 10–11, but was 8–4 in the second half giving hope for 1949. Pollet finished at 13–8, but his ERA was 4.55 so his problem was still not completely solved. Hope springs eternal and now the Redbirds would wait for next spring to try and return to the World Series.

Musial was an easy winner for the MVP as he led the league in every major category but home runs, missing by one. He lost a home run early in the season in a rained out game in New York against the Giants. With that he would have copped the triple crown and been the only player to lead in every major category. He led with batting (.376), runs (135), doubles (46), triples (18), RBIs (131), slugging percentage (.702), on base percentage (.450), total bases (429), and extra base hits (103). He also fanned just 34 times, thus having more home runs than strikeouts.

TEN

1949

One Week Too Long

The Cardinals had finished second in 1948, the fourth time in the decade. The other five years they had won four pennants and finished third in 1940. Entering this season they had a string of eight straight seasons in first or second. As history had shown us they could have won at least two more pennants, but then you must also give the other team credit.

Stan Musial had the greatest season of his career as he hit .376 with 39 home runs and 131 RBIs. He led the league in runs scored, hits, doubles, triples, RBIs, average, total bases, extra base hits and slugging percentage. He missed the triple crown by one home run. In a game early in the season he hit a home run, but the game was rained out and since five innings weren't played, none of the statistics counted. That cost him a tie for the home run title. He also missed by two triples becoming the fourth player and second Cardinal to have 20 doubles, triples and home runs in a season.[1]

Enos Slaughter also put together a fine season, hitting .321 with 90 RBIs. After that the numbers fell dramatically. Whitey Kurowski hit just .214 as his crippled arm gave him problems and he was limited to 77 games and hit just two home runs. In 1947 he had batted .310 with 27 home runs and 104 RBIs. What a difference that would have made in 1948.

Terry Moore's legs gave out on him and he retired at the end of the season. Red Schoendienst missed almost 40 games because of a sore arm. He literally couldn't throw. Del Rice, an excellent defensive catcher, batted just .197. The replacements for Kurowski, Moore and Schoendienst were found wanting.

On the bright side Harry "The Cat" Brecheen had his best season, finish-

242

ing 20–7 with the league's best ERA at 2.24 and a league best seven shutouts.[2] However, after that the pitching dropped off dramatically. Murray Dickson was 12–16 with a 4.14 ERA and a record 39 home runs allowed. Howard Pollet was 13–8, but with a 4.54 ERA. Al Brazle was 10–6, starting and relieving, with a so-so 3.80 ERA.

The Cardinals had been waiting since George "Red" Munger returned in late August 1946 to deliver on the promise he showed in 1944 when he was 11–3 with a 1.34 ERA at mid-season and then called into the army. He had been 16–5 with a 3.37 ERA in 1947, but still wasn't the pitcher of 1944. Last year he fell to 10–11 with a 4.50 ERA. Jim Hearn, who had showed promise with a 12–7 record in 1947, fell to 8–6 with a 4.22 ERA. Ted Wilks continued his great relief pitching, appearing in 57 games, and was 6–6 with a 2.61 ERA and 13 saves.

The team had a lot of rebuilding to do for 1949. They needed a center fielder, third baseman and catcher. On the pitching staff they needed some of the veterans, i.e. Pollet, Dickson and Munger, to regain their previous winning form. Or they needed some young pitchers to come forward and take charge as the Ernie Whites and Johnny Beazleys did in the first half of this decade.

The other need was a first baseman as Musial preferred playing right field and that was where manager Eddie Dyer wanted him. Vernal "Nippy" Jones had 81 RBIs last season, but hit just .254. It would be a trial between him and Glenn "Rocky" Nelson for the first base job.

When it came to salaries the major league owners were adopting a retrenchment mode. Attendance was over 20,000,000 in 1948 so the owners were quite happy and didn't want to do anything to rock the boat. They were anxiously awaiting the outcome of the contracts for the big boys. They were to set the pattern for all other players.

There are five players on whom all eyes were cast. They were Joe DiMaggio, Ted Williams, Bob Feller, Johnny Mize and Stan Musial. All but Feller came off great seasons in 1948. Feller won 19 games, but it was a comedown for him from prior seasons. He had an $80,000 package last year, but approximately half was a bonus tied to attendance. It would be interesting to see what type of contract he was offered for 1949 after going 19–15 with an ERA in the mid threes and no World Series win in two starts. He was in line for a potential pay cut.

Dyer said the Cardinals cripples were ready to go. Marty Marion's back was reported in good shape and he was ready for the season. Last year he hit just .252 in 144 games with just 43 RBIs. The prior season he batted .272 with 74 RBIs in 149 games. Schoendienst said his arm was fine and ready for a big season. He and Marion had added 13 and 10 pounds respectively. It was weight both needed.

Marion said the failure to make the double play last season cost the team several games. He said when Red was out his replacements had trouble turning the double play. The team needed better reserves. The two of them both hoped to play every game.

The big hope was that Kurowski's arm was healthy again and that he could play third base. They needed his big bat in the lineup. He hit over .300 from 1945–47 and averaged almost 20 home runs and over 92 RBIs a year from 1943–47. His presence in the lineup with Musial and Slaughter forced the other team to pitch to the two of them. It also helped nullify the left handers other teams saved for St. Louis.

Some of the experts said the Cardinals' real problem was they were getting old. A ballplayer's best years were supposed to be between the ages of 28–32. Of the eight players considered as regulars only Slaughter was over 30. He was 33. The others ranged from 24 to 29. Three of the Cardinals' first five pitchers were over 32. Brazle was 35, Brecheen 34 and Wilks 33. Munger was 30 and Pollet 28. Dyer didn't believe he needed additional players; he just needed the ones he had to stay relatively injury free. With that, the team could go all the way, he contended.

The major leagues didn't see any real flux of Negro players into the majors. Most would have to spend some time in the minors before coming to the majors. The owners basically felt they were an unproven commodity and were not willing to accept them from the Negro League. They would have to spend a few years in the minors just as the white players did.

Seven players had been brought into the majors and only two had made it so far. They were Jackie Robinson and Larry Doby. In fact Doby was dubbed the "rookie flop of 1947" when he hit .158 after being brought to Cleveland in midseason. Willard Brown, Dan Bankhead and Henry Thompson had all been set back to the minors.

The jury was still out on Roy Campanella. He proved he was a good defensive catcher, but hit just .258. If he couldn't hit anymore than that he might not last. Satchel Paige might stick, as he was a fan attraction, but was close to 45 so his usefulness was limited. Most of the black players from the Negro League were 25–30 and some older. So the chances were slim of their making it to the majors.

If it were not for Marion on the team Schoendienst would be the shortstop. This was the position he broke into in the minors, but with Marion at short, he quickly realized he would have to learn another position if he were to play for the Cardinals. His rookie season in 1945 saw him in the outfield and then in 1946 when all the veterans returned he became the second baseman.

Griesedieck Brothers beer purchased the broadcasting rights of the Cardinals' games for $150,000. Harry Caray and Charles "Gabby" Street would do the play by play again. The team wanted a more powerful station than WMTV radio. It had 54 stations and the Cardinals wanted a larger network.

They want someone who had broadcasting rights to the complete territory that they served.

The argument over bonus babies continued. The owners wanted to have the rule changed. Under present rule the player had to be on the major league roster. In most cases they lacked experience so they just sat on the major league bench. They were of no value to themselves, as they weren't getting playing time or being developed. They didn't benefit the club as that position could be filled by a more experienced ball player.

The owners argued if they were sent to the minors they could gain the valuable experience needed and return to the majors. The player would benefit and the team would benefit. It would be all winners, no losers. The fans in minor league towns would come out to see the player, because he had become a "celebrity" after signing the bonus contract. Attendance in minor league towns would rise. Most baseball people figured it took five years to bring a player through the ranks and to the majors.[3]

Fred Saigh bought out partner Robert E. Hannegan on advice of the latter's physician. Hannegan said he sold his interest because of medical reasons. The tension and pressure of running the ball club was too demanding and his physician advised him to sell. Saigh would take over formal running of the team.

When the two purchased the club in November 1947 from Sam Breadon they paid $4,060,000 with the stock valued at $400 per share. Each owned 50 percent of the team. Saigh had now bought 40 percent of the 50 percent Hannegan owned and would have 90 percent ownership of the team. Saigh and Hannegan both said when they bought the team, "The Cardinals were here to stay. They would never leave St. Louis."[4]

There was no concern about the Cardinals having a new manager as Dyer had a two year contract and Saigh said he was satisfied with the way Dyer had handled the club. He realized the adversity that was encountered last season. If all the players had been healthy, even with some of the pitchers not performing up to par, they still would have won the pennant.

Breadon said his biggest thrill in baseball was when Pete Alexander fanned Tony Lazzeri with the bases loaded in game seven of the 1926 World Series. While his teams won nine pennants and six World Series, it was that first one that gave him the biggest thrill. Breadon owned and ran the Cardinals from 1920 through 1947. He was not only the owner, but a great Cardinals fan as well. When they lost a little of him died inside. When they won he was like a kid with an ice cream cone.

Contracts were sent to all players on January 28, but Musial and Slaughter had not returned theirs. Saigh said it was important that these two sign as they were the top two along with Brecheen, Marion and Schoendienst forming the nucleus of that team. Around them the ball club was built.

Brecheen in 68 games pitching at night had a marvelous 43–12 record.

He had pitched nine shutouts and had 10 games in which he allowed five hits or less. On May 8, 1948, he almost pitched a perfect game. Brecheen pitched a one hitter against Philadelphia. Johnny Blatnik got the only hit. It was on the infield. He hit a ground ball to Kurowski, who had trouble getting the ball out of his glove, and then because of his bad arm could not make a good throw to first base. It was ruled a hit. This writer was a very young teenager attending the game.

The Cardinals were keeping a close eye on the developments with Kurowski. He had an operation on his arm over the winter and believed it would allow him to play baseball. Dyer was hoping he could recover and perform as he did in 1947. The other big need was a right hand hitting center fielder. The team had Charles "Chuck" Diering, a excellent outfielder with a good arm, but so far he had not been able to solve major league pitching.

There were two other potential center fielders. Erv Dusak had been up and down with the Cardinals since 1941. He was another good defensive outfielder with a strong arm, but had not been able to solve major league pitching with any degree of consistency. In 1947 he platooned in right filed with Ron Northey. The latter hit .293 with 15 home runs, while Dusak hit .284. He slipped to .209 last season.

The other center fielder was Musial. He played it in the minors and had done so in the majors, but he preferred to be in right field and that was where Dyer wanted him to play. If Musial played center then there had to be some type of platoon tandem of Northey and a right hand hitter. If neither Jones nor Nelson made it at first base, then Musial could move there, further complicating the outfield situation. Dyer had a lot of problems to work out before his team could challenge.

The sale of two clubs in one week made major league history. After the Cardinals had been sold the DeWitt brothers bought 58 percent of the St. Louis Browns stock for an estimated $800,000 to $1,000,000. They said the team would remain in St. Louis. Not only were two major league teams sold in one week, but both were from the same city.

On January 29 the Cardinals sold Dickson to the Pittsburgh Pirates. He had set a major league mark last season when he allowed 39 home runs. Pittsburgh defeated him five times in 1948. He appeared in eight games (as a starter and reliever) against Pittsburgh last year and posted a fine 1.99 ERA, but still lost five times. Dickson had a horrible first half, but did much better in the second half of the season.

The sale of Dickson (who was 31) forced the club to use younger pitchers like Hearn, Ken Johnson, Bill Reeder from Rochester, Kurt Krieger from Columbus or Cloyd Boyer from Houston. With Dickson gone one or more of those pitchers would have a chance to win a big league starting job. Johnson had a good fastball, but in 45 innings last year he walked 30 and didn't complete any of his four starts.

Dickson had a fine season in the pennant winning year of 1946 when he was 15–6 with 2.89 ERA. The last two years he didn't perform as well. He had a good ERA (3.06) in 1947 but was just 13–16. Then last year his ERA climbed to 4.02 and he was 12–16. Based on that and his home run record the decision was to sell or trade Dickson. Dyer found out about it after the fact. Saigh offered to call off the deal, but Dyer said no. He had been through a lot with Dickson as he helped him win the pennant at Houston in 1939 and then was one of the 1946 mainstays.

The fans were asking why he was sold for cash when the team needed a hard hitting outfielder? The question being asked was couldn't the Cardinals have gotten an infielder, outfielder or catcher, not just cash? The answer was no. Pittsburgh wasn't willing to part with any players. For them it was a cash only deal. Management had also assured Dyer he would know about all deals in advance in the future.

Dyer said he saw a nice blend of veterans and young players developing on the team for the season. He wanted to add young players with veterans like Musial, Slaughter, Schoendienst and Marion. If Kurowski couldn't make it at third, then it would be a battle between Tommy "Harpo" Glaviano or Solly Hemus for third base. Glaviano's nickname comes from his hairdo that was similar to one of the Marx Brothers.

He also saw as a possibility the platooning of Hal Rice and Ed Sauer in the outfield. The only problem with that was Sauer could play center, but Rice couldn't. Rice was a left hand hitter, so he would be in more games. That would mean Musial would have to play center field for about 100 games. Dyer didn't particularly like that arrangement, although it could be forced on him. It also depended on how well Diering performed and what happened with Jones and Nelson at first base. It did get a little complicated.

Dyer called up 33 year old reliever Jack Creel. He had pitched for St. Louis in 1945 and was 5–4 with 4.14 ERA. Dyer had planned on using Dickson in the bullpen to help Wilks, but with his sale other arrangements had to be made. Dyer didn't know if Creel could make the team, but would give him a try.

Dyer was proud of the players he had sent to the majors. They included Dickson, Brecheen, Wilks and White. A pretty fair pitching staff. He also sent Eddie Lake, Johnny Hopp and catchers Joe Schultz Jr. and Tom Turner. Dyer was a good judge of talent and handler of men. One of the things Dyer liked about Dickson was his rubber arm. He could start and relieve. From 1942, sans two years in the army in 1944–45, through 1956 Dickson never pitched in fewer than 31 games, starting and relieving. From 1946–55 the fewest games he pitched in was 40 and the high was 51. During that time he started between 19 and 35 games every year.

Dyer said that the rookies and youth would instill a Gas House spirit in the team. He wanted a running ball club. He didn't want Musial or Slaughter taking any unnecessary chances as he couldn't risk their getting injured. He was well aware of what Slaughter's injury had meant to the 1941 team. He didn't want a repeat like that with this year's edition.

Dyer was hopeful that Jones could make it at first base as he would add a right hand bat to the lineup. Another option open to Dyer was if Hemus could play well enough to take over second base, Schoendienst could go back to the outfield, where he played in 1945. There were two problems with that. It meant putting the best second baseman in the league in the outfield and Red couldn't play center because of his arm. That meant Musial in center if Red was in the outfield. Dyer still didn't know what he would do. He did have a few weeks in which to decide.

One last item to consider about Dickson. In the first half of the season he was trying to be to cute with his pitches and that was how he got in trouble. His ERA was 5.75 at midseason. He had a 2.50 ERA the rest of the way. Dickson said some advice that Dizzy Dean gave him made the difference and he was a much better pitcher in the second half of the season. Pittsburgh had their choice of Dickson, Munger, Pollet and Wilks. Ironically all four would eventually pitch for Pittsburgh, with mixed success, before their careers were finished.

The Cardinals' other problem was catching. Rice was an excellent receiver and handler of pitchers, but a poor hitter. Joe Garagiola had a good season in the minors and would challenge for the job. The word was he was a much improved catcher. Going into the World Series at age 20 put a lot of pressure on him. There was too much expected of him and that was where his troubles began. Another candidate was Larry Ciaffone who hit .373 with 14 home runs and 92 RBIs in 402 at-bats at Allentown last season.

The team continued its search for a right hand hitter. Much would depend upon the progress of Kurowski. A deal might be delayed until spring. Other clubs wanted to wait until spring or after the season started. The more critical the Cardinals' situation, the higher the asking price.

There was a possibility that Max Lanier, Freddie Martin and Lou Klein could come back from the Mexican League, as the situation didn't develop the way the players were promised. There was still the hurdle of the five year ban. Breadon had said he would never take them back, as they violated their contracts. Saigh would be willing to give them a chance. Cardinals players, including some who objected to what they did, said let them come back. They had suffered and paid enough.

Dyer predicted a dogfight for 1949. He thought Boston, who won in 1948, was the team to beat. They had Johnny Sain and Warren Spahn heading a strong pitching staff. Sain had won 65 games the past three seasons and Spahn had 36 for the last two. They had a newcomer in Vern Bickford, who was 11–5 last year. Dyer also saw the Dodgers, Phillies and Giants as tough competition, but added the Cardinals would be right in the thick of the race.

As if the team didn't have enough to worry about in trying to fill the holes in their lineup, now there was a battle brewing with the St. Louis Browns. The Browns owned Sportsman's Park and the Cardinals had always been tenants. In 1940 Breadon signed a ten year contract calling for $35,000 per year plus one half of the playing season's costs. Any remodeling would be done at the Browns' expense, unless requested by the Cardinals. The contract still had two years to run. The DeWitts wanted the park maintenance to be based on attendance. This meant the Cardinals, based on last year's attendance, would pay about 70 percent. Saigh said no, they had a contract. The next move was up to the Browns.

The reserve clause was the cornerstone of organized baseball. It was the bedrock, the foundation on which the game was structured. Without it utter chaos would reign. The vast majority of players supported the reserve clause. Joe Gordon, speaking for the American League players, said without it the game would suffer. The farm system's fate hung on this clause. If the reserve clause didn't exist there would be unbridled bidding for players. All the wealthy teams would have the best players and the poorer clubs would be perennial also rans. They saw into the future 25 years.

Connie Mack said the pay orgy was hurting the game. There was no sign of discontent among the players. They were well paid, had a pension plan and basically were satisfied. What had brought about all the furor was that Danny Gardella (a New York Giants outfielder who jumped to the Mexican League in 1946) was suing organized baseball for $300,000. Most players thought he was unjustified in his lawsuit.

Gardella jumped to the Mexican League and it didn't work out and now he wanted to sue major league baseball for something he did. It was not major league baseball's fault that he jumped and it didn't work out in Mexico. All players were warned of the consequences if they took that action. He resented being disciplined when he wanted to return. The players did not sympathize with him. When he returned he refused to sign an appeal to Commissioner Chandler for reinstatement. There were 18 major league players banned for jumping. Chandler insisted he wouldn't cut the five year suspension of jumpers. Gardella, only 29, would have just one more at-bat in the majors. He had a pinch-hitting appearance with the Cardinals in 1950. His actions and attitude basically blacklisted him in the game.

The battle between the two St. Louis teams continued. The Browns, although in need of cash, had refused to cash the last five checks sent by the Cardinals. They wanted a new deal. The Browns send an eviction notice, saying be out by April 1. The Cardinals would have to go to court if necessary. The Browns said that the Cardinals broke the lease when the team was sold because of the attempted assignment of the contract to the new owner.

Kurowski took a pay cut, but with a promise it would be restored if he could play in 1949. He had reduced his weight and was in the best playing shape in several years. Dyer said the team would have won last season if Red and Whitey could have played 140 games at their usual level.

Dyer said Boston and Brooklyn would be the two toughest teams in the league. The Braves now had Pete Reiser and if he was healthy they had the best outfield in the league. Add that to their pitching and they were going to be a tough team with which to contend.

A peace effort by Chandler failed. Martin and Lanier had a $2,500,000 suit against organized baseball. Gardella said they were wrong for two reasons. First they were contract jumpers, which he never was. Secondly they got $5,000 bonuses. Gardella got zero.

The Cardinals continued to weigh their options in center field and the more Dyer looked at it the more complicated and frustrating it became. He had Dusak who was a good fielder, but not a hitter. Rice and Larry Miggins could hit, but neither could play center field. If Red played center field, that made for a hole at second base. Kurowski had to come back for Glaviano to be a candidate with Hemus at second base. Diering could play center excellently, but he couldn't hit. It seemed like a merry go round.

Lou Perini, owner of the Boston Braves, said it was not the reserve clause that was the problem, but low pay, especially in the minors, that was the real danger to organized baseball. National League players had voted that the reserve clause should be kept. American League players hadn't voted yet, but the sentiment was they favored keeping the clause.

Dyer said he had several combinations for the outfield. Against right hand pitching he would have Slaughter in left, Musial in center and Northey in right. Against left hand pitching Slaughter would be in left, Sauer in center and Musial in right. If Kurowski could play third, then Hemus or Glaviano would take second and if Schoendienst's arm held out he could play center. As opening day approached Dyer was still uncertain.

Chandler said the five year ban was right. The players broke their contracts. If you break a civil or business contract you can be sued and pay damages. He didn't think any court would support contract breaking. Many ex-players said the jumpers were wrong and they also supported the reserve clause. Without it rich clubs would get all the best talent. Lanier said he knew he was breaking his contract, but could make so much money it would be worth it even if he never played in the majors again. This was a very selfish approach.

Dyer said his opening lineup would probably be Slaughter in left, Musial in center and Northey and Sauer platooning in right field. Diering and Rice would probably be outfield reserves. Kurowski had stiffness in his shoulder and couldn't bat and hit like he did in 1947. Glaviano had been impressive. He would stay with the team. Del Rice dislocated his right thumb and would be out for two weeks. He could miss opening day. Pollet looked like the Pollet of 1946. Hearn had also been impressive in the spring.

Judge Edward Conger denied reinstatement to Lanier and Martin. Congress was asked to uphold the reserve clause. It was pointed out that most Federal League jumpers found coming back to the majors very rough. Only Jack Quinn and Bill Rariden were able to have scintillating years after they returned.

A newcomer had entered the infield picture. He was third baseman Eddie Kazak. He was hitting and fielding well and would probably play third as Kurowski couldn't bat or throw because of his arm. Kazak also had an arm ailment. It was injured during the war and he spent 18 months in hospitals. Everyone told him he would never play baseball again. Here he was at a major league camp and would be the starting third baseman on opening day.

The Cardinals decided to keep Glaviano as a reserve and send Hemus back for more seasoning. Jones and Nelson would probably platoon, but it was expected that the former would get more playing time because he was the better hitter. Rice would be out until at least May 1 so Garagiola would be the number one catcher. Dyer said after Musial, Slaughter, and Brecheen the team was unpredictable. There were a lot of "ifs."

Dyer said his pitching was in this order: Brecheen number one; Pollet had looked good and would be number two; Brazle seemed to have his knuckler under control and would be number three. After that it became a flip the coin game. Munger had never lived up to his full potential. One of the raps was he was too nice a guy and just wouldn't rare back and throw the high hard one to chase the batter off the plate.

Hearn had tried to learn about pitching in the majors what most pitchers used to take five and six years to learn in the minors. Staley had exhibited a lot of potential and could be one of those pitchers that can start or relieve. Wilks was the number one man in the bullpen. After that it was Reeder, Boyer, Johnson. Take your pick. Munger and Staley could be the keys to a successful season.

The baseball writers made their annual choices and it was Brooklyn, Boston, Pittsburgh, St. Louis and New York, in that order. This was despite the fact the Cardinals had won one pennant and finished second twice the last three seasons. Most believed the team was getting old and had too many unanswered questions and problems. Dyer, while not making any flag predictions, said, "Pardner, we would be in the race all year." He had said there were too many ifs to predict a flag.

There was a trade rumor involving the Cardinals and the New York Giants. The Giants would receive Jones, Schoendienst, Munger or Pollet, while the Cardinals would receive Walker Cooper, Willard Marshall and Johnny Mize. On the surface the trade would favor St. Louis.

While St. Louis would have given up the very popular Schoendienst, who was also the best second baseman in the league, they would have solved their first base, outfield and catching problem. Marshall had 14 home runs and 86 RBIs last year and 36 home runs and 107 RBIs the previous season. As a left hand hitter he would have found that right field wall very inviting.

Although Mize was 36, he too could have taken advantage of that right field wall. He hit 91 home runs the past two seasons to tie for the home run lead each year. Cooper had 35 home runs and 122 RBIs in 1947, but a knee injury reduced his effectiveness last year. He was supposedly fully recovered. Cooper was traded to Cincinnati when the deal fell through and hit 20 home runs with 83 RBIs. Marshall would hit .307 and Mize had 18 home runs before he was waived out of the league to the Yankees in late August. Those three bats would have made a significant difference in the Cardinals' lineup.

As the season opened several problems remain unsettled. The club still didn't know if Kurowski could play. They had no suitable replacement for Marion except Schoendienst which then created a hole at second. The pitching staff was still unsettled. The outfield question remained a mystery. Kazak had looked good and would probably open at third. Dyer would still like to play Schoendienst in center, so Musial could play right. It depended on Glaviano being able to play second base.

Gardella's request for reinstatement was denied. A hearing on the request would be held in June. The Browns and Cardinals signed a truce. The Cardinals would remain as tenants and the Browns cashed their checks for $80,000. Chandler ruled that the Cardinals couldn't send Al Papai to the minors, as it would be his fourth option. They must either keep him or ask for waivers.

The Cardinals lost their first two games of the season to Cincinnati as left handers Kenny Raffensberger and Johnny Vander Meer held them to one run. The lone run was a home run by Slaughter. In that game Brecheen lost 3–1 on three unearned runs. Dyer said he needed a right hand punch like Kurowski to help offset those left handers. He used Glaviano at third and Jones at first in the opening series.

The team recovered and won four of six on their first homestand against the Cubs, Pirates and Reds. Dyer said he would give Reeder, Boyer and Johnson starting assignments on the next road trip. He did not believe it was a good policy to experiment at home with young pitchers. Fans got impatient if rookie pitchers had problems. Better to let him get his introduction on the road. The three were considered the Pollets and Mungers of tomorrow, however none of them ever made it. Dyer was hopeful they could join Pollet, Brecheen, Brazle and Munger by the time the team returned home.

While the Nelson-Jones battle continued, Dyer said that Kurowski would soon get another chance at his old job. If he couldn't make it then there was Kazak and Glaviano ready to take over. Dyer wouldn't gamble on a hurt Kurowski like he did last season. He had to make a decision by May 19, which was the deadline for getting to the 25 player limit.

The home run in the glove incident occurred in Chicago on April 30 before 30,775. Bob Rush was leading 3–1 in the ninth inning. He fanned Musial and then Slaughter doubled, but Northey bounced back to Rush. Kazak singled to make the score 3–2. Diering ran for Kazak and Nelson lined to left field. Umpire Al Barlick ruled that Andy Pafko, an excellent outfielder, trapped the ball. Pafko ran in to argue while Diering and Nelson were circling the bases. By the time Pafko realized what had happened Nelson had crossed the plate with what proved to be the winning run. It was then called the "inside the glove home run."

Musial said he was not going to try for the home run title. The way to have a big year was to have a high average for the first 150 times at bat. After that a batter fluctuated only three or four points per game. However he was off to a very slow start, hitting below .250 with just six RBIs in the first 13 games.

Boyer and Johnson failed in their first starting assignments. On the good side Kazak was now playing third and batting .395, while Schoendienst was hitting .356. The team released Papai to the St. Louis Browns. Brazle and Brecheen were each 2–1, while the Cardinals were in fourth at 7–7, two games behind Boston.

Breadon died of cancer on May 10. With Rickey he had developed the farm system. They won nine pennants and six World Series. From 1925–47 the team finished below .500 just twice. Breadon sold the club after the 1947 season, citing health reasons why he was stepping down from the game and team that he loved.[5]

As the middle of May approached it looked like the experts were correct about St. Louis. Perhaps they were overly optimistic about the team finishing fourth. The club was in seventh place with an 8–11 record, three games behind Boston and New York. From this date forward the team was 88–47, a .652 winning percentage or better than Brooklyn's final mark of .630.

Northey had started off in a slump, hitting around .200. He started copying Musial and was out of his slump. Musial said, "Now I'll have to see who I can copy." Musial was hitting less than .250 and not driving in runs.

The team had been struggling and did not have a set lineup. Dyer was trying to sort through his players and decide who to keep and who to send out. In a nine day span he used nine lineups. Dyer was giving everyone a chance to play. He even benched Slaughter for two games as he wasn't hitting. Musial was batting .360 a year ago at this time. He was hitting .254 today. Schoendienst was at .367, Kazak at .355 and Marion at .329 and had yet to make an error. Pitching was still not up to par. He had used 50 pitchers in the first 19 games with just five complete games. Wilks had already appeared in nine games.

Kurowski was placed on the 60 day disabled list and Kazak was made the permanent third baseman. He also had arm problems, but had been able to overcome his. Kazak had a plastic right elbow as shrapnel had shattered his in World War II. He was told he would never play baseball again, but he fooled everyone. He shifted from second to third base, as it was easier on his arm.

The Cardinals became embroiled in a feud with Pittsburgh. It began in St. Louis on April 27 when shortstop Stan Rojek was beaned by wild man Ken Johnson. The Pittsburgh fans took exception and when the Cardinals got to Pittsburgh they hissed Garagiola, blaming him. On May 3 34,893 turned out for the game.

Rip Sewell was losing 2–1 when Garagiola bunted and Sewell, sensing what he was going to do, blocked the baseline and hipped him as he went by. It sent Garagiola flying. The umpire ruled interference and Sewell was charged with an error. The dugouts emptied, but soon peace was restored. When play continued Brecheen and Schoendienst followed with hits, but Garagiola, hurting from the bumping, was out at home. It cost the Cardinals the game. Instead of leading 3–1 and maybe a chance for more, the inning was ended. In the bottom of the ninth with Munger in relief he gave up a home run and the Cardinals lost 3–2. The game didn't seem to be critical in May, but it would loom much larger at season's end.

The next day the fans continued jeering and booing Garagiola. He responded by throwing out two would be base stealers, getting a walk, single and two doubles with two RBIs in a 4–3 victory. To show that the Pittsburgh fans were fair, his performance turned their jeers into cheers.

Dyer was still looking for starting pitching. The team was mired in seventh place, but Dyer said they wouldn't stay there. They might not win the pennant, but they would finish in the first division. Only Brecheen, Pollet and Brazle were dependable. Hearn, Munger and Staley had been inconsistent and Johnson couldn't get his control. Dyer said Reeder would start, but needed hot weather. Wilks was in and out, but Dyer believed he would be okay.

Diering was now playing center field and if he could hit .260 he would probably stay there as he was an excellent outfielder. Saigh could have sold Kurowski on waivers for $40,000 and saved his $15,000–$18,000 salary, but because of past service and performance he declined to do it.

Marion had been errorless until May 17 when he committed three in one game against Philadelphia in St. Louis. The St. Louis fans were so frustrated with the team's performance that they booed Marion, something he was unaccustomed to hearing, especially in St. Louis. Dyer said they would be okay once Musial and Slaughter started hitting. Through May 17 Musial was hitting .241 and Slaughter not much higher. The team was mired in seventh place at 10–15. They would be 86–43 the rest of the way.

Schoendienst continued his fine play, as he was batting over .350 and had made no errors. In June 1948 Schoendienst had set two records. He had eight doubles in three games and seven long hits in two games. On June 5 against Brooklyn, Schoendienst had three doubles and a single. The next day in the first game of a double-header against Philadelphia he had three doubles and a home run. In game two Schoendienst hit two more doubles.

Schoendienst set a new National League fielding mark. He played 39 consecutive games and handled 236 chances (136 assists) without an error. He exceeded the mark of 38 games by Buck Herzog of Chicago in 1919 and the 196 chances by Hughie Critz of New York in 1932. His last error was on September 15, 1948, on a ground ball by Willie Jones of Philadelphia.

Schoendienst came up as a shortstop but that path was blocked by Marion so he played the outfield in 1945. He was classified as a utility player in 1946 when the veterans returned. He then won the second base job. The major league mark was held by Boston's Bobby Doerr at 73 games and 414 chances, covering the period of June 24, 1948, through September 19, 1948.

Pollet was hammered out in his first two starts against Cincinnati and Pittsburgh, allowing nine runs in six innings. He was sent to the bullpen to straighten himself out. He was in the bullpen for 17 days and pitched effectively in three games, covering nine innings. Given another chance he pitched a complete game win, 4–3 over Pittsburgh on May 14. Then he lost a complete game, 2–0 to Brooklyn in St. Louis on May 19. Then on May 25 he pitched his first shutout since 1946, beating Boston 3–0. Over 35 innings covering his three starts and three relief appearances he allowed just five runs. He looked like he was ready to help the team.

Staley had been doing a much better job in relief, posting a 1.18 ERA for 20 innings. He might get a starting opportunity very soon. He now had a 2–1 record, while Brazle and Brecheen were each 3–2. The team was still below .500 at 15–17, four games behind Boston.

Lanier was now pitching for Drummondville (a city of 30,000) in the independent Quebec Provincial League. Other former big leaguers and Mexican jumpers were also there, including Martin and Adrian Zabala. Lanier was earning $10,000 per season, but the team could afford to pay him only $6,000. They took up a collection from the fans who made up the difference.

Eventually all good things end and so did Schoendienst's errorless streak. On May 28 at 268 chances and 44 games it ended in the fourth inning in a game at St. Louis, who was playing Pittsburgh. Ralph Kiner was on third and Ed Stevens was on second. Eddie Bockman grounded to Marion, who had no chance to get Kiner who scored. Marion pitched the ball to Schoendienst to get Stevens trying to get back to second. He was called out and then safe when the ball was jarred out of his glove. It was called an error and that ended the streak.

When the Cardinals won the Memorial Day double-header against Cincinnati they finished their homestand at 9–6, but more important they had won seven of their last eight games. Slaughter had been a driving force in that streak. On the homestand he accounted for the winning run in three of the games. For the first 17 games Slaughter batted just .254. Rested for two games he hit .363 in the next 18. As the team embarked on its eastern trip he was forced out of the action because of a very painful muscle strain in his back.

Musial was still running considerably behind last season's pace, especially on his batting average and RBIs. He had eight home runs, helped by two he got in a 6–3 win over Brooklyn on June 1. Last season when he hit 39, Musial had only one game where he had more than one home run.

Wilks was hit by a line drive on the right forearm in the first game of the Memorial Day double-header. This was the third time Wilks had been battered out in his six year career. In 1944 he was hit on the right side of the head by a line from Steve Mesner of Cincinnati. In 1947 his jaw stopped a smash from Brooklyn's Harry Taylor. Both times he was physically knocked out. He came back two days later to save Hearn's win over Brooklyn. He retired the last three batters of the game with the bases loaded.

All Mexican jumpers were reinstated and were free to sign with their respective teams. The Cardinals players friendly attitude to the jumpers turned to resentment when following reinstatement they made high salary demands. Slaughter said Lanier and Klein had cost us two pennants. Lanier wanted $15,000.

"We'd still like to see those boys with us, but if they think the Cardinals owe them something for the time they had been gone, we think they're wrong," said Slaughter. Lanier said he had considerable expense and needed to make up for lost time. "Those fellows ought to be tickled to death just to get back," said Musial. The players were glad to have them back, but they had to prove themselves before they started demanding more money. Lanier said he was waiting for a suitable offer.

Southpaws pitched the Cardinals into pennant contention. Pollet beat the Braves 2–1 on June 4. It was his fifth victory and fourth in a row. He had allowed just three runs in his last 35 innings and only eight in his last 56⅔ innings. The next day Brazle gained his sixth win with an 8–1 triumph over Boston. Brecheen, pitching like his 1948 version, shut out New York on June 7. It was reminiscent of the 1930 team. They beat Brooklyn two out of three and then swept three from Boston. The Cardinals had lost 17 of their first 29 and were outscored 147 to 119. They then won 12 of their next 14 and outscored their opponents 76 to 39.

Staley might be the right hand starter Dyer had been looking for as he blanked New York 2–0. Dyer believed that Lanier and Klein could mean the pennant for St. Louis. Musial finally reached .300; he was at .301. Schoendienst, Slaughter and Kazak were all over the .300 mark. St. Louis was now in second, one-half game behind Brooklyn.

In 1948 the Cardinals rode the bats of Musial, Slaughter and Northey to victory. If they didn't hit the team didn't win. On June 15, 1948, they were

27–23 and in fourth place and didn't right themselves until September to finish second. This year, with the three not hitting early, the team was 30–22 on the same date (they had won 19 of the last 25). Slaughter was now at .316, but Musial had slipped below .300 at .294 and Northey was just .209. However the hitting of Schoendienst, Kazak, Marion and Jones had made the difference.

Pollet's comeback was the big success story of the year. His courage and Dyer's skillful handling led to his recovery. Dyer had often been accused of pitching and favoring his pets, Pollet and Munger. They went back with him to 1940 when he was at Houston. He nurtured and helped develop both pitchers. As a major league manager Pollet was his ace in 1946. A bad back caused his problem in 1947 and he was partly recovered last season with a 13–8 record. Munger was 16–5 in 1947 for Dyer. When Pollet beat Philadelphia on June 18 it was his seventh win and sixth complete game in seven starts.

Klein signed for $6,500 and Saigh said the price could be higher if he proved himself. Klein was glad to be back with the Cardinals. He was accepted by the players and made to feel welcome. He stepped in and did a good job replacing an ailing Marion. Lanier's situation was different. He wanted a release from the Cardinals so he could negotiate with whomever he wanted. Also he was keeping the lawsuit viable. Chandler's edict said players were reinstated only if they returned to the teams they left. Martin was ready to come back to St. Louis.

The Cardinals received good news as Lanier was to return to the team. He was needed as Brazle had been knocked out four straight times and Brecheen three. Lanier signed for $11,500 and if he proved himself he could earn more. Dyer was anxious to have him. He planned to use Lanier only as a starter. He would give him regular rest.

Saigh was true to his word and gave Klein a $2,500 increase for the fine job he had done filling in for Marion. Klein commented that the organization sure had changed since he was here before. The hitting of Schoendienst, Slaughter, Kazak, Jones and Musial was fueling the Cardinals' drive. Musial was now at .305 and thought he could still win the batting title.

Dyer was still not satisfied with the pitching. There had been only 24 complete games in the first 65. This phase of the staff needed marked improvement. He would probably send either Hearn or Johnson to the minors as neither had been impressive. Despite all the early problems they were just one game behind Brooklyn at 40–27 as the first of July approached.

The key question was, could Lanier regain the form of 1941–46? He was 63–37 during that time, but he was in just four games in 1945 before going into the service. Then he was 6–0 with six complete games in 1946 when he jumped to the Mexican League. From 1942–44 he averaged 15 victories a season and a sore arm kept him from winning 20 or more in 1944.

Dyer admitted the Dodgers had the Cardinals on power, speed and even defense, but the Cardinals had the pitching edge. The Cardinals had a slightly higher team batting average, but Brooklyn, because of their home run power, had scored almost one run per game more. If Lanier was okay, that could be St. Louis' edge. He was unimpressive in his first start against Chicago. The Cardinals won 9–4, but he left in the third inning.

The key was for Lanier to be able to team with Pollet as a one-two combination. Brecheen had been having his problems while Munger and Brazle had been inconsistent. Staley and Wilks had been very dependable and Dyer wanted to leave the former in the bullpen.

Brooklyn was the pacesetter in 1940, '41, '42, '45, '46, '47 at the fourth of July holiday, yet won only twice, in 1941 and 1947. They had a history of fading in the stretch. The Cardinals overtook them in 1942 and 1946, while Cincinnati passed them in 1940 and Chicago in 1945. In fact, St. Louis was second in 1945. The Cardinals also lost in 1941 because of a large number of injuries.

Dyer wouldn't name the biggest disappointments of the first half, but they would have to be Brecheen and Musial; the latter had trouble staying over .300 and wasn't driving in runs like he should. If he had hit like in 1948 the team would be several games in front. There was still the second half and the team was only two games behind Brooklyn. There was plenty of time to turn the tide.

The Cardinals had done well against Brooklyn (6–5) and Boston (7–2), but only 4–4 versus Cincinnati and 7–5 against Chicago, both second division teams. They were 25–16 at home and 17–14 on the road. Saigh handed out raises to Kazak, Glaviano, Pollet and Hal Rice for fine first half performances. They received theirs the same time as Klein.

On July 8 the Cardinals defeated Cincinnati 6–1, but Musial was involved in a very unusual play. He had doubled to drive in a run in the first inning, but then overran second base. Before he could be retired it took seven players handling the ball to get him out. Finally catcher Cooper tagged him out at third base in one of the most unusual plays of the season.

After the All Star break the Cardinals swept Cincinnati in four games as the pitching really hit its groove. Brecheen got a complete game victory, while Pollet picked up win number 11. Lanier pitched good ball for six and two-thirds innings and Wilks picked up the victory in relief. The team also had strong pitching from Munger, Brazle and Staley. Musial hit his 15th home run on July 8 and it was his first in 18 games. As the middle of July approached the team was one and one-half games off the pace.

Musial had dipped below .300 again. He was at .293, over 55 points below his career average. However, Kazak, Schoendienst, Jones, Marion and Slaughter were all over .300. Pollet had 12 victories, while Brazle and Wilks had eight each. Munger, Staley and Brecheen each had six wins. All were over .500.

The pension plan was a major concern of all players and owners. Various proposals had been made. Some had suggested two All Star games, with the revenue going into the pension plans. Other had suggested a portion of TV revenue go into the plan. Another suggestion was raising the age limit to 55 from 50 before a player could draw. The problem developed when 60 players qualified for the $100 per month maximum by making a one time payment of $250 to the fund. No one realized it would be that many players. The thinking was there might be 10 or 15. The situation had to be solved, all parties agreed.

Neither the Cardinals nor the Dodgers had lost a double-header. The Cardinals were 2–0–3 and the Dodgers were 1–0–3. The number of double-headers had been greatly reduced since the early and mid–1940s.

Dyer said except for Lanier and Wilks he didn't rate pitchers as starters or relievers, but as pitchers to be used as needed. Thus if he needed Pollet or Munger in relief, he would use them accordingly. Likewise Staley or Brazle could start a game or relieve. He liked the flexibility it gave him with the pitching staff. The Cardinals' pitching allowed an average of just two runs in 10 games, but the team was just 6–4.

They had the top team average, but not hitting with men on base. An example was Musial, who had 52 RBIs in 83 games, a pace that would give him 96 for the season. That number was good from anyone else, but under par for Musial, who drove in 131 last year. He would drive in 71 runs in the last 71 games.

Slaughter had been a Cardinals regular since 1938 and had always said they would have to tear the uniform off him before he quit playing baseball. He almost didn't become a Cardinal. Back in 1935 at the Cardinals youth training camp Rickey was going over the list of players with his squad of 24 scouts and they were deciding who to keep. When they came to Slaughter 23 of the scouts said no, but Joe Schulz Sr. said keep him. So Rickey did.

In 1937 he hit .382 at Columbus and other teams were bidding for his services and that of another Columbus star, Johnny Rizzo. Rickey said, "Rizzo I will trade. The other man I want for myself." In his first year Rizzo drove in 111 runs and set the Pittsburgh home run record with 23, since broken by Ralph Kiner. Slaughter hit .276 with just eight home runs.

Since then he had hit .300 or better in six of the seasons, and .294 in the seventh. He had been an All Star five times and with Terry Moore and Musial formed one of the greatest outfields of all time. Rizzo played through 1942 and never duplicated that rookie year. Slaughter led the league in RBIs in 1946 and made that now famous dash from first to home on a single in game seven of the 1946 World Series. He was known as Mr. Hustle. And today he was a Cardinal because of one man, Joe Schulz Sr.

Wilks was considered the best relief pitcher in the game. He had been in 35 of the team's first 90 games. The failure of management to recognize the value of relief pitching is why most pitchers shied away from it. Wilks had made a career of it. He was 41–17 entering this season, appearing in 178 games, starting 43 and completing 21. This season he was 8–3 with a 2.08 ERA, all in relief.

The Cardinals took over first place by defeating co-favorites Boston (two of three) and Brooklyn (three of three). The charge was led by 33 year old Slaughter. He may have lost some speed and arm strength, but he kept chugging along. He was currently hitting .336.

The Redbirds had just completed a 21 game road trip during which they were 13–7–1. The tie game was a 4–4 affair with Brooklyn on July 25 when both teams had to catch a train. In that Brooklyn series Musial hit for the cycle on July 24. In that series St. Louis took the first three games by scores of 3–1, 5–4 and 14–1. During that trip they outscored their opponents 88 to 64. They would now open a 19 game homestand.

Another factor in the Cardinals' winning ways had been the play of their reserves. Klein had done an excellent job in relieving Kazak, Marion and Schoendienst as needed. The pony infield (Glaviano, Klein and Nelson) had also been a contributor. Another factor was St. Louis' record against first division teams. They were 24–17, while Brooklyn was 15–21. The Cardinals had Slaughter, Schoendienst, Musial and Kazak over .300, while Pollet was 13–5, Brazle 10–5, Munger 9–4 and Wilks 9–3. As August approached St. Louis was 59–36, one and one-half games ahead of Brooklyn (57–37).

Dyer had the team winning because he had the ability to make the players feel at ease and relaxed. He had many of them in the minors. He got Pollet and Munger back on stride by warning them they would be in the bullpen or worse if they didn't pitch like he knew they could. He told Jones and Kazak to relax and not worry about their hitting, because he knew they could do it. As a result Kazak had been over .300 all season and Jones between .285 and .300.

The Cardinals were not an old team, they had just been around a long time. Marion at 30 and Slaughter at 33 were the oldest among the regulars. Slaughter had been with the team since 1938, Marion since 1940, Musial since 1941 and Schoendienst since 1945. If Marion's back held out he could play another six to eight seasons.

Munger tired of throwing junk pitches and began pitching like he did in 1944 and everyone knew he could. Since June 6 he had been the best right hand pitcher in the league. At that time he had a 6.69 ERA and was 3–2 (through sheer luck) with two complete games in eight starts. Since that time he had completed six of ten starts and compiled a 7–2, 2.92 ERA mark.

Schoendienst booted his first ground ball since September 15, 1948, on July 31. His only errors this year had occurred on throws. When Brooklyn defeated St. Louis in the final of their series they ended two streaks. St. Louis had been 9–0–2 and also had won eight straight from Brooklyn.

The Cardinals got a bad break in early August when Kazak, hitting .304, broke his ankle and would be lost for most of the season. Glaviano took over at third and did a creditable job, but the team missed Kazak. Glaviano did not have the range of Kazak and hit almost 40 points less.

On August 6 the Cardinals suffered another tough loss, this time to New York 3–1. In the first inning with two out and Schoendienst on first Jones hit an apparent home run into the left field bleachers off Giants pitcher Adrian Zabala (a Mexican jumper). However, the umpire ruled Zabala had balked before making the delivery and under the rules of the day the home run was nullified. On the next pitch Jones grounded out and the Cardinals lost the game.

Under today's rules the Cardinals would have had the option and naturally would have taken the home run. Thus instead of having a 2–0 lead at the end of the first it was a scoreless game. Dizzy Dean, who was at the game, said, "I always knew I stopped pitching too soon. Boy now you can even call back a home run." Your writer was a young teenager sitting in the left field bleachers and Jones' "home run" landed about ten feet from me.

Diering had been playing center field and batting around .280 with 19 doubles, six triples and one home run. As long as he continued to play center field the way he did and hit in the .260–.280 range he would remain in the lineup. The outfield of Slaughter, Diering and Musial was the best defensive one they had had since the heydays of Slaughter, Moore and Musial.

For the middle two weeks of August the Cardinals would play the second division teams. They hoped they could feast on them like the Dodgers did. The Cardinals were 41–25 against clubs with winning records and 25–14 against those with losing marks.

Before Kazak broke his ankle, Glaviano was subbing for him as Kazak had been hit by a pitch one day, spiked the next and then hit by another pitch the next night. Pollet was now 15–5 and had six straight victories while Munger was at 11–5 with five consecutive complete games. Musial went on a hitting tear, getting seven doubles in eight games and hitting the right field screen five times in his first at-bat in five of the games during that streak.

The team had lost another tough game in July at Pittsburgh. The Pirates had a young outfielder named Dino Restelli, who had broken in with a flurry of home runs. It had made him an overnight hero, briefly, and a little cocky. The game was a scoreless duel between Ernie Bonham and Gerry Staley.

Restelli had complained bitterly about called strikes to umpire Larry Goetz, one of the best in the game. He finally got irritated and motioned to Staley to pitch to Restelli who had twice stepped out of the batters' box to complain. Staley was daydreaming and didn't fire the ball over the plate for an easy third strike. It took Garagiola firing the ball back to him to make him understand what Goetz wanted.

Still he hesitated, checking the runners on base, which he didn't need to do. He just lobbed the ball to the plate and Restelli, now realizing what was happening, stepped back in and hit it for a double which led to a Cardinals defeat. Goetz, when asked for an explanation by the press, said frankly, "I was trying to put the fresh busher in his place, but St. Louis wouldn't let me." The defeat in Pittsburgh, the one on Jones' disallowed home run and the earlier one this season to Pittsburgh would all loom big in late September.

Musial said he tried pulling the ball too much earlier in the season, going for home runs, even though he said he wasn't going to do that. It threw his timing off and took him a couple of months to get it back. He now had his average on the rise as he quit trying to hit home runs, but now they were coming.

The Cardinals had an excellent homestand at 13–5, but lost ground to Brooklyn. They came home on July 26 one-half game out and when they left three weeks later they were one game out. The Cardinals' pennant drive was pitching based. During one stretch their pitchers went 41 innings without allowing a walk. They had three complete games by Brecheen, Brazle and Staley, nine innings by Munger and Wilks and five by Pollet. Martin allowed the first pass on August 14 to Jack Phillips of Pittsburgh leading off the sixth inning.

When Dickson beat Munger 6–3 he stopped the Redbird's winning streak at five and it marked the third time this season he had beaten his former teammates. Then Cliff Chambers defeated Pollet 3–0 to end his six game winning streak. St. Louis was just 7–7 versus Pittsburgh while Brooklyn was 14–3 against them. This was a key reason the Cardinals were one game back instead of several in front.

Dyer saw a fight to the finish. Six of the Cardinals' nine pennants were squeakers. Only in 1931, 1943 and 1944 did they have easy pennant wins. The hitting had slowed, causing a drop in the Cardinals' performance. They had just been 5–7 while Brooklyn had been 4–8. Both teams hit a slump at the same time. Hemus was called up as Kazak was out with a broken ankle, Marion had back trouble and Glaviano had some minor injuries. As the last week of August dawned St. Louis was one and one-half games ahead of Brooklyn.

Boston's pennant drive was virtually killed as they lost three of four to St. Louis. The Cardinals' home run drought ended as a hurricane of home runs were hit by Redbird hitters. Musial led the parade by hitting six in eight games, to equal what he had hit in the previous 56. That raised his season's total to 26.

The rest of the lineup joined in the fun. Jones hit two in the August 28 double-header at Boston, raising his season's total to seven. Marion hit two in the New York double-header the prior day, raising his total to three. They hit 10 home runs in a double-header, 13 in six games and 15 in nine games after hitting just 12 from June 25. When the team scored 11 runs in the second game of the double-header at New York it was the first time since August

12 they had scored more than five runs in a game. They had defeated Pittsburgh 8–2 that day and when they scored five runs in the third inning it was more than they had scored in any of the previous 17 games.

Dyer had fretted about the back to back double-headers with New York and Boston for two months. He had talked about them for the two weeks prior. The team was to play New York on the 27 and Boston on the 28. They won both double-headers and Dyer then wondered what all his worrying was about.

When Lanier pitched a three hitter over Boston in his 7–1 victory, it was his first one since 1946. The next day he and Martin dropped their $2,500,000 suit against organized baseball. Lanier and Martin wanted to remain Cardinals forever. Saigh didn't want any player making just the $5,000 minimum. The least he would pay was $6,000. He helped arrange the dropping of the lawsuit for Lanier and Martin.

The Cardinals had a sold five man pitching staff, including their fireman Wilks. Pollet was 16–8, headed for his second 20 win season. Munger was 12–5, Brazle in his best season was 14–6 and Brecheen had started pitching like "The Cat" of old and was now 11–9. Wilks sported a 10–3 record. Musial was at .321 and Slaughter at .327, as he had ambitions for a batting title. The Cardinals were 79–48, two games ahead of Brooklyn (77–50) as September rolled around.

The Cardinals were only 10–10 versus Pittsburgh while Brooklyn was 16–4. What a difference that made in the standings. The feud with the Pirates had riled them up and they played very heady baseball against the Cardinals. It started with the beaning of Rojek on April 27. Then a second incident occurred in the second game of the Labor Day double-header. The Cardinals were ahead and Slaughter spiked Murtaugh when sliding into him. There were words exchanged, but this incident coupled with the one in April seemed to add fuel to the fire and Pittsburgh pulled out a 5–4 victory.

Musial was the recipient of several gifts as he was honored. On August 21 he was given a Cadillac by fans from his hometown of Donora, Pennsylvania. Then on September 7 in St. Louis he received a De Soto station wagon plus six $1,000 savings bonds.

Slaughter was now at .340, a few points behind Jackie Robinson (who said the Cardinals were the toughest team in the league to steal on). Musial had moved up to .326 as he was making a belated run for the batting title. He was also second in the league with 28 home runs. From a season that looked like a disaster he was having another banner year.

The Cardinals finished the season 7–4 at New York and Brooklyn and 8–3 at Boston. However, they were just 4–7 at Philadelphia and held only a 10–9 edge on them for the season. The team had not lost a double-header as they were 5–0–5. With 14 home games left the Cardinals had outdrawn last season. They were at 1,140,394. With three weeks to play St. Louis and Brooklyn had each won 84, but Brooklyn had lost two more (51).

The Cardinals started the season 4–10 on the road, but had been 40–18 for the last 58 games making their overall road record 44–28, while at home the team was 45–22. With less than two weeks to go the team had a one and one-half game edge on Brooklyn. St. Louis was 89–50 and Brooklyn was 88–52. Musial had come on strong and was now at .333 with 32 home runs. He had hit two home runs in five different games this season.

The pennant was going to go down to the wire as the Cardinals lost a crucial series to Brooklyn at home. They took the first game 1–0 on September 19 behind Lanier. This victory assured St. Louis of the lead at the end of the series. Unfortunately Brooklyn took the next two. In the next game the Dodgers started Joe Hatten, who had not beaten the Cardinals in six tries. He was opposed by Munger, who had defeated them three straight times. It looked like an easy win for St. Louis.

It turned out it wasn't as Brooklyn humiliated St. Louis 19–6 in their worse defeat of the season. The next night Roe defeated Brecheen 5–0. Brooklyn left town, trailing St. Louis by one-half game. Each team had won 93, but St. Louis had lost 54 compared to Brooklyn's 55. The Cardinals won the season series with the Dodgers, 12–10, but lost five of the last seven played.

Going into the final week the Cardinals had five games to play, two with Pittsburgh and three with Chicago, while Brooklyn had four. On September 28 Dickson defeated the Cardinals 7–2 and knocked them out of first place. The next day Bill Werle and the Pirates beat Munger and the Cardinals 6–4. For the year Musial hit .250 at Pittsburgh in 1948 and just .159 in 1949.

The Cardinals had three left with Chicago and lost the first to Bob Chipman (who had been winless for two and one-half months) 3–1. The Redbirds left 12 men on base. The next day Bob Rush defeated Lanier 6–5. The Cardinals were a game out and won on the final day 13–5 as Musial hit two home runs and Pollet gained his 20th victory, but it wasn't enough as Brooklyn also won.

It was a bittersweet season for St. Louis. They won 96 games, the most since 1946, but lost a pennant they should have won. Once again injuries played a major part in their failure to win the pennant. Losing Kazak for the last two months was a crucial blow. By the end of the season Marion, Slaughter and Schoendienst were worn to a frazzle. The Redhead had lost 10 pounds. All were fatigued and needed a rest. Once again the reserves weren't up to par and able to relieve the starters.

The failure of the Cardinals to defeat Pittsburgh was a key factor. The Cardinals finished 10–12 against Pittsburgh while Brooklyn was 16–6. Reverse the Cardinals' record with Pittsburgh and they had the pennant by one game. If you looked back you saw two defeats to Pittsburgh, one on Labor Day and the Restelli double, plus the game where the home run was called back against the Giants, and that made the difference. They all loomed large at the end.

No one could fault the team; they put up a spirited fight and never quit.

They played hard until the very end. The season did point up a key weakness and that was the need for a strong right hand batter to support Musial and Slaughter. It was a shame that Kurowski couldn't play. They needed his bat. Jones hit .300, but had just eight home runs and 62 RBIs. Not Kurowski type numbers.

The other pressing need was infield reserves, as Marion was going to need more rest and perhaps Schoendienst too. Another question to be answered was whether Kazak would be able to recover from his injury and play as he did in the first half of the season. Finally, could Slaughter keep grinding it out? Time would tell.

There was some concern about the pitching staff as next season Brazle would be 36, Brecheen 35, Wilks 34, Lanier 34 and Martin 35. That didn't mean the entire staff would collapse, but younger pitchers were needed if the team was to continue to be a strong pennant contender. Staley showed he could be one of the pitchers of the future.

Nobody realized it at the time, but it would be 15 years before a pennant and World Series flag would fly atop the flag pole in center field in St. Louis. There was age on the team and starting in 1950 it began to show. The team was in first place through middle June and until after the All Star break was second. Then it collapsed, finishing fifth at 78–75.

Pollet was 14–13, despite a respectable 3.29 ERA. He would be traded to Pittsburgh early in 1951. He would pitch through 1956 and be just 34–54 for those years. He was 97–62 for St. Louis. Munger was 7–8 with a 3.90 ERA. After a 4–6 season in 1951 he would be traded to Pittsburgh. Staley was 13–13 with a 4.99 ERA. He would then win 54 games over the next three seasons for St. Louis.

Even Brecheen fell as he had his only losing season in 10 for the Cardinals at 8–11. He would be 8–4 and 7–5 the following two years before ending his career with the St. Louis Browns as they ended theirs in St. Louis in 1953. Wilks was 2–0 with a 6.66 ERA. Lanier was 11–9 with a 3.13 ERA. He would be the same in 1951 and then was traded to New York.

Musial had another great season, leading the league at .346 and hitting 28 home runs with 105 RBIs. Slaughter hit .290 with 101 RBIs. Schoendienst fell to .276, but led the league in doubles. There wasn't enough other fire power to support a staff ERA of 3.97, one-half run higher than in 1949, while the team scored almost one-half run per game less. That about told the story.

We need to make one last comment about Lanier before closing the chapter on 1949. His story was a tragic one in many ways. He never fully regained his form after returning from the Mexican League. Age and three and one-half years away from major league baseball had its effects. He was 5–4, 11–9 and 11–9 for St. Louis before ending his career with the St. Louis Browns at 0–1 in 1953.

The three full seasons he pitched (1942–44) prior to jumping to the

Mexican League he had averaged 15 wins. In 1944 he was 17–5 when he developed a sore arm and lost his last seven decisions. He could have won 20 or more that season. Then before he left for service in 1945 he was 2–2 with 1.73 ERA and three complete games in four starts.

He started 1946 with a 6–0, a 1.93 ERA and six complete games in six starts. He was headed for his greatest season. Had Lanier not jumped it was safe to assume he could have won 50–60 games for St. Louis from 1946–48 and would have been a much better pitcher in 1949 and ensuing seasons. His actions probably cost the Cardinals at least one and maybe as many as three pennants in the period 1947–49.

It also cost him in his career. Lanier finished at 108–82, 101–69 with St. Louis. His St. Louis record was a .594 winning percentage. It is quite conceivable he could have ended his career with double the victory total. Lanier had said one of the reasons for his high salary demands when he returned was all the expenses he had. Yes, Lanier paid a high price for his jumping to the Mexican League.

This ended the greatest period in Cardinals history. Some might say it ended on a sad note and perhaps in a way it did, but then remember this team was picked to finish fourth or fifth and almost won it all. It would have been great to go out as champions, but then things don't always work out the way you want.

Let us sum up the past ten seasons. They won four pennants, three World Series championships, five second place spots and one third. They averaged 96 wins per season for the best record in baseball during the decade. As we have seen over the last ten chapters with a few breaks (mainly fewer injuries) the Cardinals could have added three or four more pennants to the impressive list. Certainly 1941, '45 and '49 could have been in that category. When we review 1947 we see that a better handling of the Dodgers and a healthy Musial and Pollet would have made the difference. In closing it had been a great run and was just too bad it couldn't last into the 1950s, but by that time the well had run dry as they no longer had the old master Rickey to guide the farm system. The biggest mistake Breadon made was letting Rickey leave as he let his own ego get in the way and Rickey built a dynasty for Brooklyn (1947–56) that could have just as easily been for St. Louis. Well, so long, folks, until the next chapter is written.

Appendix: Statistics

Listed below are the season by season statistics for each Cardinals player. An asterisk by a number indicates the player led the league in that category

1940

Players	G	AB	R	H	2B	3B	4B	RBI	Ave	SLP
Johnny Mize	155	579	111	182	31	13	43*	137*	.314	.636*
Joe Orengo	129	415	58	119	23	4	7	58	.287	.412
Marty Marion	125	435	44	121	18	1	3	46	.278	.345
Stu Martin	112	369	45	88	12	6	4	32	.238	.336
Enos Slaughter	140	516	96	158	25	13	17	73	.306	.504
Terry Moore	138	537	92	163	33	4	17	64	.304	.475
Ernie Koy	93	348	44	108	19	5	8	52	.310	.463
Mickey Owen	117	307	27	81	16	2	0	27	.264	.329
Jimmy Brown	107	454	56	127	17	4	0	30	.280	.335
Don Padgett	93	240	24	58	15	1	6	41	.242	.388
Pepper Martin	86	228	28	72	15	4	3	39	.316	.456
Johnny Hopp	80	152	24	41	7	4	1	14	.270	.388
Don Gutteridge	69	108	19	29	5	0	3	14	.269	.398
Joe Medwick	37	158	21	48	12	0	3	20	.304	.437
Eddie Lake	32	66	12	14	3	0	2	7	.212	.348
Bill DeLancey	15	18	0	4	0	0	0	2	.222	.222

Players (1940 cont.)	G	AB	R	H	2B	3B	4B	RBI	Ave	SLP
Red Jones	12	11	0	1	0	0	0	1	.091	.091
Hal Epps	11	15	6	3	0	0	0	1	.200	.200
Harry Walker	7	27	2	5	2	0	0	6	.185	.259
G. Gillenwater	7	25	1	4	1	0	0	5	.180	.200
Walker Cooper	6	19	3	6	1	0	0	2	.316	.368
Creepy Crespi	3	11	2	3	1	0	0	0	.273	.364
Totals	156	5499*	747	1514	296	61	119*	709	.275	.411*

Pitchers	G	GS	CG	W	L	PCT	ERA	SHO	Saves
Bill McGee	38	31	11	16	10	.615	3.80	3	0
Lon Warneke	33	31	17	16	10	.615	3.14	1	0
Clyde Shoun	54*	19	13	13	11	.542	3.93	1	5
Mort Cooper	38	29	16	11	12	.478	3.62	3	3
Max Lanier	35	11	4	9	6	.600	3.24	2	3
Bob Bowman	28	17	7	7	5	.583	4.34	0	0
Ira Hutchinson	20	2	1	4	2	.667	3.14	0	1
Carl Doyle	21	5	1	3	3	.500	5.89	0	0
Jack Russell	26	0	0	3	4	.429	2.50	0	1
Newt Kimball	2	1	1	1	0	1.000	2.57	0	0
Ernie White	8	1	0	1	1	.500	4.09	0	0
Gene Lillard	2	1	0	0	1	.000	12.60	0	0
Curt Davis	14	7	0	0	4	.000	5.17	0	1
Harry Brecheen	3	0	0	0	0	.000	0.00	0	0
Murray Dickson	1	1	0	0	0	.000	13.50	0	0
Bob Wieland	1	0	0	0	0	.000	27.00	0	0
Totals	324	156	71	84	69	.549	3.83	10	14

1941

Players	G	AB	R	H	2B	3B	4B	RBI	AVE	SLP
Johnny Mize	126	472	67	150	39*	8	16	100	.317	.535
Creepy Crespi	146	540	55	156	24	2	4	46	.279	.350
Marty Marion	155	547	50	138	22	3	3	56	.252	.320

Players *(1941 cont.)*	G	AB	R	H	2B	3B	4B	RBI	Ave	SLP
Jimmy Brown	132	549	81	168	28	9	3	56	.306	.406
Enos Slaughter	113	425	71	132	22	9	13	76	.311	.496
Terry Moore	122	493	86	145	26	4	6	68	.294	.400
Johnny Hopp	134	445	83	135	25	11	4	50	.303	.436
Gus Mancuso	106	328	25	75	13	1	2	37	.229	.293
Don Padgett	107	324	39	80	18	0	5	44	.247	.349
Estel Crabtree	77	167	27	57	6	3	5	28	.341	.500
Coaker Triplett	76	185	29	53	6	3	3	21	.288	.400
Walker Cooper	38	200	19	49	9	1	1	20	.245	.315
Eddie Lake	45	76	9	8	2	0	0	0	.105	.132
Steve Mesner	24	69	8	10	1	0	0	10	.145	.159
Ernie Koy	13	40	5	8	1	0	2	4	.200	.375
Stan Musial	12	47	8	20	4	0	1	7	.426	.574
Harry Walker	7	15	3	4	1	0	0	1	.267	.333
Erv Dusak	6	14	1	2	0	0	0	3	.143	.143
W. Kurowski	5	9	1	3	2	0	0	2	.333	.556
Totals	155	5457	724	1482	254	56	70	664	.272	.371

Pitchers	G	GS	CG	W	L	Pct	ERA	SHO	Saves
Ernie White	32	25	12	17	7	.708	2.40	3	2
Lon Warneke	37	30	12	17	9	.654	3.13	4	0
Mort Cooper	29	25	12	13	9	.591	3.90	0	0
Harry Gumbert	33	17	8	11	5	.688	2.75	3	1
Howie Krist	37	8	2	10	0	1.000	4.03	0	2
Max Lanier	35	18	8	10	8	.556	2.82	2	3
Sam Nahem	26	8	2	5	2	.714	2.96	0	1
Howie Pollet	9	8	6	5	2	.714	1.93	2	0
Clyde Shoun	26	6	0	3	5	.375	5.66	0	0
John Grodzicki	5	1	0	2	1	.667	1.38	0	0
Hank Gornicki	4	1	1	1	0	1.000	3.28	0	0
John Beazley	1	1	1	1	0	1.000	1.00	0	0
Bill Crouch	18	4	0	1	2	.333	3.63	0	6
Ira Hutchinson	29	0	0	1	5	.167	3.83	0	5
Bill McGee	4	3	0	0	1	.000	5.14	0	1

Pitchers *(1941 cont.)*	G	GS	CG	W	L	Pct	ERA	SHO	Saves
Hersh Lyons	1	0	0	0	0	.000	0.00	0	0
Totals	326	155	64	97	56	.634	3.19	15	20

1942

Players	G	AB	R	H	2B	3B	4B	RBI	Ave	SLP
Johnny Hopp	95	314	41	81	16	7	3	37	.258	.362
Creepy Crespi	93	292	33	71	4	2	0	35	.243	.271
Marty Marion	147	485	66	134	38*	5	0	54	.276	.375
W. Kurowski	115	366	51	93	17	3	9	42	.254	.391
Enos Slaughter	152	591	100	190*	31	17*	13	98	.318	.494
Terry Moore	130	489	80	141	26	3	6	49	.288	.391
Stan Musial	140	467	87	147	32	10	10	72	.315	.490
Walker Cooper	125	438	56	123	32	7	7	65	.281	.434
Jimmy Brown	145	606*	75	155	28	4	1	71	.256	.320
Ray Sanders	95	282	37	71	17	2	5	39	.252	.356
Harry Walker	74	191	38	60	12	2	0	16	.314	.398
Coaker Triplett	64	154	38	42	7	4	1	23	.272	.390
Ken O'Dea	59	192	22	45	7	1	5	32	.234	.359
Buddy Blattner	19	23	3	1	0	0	0	1	.043	.043
Erv Dusak	12	27	4	5	3	0	0	3	.185	.296
Sam Narron	10	10	0	4	0	0	0	1	.400	.400
Estel Crabtree	10	9	1	3	2	0	0	2	.333	.556
Gus Mancuso	5	13	0	1	0	0	0	1	.077	.077
Jeff Cross	1	4	0	1	0	0	0	1	.250	.250
Totals	155	5421*	755*	1454*	282*	69*	60	692*	.268*	.379*

Pitchers	G	GS	CG	W	L	Pct	ERA	SHO	Saves
Mort Cooper	37	35*	22*	22*	7	.759	1.77*	10*	0
John Beazley	43	23	13	21	6	.778	2.14	3	3
Howie Krist	34	8	3	13	3	.813	2.52	0	1
Max Lanier	34	20	8	13	8	.619	2.96	2	2
Harry Gumbert	38	19	5	9	5	.645	3.26	0	5

Pitchers (1942 cont.)	G	GS	CG	W	L	Pct	ERA	SHO	Saves
Howie Pollet	27	13	5	7	5	.583	2.89	2	0
Ernie White	26	19	7	7	5	.583	2.53	1	2
Murray Dickson	36	7	2	6	3	.667	2.90	0	2
Lon Warneke	12	12	5	6	4	.600	3.29	0	0
Bill Beckmann	2	0	0	1	0	1.000	0.00	0	0
Bill Lohrman	5	0	0	1	1	.500	1.39	0	0
Whitey Moore	9	0	0	0	1	.000	4.50	0	0
Clyde Shoun	2	0	0	0	0	.000	0.00	0	0
Totals	305	156	70	106*	48	.688*	2.53*	18*	15

1943

Players	G	AB	R	H	2B	3B	4B	RBI	Ave	SLP
Ray Sanders	144	476	69	134	21	5	11	73	.280	.414
Lou Klein	154	627	91	180	28	14	7	62	.287	.410
Marty Marion	129	418	38	117	15	3	1	52	.280	.337
W. Kurowski	139	522	69	150	24	8	13	70	.287	.439
Stan Musial	157	617	108	220*	48*	20*	13	81	.357*	.562*
Harry Walker	148	564	76	166	28	6	2	53	.295	.376
Danny Litwhiler	80	258	40	72	14	3	7	31	.279	.438
Walker Cooper	122	449	52	143	30	4	9	81	.319	.463
Johnny Hopp	91	241	33	54	10	2	2	25	.224	.307
Debs Garms	90	249	26	54	10	2	0	22	.257	.313
Ken O'Dea	71	203	15	57	11	2	3	25	.281	.399
Frank DeMaree	39	86	5	25	2	0	0	9	.291	.314
George Fallon	36	78	6	18	1	0	0	5	.231	.244
Jimmy Brown	34	110	6	20	4	2	0	8	.182	.255
Sam Narron	10	11	0	1	0	0	0	0	.091	.091
Coaker Triplett	9	25	1	2	0	0	1	4	.080	.200
Buster Adams	8	11	1	1	1	0	0	1	.091	.192
Totals	157	5438*	679	1515*	259	72	70	638	.279*	.391*

Pitchers (1943 cont.)	G	GS	CG	W	L	Pct	ERA	SHO	Saves
Mort Cooper	37	32	24*	21*	8	.724*	2.30	6	3
Max Lanier	32	25	14	15	7	.682	1.91	2	3
Howie Krist	34	17	9	11	5	.688	2.91	2	3
Harry Gumbert	21	19	7	10	5	.667	2.84	2	0
George Munger	32	9	5	9	5	.643	3.97	0	2
Harry Brecheen	29	13	8	9	6	.600	2.27	1	4
Murray Dickson	31	7	2	8	2	.800	3.57	0	0
Al Brazle	13	9	8	8	2	.800	1.53	1	0
Howie Pollet	16	14	12	8	4	.667	1.75*	5	0
Ernie White	14	10	5	5	5	.500	3.76	1	0
Bud Byerly	2	2	0	1	0	1.000	3.46	0	0
Totals	261	157	94*	105*	49	.682*	2.57*	21*	15

1944

Players	G	AB	R	H	2B	3B	4B	RBI	Ave	SLP
Ray Sanders	154	601	187	177	34	9	12	102	.295	.441
Emil Verban	146	488	51	128	14	2	0	43	.257	.293
Marty Marion	144	506	50	135	28	2	6	63	.267	.362
W. Kurowski	149	555	95	150	25	7	20	87	.270	.449
Stan Musial	146	568	112	197*	51*	14	12	94	.347	.548*
Johnny Hopp	139	527	106	177	35	9	11	72	.336	.499
Danny Litwhiler	140	492	53	130	25	5	15	82	.264	.427
Walker Cooper	112	397	56	126	25	5	13	72	.317	.504
Ken O'Dea	85	265	39	66	11	2	6	37	.248	.374
Augie Bergamo	80	192	35	55	6	3	2	19	.286	.380
Debs Garms	73	149	17	30	3	0	0	5	.201	.221
George Fallon	69	141	16	28	6	0	1	9	.199	.262
Pepper Martin	40	86	15	24	4	0	2	4	.279	.395
John Antonelli	8	21	0	4	1	0	0	1	.190	.238
Bob Keely	1	0	0	0	0	0	0	0	.000	.000
Totals	157	5475*	772*	1507*	274*	59	100*	720*	.275*	.402*

Pitchers (1944 cont.)	G	GS	CG	W	L	Pct	ERA	SHO	Saves
Mort Cooper	34	33	22	22	7	.759	2.46	7*	1
Ted Wilks	36	21	16	17	4	.810*	2.64	4	0
Max Lanier	33	30	16	17	12	.586	2.65	5	0
Harry Brecheen	30	22	13	16	5	.762	2.86	3	0
George Munger	21	12	7	11	3	.786	1.34	2	2
Freddy Schmidt	37	9	3	7	3	.700	3.14	2	5
Al Jurisch	30	14	5	7	9	.438	3.39	2	1
Harry Gumbert	10	7	3	4	2	.667	2.51	0	1
Blix Donnelly	27	4	2	2	1	.667	2.13	1	2
Bud Byerly	9	4	2	2	2	.500	3.43	0	0
Bill Trotter	2	1	0	0	1	.000	13.50	0	0
Mike Naymick	1	0	0	0	0	.000	4.50	0	0
Totals	300	157	89	105*	49	.682*	2.67*	26*	12

1945

Players	G	AB	R	H	2B	3B	4B	RBI	Ave	SLP
Ray Sanders	143	537	85	148	29	3	8	78	.276	.385
Emil Verban	155	597	59	166	22	8	0	72	.278	.342
Marty Marion	123	430	63	119	27	5	1	59	.277	.370
W. Kurowski	133	511	84	165	27	3	21	102	.323	.511
Johnny Hopp	124	446	67	129	22	8	3	44	.289	.395
Buster Adams	140	574	98	169	26	0	20	101	.292	.441
R. Schoendienst	137	565	89	157	22	6	1	47	.276	.343
Ken O'Dea	100	307	36	78	18	2	4	43	.254	.365
Augie Bergamo	94	304	51	96	17	2	3	44	.316	.414
Del Rice	83	253	27	66	17	3	1	28	.261	.364
Debs Garms	74	146	23	49	7	2	0	18	.336	.411
Pep Young	27	47	5	7	1	0	1	4	.149	.224
Art Rebel	26	72	12	25	4	0	0	5	.347	.403
Dave Bartosch	24	47	9	12	1	0	0	1	.255	.277
George Fallon	24	55	4	13	2	1	0	7	.238	.309

Players *(1945 cont.)*	G	AB	R	H	2B	3B	4B	RBI	Ave	SLP
Lou Klein	19	57	12	13	4	1	1	6	.228	.386
Jim Mallory	13	43	3	10	2	0	0	3	.233	.279
Gene Cruming	6	12	0	1	0	0	0	1	.083	.083
Walker Cooper	4	18	3	7	0	0	0	1	.369	.369
Totals	155	5487*	756	1498*	256	44	64	698	.273	.371

Pitchers	G	GS	CG	W	L	Pct	ERA	SHO	Saves
Red Barrett	34	29	22	21	9	.700	2.73	3	0
Ken Burkhart	42	22	12	18	8	.692	2.90	4	2
Harry Brecheen	24	18	13	15	4	.769*	2.52	3	2
George Dockins	31	12	9	8	6	.571	3.21	2	0
Blix Donnelly	31	23	5	8	10	.444	3.52	4	2
Jack Creel	26	8	2	5	4	.556	4.14	0	2
Bud Byerly	33	8	2	4	5	.444	4.74	0	0
Ted Wilks	18	16	4	4	7	.367	2.94	1	1
Glenn Gardner	17	4	2	3	1	.750	3.27	1	0
Al Jurisch	27	6	1	3	3	.500	5.13	0	0
Mort Cooper	4	3	1	2	0	1.000	1.50	0	0
Max Lanier	4	3	3	2	2	.500	1.75	0	0
Bill Crouch	6	0	0	1	0	1.000	3.46	0	0
Art Lopatka	4	1	1	1	0	1.000	1.50	0	0
S. Parkenheimer	8	2	0	0	0	.000	6.29	0	0
Totals	309	155	77	95	59	.619	3.24	18*	9

1946

Players	G	AB	R	H	2B	3B	4B	RBI	Ave	SLP
Stan Musial	156	624*	124*	228*	50*	20*	16	103	.365*	.591*
R. Schoendienst	142	606	94	170	28	5	0	34	.281	.343
Marty Marion	146	498	51	116	29	4	3	46	.233	.325
W. Kurowski	142	519	76	156	32	5	14	89	.301	.462
Enos Slaughter	156	609	100	183	30	8	18	130*	.300	.465
Terry Moore	91	278	32	73	14	1	3	28	.263	.353

Players *(1946 cont.)*	G	AB	R	H	2B	3B	4B	RBI	Ave	SLP
Harry Walker	112	346	53	82	14	6	3	27	.237	.338
Joe Garagiola	74	211	21	50	4	1	3	22	.237	.308
Erv Dusak	100	275	38	66	9	1	9	42	.240	.376
Dick Sisler	83	235	17	61	11	2	3	42	.260	.362
Buster Adams	81	173	21	32	6	0	5	22	.185	.306
Del Rice	55	139	10	38	8	1	1	12	.273	.367
Clyde Klutz	52	136	6	36	7	0	0	14	.265	.316
Jeff Cross	49	69	17	15	3	0	0	6	.217	.261
Lou Klein	23	83	12	18	3	0	1	4	.194	.258
Ken O'Dea	22	57	2	7	2	0	1	3	.123	.211
Bill Endicott	20	20	2	4	3	0	0	3	.200	.350
Nippy Jones	16	12	3	4	0	0	0	1	.333	.333
Walt Sessi	15	14	2	2	0	0	1	2	.143	.367
Totals	156	5372*	712*	1426*	265*	56	81	665*	.265*	.391*

Pitchers	G	GS	CG	W	K	Pct	ERA	SHO	Saves
Howie Pollet	40	32	22	21*	10	.677	2.10*	4	5
Murray Dickson	47	19	12	15	6	.714	2.89	2	1
Harry Brecheen	36	30	14	15	15	.500	2.49	5	3
Al Brazle	37	15	6	11	10	.524	3.29	2	0
Ted Wilks	40	4	0	8	0	1.000	3.41	0	1
John Beazley	19	18	5	7	5	.563	4.46	0	0
Max Lanier	6	6	6	6	0	1.000	1.93	2	0
Ken Burkhart	25	13	5	6	3	.667	2.88	2	2
Red Barrett	23	9	1	3	2	.600	4.03	1	2
Freddie Martin	6	3	2	2	1	.667	4.03	0	0
George Munger	10	7	2	2	2	.500	3.31	0	1
Freddy Schmidt	16	0	0	1	0	1.000	3.33	0	0
Blix Donnelly	13	0	0	1	2	.333	3.86	0	0
John Grodzicki	3	0	0	0	0	.000	9.00	0	0
Howie Krist	15	0	0	0	2	.000	6.63	0	0
Totals	156	156	75*	98*	58	.629*	3.01*	18*	15

1947

Players	G	AB	R	H	2B	3B	4B	RBI	Ave	SLP
Stan Musial	149	587	113	183	30	13	19	95	.312	.504
R. Schoendienst	151	639*	91	167	25	9	3	48	.253	.332
Marty Marion	149	540	57	147	19	6	4	74	.272	.352
W. Kurowski	146	513	108	156	27	6	27	104	.310	.544
Erv Dusak	111	326	56	93	7	3	6	28	.284	.376
Terry Moore	127	460	61	130	17	1	7	45	.283	.370
Enos Slaughter	147	551	100	182	31	13	10	86	.294	.452
Del Rice	97	291	28	57	7	3	12	44	.218	.406
Ron Northey	110	311	52	91	19	3	15	63	.293	.518
Chuck Diering	105	74	22	16	3	1	2	11	.216	.365
Joe Garagiola	77	183	20	47	10	2	5	25	.257	.415
Joe Medwick	75	150	19	46	12	0	4	28	.307	.447
Del Wilber	51	99	7	23	8	1	0	12	.232	.333
Jeff Cross	51	49	4	5	1	0	0	3	.102	.122
Dick Sisler	46	74	4	15	2	1	0	9	.203	.257
Nippy Jones	23	73	6	18	4	0	1	5	.247	.342
Bernie Creger	15	16	3	3	1	0	0	0	.188	.250
Harry Walker	10	25	2	5	1	0	0	0	.200	.240
Totals	156	5422*	780	1462*	235	65*	115	718	.270	.401

Pitchers	G	GS	CG	W	L	Pct	ERA	SHO	Saves
George Munger	40	31	13	16	5	.762	3.30	6	3
Harry Brecheen	29	28	18	16	11	.593	3.31	1	1
Al Brazle	44	19	7	14	8	.636	2.84	0	4
Murray Dickson	47	25	11	13	16	.448	3.06	4	3
Jim Hearn	37	21	4	12	7	.632	3.22	1	1
Howie Pollet	37	24	9	9	11	.450	4.35	0	2
Ted Wilks	37	0	0	4	0	1.000	5.04	0	5
Ken Burkhart	34	6	1	3	6	.333	5.21	0	1
Ken Johnson	2	1	1	1	0	1.000	0.00	0	0
Gerry Staley	18	1	1	1	0	1.000	2.79	0	0
Freddy Schmidt	2	0	0	0	0	.000	2.25	0	0

Pitchers *(1947 cont.)*	G	GS	CG	W	L	Pct	ERA	SHO	Saves
John Grodzicki	16	0	0	0	1	.000	5.46	0	0
Totals	309	156	65	89	65	.576	3.53*	12	20

1948

Players	G	AB	R	H	2B	3B	4B	RBI	Ave	SLP
Nippy Jones	132	481	58	122	21	9	10	81	.254	.397
R. Schoendienst	119	408	64	111	21	4	4	36	.272	.373
Marty Marion	144	567	70	143	26	4	4	43	.252	.333
Don Lang	117	323	30	87	14	1	4	31	.269	.356
Enos Slaughter	146	549	91	176	27	11	11	90	.321	.470
Terry Moore	91	207	30	48	11	0	4	18	.232	.343
Stan Musial	155	611	135*	230*	46*	18*	39	131*	.376*	.702*
Del Rice	100	290	24	57	10	1	4	34	.197	.279
Erv Dusak	114	311	60	65	9	2	6	19	.209	.309
Ron Northey	96	246	40	79	10	1	13	64	.321	.528
Ralph LaPointe	87	222	27	50	3	0	0	15	.225	.239
W. Kurowski	77	220	34	47	6	0	2	33	.214	.277
Bill Baker	45	119	13	35	10	1	0	15	.294	.395
Murray Dickson	43	96	7	27	2	0	0	11	.281	.302
Babe Young	41	111	14	27	5	2	1	13	.243	.351
Del Wilber	27	58	5	11	2	0	0	10	.190	.224
Joe Garagiola	24	56	9	6	1	0	2	7	.107	.232
Joe Medwick	20	19	0	4	0	0	0	2	.211	.211
Hal Rice	8	31	3	10	1	2	0	3	.323	.484
Chuck Diering	7	2	2	0	0	0	0	0	.000	.000
Eddie Kazak	6	22	1	6	3	0	0	2	.273	.409
Totals	155	5302	742	1396	238	58*	105	680	.263	.369

Pitchers	G	GS	CG	W	L	Pct	ERA	SHO	Saves
Harry Brecheen	33	30	21	20	7	.741*	2.34*	7*	1
Howie Pollet	36	26	11	13	8	.619	4.55	0	0
Murray Dickson	42	29	11	12	16	.429	4.14	1	1

Pitchers *(1948 cont.)*	G	GS	CG	W	L	Pct	ERA	SHO	Saves
Al Brazle	42	23	8	10	6	.625	3.81	3	1
George Munger	39	25	7	10	11	.476	4.50	2	0
Jim Hearn	34	13	3	8	6	.571	4.20	0	1
Ted Wilks	57	2	1	6	6	.500	2.61	0	13
Gerry Staley	31	3	0	4	4	.500	6.92	0	0
Ken Johnson	13	4	0	2	4	.333	4.80	0	0
Ken Burkhart	20	0	0	0	0	.000	5.59	0	1
Clarence Beers	1	0	0	0	0	.000	13.50	.0	0
Erv Dusak	1	0	0	0	0	.000	0.00	0	0
Ray Yochim	1	0	0	0	0	.000	0.00	0	0
All Papai	10	0	0	0	1	.000	5.06	0	0
Totals	360	155	60	85	69	.552	3.91	13	18

1949

Players	G	AB	R	H	2B	3B	4B	RBI	Ave	SLP
Nippy Jones	110	380	51	114	20	2	8	62	.300	.426
R. Schoendienst	151	640	102	190	25	2	3	54	.297	.356
Marty Marion	134	515	61	140	21	2	5	70	.272	.369
Eddie Kazak	92	326	43	99	15	3	6	42	.304	.423
Stan Musial	157	612	126	207*	41*	13*	36	123	.338	.624
Chuck Diering	131	369	60	97	21	8	3	36	.263	.388
Enos Slaughter	151	568	92	191	34	13*	13	96	.336	.511
Del Rice	92	284	25	67	16	1	4	29	.236	.342
Ron Northey	90	265	28	69	18	2	7	50	.260	.423
Tom Glaviano	87	256	32	69	16	1	6	36	.267	.407
Rocky Nelson	82	244	28	54	8	4	4	32	.221	.337
Joe Garagiola	81	241	25	63	14	0	3	26	.261	.357
Lou Klein	58	114	25	25	6	0	2	12	.219	.325
Hal Rice	40	46	3	9	2	1	1	9	.198	.348
Ed Sauer	24	45	5	10	2	1	0	1	.222	.311
Bill Baker	20	30	2	4	1	0	0	4	.133	.167
Solly Hemus	20	33	4	11	1	0	0	2	.333	.364

Players *(1949 cont.)*	G	AB	R	H	2B	3B	4B	RBI	Ave	SLP
W. Kurowski	10	14	0	2	0	0	0	0	.143	.143
Bill Howerton	9	13	1	4	1	0	0	1	.308	.385
Totals	157	5463*	766	1513*	281*	54	102	720	.277*	.404

Pitchers	G	GS	CG	W	L	Pct	ERA	SHO	Saves
Howie Pollet	39	28	17	20	9	.690	2.77	5*	1
George Munger	35	28	12	15	8	.652	3.88	2	2
Al Brazle	39	25	9	14	8	.636	3.19	1	0
Harry Brecheen	32	31	14	14	11	.560	3.35	2	1
Ted Wilks	59*	0	0	10	3	.769	3.74	0	9*
Gerry Staley	45	17	5	10	10	.500	2.74	2	6
Freddie Martin	21	5	3	6	0	1.000	2.44	0	0
Max Lanier	15	15	4	5	4	.556	3.82	1	0
Bill Reeder	21	1	0	1	1	.500	5.03	0	0
Jim Hearn	17	4	0	1	3	.250	5.14	0	0
Cloyd Boyer	4	1	0	0	0	.000	12.00	0	0
Ray Yochim	3	0	0	0	0	.000	18.00	0	0
Kurt Krieger	1	0	0	0	0	.000	0.00	0	0
Ken Johnson	14	2	0	0	1	.000	6.35	0	0
Totals	345	157	64	96	58	.623	3.44*	12	19*

Chapter Notes

Chapter One

1. *The Sporting News*, October 12, 1939, pp. 6, 7.
2. Ibid., November 2, 1939, p. 5.
3. Ibid., November 30, 1939, p. 1.
4. Ibid., p. 3.
5. Ibid., January 18, 1940, pp. 1 and 6.
6. Ibid., February 8, 1940, pp. 1, 5.
7. Ibid., April 4, 1940, p. 5.
8. Broeg and Vickery, *St. Louis Cardinal Encyclopedia*, p. 37.
9. Ibid., P. 38.
10. *The Sporting News*, June 20, 1940, pp. 1 and 2.
11. Thorn and others, *Total Baseball*, p. 2150.
12. *The Sporting News*, August 29, 1940, p. 1.
13. Ibid., September 12, 1940, p. 1.
14. Ibid., p. 3.

Chapter Two

1. *The Sporting News*, October 24, 1940, pp. 1, 9.
2. Ibid., October 31, 1940, pp. 1, 2.
3. Ibid., p. 3.
4. Ibid., November 7, 1940, p. 10.
5. Ibid., December 19, 1940, p. 1, 8.
6. Ibid., November 28, 1940, p. 8.
7. Ibid., December 12, 1940, p. 2.
8. Ibid., February 27, 1941, p. 3.
9. Ibid., January 30, 1941, p. 8.
10. Ibid., February 4, 1941, p. 1.
11. Ibid., February 6, 1941, pp. 1, 7.

12. Ibid., February 10, 1941, p. 2.
13. Ibid., March 13, 1941, p. 1.
14. Ibid., April 24, 1941, p. 1.
15. Broeg and Vickery, *St. Louis Cardinal Baseball Encyclopedia*, p. 38.
16. *The Sporting News*, June 26, 1941, p. 6.
17. Broeg and Vickery, p. 39.
18. Broeg, *Stan Musial*, p. 47.

Chapter Three

1. *The Sporting News*, October 23, 1941, p. 7.
2. Ibid., October 3, 1941, p. 1.
3. Ibid., November 6, 1941, p. 7.
4. Ibid., November 22, 1941, p. 2.
5. Thorn and others, *Total Baseball*, p. 906, 2392.
6. *The Sporting News*, December 11, 1941, pp. 1, 12.
7. Ibid., December 18, 1941, pp. 1, 2.
8. Ibid., January 18, 1942, p. 6.
9. Ibid., January 22, 1942, pp. 1, 2.
10. Ibid., February 5, 1942, pp. 1, 2.
11. Ibid., February 26, 1942, p. 10.
12. Ibid., March 5, 1942, p. 1.
13. Ibid., April 16, 1942, p. 7.
14. Ibid., pp. 1, 12.
15. Ibid., May 7, 1942, pp. 1, 2.
16. Freese, *Glory Years*, p. 106.
17. *The Sporting News*, June 18, 1942, p. 8; July 2, 1942, p. 4; August 13, 1942, p. 3.
18. Ibid., July 2, 1942, p. 4; July 16, 1942, p. 9; August 13, 1942; p. 3.
19. Freese, *Glory Years*, pp. 111–112.

20. Ibid., p. 113.
21. Broeg, *Stan Musial*, p. 60.
22. *The Sporting News*, August 20, 1942, pp. 1, 5.
23. Ibid., September 24, 1942, p. 5.

Chapter Four

1. *The Sporting News*, October 8, 1942, p. 1; October 22, 1942, pp. 1, 14.
2. Ibid., October 15, 1942, pp. 1, 12.
3. Neft and Cohen, *Sports Encyclopedia: Baseball*, p. 214.
4. Hoppel, *Baseball*, p. 206.
5. *The Sporting News*, November 5, 1942, pp. 6, 8.
6. Ibid., October 29, 1942, p. 5.
7. Ibid., November 5, 1942, pp. 1, 8.
8. Ibid., November 19, 1942, pp. 1, 8.
9. Thorn and others, *Total Baseball*, p. 817.
10. Neft and Cohen, p. 218.
11. Freese, *Glory Years*, pp. 9, 122–123.
12. *The Sporting News*, April 8, 1943, pp. 1, 2.
13. Ibid., April 8, 1943, pp. 1, 2.
14. Ibid., April 15, 1943, pp. 1, 7.
15. Broeg, *Stan Musial*, p. 77.
16. *The Sporting News*, June 24, 1943, pp. 1, 16.
17. Ibid., June 10, 1943, p. 1.
18. Ibid., July 8, 1943, p. 1.
19. Ibid., July 15, 1943, p. 1.
20. Broeg and Vickery, *St. Louis Cardinal Baseball Encyclopedia*, p. 46.

Chapter Five

1. *The Sporting News*, October 21, 1943, p. 7.
2. Broeg, *Stan Musial*, p. 81.
3. *The Sporting News*, November 4, 1943, pp. 1, 6.
4. Ibid., p. 9.
5. Ibid., November 11, 1943, p. 7.
6. Ibid., November 18, 1943, pp. 3, 14.
7. Ibid., p. 3.
8. Ibid., November 25, 1943, pp. 2, 4, 7 and 17.
9. Ibid., December 9, 1943, p. 11.
10. Ibid., December 23, 1943, p. 7.
11. Ibid., January 20, 1944, p. 4.
12. Ibid., February 3, 1944, pp. 1, 2.
13. Freese, *Glory Years*, p. 135.
14. Neft and Cohen, *Sports Encyclopedia: Baseball*, pp. 214, 218.

15. *The Sporting News*, June 1, 1944, pp. 1, 2.
16. Thorn and others, *Total Baseball*, p. 2166.
17. *The Sporting News*, July 20, 1944, p. 3.
18. Ibid., August 17, 1944, p. 2.
19. Freese, *Glory Years*, p. 145.
20. Ibid.
21. Ibid., pp. 151, 152.

Chapter Six

1. Broeg and Vickery, *St. Louis Cardinal Encyclopedia*, pp. 47–48.
2. *The Sporting News*, October 12, 1944, p. 1.
3. Ibid., October 19, 1944, p. 3.
4. Ibid., October 26, 1944, p. 3.
5. Ibid., p. 9.
6. Ibid., November 16, 1944, pp. 1, 2.
7. Ibid., p. 7.
8. Ibid., November 30, 1944, pp. 1, 4–7.
9. Ibid., December 7, 1944, pp. 1, 2.
10. Ibid., December 14, 1944, pp. 1, 2.
11. Ibid., p. 1; December 28, 1944, p. 3.
12. Ibid., January 4, 1945, pp. 1, 2, 4, 6.
13. Ibid., January 18, 1945, p. 5; February 15, 1945, pp. 1, 2.
14. Ibid., April 12, 1945, pp. 1, 2.
15. Ibid., May 24, 1945, p. 2.
16. Ibid., May 25, 1945, p. 2.
17. Ibid., June 21, 1945, p. 2.
18. Broeg and Vickery, p. 49.
19. Neft and Cohen, *Sports Encyclopedia: Baseball*, pp. 174, 179, 183, 187, 191, 195, 199, 203, 207, 211, 215, 219, 223.
20. *The Sporting News*, August 2, 1945, pp. 1, 2, 4.

Chapter Seven

1. *The Sporting News*, October 11, 1945, p. 1.
2. Ibid., October 25, 1945, p. 9.
3. Ibid., p. 12.
4. Ibid., November 1, 1945, pp. 4, 5.
5. Ibid., November 8, 1945, p. 1.
6. Ibid., November 29, 1945, p. 6.
7. Ibid., December 13, 1945, p. 2.
8. Broeg, *Stan Musial*, p. 87.
9. Broeg and Vickery, *St. Louis Cardinal Encyclopedia*, p. 50.
10. *Sporting News*, February 7, 1946, p. 11.
11. Broeg and Vickery, p. 50.
12. *The Sporting News*, February 28, 1946, p. 2.

13. Ibid., p. 18.
14. Ibid., March 7, 1946, p. 2.
15. Ibid., April 4, 1946, p. 4.
16. Ibid., April 18, 1946, pp. 1, 2.
17. Ibid., April 25, 1946. pp. 1, 3.
18. Ibid., May 23, 1946, p. 2.
19. Freese, *Glory Years*, pp. 167–168.
20. *The Sporting News*, June 12, 1946, p. 2.
21. Ibid., June 19, 1946, p. 3.
22. Ibid., June 6, 1946, p. 2.
23. Ibid., July 17, 1946, pp. 1, 2.
24. Ibid., July 31, 1946, p. 3.
25. Ibid., August 7, 1946, pp. 1, 5.
26. Ibid., September 4, 1946, p. 1, 2.
27. Ibid., September 11, 1946, p. 1.
28. Broeg, *Stan Musial*, p. 93.
29. Broeg and Vickery, p. 54.
30. Ibid., p. 55.

Chapter Eight

1. *The Sporting News*, October 30, 1946, pp. 12, 40.
2. Ibid., November 11, 1946, p. 14.
3. Ibid., January 1, 1947, p. 2.
4. Ibid., January 8, 1947, pp. 15; January 22, 1947, p. 16.
5. Ibid., January 22, 1947, p. 17.
6. Ibid., February 12, 1947, p. 3.
7. Ibid., February 19, 1947, pp. 1, 2.
8. Ibid., April 16, 1947, pp. 1, 18.
9. Ibid., pp. 1, 4.
10. Ibid., April 23, 1947, p. 3.
11. Thorn and others, *Total Baseball*, p. 958.
12. Broeg and Vickery, *St. Louis Cardinal Encyclopedia*, pp. 58–59.
13. Broeg, *Stan Musial*, p. 105.
14. *The Sporting News*, May 21, 1947, pp. 3, 5.
15. Story told to author by sportswriter Bob Broeg.
16. *The Sporting News*, June 11, 1947, p. 19.
17. Ibid., June 18, 1947, p. 2.
18. Ibid., June 25, 1947, p. 5.
19. Ibid., July 2, 1947, p. 1.
20. Ibid., July 9, 1947, p. 3.
21. Ibid., July 30, 1947, p. 1.
22. Ibid., p. 5.

23. Ibid., p. 9.
24. Broeg, p. 107.
25. *The Sporting News*, August 6, 1947, pp. 1, 6.
26. Ibid., p. 9.
27. Ibid., September 10, 1947, pp. 1, 4.

Chapter Nine

1. *The Sporting News*, September 22, 1947, p. 18.
2. Ibid., November 19, 1947, pp. 1, 6.
3. Ibid., December 3, 1947, pp. 6–8.
4. Ibid., December 10, 1947, p. 4.
5. Ibid., December 17, 1947, pp. 1, 5.
6. Ibid., December 31, 1947, p. 6.
7. Ibid., January 7, 1948, pp. 1, 2.
8. Ibid., January 28, 1948, pp. 1, 2.
9. Ibid., p. 8.
10. Ibid., February 4, 1948, p. 6.
11. Ibid., February 25, 1948, pp. 1, 2.
12. Broeg and Vickery, *St. Louis Cardinals Encyclopedia*, p. 59.
13. *The Sporting News*, May 5, 1948, pp. 1, 2.
14. Ibid., May 19, 1948, pp. 1, 6.
15. Ibid., May 26, 1948, p. 7.
16. Ibid., June 23, 1948, pp. 4–6, 7.
17. Ibid., June 30, 1948, pp. 1, 2.
18. Broeg, *Stan Musial*, pp. 113–114.
19. *The Sporting News*, July 7, 1948, pp. 2, 4.
20. Ibid., August 18, 1948, pp. 1, 6.
21. Broeg and Vickery, p. 62.
22. *The Sporting News*, August 25, 1948, Section 2, pp. 1–10.
23. Ibid., September 8, 1948, p. 7.
24. Hoppel, *Baseball*, pp. 230–231.

Chapter Ten

1. Hoppel, *Baseball*, pp. 230–231.
2. Neft and Cohen, *Sports Encyclopedia: Baseball*, p. 276.
3. Broeg and Vickery, *St. Louis Cardinals Encyclopedia*, pp. 59–60.
4. Ibid., p. 62.
5. Ibid.

Bibliography

Books

Broeg, Bob. *Stan Musial: "The Man's" Own Story.* Garden City, NY: Doubleday, 1964.
_____, and Jerry Vickery. *St. Louis Cardinals Encyclopedia.* Indianapolis: Masters Press, 1998.
Freese, Mel. *The Glory Years: The Championship Seasons of the St. Louis Cardinals.* St. Louis: Pamerston & Reed, 1999.
Hoppel, Joe. *Baseball: 100 Years of the Modern Era: 1901–2000.* New York: McGraw-Hill, 2001.
Neft, David S., and Richard M. Cohen. *The Sports Encyclopedia: Baseball, 1995,* 15th ed. New York: St. Martin's Press, 1995.
Thorn, J., M. Gershman, P. Palmer, and D. Pietrusza, eds. *Total Baseball,* sixth edition. New York: Total Sports, 1999.

Newspapers

The Sporting News (1940–1949)

Index